GEORGE I, THE BALTIC
AND THE
WHIG SPLIT
OF 1717

GEORGE I, THE BALTIC AND THE WHIG SPLIT OF 1717

A Study in Diplomacy and Propaganda

by

JOHN J. MURRAY

The University of Chicago Press

Library of Congress Catalog Card Number: 68–54009

The University of Chicago Press, Chicago 60637
Routledge & Kegan Paul Ltd, London E.C.4

DA
499
. M8
1969 b

To

Betty

Wife, mother, and good companion

CONTENTS

PREFACE

THIS study is intended to show how diplomacy, naval and military actions (especially the use of the 'fleet in Being'), trade considerations, internal politics, and the use of the press all worked together so that George I could utilize the resources of Great Britain in the Baltic. It is hoped that this effort will complement the labors of James F. Chance, Ragnhild Hatton, J. H. Plumb, Karl Hartman, Sigurd Schartau, Gabriel Syveton, Wolfgang Michael, Basil Williams, Edvard Holm, Jerker Rosén, Walther Mediger, Theodore Bussemaker, and a whole host of other historians who have made it possible for me to weave together my story.

I am grateful to the many friends who read parts of the manuscript and gave pertinent advice. My debt to the late Waldemar Westergaard is invaluable; for years Professor Westergaard not only furnished encouragement and guidance, but he loaned me many rare books and microfilms from his own magnificent personal collection. To me he was both friend and teacher. My thanks to Dr. Ragnhild Hatton of the London School of Economics and Political Science cannot be measured. She read the entire manuscript, called my attention to new materials, and urged me to get on with the work when I became side-tracked by other interests. She has indeed been a friend throughout the years.

Students, colleagues, archivists, and librarians all rendered invaluable assistance, but the responsibility for errors is mine and mine alone. I would be amiss if I did not express my appreciation to the trustees and administrators of Coe College for the encouragement they have constantly shown during my research.

ix

President Joseph McCabe and Dean Howard Greenlee were most generous in the matter of leaves, teaching assignments, and in keeping committee assignments to a minimum so that I might have time both for research and writing. In this work and others, they have been most coöperative. They have helped make the ideal academic life of teaching and learning a reality. I am also indebted to the Margaret Pilcher Fund of Coe College for providing funds which helped to make the publishing of this book possible. Mrs. Glen Harvey, Mr. John Reed, and Mrs. Linda Rice helped with the indexing, and for their assistance I am most grateful.

Last, but by no means least, I should like to express my indebtedness to my wife who made sacrifices, financial and otherwise, so that this book would be completed. Only I know what some of those sacrifices were.

J.J.M.

A NOTE ON THE SOURCES

BOTH printed and manuscript sources were consulted, and whenever possible I have used archival materials and so cited them, although some of the same materials have been printed. Usually the printed collection is mentioned the first time that the archival material is cited, but in the interest of space subsequent citations are ordinarily from the manuscript source itself. This procedure has been followed throughout.

Pamphlet and printed sources need little comment, but perhaps some comment on the best archive materials might be pertinent. From the British museum in the Additional Manuscripts were letters and materials that gave an insight into the position of Sir John Norris. These same letters were used by Chance, Hatton and others. The most valuable were Add. MSS. 28,143; Letter Books, Baltic, Portsmouth and Channel, May 31–Sept. 10, 1715; Add. MSS. 28,144; Letter Books (Baltic) May 4–Sept. 17, 1715; Add. MSS. 28,145: Letter Book of Sir John Norris, 1716; and Add. MSS. 28,154: Letters to Sir John Norris. These among other things also had minutes of councils of war and illustrate the delicate position of Norris as he tried to serve two masters in one, George I as King of England, and George as Elector of Hanover. The Stowe MSS. 227–230 are the Hanover Papers (Robethon and Castle Papers) and were disappointing. Much of the material used on the Hanover side was culled from secondary accounts.

So far as the collections of the Public Record Office are concerned one hardly knows where to begin. In these gold mines of information was found much of the material dealing with the diplomacy and some treating the politics. A list of the most valuable State Papers found in the P.R.O. follows:

State Papers Domestic, Baltic, 1711–1718 (Ad. 1/2). Admiralty, Secretary's Dispatches.

State Papers Domestic, Naval (S.P. 42/70). Secretary of State's Out Letters With Naval Commanders (Baltic).

State Papers Domestic, Regencies, Entry Books (S.P. 44/267). Letter Books by Methuen and Townshend, 1716–1719.

State Papers Domestic, Regencies, Hanover (S.P. 43/1). Incoming Letters from Hanover, 1716–1720, by Stanhope, Townshend and Carteret.

State Papers Foreign, Denmark (S.P. 75/36 & S.P. 75/37). Letters of Alexander, Lord Polwarth, 1716 and January to June, 1717.

State Papers Foreign, Denmark (S.P. 75/35). Letters of Daniel Pulteney, 1715.

State Papers Foreign, Flanders (S.P. 77/66 & S.P. 77/67). Letters and papers of William, Lord Cadogan, 1715–March, 1715 and April–December, 1715.

State Papers Foreign, German Empire and Hungary (S.P. 80/33). Letters of Luke Schaub, 1716.

State Papers Foreign, German Empire and Hungary (S.P. 80/32). Letters of Lord Cobham, James Stanhope and Luke Schaub, 1714–1715.

State Papers Foreign, Holland (S.P. 84/252 & S.P. 84/253). Letters and Papers of Horatio Walpole, 1715 January to April, and 1715–1716.

State Papers Foreign, Holland (S.P. 84/254). Letters and papers of Horatio Walpole and Lord Cadogan, May to October, 1716.

State Papers Foreign, Holland (S.P. 84/255). Letters and papers of Lord Cadogan and W. Leathes, 1716–1717.

State Papers Foreign, Prussia (S.P. 90/7). Letters and papers of Charles Whitworth, August, 1716–April, 1717.

State Papers Foreign, Sweden (S.P. 95/17). Letters and papers of James Jefferyes, 1707–1715.

State Papers Foreign, Sweden (S.P. 95/18–21). Letters and papers of Robert Jackson, 1707–1717.

State Papers Foreign, Confidential, Sweden (S.P. 107/13). Intercepted Letters (Sweden), 1716–1717.

State Papers Foreign, Denmark, Foreign Entry Books (S.P. 104/245). Foreign Ministers in England, Secretary's Letter Book, 1715–1726.

State Papers Foreign, Denmark, Foreign Entry Books (S.P. 104/5). Secretary's Letter Book, 1711–1725.

State Papers Foreign, Hanover, Foreign Entry Books (S.P. 104/48). Secretary's Letter Book (Hanover), 1704–1711.

State Papers Foreign, Holland, Foreign Entry Books (S.P. 104/249). Foreign Ministers in England, Secretary's Letter Books, 1715–1728.

State Papers Foreign, Holland, Foreign Entry Books (S.P. 104/81–82). Secretary's Letter Book, 1714–1717 & 1716–1717.

State Papers Foreign, Prussia, Foreign Entry Books (S.P. 104/53). Secretary's Letter Book, 1713–1725.

State Papers Foreign, Sweden, Foreign Entry Books (S.P. 104/155). Secretary's Letter Book, 1714–1725.

State Papers Foreign, Sweden, Foreign Entry Books (S.P. 104/256). Foreign Ministers in England, Secretary's Letter Book, 1714–1727.

State Papers Foreign, Foreign Entry Books (S.P. 104/265). Foreign Ministers in England, Ambassador's Privileges (Northern), 1713–1738.

State Papers Foreign, Foreign Entry Books (S.P. 104/268). Foreign Ministers in England, Ambassador's Privileges (Southern), 1709–1726.

State Papers Foreign, Denmark, Foreign Ministers in England Book, 1684–1780 (S.P. 100/1).

State Papers Foreign, Holland, Foreign Ministers in England Book, 1713–1720 (S.P. 100/22).

State Papers Foreign, Sweden, Foreign Ministers in England Book, 1714–1716 and *Ibid.*, 1717–1728 (S.P. 100/62 & 63).

State Papers Foreign, Holland, Newsletters, 1714–1715 and *Ibid.*, 1716–1719 (S.P. 101/67 & 68).

State Papers Foreign, Treaty Papers (S.P. 103/50 & 51).

Of special value were the letters of Jackson and Jefferyes along with the intercepted dispatches of Görtz and Gyllenburg so far as Sweden was concerned. The Foreign Entry Books to ministers in Sweden, the States and Denmark along with the State Papers for these countries were invaluable.

The rich resources of the Algemeen Rijksarchief were surpassed only by its staff, especially Dr. B. van't Hoff and

Messrs. Hardenberg and Brouwer. A list of the important materials in the Archief Anthonie Hensius shows in part the mass of material that passed over the desk of the Grand Pensionary of Holland. Needless to say, his correspondence with Wassenaer van Duevenvoorde and P. J. Borssele van der Hooghe were the most valuable. A list of those items used, along with their archive numbers, follows:

1892. Borssele van der Hooghe, (P. J. van); uit London.

1894. Buys, (W.); uit Parijs.

1922. Robethon, (J. de); uit London.

1923. Rumpf, (J. W.); uit Stockholm.

1928. Veth, (L. de); van de vleet in de Oostzee en de Sont.

1929. Walpole, (H.); uit 's-Gravenhage.

1930. Wassenaer van Duivenvoorde, (A. van); uit Brielle en London.

1715b. Borssele van der Hooghe, (P. J. van).

1934. Borssele van der Hooghe, (P. J. van).

1935. Buys, (W.).

1943. Wassenaer van Duivenvoorde, (A. van).

1948. Borssele van der Hooghe, (P. J. van); uit London.

1949. Buys, (W.); uit Amsterdam.

1957. Goes, (R.); uit Kopenhage, Lübeck, Hamburg en andere plaatsen in Noord-Duitsland.

1968. Robéthon, (J. de); uit 's-Gravenhage.

1971. Walpole, (H.); uit 's-Gravenhage.

1972. Wassenaer van Duivenvoorde, (A. van); uit London, Breda en Duivenvoorde.

1978. Borssele van der Hooghe, (P. J. van).

1979. Buys, (W.).

1986. Wassenaer van Duivenvoorde, (A. van).

The Archief of Simon van Slinglandt contained considerable materials treating Anglo-Dutch, Baltic affairs, while the Archief of Francois Fagel contained information on the Görtz affair. Of much greater importance was the Archief Staten

Generaal which contained letters both secret and public dealing with the diplomacy of the period. The Legatie Archief contained the Verbaal or diplomatic reports of both Borssele and Duivenvoorde. The materials from the Rigsarkiv in Copenhagen were microfilmed for me by the late Professor Waldemar Westergaard of U.C.L.A. and included the letters of Hendrick Frederik Sohlenthal, minister to England and those of Georg von Westphal, minister to the Czar. Also of considerable importance were the minutes of the Danish Privy Council which shed light on those meetings, both military and diplomatic, where Britishers and Hanoverians, were in attendance.

Printed sources and specialized material abound and have been duly cited in the footnotes. Many new works continue to appear on this subject and much of the printed material has been incorporated. Some authorities not mentioned have ordinarily been consulted, but if they made no real change in interpretation they perhaps have not been cited. To all these the author expresses his apologies, but printing costs preclude a definitive bibliography.

I

A NEW KING AND
AN OLD WAR

Let Royal George, the Papists' scourge
To England quickly come;
His health till then, let honest men
Drink all in Brunswick mum.[1]

DRUMS rolled and trumpets sounded. Before the gate of St. James's, at four other places in the city of London, it was announced that 'the high and mighty Prince George, Elector of Brunswick-Luneburg, is now by the death of our late Sovereign of happy memory, become the lawful and rightful liege Lord, George, by the Grace of God, King of Great Britain.'[2] At York there were great illuminations accompanied by the ringing of bells to proclaim the happy event. Lighted by the numerous bonfires and inflamed by the spirit and spirits of the occasion, the joyous mob shouted 'Liberty and property' and 'Long live King George.'[3] On that day of August 1, 1714, the hopes of Henry St. John, Viscount Bolingbroke, and other Stuart adherents received a harsh blow from the bantering of fortune.[4] As the ardent Jacobite and Bishop of Rochester,

[1] James Hogg, *The Jacobite Relics of Scotland* (Edinburgh, 1819–1821), II, 415.
[2] Abel Boyer, *The Political State of Great Britain* (London, 1711–1740), VIII, 116.
[3] James A. Stuart-Wortley Mackenzie, Baron Wharncliffe (ed.), *The Letters and Works of Lady Mary, Wortley Montagu* (London, 1837), I, 209.
[4] Bolingbroke to Swift, August, 1714, Jonathan Swift, *Works*, John Hawkesworth *et al.* (ed.) (London, 1755–1779), XVI, 178. 'The Earl of Oxford was removed on Tuesday, the Queen died on Sunday; what a world this is and how does fortune banter us.'

Atterbury, remarked, 'The grief of my soul is this, I can see plainly that the Tory Party is gone.'[1] A new era of English history was to begin. The period of 'the Whig supremacy' was at hand.

The accession of George I to the Stuart throne in England had vast constitutional and political influence upon the internal history of England. It also had marked repercussions upon the state system of Europe. This was especially noticeable in the troubled decades following the Utrecht settlement of 1713. These years were ones of flux and constituted a period during which Europe changed from old diplomatic principles to new ones. Changing conditions resulting from aggrandizement under the guise of a 'quest for security' constantly upset the balance of power, the goal for which most European diplomats strove.

The result of their diplomatic juggling was the rebuilding of a different Europe. Russia emerged as a permanent factor in European affairs, while the United Provinces (or States) and Turkey along with Sweden passed from the ranks of the first-rate European nations. Prussia and Hanover increased their prestige in the Empire, with the former consolidating and constructing a strength which was to be utilized later by Frederick the Great. France, in the meantime, because of dynastic and internal difficulties, did a *volte-face*—before the more publicized diplomatic revolution of the reversal of alliances in 1756—and signed treaties with its two arch enemies, England and Austria. Spain's attempts to raise itself by the bootstraps soon became mired in the morass of Italian politics, and the endeavors of the Spanish queen, Elizabeth Farnese, to find Italian crowns for her sons were constant threats to the peace of Europe.

Granted that Cardinal Guilio Alberoni's[2] statement that the 'peace of Utrecht has left the seeds of endless wars'[3] is somewhat

[1] James Macpherson, *Original papers, containing the secret history of Great Britain ...* (London, 1775), II, 65.

[2] Alberoni was born in Piacenza on March 21, 1664. After a brief career in the Church he became a trusted diplomatic agent of the Duke of Parma and when the latter's daughter in 1714 became queen of Spain, Alberoni shortly was raised to the rank of chief minister of Spain, a post he held until late 1718. A popular and fairly lucid biography is Simon Harcourt-Smith, *Cardinal of Spain* (New York, 1944).

[3] *Lettres intimés de J. M. Alberoni*, Émile Bourgeois (ed.) (Paris, 1893), p. 306.

exaggerated, yet there can be no doubt that the pacification ending certain phases of the War of the Spanish Succession came far short of solving the many problems facing Europe. Not until the next year did the Houses of Hapsburg and Bourbon settle their Spanish succession differences at Rastadt and Baden. Still, more than another twelve months were to elapse before the Austrians and the Dutch could work out the complicated provisions of the Barrier Treaty, whose aim was to protect the Low Countries from further French aggression.[1]

There were other trouble spots not connected directly with the Utrecht settlement. In 1716 the Empire went to war with Turkey, a conflict that was to last until 1718.[2] France, England, and Austria in 1718 turned their military and naval might against the Spain of Alberoni and Elizabeth Farnese. In addition, other states within and without the Empire were juggling among themselves and with other European powers to insure for themselves as great a profit as possible from the Great Northern War, which had been raging since the turn of the century, and was to continue until 1721.

George I, king of England and elector of the Empire, was one such manœuverer; and regardless of his English office, was German in taste and sympathy. As one writer has said, 'Despite his Stewart Blood, George Lewis was a German without alloy.'[3] His heart was constantly in Hanover and his main objective was the continued prosperity of that electorate, which had progressed remarkably well under the rule of his house. He and his Hanoverian ministers had an excellent understanding of German politics and were not loath to do all in their power to raise the prestige of the Brunswick-Luneburg house in Germany. Although Lord Chesterfield might remark that George's

---

[1] Roderick Geikie and Isabel Montgomery, *The Dutch Barrier, 1750–1719* (Cambridge, Eng., 1930) is the fullest treatment in English of the complicated negotiations which led up to the Dutch Barrier Treaty. See also Ragnhild Hatton, *Diplomatic Relations between Great Britain and the Dutch Republic, 1714–1721* (London, 1950), and Thomas Bussemaker, 'De Republiek van de Vereenigde Nederlanden en de Keurvorst Koning George I,' *Bijdragen voor Vaderlandsche geschiedenis en oudheidkunde*, 4th series I (The Hague, 1898). Cited hereafter as Bussemaker, 'De Republiek en de Keurvorst.'

[2] J. Zinkeisen, *Geschichte des Osmanischen Reiches in Europa* (Hamburg and Gotha, 1840–1863), V, 461ff.

[3] Frederick S. Oliver, *The Endless Adventure* (Boston and New York, 1931), I, 170.

'views and affections were singly confined to the narrow compass of the Electorate' and that 'England was too big for him,' nevertheless, the king was astute and had a shrewd eye for that which could be practically obtained. He realized his potential capacities and limitations and listened to competent advisers. His judgement was excellent.[1] He was however highly suspicious, and may have been stupid on English matters as Professor Plumb has pointed out in his brilliant study of Robert Walpole.[2] It is possible that his ministers had the brain power. Whatever the source of origin, George I and his Hanoverian advisers were to influence English foreign policy for the next few years.[3]

Like other German princelings, George entertained expansionist ideas, and constantly sought ways and means to increase his holdings in and out of the Empire. His advent from the comparative rags of Hanover to the riches of Great Britain presented him with an excellent opportunity to employ the resources of his new kingdom to pull his Hanoverian chestnuts out of the diplomatic fires in the Empire. Among other things he hoped to add with British help the Swedish possessions of Bremen and Verden to his electoral domains. Those principalities would give him an outlet to the Baltic.

Although such intentions were directly contrary to the Act of Settlement of 1701, upon which his succession rested, yet there were ways and means by which an able sovereign could operate to violate the spirit, if not the letter, of the shackling laws imposed upon him by the parliament of his new subjects. It was an age when kings had considerable power, even an English one.

There was ample opportunity for George and his contemporaries to fish

> In Northern Climes where furious Tempests blow,
> And men more furious raise worse Storms below.[4]

Perhaps from the resulting troubled waters they might gain, for

---

[1] Walther Mediger, *Moskaus Weg Nach Europa* (Braunschweig, 1952), p. 13.

[2] J. H. Plumb, *Sir Robert Walpole, The Making of A Statesman* (Boston, 1956), p. 202.

[3] Wolfgang Michael, *England under George I: the beginnings of the Hanoverian Dynasty* (London, 1936), I, 81.

[4] Daniel Defoe, *The Dyet of Poland: a Satyr* (London, 1701), p. 1.

their states, a few additional square feet of German territory. The Elector of Hanover by late 1714 had literally set his heart upon the bishopric of Bremen and the principality of Verden. The owner Sweden engaged in a life and death struggle against overwhelming odds was too weak to defend them. On the surface it appeared in 1714 that the Swedes might lose all their German possessions without being able to put up any resistance whatsoever, for Sweden was exhausted by fifteen years of warfare. Why should not George spear a fish for himself? The Great Northern War was moving rapidly towards a climax. The time for poaching was opportune. The weir owner, Charles XII, was occupied elsewhere.

Yet that landlord had had a whirlwind career. As a mere boy of fifteen he had in 1697 assumed the Swedish throne. Shortly thereafter Paul Heins, Danish ambassador to Russia presented a plan to Moscow for the despoiling of Sweden's Baltic possessions. Somewhat later Augustus II of Saxony, king of Poland and one of the more adventurous political busybodies who were concerning themselves with the affairs of northern Europe, began to listen to the machinations of a Livonian malcontent, one John Reinhold Patkul. At the time (1699), Augustus was at odds with his Polish subjects and was seeking a plausible excuse to maintain his Saxon army in Poland proper.[1] The honeycombed schemes of Patkul for depriving Sweden of her Baltic provinces of Esthonia, Livonia and Courland fitted perfectly with the ideas of Augustus, who liked to imagine himself playing in eastern and northeastern Europe the role of a Polish Louis XIV.

Patkul, the siren of the Polish king, was an exiled Swedish subject from Livonia. He could sing his song to Sweden's enemies in four languages and could write both Latin and Greek. He dreamed of a 'free' Livonia where a handful of nobles like himself would play the part of irresponsible landlords tyrannizing a race of serfs. A cultured gentleman, endowed with an excellent physique, a dogged determination, and a sufficient store of courage, Patkul was a man whose better parts were more than balanced by narrow selfish pride, by greed,

[1] Carl Hallendorf and Adolf Schück, *A History of Sweden*, Delaware edition (Stockholm, 1938), p. 293. Reinhard Wittram, *Peter I, Czar und Kaiser*, 2 vols. (Göttingen, 1964), I, 199.

and by unbearable insolence. Vindictive hatred was the guiding principle of his life; faithlessness and treachery the signposts of his conduct. 'With an energy and an ability worthy of a better cause' Patkul labored constantly and mightily to erect a grand coalition which would bring about a partitioning of the Swedish empire.[1]

According to the glib-tongued tempter, the rewards of the trespassers would be great; the risks involved would be correspondingly small. Concerted action by Sweden's many enemies would topple the colossus of the North, and the fragments could be gathered up by the scavengers. Russia would gain a 'window on the Baltic,' Poland a part of the Baltic provinces, while Denmark's share of the plunder was to be Holstein and the provinces in southern Sweden of Skåne, Halland, and Bleking. Brandenburg-Prussia was to be lured into the plot by a promise of Swedish Pomerania. To accomplish these objectives, Denmark was to invade Skåne and Holstein; Brandenburg was to overrun Pomerania; and Russia was to launch an offensive against Finland, Ingria, and other Swedish holdings in eastern Europe. Augustus was to throw his Saxon army into Livonia, where, according to Patkul, the population was prepared to greet the Polish king as a liberator freeing them from the oppressive yoke of Sweden. The Baltic nobles did side with the Czar. They hoped that they might profit from the presence of the Russian army and regain their traditional privileges.[2]

It would appear that Peter was the most enthusiastic of the allies. To him Sweden's possessions on the Baltic robbed Russia of necessary harbors and cut off his connections with the whole world. Thus, Russia was thwarted in its natural growth and Sweden's expulsion from the Baltic was an absolute necessity for the serenity of Peter's empire.[3]

Definite agreements for executing the grand design were

---

[1] R. Nisbet Bain, *Charles XII and the Collapse of the Swedish Empire* (New York and London, 1895), p. 53.

[2] Claude J. Nordmann, *La Crise du Nord un début du XVIIIe Siècle*, in *Bibliothèque d'Histoire du Droit et Droit, VIIe* (Paris, 1962), p. 16, cited hereafter as *La Crise du Nord* cf Gabryelle van den Haute, *Les Relations Anglo-Hollandais au début du XVIIIe Siècle d'Apres la Correspondance d'Alexandre Stanhope 1700–1706* (Louvain, 1932), pp. 11ff.

[3] Mediger, *Moskaus Weg*, pp. 7–8.

reached in 1699 by Denmark, Saxony-Poland, and Russia.[1] Brandenburg-Prussia remained aloof from the conspiracy because the Elector of Brandenburg did not want to place any difficulties in the way of negotiations he was carrying on with the Emperor with a view towards the latter investing him with the title 'King in Prussia.' Moreover, Brandenburg was much disturbed by the threatening international situation which was developing on the horizon as the powers of western Europe moved towards the War of the Spanish Succession.[2] Hers was to be a game of watchful waiting. Sixteen years were to elapse before changing conditions made it possible for Brandenburg-Prussia to join actively the enemies of Sweden in order to obtain its share of the booty. The others, however, were not so patient. The Great Northern War began in 1700, and soon picked up momentum.

The government of Hanover although it wanted Swedish Bremen and Verden remained pro-Swedish as it had a real fear of Russian designs on Europe which went back to Peter's European trip in 1697. Through its diplomats at the Hague it predicted that Peter would incite old differences between Sweden and Denmark and suggested to William III that steps be made to prevent a Danish-Russian attack in Sweden. In addition, Hanover feared Danish expansion in the Bremen-Verden areas.[3]

While his enemies prepared their trap, the new Swedish king amused himself with wild rides, bear hunts, and mad escapades. When war commenced, however, he tore himself from his youthful pleasures and administered in turn crushing defeats upon his many foes. The hunted became the hunter. Denmark made peace in 1700 at Travendal; Saxony followed suit in 1707 at Alt-Ranstädt. Charles XII then resolved to carry the conflict into the very heart of Russia. On the plains of Poltava in 1709, he suffered a terrific setback, and was barely able to escape from the battle with his life. The situation once more

[1] Eugene Schuyler, *Peter the Great, Emperor of Russia*, 2 vols. (New York, 1884), I, 372–373.
[2] Bernhard Ermannsdörffer, *Deutsche Geschichte vom Westfälsschen Frieden bis zum Regierungsantritt Friedrichs des Grossen, 1648–1740*, in *Allgemeine Geschichte in Einzeldarstellungen*, Wilhelm Oncken (ed.) (Berlin, 1893), Part III, Vol. VII, 157.
[3] Mediger, *Moskaus Weg*, pp. 9–10, Haute, *Les Relations Anglo-Hollandais*, p. 13 traces the designs of the maritime powers and their willingness to uphold the treaty of Altona.

reversed itself. The arbiter of eastern Europe now became the exiled Swedish king in Turkey. Denmark and Saxony quickly resumed the war against Sweden in order to realize an advantage from Russian successes. Sweden's Baltic holding on the continent slowly began to dwindle.

After five years of adventures and mis-adventures, which ranged from the capitulation at Pruth[1] to the debacle at Bender,[2] Charles by late 1714 was preparing to leave Turkey and to return to his own country. Such was the situation when George I became king of England. The new sovereign was, therefore, presented with a golden opportunity to realize his ambitions regarding Bremen and Verden. All that was necessary was to find some pretext for employing English gold and the English fleet to carry out his designs. The excuse, however, would have to be a good one, for the terms of the Act of Settlement categorically stated:

> that in case the crown and imperial dignity of this realm shall hereafter come to any person, not being a native of this kingdom of England, this nation be not obliged to engage in any war for the defense of any dominions or territories which do not belong to the crown of England without the consent of Parliament.[3]

If only the Parliament and the British people could be prevailed upon to espouse an anti-Swedish policy, the greed and political ambitions of the elector-king could be satiated! Perhaps he could uncover ways and means to win his new subjects over to his desires. By exploiting minor Anglo-Swedish differences and dwelling upon them until they became major issues, an unscrupulous ruler could accomplish much. If the governing classes in England could be sufficiently aroused against Sweden, they might be persuaded to expend treasure and manpower against

[1] Peter in 1711 at Pruth made a peace with the Turks in which he ceded Azov to them. He did this to prevent his army from being crushed by a Swedo-Turkish army.

[2] After the capitulation at Pruth, Charles XII when requested by the Turks to leave Turkey refused. He became embroiled at Bender with Turkish officials over the matter. This affair of 1713 degenerated into little better than a street brawl, and it did much to lessen the prestige of the Swedish king throughout Europe. For a full and lurid account of the Bender affair, see Jefferyes to Bolingbroke, February 12, 1713, Public Record Office (P.R.O.), State Papers, Sweden, 95/17.

[3] Extract of Act, 12 and 13 William III in *Calendar of State Papers, Domestic series, 1660–1704* (London, 1860–1938), volume for 1700–1702, p. 481.

Sweden in such a way that his own ambitions could be realized. An angry populace might also stimulate the governing classes to action.

Fortunately for George I, the early part of the eighteenth century saw an increasing use of the press by rulers and nations to foster political objectives. To be sure, the use of the pamphlet was not new to the eighteenth century, but that period did see the employment by governments of the pamphleteer on an unprecedented scale. Throughout the War of the Spanish Succession and the Great Northern War, the press came to play a more important role. Increasingly at home and abroad the states of Europe presented their causes before the bar of public opinion, and more and more did the pamphlets and the newsletters contain carefully selected official materials, which could have reached the hacks of London and the Hague only through the coöperation of those in high official positions. Just before George I was able to achieve his objective in 1717 and bring about a rupture of diplomatic relations between England and Sweden, he had circulated throughout Europe a 'whitebook' which would have done credit to the Foreign Office productions of the twentieth century.

Another factor advantageous to George I was the fact that the bulk of the propaganda released for European consumption originated either in England or in the United Provinces, countries which enjoyed a relatively free press.[1] The latter was a much more important center for the distribution of pamphlets and newsletters than was England and a good deal of the material appearing in England was copied from releases at the Hague or at Amsterdam. In Britain, however, there was a relatively wide reading public which exerted a considerable role in political affairs. To both countries flocked French Huguenot refugees whose facile pens and keen and penetrating minds could be bought by princes.[2] Such an exile was Jean Roberthon, the King of England's private secretary who was to be the editor and compiler of a 'whitebook' that appeared in

[1] Sven G. Haverling, 'Huvuddrag i svensk och antisvensk propaganda i västeuropa på 1710-talet,' *Karolinska Förbundets Årsbok, 1952* (Stockholm, 1952), p. 81. Cited hereafter as Haverling, 'Huvuddrag i . . . propaganda.'

[2] J. Texte, *Jean-Jacques Rousseau et les origines du cosmopolitisme littéraire* (Paris, 1909), p. 18.

9

1717.[1] George I could also exert political and financial pressures in both England and the States in order to insure that the majority of the pamphlets issued would be slanted on his behalf.[2] Before any detailed study of George's propaganda efforts can be made, some sort of a survey should perhaps be undertaken to show what the attitudes of the British people had been to the belligerents of the Great Northern War.

It was true that the British of all classes had little love for the Swedes. In fact, their feeling bordered on contempt. Still British insular self-satisfaction and provincialism extended to all foreigners,[3] and there were many in England who were ever ready to remind the King that he too lacked the blessings of an English birth. On the other hand a goodly percentage of the realm's inhabitants could not be classed as isolationists; for in press and in coffee-house talk, they followed European affairs closely, and they gloried in the fact that William and Anne in their time had been arbiters of the continent. The Whigs were especially interested in reviving England's favored diplomatic position as it had existed in the reign of William III, and many of them actually wanted to renew the war with France.[4] It was not until 1721 with the advent of Sir Robert Walpole to power, that the 'little Englanders' among the Whigs came to control English foreign affairs. It had to be admitted, however, that when the Northern War began, William III was pro-Swedish and had bent every effort to win over a peace party to an understanding of the dangers that threatened England and Holland if the entire Spanish inheritance went to the house of Bourbon.

At the turn of the century, the English had definite thoughts on northern and eastern Europe and the inhabitants of those areas. British sentiments and ideas about Scandinavia were based upon numerous writings, the most influential being the *Account of Denmark* by Lord Molesworth, and an *Account of Sueden* by Dr. John Robinson. The former was published anonymously in 1694, and went through three editions in less than

[1] John J. Murray, 'An Eighteenth-Century Whitebook,' *The Huntington Library Quarterly*, XIII (1950), p. 376.
[2] Haverling, 'Huvuddrag i . . . propaganda,' p. 81.
[3] Basil Williams, *The Whig Supremacy, 1714–1760* (Oxford, 1939), p. 1.
[4] Michael, *England under George I*, I, 249.

an equal number of months.[1] The latter, also anonymous, appeared in the same year, and was written ostensibly at the request of many Englishmen who desired a survey of Sweden similar to the one that Molesworth had drawn up for Denmark.[2] Robinson's account was not so controversial as was that of Molesworth's. The two 'authorities' had one thing in common. They both had served England as diplomatists to the country and courts about which they wrote.[3]

Neither book presented a completely accurate picture, but as is often the case when human emotions decide the course of history—and they far too often do—what people think to be true is apt to be more influential at a given time than the truth itself. The Swedes were considered by Robinson to have vigorous constitutions, which accounted for their excellence as soldiers. Such fine physiques made the Swedes more fitted for hard labor and camp life than for intellectual pursuits. Robinson was of the opinion that the climate influenced their minds to such a manner that they were seldom found 'endued with any eminent share of Vivacity or Pregnancy of Wit.' They were men of courage and loyal to the monarchy. They were 'grave even to formality; sober, more out of necessity, than principles of temperance.' Devoted to the Lutheran Church, they were narrow in their viewpoint and little given to original thought.[4]

The good doctor—called 'that Holy Black Swede' by Bolingbroke—did not ignore the ladies of that land of snow and ice about which a French ambassador said jokingly 'there were in Sweden only nine months winter, and all the rest were summer.'[5] Robinson noted that the Swedish girls did not marry until their late twenties or early thirties. He deplored the levity

[1] Dr. John Robinson, An Account of Sueden; together with an Extract of the History of that Kingdom (London, 1694), p. 1. There were English editions in 1711, 1717, and 1738 plus two Dutch and three French editions. Ragnhild Hatton, 'John Robinson and "The Account of Sueden," ' The Bulletin of the Institute of Historical Research, XXVIII (1955), p. 140.

[2] Robinson, Account of Sueden, p. ii–iv.

[3] Robert, first Viscount Molesworth, was sent on a special mission to Denmark in 1689–90. In 1692 he returned there as envoy extraordinary. He offended the Danish court, and within the year left without the usual formality of an audience of leave. Dr. John Robinson was sent as chaplain to the British embassy in Sweden in 1680. He rose to be envoy extraordinary and did not sever his connection with Sweden until 1710 when he was succeeded by his secretary, Robert Jackson.

[4] Robinson, Account of Sueden, pp. 45–52.

[5] Ibid., p. 12.

displayed at Swedish weddings, and funerals, and soberly pointed out that the marriage festivities often were so expensive that for many years the young couple were plunged into debt. He admired the felicity of Swedish married life and the domestic capabilities of the Swedish women. He was, moreover, not blind to their sexual appeal.

> the women, while young, have generally fair complexions, tolerable features, and good shapes; and some of them are accounted more eminent for chastity before marriage, than fidelity after; they are fruitful, and seldom fail of a numerous issue.[1]

Robinson opposed the arbitrary government of Sweden and deplored the fact that the estates, Sweden's representative body, was left with little more than 'its ancient name and a power of consent to such impositions as the King's occasions require.'[2] He especially criticized the resumption of the crown lands on the part of the Swedish king in order to raise revenues for the crown.[3] Robinson was not alone in his attitude on this point.[4] Such tactics must have been extremely distasteful to such men as those who at York shouted 'Liberty and Property' upon hearing the announcement of George I's accession to the throne.

William Benson, a Whig, is an excellent example of his party's animosity to Swedish absolutism. In a *Letter to Sir J ... B ...* he could therefore write to an expatriate Swede:

> It might have been imagin'd, that you had renounc'd that kingdom, [Sweden] because it had utterly lost its *Liberty*; and 'tis very strange that you, who are happily escap'd out of the *House of Bondage* into a blessed Cannaan should be hankering after the Leeks of Egypt.[5]

[1] *Ibid.*, p. 69.
[2] *Ibid.*, p. 116.
[3] *Ibid.*, p. 102.
[4] William Benson, *A letter to Sir J ... B ... by birth a Swede but naturaliz'd and now a M ... of the present P ... t* (London, 1711), p. 18. J ... B ... is Sir Jacob Banks who was later arrested as a Jacobite.
[5] *Ibid.*, pp. 2–3. William E. H. Lecky, *A History of England in the Eighteenth Century* (London, 1892), I, 76 says this pamphlet issued at the time of the Sacheverell trial sold as many as 60,000 copies in London. It ran through at least ten editions. Cf. Haverling, 'Huvuddrag i ... propaganda,' p. 83; and S. Rydberg, *Svenska Studieresor till England under frihetstiden* (Uppsala, 1951), p. 80. In the pamphlet Benson, the Whig, was attacking the Tory, Banks, who was a member of Parliament.

Yet the Tory, Robinson, had his misgivings over Swedish disregard for property and commented that Charles XII had recovered a good revenue by seizing those lands which had once been the property of the crown.

> tho with the impoverishing of most families in Sweden and many of them, such whose ancestors, and themselves had spent their lives and fortunes in the Crown's service.[1]

This English dislike for Swedish absolutism almost made Patkul an English hero. That usually Whiggish Defoe, who wrote a laudatory biography of Charles XII in 1715, but who in the *Review* had earlier criticized Swedish military tactics, had misgivings over the fact that the Swedish king broke Patkul on the wheel in 1707.[2] Benson in a *Second Letter to J . . . B . . .* set forth a violent defense of the traitor whom he called 'Brave Patkul (that noble Foreign Whig, who took up arms for the liberty of his country).'[3] According to Benson, Charles had been victorious so long as he fought a just war 'but he had no sooner embru'd his hands in the blood of one of his own subjects [Patkul] . . . but he became as unfortunate as he was before successful.'[4]

Robinson, churchman and Tory, pointed out that the Swedish clergy exercised considerable power in Sweden and that they were mainly responsible for insuring the domestic tranquility in the kingdom. According to Robinson, himself a churchman, 'the priests have very great and uncontroulable interest and authority among the common people (who only can make disturbances) and can at their pleasures inflame or appease them.'[5] The Whig, Benson, a year later, showed his party colors. Relying upon the cleric, Robinson, whom he called 'an irresistible authority'[6] well disposed to episcopacy and monarchy, Benson pointed out that Charles XI, a pious and religious man, became absolute through the coöperation of the clergy, who as was their delight had delivered the nation over to a tyrant.[7] It takes little

---

[1] Robinson, *Account of Sueden*, pp. 102–103.
[2] Daniel Defoe, *The History of the Wars of His Present Majesty Charles XII, King of Sweden* (London, 1715), p. 275.
[3] William Benson, *A Second Letter to J . . . B . . .*, etc. (London, 1711), p. 21.
[4] *Ibid.*, p. 21.
[5] Robinson, *Account of Sueden*, pp. 111–112.
[6] Benson, *A Letter to J . . .*, p. 4.
[7] *Ibid.*, p. 27.

imagination to comprehend how little sympathy Whig and dissenter in England would have for the alliance of church and state in Sweden. And it was to be the Whigs who were to maintain the house of Hanover on the British throne.

The anti-French sentiments of the Swedish people, however, found a kindred response in the breast of Englishmen. Robinson was much pleased with the bias maintained by Charles XI towards France and French customs. His nationalism, however, did not prevent him from admitting that the aversion of the Swedish king to the French language made it difficult for foreign diplomats to conduct negotiations at the Swedish court.[1] It was a mutual distrust of Louis XIV and Versailles by Sweden and England that was to put England on the side of Sweden during the early stages of the Great Northern War in spite of the fact that many things about the Swedes and Sweden were distasteful to the ordinary Englishmen. The differences, however, were still such that clever propaganda by George and his Hanoverian ministers might widen the cleavage. The new Whig government would have less in common with Swedish ideas than did the Tories who had been swept from power.

The Danes on the other hand were pro-French. If Molesworth is to be believed, and he was by a considerable portion of the English people, the King of Denmark preferred France to all his other allies. Moreover, he aped French ideas and customs even though they were causing the total ruin of the kingdom.[2] French example, French advice, French assistance had been instrumental in the Danish adoption of absolutism,[3] and in the overthrow of Danish liberty.

> This notion of Jus Divinum of kings and princes was never known in these northern parts of the world, till these later ages of slavery: even in the eastern countries, though they adore their kings as Gods, yet they never fancied they received their right to reign immediately from heaven.[4]

---

[1] Robinson, *Account of Sueden*, pp. 76–77.

[2] Robert (Viscount) Molesworth, *An Account of Denmark as it was in the Year 1692* (London, 1694), pp. 223–225. The first edition probably appeared in December, 1693. C. H. Brasch, *On Robert Molesworth's 'An Account of Denmark as it was in the year 1692'* (Kjøbenhavn, 1879), p. 41.

[3] Molesworth, *Account of Denmark*, pp. xlvi–xlvii.

[4] *Ibid.*, pp. xxvii–xxvix.

How the men of 1688 who had set aside the divine right theory of kingship must have revolted at the ideas held by the Danish king! Whig sentiments on the place of kings in the political structure of the state were at odds then with the trends in both Scandinavian countries which were based on the principle of *Rex Legis*, found in Roman Law.

Molesworth bemoaned the changes which had taken place in Danish government over the past thirty years, and his Whig humours were infuriated that the meetings of the Danish estates had been abolished. As a result of the suspension of parliamentary privileges, the Danish people in peace time had been burdened with frequent and arbitrary taxes, and the value of property had fallen seventy-five percent. Poverty was rampant among the gentry; extreme misery and want was the condition of the peasantry.[1] Land and gentry, the very foundations of Whiggery, had thus been destroyed in Denmark, and Englishmen could take warning for

> Slavery, like a sickly constitution, grows in time so habitual, that it seems no burden nor disease; it creates a kind of laziness, and idle despondency, which puts men beyond hopes and fears.[2]

Church and army, those two pillars of absolutism, were attacked by Molesworth, who asserted that the Lutheran church was as much a bulwark of tyranny in Denmark as the Catholic church was in France.[3] The Danish army was larger than the country could afford, and the Englishman took issue with the belief that the wealth of a country was measured by the size of its army. Molesworth blamed France for this erroneous concept of national well-being and pointed out in true English fashion that when the peoples of a nation paid taxes to maintain a standing army they 'are contributors to their own misery; and their purses are drain'd in order to their slavery.'[4] Englishmen whose liberties were based on the Petition of Right and the Declaration of Rights could in no way stomach the quartering of Danish soldiers upon the population. As Molesworth put it,

[1] *Ibid.*, p. 74.
[2] *Ibid.*, p. 75.
[3] *Ibid.*, pp. 258–259.
[4] *Ibid.*, pp. 123, 125.

15

'the charge was bad, but the plague of insolent and uncouth soldiery was worse.'[1]

He was uneasy as to how the King of Denmark would subsequently employ his troops, because soldiers after eating out of house and home their own people are forced 'to make use of a hundred cruel and unjust shifts to the ruin of their neighbors.'[2] He admitted that Anglo-Danish diplomatic relations on the whole had been good and that the trade between the two countries had been heavy. He attributed the apparent friendship to English naval supremacy and to the effectiveness of the North Sea as a protective barrier between the two countries. Yet Molesworth warned his countrymen that Denmark, to maintain a balance of power in the Baltic and to preserve freedom of commerce, would 'leave no stone unturned to do us a mischief, in order to humble us to such a degree as may put them out of fears that we shall give law to the ocean.'[3] No wonder the English at the outset of the Great Northern War favored Sweden! Still it was Denmark rather than Sweden that contributed men to swell the troop contingents serving under Marlborough in the War of the Spanish Succession.

Denmark, however, was not without her defenders among the pamphleteers of England, although it must be admitted that the Molesworth endeavor was by far the most influential in deciding public opinion. The possibility that a defense of Denmark might bring political rewards from Anne Stuart and her husband Prince George of Denmark was not ignored by those gentlemen of England who lived by their wits and by their pens. William King in his *Animadversions on the pretended account of Denmark* (1694) and Jodocus Crull in *Denmark Vindicated* (1694) were among the writers who attempted to answer Molesworth. Crull's account was indeed scathing.

Lashing at the anonymity of the Molesworth *Account*, Crull asserted:

> Books without their author's names, being like bastards, who cannot claim the least prerogative from their parentage, ought

---

[1] *Ibid.*, p. 87. The Swedes also quartered soldiers upon the inhabitants. Robinson, *Account of Sueden*, pp. 126ff.

[2] Molesworth, *Account of Denmark*, p. 124.

[3] *Ibid.*, 190–191.

questionless to challenge no other authority, but what is derived from their own deserts.[1]

Small factual errors made by Molesworth were enlarged and the Whig attack on the power of the clergy was answered with the statement 'Here is a general charge against the whole body of the clergy (except the Calvinists and their proselytes) . . . concerning the miseries that have befallen Europe these two hundred years.'[2] As for the monopoly of the Danish clergy over the minds of the Danish youth, Crull claimed that Molesworth had stated the facts incorrectly.[3]

In discussing the loss of Danish liberties, high taxes, and a resumption of crown lands by the Danish monarchy, Crull exhibited a better understanding of Danish affairs than did the more widely influential Molesworth. The latter had expressed surprise that the clergy and the burgher-peasant groups had parted so easily with their liberties. Crull aptly pointed out that Denmark in the seventeenth century could hardly be called a land of liberty because only the second estate had enjoyed power. With it in the saddle, the lives of burgher and peasant had been a sorry one. Many of the late calamities of Denmark could be laid at the door of the nobility, whose wings had been clipped by the crown to avoid a recurrence of the disasters the Danes had suffered in the long war with Sweden which had ended in 1660.[4] In fact Crull was of the opinion that the four estates in Denmark of the clergy, nobility, burghers and peasants had 'not surrendered anything of their native rights, tho perhaps some particular persons have felt the smart of it.'[5] The high taxes were only the consequences and effects of the long series of wars in which Denmark had been engaged in the early part of the seventeenth century.[6] Crull in many respects was closer to the truth than Molesworth, but the virtue of truth—with all due respect to those who mouth cliches—is

[1] Jodocus Crull, *Denmark Vindicated* (London, 1694), p. 1. Crull is substantiated in the anonymous *Defense du Danemark* (Cologne, 1696) and the better known William King, *Animadversions on the pretended account of Denmark*, printed in *The Original Works of William King, LL.D.*, 3 vols. (London, 1776), I, 35–132. King received his information from the Danish minister to the English Court.

[2] Crull, *Denmark*, pp. 28–29.

[3] *Ibid.*, p. 55.

[4] *Ibid.*, p. 192.

[5] *Ibid.*, p. 154.

[6] *Ibid.*, p. 187.

often not triumphant when the collective mind of a nation arrives at a conclusion.

King, who because of his defense of Denmark was appointed to be Anne's secretary,[1] was even harsher on Molesworth. In the prefatory letter to the *Animadversions*, it was pointed out that Molesworth had failed in his embassy, because he insisted that he should be allowed privileges reserved for the Danish king.[2] Many contradictions in Molesworth's account were brought to light and Englishmen were reminded that in Denmark all bore their just burden of taxes.[3] Molesworth's defense of the Duke of Holstein-Gottorp was also attacked.[4]

Poland, in contrast with Denmark and Sweden, had too much liberty for the ordinary English gentry and citizenry to stomach.[5] Defoe, who was pro-Augustus, blamed the Polish Diet for that country's many ills.[6] An anonymous pamphlet entitled *The Ancient and Present State of Poland* (1697) claimed that the nobles had a life and death power over the inhabitants who were treated like slaves.[7] Crull and King considered the *Liberum Veto* to be the curse of Poland, and the former in his defense of Denmark cited Poland as an example where 'too much liberty is frequently the spring of fatal diseases in the government.'[8]

Russia then as in the present day was the great enigma of western Europe. Restrictions on travel both into and from Russia had given Englishmen little opportunity to study the inhabitants of Muscovy and their customs.[9] It was not until after Peter the Great's advent to the throne in 1682 that Russia's 'iron-curtain' was even partially lifted. That monarch

[1] Anthony à Wood, *Athenae Oxonienses* (1691–92), II, 914.
[2] King, *Animadversions*, I, 42.
[3] *Ibid.*, I, 75.
[4] *Ibid.*, I, 116.
[5] *Ibid.*, I, 70.
[6] Defoe, *Dyet of Poland*, p. 36. When using this pamphlet, one should remember that its reason for being was an attack upon the Church of England party which was opposed to England's intervention in European affairs. Defoe in some of his later writings changed his estimate of Augustus II. Cf. Defoe, *History of Charles XII*, p. 55.
[7] Anon., *The Ancient and present state of Poland, giving a short but accurate account of the situation in that country* (1697), pp. 3–4.
[8] Crull, *Denmark*, p. 6; cf. King, *Animadversions*, I, 70.
[9] Molesworth, *Account of Denmark*, pp. xxxv–xxxvi and Daniel Defoe, *An Impartial History of the Life and Actions of Peter Alexowitz* (London, 1723), p. 6.

had the penetrating judgment to realize that ignorance of one's neighbors and their customs was something not to be sought nor cherished, and for that attitude Defoe in 1723 was to commend Peter.[1] One of Peter's accomplishments for which posterity has given him the title 'Great,' was to change the Russians from 'greatest contemners of knowledge' to 'searchers after wisdom.'[2] The breakdown of restrictions on the exchange of information between Russia and the rest of Europe, however, had just commenced when the Great Northern War began, and it was not until the middle of the war that the English gained any clear-cut knowledge of Russia and Russian institutions. Concerning Russian trade and trade practices, the British had ample information, most of which was not conducive to the establishing of friendly relations, commercial or otherwise, between Russians and Englishmen. For example, Captain John Perry's *State of Russia* (1716) attempted to show the inherent dishonesty of most Russians[3] while British merchants continually complained about shady Russian traders. The former pointed out that the Russian language was actually devoid of the word 'Honour,' and that a common saying among foreigners in Peter's domains was:

that if you would know if a Russ be an honest man you must look if he has Hair grown on the Palm of his Hand; but if you find none there, don't expect it [honesty][4]

Defoe in *The Consolidator* credited Peter's European travels as being the reason for Russian military successes against Sweden, and bursting with nationalism, he was elated that Peter had

transmitted most of our general practice, especially in war and trade, to his own unpolite people, and the effects of this curiosity of his, are exceedingly visible in his present proceedings.[5]

[1] Defoe, *Peter*, pp. 6–7.
[2] *Ibid.*, p. 3.
[3] Captain John Perry, *The State of Russia under the present Czar* (London, 1716), *passim*. Perry had served Peter in many capacities and had not received payment for his hire. Russian attempts to keep Perry at what was practically forced labor besmack of current Soviet practices regarding German, Baltic, and Polish scientists. Perry fortunately was saved from such a fate by the British embassy.
[4] *Ibid.*, pp. 216–217.
[5] Daniel Defoe, *The Consolidator, or Memoirs of Sundry Transactions from the World in the Moon* (London, 1705), p. 1.

The 'self-styled author of *The True-Born Englishman*' gloried in the fact that Russia had built her excellent fleet through the efforts of Dutch and English artisans, and he paid St. Petersburg one of the finest compliments that could be bestowed by an eighteenth-century Englishman, namely, that it began 'to look like our Portsmouth.'[1] Defoe, however, sounded a note of warning which more and more Englishmen took to heart as the war progressed, and as the balance in the North became more one-sided. According to Defoe, the vast and incredible advancement of the Russians 'may serve to remind us, how we once taught the French to build ships, till they are grown able to teach us how to use them.'[2] At a relatively early stage in the war, it was possible to note in England a growing uneasiness that Russia would replace Sweden as the dominant Baltic power and thereby upset the diplomatic equilibrium even more than it had been out of balance during the days of Swedish hegemony. After Poltava that uneasiness was to increase remarkably. As Sir Josiah Burchett, Secretary of the Admiralty (1666?–1746) well illustrated English misgivings:

> What will be the event of the Accession of so great a Power by Sea and Land, in the Hands of a Prince, Master of so wide a Dominion, peopled with such infinite Multitudes, and what Alterations in the Affairs and Interests of Europe it may occasion, I leave to the Politicians to discuss.[3]

Russian tyranny and brutality were distasteful to the Whig Molesworth, who felt that the Russian clergy had contributed to the enslavement of the people.[4] Defoe considered Russia to be an aggressor in the Great Northern War, and condemned Peter for his perfidy in professing peace to Sweden at a time he was making military preparations to dismember her,[5] 'which renders the character of those who made those protestations sufficiently contemptible to all the christian princes of Europe....'

[1] *Ibid.*, p. 2.
[2] *Ibid.*, p. 3.
[3] Sir Josiah Burchett, *A Complete History of the Most Remarkable Transactions at Sea* ... (London, 1720), p. 19.
[4] Molesworth, *Account of Denmark*, p. xxv.
[5] Defoe, *Peter*, pp. 94, 96. In the *History of Charles XII*, p. 56, Defoe asserted 'It was a war begun without the least provocations given on the part of the Swedes.'

Peter, however, was not so bad as Augustus II because 'he did not fall on without saying Grace.'[1]

George I could thus measure the feelings of his subjects by the writings of the pamphleteers. In fact many of them whose pens were for sale would be utilized by him in the future. He could consider also the foreign policy of his predecessors and their attitudes towards events in northern Europe. On the surface it appeared that the British, all things being weighed, favored Sweden over the other belligerents in the North. Yet there was a loophole whereby petty British grievances towards the Swedes might be enlarged especially if effective propaganda were employed. The opening wedge for exploitation was trade, for English commercial sentiments were at times directly opposed to British political opinions.

[1] Defoe, *History of Charles XII*, p. 55.

II

COMMERCE AND POWER
POLITICS

> The Muscovite with many a Knight
> The Swesian and Denmarke kinge
> To her good grace
> Send hither, a-pace
> For many a needful thing.[1]

GEORGE I had good reason to hope that he could use trade as a means to foster his power politics in the Baltic for the balance of power for which European diplomats strove in the eighteenth century had the 'soul of commerce.'[2] Power and economics were closely interwoven. Each country endeavored to prevent any single nation from becoming too powerful by obtaining an excess of profit and a consequent increase of power through trade,[3] which Defoe called 'the life of the world's prosperity,' and asserted that 'all the wealth that has been extraordinary, whether of nations or cities has been raised by it. . . .'[4] Trade and navigation were understood by the diplomatists of the time to be means by which pressure might

---

[1] Quoted from Swineton Ballads by Ethel Seaton, *Literary relations of England and Scandinavia in the Seventeenth Century* (Oxford, 1935), p. 27. Some of the ideas expressed in this chapter can be found in John J. Murray, 'Baltic Commerce and Power Politics in the early eighteenth century,' *Huntington Library Quarterly*, VI (May, 1943), 293–312.

[2] Louis M. Kahl, *La balance de l'Europe* (Berlin and Gottenburg, 1774), pp. 142–165.

[3] Douglas K. Reading, *The Anglo-Russian Commercial Treaty of 1734*, Yale Historical Publication, XXXII (New Haven, 1938), p. 10.

[4] Daniel Defoe, *A Plan of the English Commerce* (London, 1728), p. 32.

COMMERCE AND POWER POLITICS

be exerted to alter the international political equilibrium. Such was the basis of England's commercial policy.[1] The eighteenth century was an age of 'economic egotism.'[2] Russia attacked Sweden in order to gain access to the Baltic. Prussia seized Stettin from defeated Sweden, and later purloined from Maria Theresa the richest jewel in the Hapsburg crown, Silesia. Hanover opened the Elbe and Weser rivers by gaining Bremen and Verden. The Dutch strangled Antwerp by keeping the Scheldt River closed to navigation, while English diplomacy choked to the death the commercial prosperity of Dunkirk. When off Cape Passaro the guns of the English fleet under Sir George Byng sank the Spanish ships in 1718, they removed the only means by which Madrid could stop the English violation of Spanish laws governing South American trade. Twenty-one years later for the glory of commerce and the ear of Captain Robert Jenkins, a repeat performance was deemed necessary by the 'Boy Patriots' and other Whigs. Thus war and business commingled.

That phase of economic policy is called the 'age of mercantilism.' The state stood at the center of mercantile endeavors as they developed historically, and was both the subject and the object of mercantile economic action.[3] Whereas medieval economic policy had been aimed at plenty, that of the mercantile era aimed at power.[4] The good of the state was the prime criterion, and all wealth was examined in that light.[5] As Colbert, the great finance minister of Louis XIV, wrote, 'Trade is the source of finance and finance is the vital nerve of war.'[6] That French statesman had in the seventeenth century so diligently applied the economic principles which were to be current for the next hundred years, that 'mercantilism' and 'Colbertism' have become synonymous. His prophecy that the maritime powers, England and Holland, would attain so much

---

[1] Eli Heckscher, *Mercantilism* (London, 1935), II, 35.

[2] Reading, *Anglo-Russian Commercial Treaty*, p. 9.

[3] Heckscher, *Mercantilism*, II, 19, 21.

[4] Edmund Whittaker, *A History of Economic Ideas*, fifth edition (New York, 1940), pp. 92-93.

[5] William Cunningham, *The Growth of English Industry and Commerce* (Cambridge, 1910-1912), I, 467-470.

[6] Heckscher, *Mercantilism*, II, 11, 17. By finance Colbert meant public finance. Cf. Charles W. Cole, *Colbert and a Century of French Mercantilism* (New York, 1939) and Idem, *French Mercantilism, 1683-1700* (New York, 1943).

strength through their commercial preponderance that they would be able to 'set bounds at their pleasure to all the plans of princes'[1] was fulfilled by the military failures of Louis XIV. It was hardly surprising, then, that the eighteenth century imitators of the Grand Monarch, whether 'enlightened' or not, took to heart the precepts of his great mercantilist. As an anonymous British pamphleteer put it 'the state of War in Europe requires unusual Supplies of Money from the Subject . . . and Money is now more than ever the Nerve of War' for countries without wealth 'will be exposed to danger of becoming a Prey to some other.'[2]

According to eighteenth-century economists, the perfect commerce was one bringing bullion into the country. Trade was advantageous to a nation when it either rid a country of superfluous manufactured goods or brought in raw materials. The sole excuse for importing manufactured articles was reëxportation. In that case a country would be well remunerated for its efforts in the profit accruing from the carrying trade. The commerce of a state was in fact measured by the ratio of the bullion exchange and by the effect of the trade upon the country's entire political and economic structure.[3]

In his *Plan of the English Commerce*, Defoe (who, according to Mr. Sutherland, one of his many biographers, 'comes nearest to being a poet when he writes in impassioned prose about the expansion of English commerce'[4]) linked manufacturing and navigation together and listed the greatest services a state derived from them.[5] Three of the points are especially worthy of note, for they throw light on the power theory of mercantilism as set forth by Cunningham and Heckscher.[6] The first,

[1] *Ibid.*, II, 18.

[2] Anon., *Considerations requiring greater Care for Trade in England* (1695), p. 2–3.

[3] William Wood, *Survey of Trade* (London, 1719), pp. 81–87. Cf. Charles King, *The British Merchant or Commerce Preserved* (London, 1721), *passim*, for similar ideas.

[4] James Sutherland, *Defoe* (London, 1937), p. 47.

[5] Defoe, *Plan*, p. 69. The list is as follows: 'Manufacturing supplies merchandise,' 'Navigation supplies shipping,' 'Manufacture is the hospital which feeds the poor,' 'Navigation is the nursery which raises seamen,' 'Manufacture commands money from abroad,' 'Navigation brings it home,' 'Manufacture loads the ships out,' 'Navigation loads them in,' 'Manufacture is wealth,' 'Navigation is strength.'

[6] This theory of mercantilism carries the bullion theory a step further and claims that the reason a bullion exchange was desired from trade was to provide money to equip the armed forces and thus enhance the prestige of the state. This

'Navigation is the nursery which raised seamen,' was an observation that Defoe was not alone in making. Anthony Wood, in his *Survey of Trade* (1717) claimed that England's foreign trade and commerce were 'breeders' of sailors,[1] and called trade 'the living fountain from whence we draw all our nourishment,'[2] while the anonymous pamphlet *Considerations requiring greater Care for trade in England* called sea power a 'Wall of Brass and the greatest Bulwark of our Religion, Laws and Properties.'[3] The Newfoundland fisheries were the chief source for the sailors who manned what Mahan called 'the wooden walls of England,'[4] but as Joshua Gee in his *Trade and Navigation Considered* shows the timber trade was the second most important school for seamen.[5] Whatever the substance of Britain's 'sea walls,' George I could take heart that the Baltic was the queen of the timber trade and as such directly influenced Britain's political economy.

The second point expounded by Defoe was: 'Manufacture is wealth.' That idea, allied with those of Defoe which explained how navigation and manufacturing brought riches to a country, was a pertinent one, and was uppermost in the minds of the late seventeenth- and early eighteenth-century economists. Sir Charles D'Avenant, an important statistician of his time and an inspector-general of the English customs, went to great lengths to illustrate that the balance of trade had a direct effect upon land prices, rates of interest, etc.[6] Sir William Temple, a leading Restoration statesman, entertained similar ideas.[7]

[1] Wood, *Survey*, p. 6.

[2] *Ibid.*, p. 4.

[3] *Considerations . . . for Trade in England*, p. 8.

[4] Alfred T. Mahan, *The Influence of Sea Power upon History, 1660–1783* (Boston, 1898), pp. 82–83; Ralph G. Lounsbury, *The British fishery at Newfoundland, 1634–1763* (New Haven, 1934), pp. 61, 206.

[5] Joshua Gee, *The Trade and Navigation of Great Britain Considered* (London, 1729), p. 7.

[6] Sir Charles d'Avenant, *Discourses on the Publick Revenues and on the Trade of England* (London, 1698), II, *passim*; his arguments can also be found in *The Political and Commercial Works of that celebrated writer Charles d'Avenant*, Charles Whitworth (ed.) (London, 1771), I. *Cf.* Daniel Defoe, *A General History of Trade* (London, 1713), p. 12 and Idem, *The Complete English Tradesman* (London, 1713), pp. 369–371.

[7] Sir William Temple, 'An Essay on the Advancement of Trade in Ireland,' in his *Miscellanea* (London, 1697), pp. 97–164.

theory, first advanced by Cunningham, has been elaborated on by Heckscher. Modern usage refers to such economic policies as 'economic nationalism.'

'Numerous merchant fleets and powerful navies,' concurred Wood, 'are not only the signs of a thriving people, but are themselves real and effectual wealth, and perhaps more useful than any other kind of riches.'[1]

The aim of such men was that England should augment her economic resources through trade and thus become politically more powerful. Defoe in a third statement, 'Navigation is strength,' showed himself to be in accord with D'Avenant, Colbert and Temple, and to espouse the idea of a system of power politics wherein commercial aspirations were knotted with diplomatic and dynastic longings. To encourage commerce, which was vital to defense,[2] England and continental countries enacted protective legislation. Gee, Defoe, Wood, and other British mercantilists all felt that a nation whose nascent industries were not protected would soon be drained of its wealth, and thus became emasculated.[3]

England had in reality little cause to worry about foreign competition, for by 1715 she was already becoming a 'nation of shopkeepers.' Defoe in the *Complete English Tradesman* pointed out with pride that a man in England could rise to a position of influence viâ the marts of commerce, whereas in other countries the highway to success traversed European battlefields.[4] He also boasted: 'We are the greatest exportation of the growth and product of our land, and of the manufacture and labour of our people; and the greatest importation and consumption of the growth, product, and manufactures of other countries from abroad, of any nation in the world.'[5]

Defoe's pride in the achievements of his compatriots was justified, because England in the period being studied was the first industrial and the first commercial state in Europe. Any attempt on the part of another European nation to destroy the

---

[1] Wood, *Survey*, p. 121; Gee, *Trade and Navigation*, p. 15.

[2] Cunningham, *Growth of English Industry*, II, 15.

[3] Gee, *Trade and Navigation*, p. 11; Defoe, *Plan*, p. 250. The Irish Woollens Act of 1696, which ruined Irish woollen manufacturing, is an excellent example of such legislation. See Cunningham, *Growth of English Industry*, I, 371–372. The mercantilist ideas expressed in the above paragraphs may also be found in Samuel Fortrey, *England's Interest and Improvement Consisting of the Increase of the Store and Trade of this Kingdom* (London, 1663); and John Cary, *An Essay on the State of England in Relationship to its Trade . . .* (Bristol, 1695).

[4] Defoe, *The Complete Tradesman*, pp. 374–375.

[5] *Ibid.*, pp. 369–370.

COMMERCE AND POWER POLITICS

English commercial predominance would have ruined the political balance of power arrived at by the statesmen who were present at the Utrecht Congress. Europe, therefore, was caught in a dilemma, and England, aiming to maintain a political equilibrium on the Continent, was annihilating all semblance of balance upon the high seas. The strength of England's economic might rested upon trade, colonies, and sea power coöperating with a government that advanced political support to serve commercial purposes. The employment of the diplomacy of the nation and the use of the country's military and naval forces for economic motives, plus a virile merchant marine, constituted the keystones to an arch upon which English commerce rested.[1]

The eighteenth century saw that commerce expanded and enlarged. Wood claimed that the English balance of trade was greater in the early part of the century than the total amount of English exports had been in the year 1663 or the year 1669.[2] According to the Custom-House books, the tonnage of shipping leaving England in 1700 amounted to 317,000 registered tons. By 1714, there had been increase to 448,843 tons.[3] Henry Martyn, Inspector-General of the English customs[4] and one of the leading economists of his age, compiled statistics in 1719 showing the relative values of English imports and exports.[5]

[1] Reading, *Anglo-Russian Commercial Treaty*, pp. 14–16. Dr. Reading's chapter on British commerce in general is a competent treatment of England's commercial aspirations and position in the early eighteenth century.

[2] Wood, *Survey*, p. 49.

[3] Paul Joseph Mantoux, *The Industrial Revolution in the Eighteenth Century*, trans. from the French by Marjorie Vernon (New York, 1928), p. 102. Mr. Mantoux calls this trade increase slow, but he is making a comparison between the early eighteenth century and the period after the industrial revolution. This increase is far from slow when compared with the commercial expansion of the seventeenth century. See Reading, *Anglo-Russian Commercial Treaty*, pp. 14–15. Sven-Erik Aström in *From Cloth to Iron, the Anglo-Baltic trade in the late seventeenth century*, Commentationes Humanarum, Litteram, XXXIII, Societas Scientiarum Finnica (Helsingfors, 1963), p. 15 points out that the Baltic Customs Accounts are good for shipping movements, but that they leave much to be desired in some other areas.

[4] George N. Clark, *Guide to English Commercial Statistics*, Royal Historical Society, *Guides and Handbooks*, II (London, 1938), p. 19.

[5] Henry Martyn, 'An essay towards finding the balance of our whole trade annually from Christmas of 1698 to Christmas in 1719,' *Ibid.*, p. 70. The errors in the third column are Martyn's. Wood, *Survey*, p. 49 set exports in 1715 at £7,739,400 9s. 10d. England's chief export was wool (Reading, *Anglo-Russian Commercial Treaty*, p. 15), and foreign countries were so dependent upon that commodity that the woollen trade flourished in spite of restrictions placed on it by foreign countries. Defoe, *Plan*, p. 250.

COMMERCE AND POWER POLITICS

YEAR	EXPORTS	s.	d.	IMPORTS	s.	d.	ENG. BALANCE	s.	d.
1700	7,302,716	17	6	5,970,175	1	10	1,080,497	5	9
1715	7,379,408	0	8	5,640,943	16	5	1,738,465	4	3
1716	7,641,985	6	11	5,800,258	7	8	1,813,826	19	3
1717	9,147,700	2	4	6,346,768	1	6	2,800,932	0	10
1718	8,225,302	14	5	6,669,390	1	1	1,555,912	13	4

It can be seen from the table above that there was a steady increase in the volume of English trade up to 1718, at which time the unstable political situation of Europe caused the volume of exports to decrease somewhat.

The regions in the Baltic Sea assumed an important place in the economics of the time. Sweden and her commerce loomed especially large in the European trade picture, for the Baltic Sea before the outbreak of the Great Northern War was little more than a Swedish lake.[1] From the days of the Hanseatic League, the wealth of Baltic shores had been known to and sought after by western Europe. Although the League had sunk into oblivion, the passage of time had not lessened the riches that might be won from the Baltic forests. The ports of Lübeck, Danzig, Königsberg, Rostock, Riga, and Stockholm, annually shipped great quantities of naval stores by sea to western European nations.[2] The Admiralty's Burchett remarked:

There are not any people better furnished with Materials for Shipping than the Swedes, their country abounding not only with useful Timber of all kinds, but with numerous Mines of the best Iron in the World, and producing great quantities of excellent Tar and Hemp.[3]

An anonymous work entitled *The Memoire of a Person Interested in Baltic Commerce* (1716) claimed that all of the hemp in the

[1] Swedish possessions in the Baltic included Finland, Ingria, Livonia, Esthonia, and Swedish Pomerania. She also possessed Bremen and Verden which controlled the mouths of the Weser and Elbe rivers.
[2] Nina Bang og Knud Korst, *Tabeller over Skibsfart og Varetransport gennem Öresund, 1661–1783, og gennem Storbaelt, 1701–1748* (Copenhagen, 1906–1922), II, 154 and *passim*. The ports enumerated were the chief shippers of naval stores. Robert B. Albion, *Forests and Sea-power; the timber problem of the Royal Navy, 1652–1862* (Cambridge, 1926), p. 140 includes Memel and Stettin as great timber ports. In Defoe, *Plan*, p. 222 Danzig, Memel, and Königsberg were considered to be the three largest naval-stores ports.
[3] Burchett, *A Complete History*, p. 18.

28

world and the best masts came from a region stretching from the Gulf of Bothnia to the coasts of Prussia.[1] Dutch bottoms carried the bulk of this lucrative trade,[2] because the individual Baltic seaports did not have sufficient commerce with the different European countries to warrant the importation of goods from the places of production. Commodities destined for the Baltic were therefore sent to Holland, center of exchange for all Europe,[3] and then transshipped. The trade with Danzig[4] and Sweden[5] was especially profitable to the States General. Naturally the ships which carried the most goods to the Baltic carried more Baltic products back to Western Europe. As Onslow Burrish remarked in his *Batavia Illustrati*, 'It would be hard to say whether the fisheries, the Indian trade, or the Northern countries ... be of most importance to the Dutch, but tis certain they are all equally necessary for the support of each other.'[6]

Next in importance to the States came England. Throughout the last half of the seventeenth century, Sweden and England came closer together politically and economically because Sweden controlled the harbors which exported the important products necessary for England's marine. For the same reasons, Russia after 1700 superseded Sweden in English commercial eyes when those same ports and products came under Russian control.[7]

[1] 'Memoire d'une personne interéssee et sensible au Commerce de la mer baltique,' in Guillaume de Lamberty, *Mémoires pour servir a l'histoire du* XVIII siècle, contenant les negociations, traitez, resolutions, et autres *documens authentiques concernant les affaires d'état* (The Hague and Amsterdam, 1700–1718), IX, 663. The work, according to Stig Jägerskiold, *Sverige och Europa, 1716–1718* (Ekenäs, 1937), p. 92 was written by Count Maurits Vellingk, the former governor of Bremen. Copies were sent to Sunderland and Stanhope. The title in Lamberty is correct. Chance, *George I and the Northern War*, p. 186 was in error by insisting that the word 'interessée' should be changed to 'désinteressée.'

[2] Bang, *Tabeller*, II, 654, 659, 664, 668.
[3] Gee, *Trade and Navigation*, p. 127; Defoe, *Plan*, p. 192.
[4] Bang, *Tabeller*, II, 660, 669. Molesworth, *Account of Denmark*, p. 117 estimated that between 1,000 and 1,100 Dutch ships passed the Sound yearly as compared with 200 and 300 British vessels.
[5] Whitworth to Polwarth, March, 18/29, 1718, in Historical Manuscripts Commission, *Reports on the Manuscripts of Lord Polwarth* (London, 1911), I, 465. Cited hereafter as *Polwarth Papers*.
[6] Onslow Burrish, *Batavia illustrati; or a view of the policy and commerce of the United Provinces, particularly of Holland*, 3 vols. (London, 1728), III, 337.
[7] Sven-Erik Åström, *From Stockholm to St. Petersburg: commercial factors in the political relations between England and Sweden, 1675–1700*, Studia Historica, II, the Finnish Historical Society (Helsinki, 1962), p. 5.

Charles Whitworth in his *Survey of the Trade of Great Britain* compiled statistics on Britain's Baltic trade, which indicate that her Baltic imports of 1715 were approximately 10.7% of her total imports.[1] When one considers the Baltic commodities were bulky and required relatively more shipping tonnage per pound sterling value than many other items, it becomes apparent that the flow of commerce between England and the Baltic was considerable so far as bulk was concerned. It was also of prime strategic importance. Whitworth figures show that the trade between England and Russia was growing, while that between England and Sweden was decreasing. Russia in 1715, by gaining possession of the Baltic Provinces, or 'the East Country' (as the area was called by contemporaries), obtained a monopoly upon the sale of certain naval stores,[2] and thus constituted a threat not only to England's economic well-being but also to her naval security. Thus it might appear that England's commercial and political policies would favor Sweden rather than her enemy Russia. Yet Sweden already had a reputation among British as an unfair monopolist, and Russian dominance lay in the future. England then in 1714 had little choice between the trade practices of the new and the old giant of the Baltic.

Such an unhappy situation brought forth loud complaints from English mercantilists. Among them was Defoe, who wrote:

> I might mention here, how unaccountable to blame we are in this Trade; that whereas a full Supply might be had of all those things, *I may say, Every one of them* from our own Colonies, the Product of the *British* proper Dominions, the Labour of the *British* people, and which is equal to it all brought by our own ships, to the vast Increase of the *British* Navigation, it should miserable be neglected or omitted, and Goods be bought with out ready Money, great part of them brought Home in foreign Bottoms, and the whole Trade managed in a wrong Place; or, as we may say, running in a wrong Channel, to the infinite Advantage of the *Danes, Swedes, Poles, Prussians* and *Muscovites,* and the enriching the (otherwise) poorest and most worthless, and I had almost said the beggerly Nations in the World.[3]

---

[1] Charles Whitworth, *The State of Trade of Great Britain* . . . (London, 1776), I, 19–21.

[2] Reading, *Anglo-Russian Commercial Treaty,* p. 26.

[3] Defoe, *Plan,* p. 222. Italics are Defoe's.

In spite of so pessimistic an outlook English–Baltic trade prospered. From Denmark–Norway came deal boards,[1] timber, spars, iron. An unfavorable exchange of trade, from an English point of view, resulted, as English shipments to the Danes were restricted to only a small amount of tobacco and a few coarse woollens having little value. In addition there was a danger that the balance would become increasingly worse after the Danes rebuilt their merchant marine, which had been sadly depleted by the ravages of the Great Northern War.[2] Moreover, the fact that all English ships passing through the Danish Sound had to pay toll occasioned disputes between the Danish government and British traders.[3] Molesworth estimated that in the latter part of the seventeenth century Denmark collected 65,000 *rigs* dollars annually at the Sound from European shipping.[4]

It was Sweden, more so than Denmark, who furnished Europe with many of the commodities that she needed, but as Robinson remarked: 'yet either the war-like temper, the idleness or ignorance of the inhabitants, has formerly kept them from being much concern'd in trade, and given strangers the management and advantage of it.'[5] The most important product exported by Sweden was iron. In the later part of the reign of Charles XII, nearly half of England's iron imports came from Sweden,[6] for England at the beginning of the eighteenth century was not the chief metal-producing country in the world; in fact, 'she could not in this respect, compare with either Sweden or Germany.'[7] Joshua Gee estimated that two-thirds of the iron wrought and consumed in England came from Sweden.[8] His figure is rather high in spite of the fact that England's iron industry was declining, and that England was probably importing more

---

[1] A deal board was used in the construction of the deck of a ship. It was usually Baltic fir or Baltic oak.

[2] Gee, *Trade and Navigation*, p. 17.

[3] Molesworth, *Account of Denmark*, p. 17.

[4] *Ibid.*, p. 121.

[5] Robinson, *Account of Sueden*, p. 142.

[6] Eli Heckscher, *Svensk Arbete och Liv Från Medeltiden till Nutiden* (Stockholm, 1941), p. 121.

[7] Mantoux, *Industrial, Revolution*, p. 277. Thomas S. Ashton, *Iron and Steel in the Industrial Revolution* (Manchester, 1924) shows the importance of Swedish iron to England during the seventeenth century. Eli Heckscher, 'The place of Sweden in Modern Economic History,' *Economic History Review*, IV (1932), pp. 14–15.

[8] Gee, *Trade and Navigation*, p. 17.

iron than she was producing. Probably Eli Heckscher's estimate that between 40 and 50 percent of England's iron needs were supplied by her northern ally is closer to the truth.[1] This figure constituted $82\frac{1}{2}\%$ of Sweden's total iron exports which between 1711–1716 yearly averaged 32,800 tons.[2] It is important to note, that when George I in 1717 attempted to ruin Sweden's economic life by forbidding imports from Sweden,[3] the hardships were so great upon England that eventually he had to allow the importation of iron from Sweden to continue.[4] The annual value of English imports of Swedish iron just before George I attempted to shackle Swedish trade was £122,700.[5]

That trade plus the traffic in planks, boards, copper, and naval stores, resulted in a lament from the author of the *Trade of Great Britain Considered* that 'the balance they drew from us amounted before the late war with Denmark to between two and three hundred thousand pounds yearly, beside the freight of their own product, which we paid them for likewise.'[6] England on the other hand sent cloth stuffs and other woolen manufactures to Sweden, which were valued at £50,000. Newcastle coal, pewter, lead, tin, fruits, sugar, and herring from Scotland were worth an equal amount as exports, which brought the British total to £100,000. But if the Swedes paid for half of what they purchased it was extraordinary.[7] Sweden, however, was to lose her lucrative exchange, during the first half of the eighteenth century, because of the Great Northern War and because the rising iron trade of Russia was more

---

[1] Heckscher, *Svensk Arbete*, p. 121. Eli Heckscher and Bertil Boëthius, *Svensk Handelsstatistik 1637–1737* (Stockholm, 1938), pp. lii–liii. Eli Heckscher, 'Un Grand chapitre de l'histoire du fer: le monopole, suédois,' *Annals d'Histoire Economique et Sociale*, IV (1932), pp. 127–138; 225–242. The latter is an excellent discussion of the Swedish monopoly of iron and the influence of the monopoly on Europe. In his article 'The Place of Sweden,' *Economic History Review*, IV, 12, Heckscher says that the lowest possible minimum was thirty percent.

[2] Heckscher in Heckscher and Boëthius, *Handelsstatistiks*, pp. lii and lv. Heckscher, 'Un grand chapitre,' *Annales d'Histoire*, IV, 234. Cf. Gösta Lindeberg, *Svensk Economisk Politik under den Görtzka Perioden* (Lund, 1941), pp. 391–393 for a slightly different statistical study of Swedish iron exports, based on among other things the Sound dues.

[3] *The Historical Register* (London, 1717–38), IV, 63, 170–173.

[4] Royal Proclamation, February 24, 1718, *The Historical Register*, V, 138–139.

[5] Reading, *Anglo-Russian Commercial Treaty*, p. 24.

[6] Gee, *Trade and Navigation*, p. 17.

[7] Robinson, *Account of Sueden*, p. 151.

amenable to English exploitation than that of Sweden.[1] When George I assumed the English throne, however, the transition was in the process of beginning.[2]

Notwithstanding the importance of iron, it was naval stores that were the most sought after of the Baltic's resources. Along the shores of that great inland sea were rich fir forests, and in the interior to the south and west lay a great oak belt. The port of Riga enjoyed the reputation of exporting the best masts in the world. They came at first from Livonia and other Baltic provinces, but as those sources of supply diminished, the lumbermen went inland. An elaborate system of canals permitted penetration to Volhynia. Even the riches of the Ukraine were tapped. Some of the best lumber known to Europe, including the famous 'Riga wainscot,' floated down the Düana to Riga[3] from places as far inland as Kiev. France, Holland, Spain, and England were all dependent upon the Baltic Provinces for their naval stores.[4]

Sweden supplied timber to the British navy, and the East Country furnished most of the hemp. From Finland came the pitch and tar so necessary for vessels of the sailing ship era. During the days of the Restoration, the mast fleets had arrived annually at Gothenburg, a staple town outside the Sound, near the Norwegian frontier. Eventually Stockholm became the chief staple center for the pitch and tar trade. After 1700 Sweden supplied the Royal Navy with less and less timber, because the protectionist policy of Charles XII shackled the trade and in time lost for Sweden the role of a great timber producing nation.[5]

Sweden's attempts to follow mercantilist concepts dear to the hearts of Englishmen brought her into sharp conflict with

---

[1] Reading, *Anglo-Russian Commercial Treaty*, p. 26.

[2] Heckscher and Boëthius, *Handelsstatistik*, p. lvi. England was Sweden's principal customer, but never predominated in the export trade to Sweden except during the years of the Continental System of the early nineteenth century.

[3] Albion, *Forests and Sea Power*, p. 141.

[4] Reading, *Anglo-Russian Commercial Treaty*, p. 19. Heckscher, *Mercantilism*, II, 39 points out that the different European countries could have saved money by having the needed ships built in the Baltic, but the economic doctrines of the day frowned upon buying finished products from other countries. Thus naval stores rather than completed vessels were imported.

[5] Heckscher, *Svensk Arbete*, p. 130 and Heckscher and Boëthius, *Handelsstatistik*, liii.

British merchants. For a long time, Sweden's lucrative commerce had been in the hands of foreigners,[1] who, although they contributed to Sweden's economic welfare, also reaped a considerable harvest by so doing. Consequently, the College of Commerce[2] which was comparable to the British Board of Trade, began to put more and more restrictions upon non-native traders.

All pertinent Swedish economic documents in the early seventeenth century concerned themselves with foreign merchants. Although the import trade was monopolized by outsiders, especially by the Dutch, there were also many complaints about the export trade. The growth of Sweden's need for money which resulted from her many military ventures did much to foster bullionism. At the same time, the outsiders were offering stiffer competition in the export trade. The Swedes consequently felt that they were nothing more than 'servants and harbor managers for the foreigners.'[3] By the end of the century, however, Robinson was to complain that were it not for the need of the Swedes for outside capital, 'merchants would have but little encouragement, or scarcely permission to live and trade amongst them, and even as the case stands, their treatment of them is as rigorous, as in any country.'[4]

About 1680 Charles XI imposed a fifty percent tax on English woollen goods, and began to encourage domestic woollen manufacturing which, according to rumors of the time, was aided by English wool exports sent to Sweden viâ Scotland.[5] By 1696 the inhabitants of Sweden looked upon the settlement of English merchants in Sweden as a direct competitive threat to the country's economic existence rather than as a boon to its commercial welfare.[6] As a result foreigners were faced with a series of restrictions, which virtually forced them out of the Swedish market. One-sixth of a merchant's estate might be

[1] Robinson, *Account of Sueden*, pp. 142–143.
[2] The College of Commerce consisted of the president of the treasury and four councillors. *Ibid.*, p. 147.
[3] Oskar Fyhrvall, 'Bidrag till Svenska handelslagstiftnings historia I, Tjärandelskompanierna,' *Historisk Bibliotek*, VII (Stockholm, 1890), p. 290. Cited hereafter as Fyhrvall, 'Tjärhandelskompanierna.'
[4] Robinson, *Account of Sueden*, pp. 148–149.
[5] 'A report concerning the general trade of England made by the Board of Trade, December the 23rd, 1698,' quoted in James F. Chance, *George I and the Northern War* (London, 1909), p. 7.
[6] Senton, *Literary Relations*, p. 43.

forfeited when he left the country. English merchants were obliged to coöperate in the quartering of soldiers and to give forced contributions to the crown. No foreigner could trade without first becoming a burgher, a restriction seemingly more obnoxious to the British than to the Dutch. Moreover, when a foreign merchant died, he forfeited to the crown one-third of all his possessions.[1] All this took place at a time when no political embargoes were laid against Swedes trading in England, although it must be admitted that the lot of the Swedish merchant there was far from easy.[2] Trade arguments and commercial sparring might furnish the opening for which George I was seeking.

Along with the commercial oppression, the favored position of Sweden at the Sound added to England's dissatisfaction. Because Swedish shares and cargoes in non-Swedish as well as in Swedish vessels were exempted from paying the Danish Sound tolls,[3] Swedish traders had a considerable advantage over their English competitors. This superiority was strengthened by the levying of great many disabilities, exactions, and burdens upon foreign ships trading in Swedish controlled ports. The result was that Sweden had a virtual monopoly of her own carrying trade before the outbreak of the Great Northern War, and English shipping consequently suffered.

From a mercantilist point of view, the loss of the freighting business was a national as well as a commercial calamity, for 'losing that trade was putting a number of ships out of employment, and consequently, paying our neighbors for work whilst our people were unemployed.'[4] Sir Josiah Child, Gee, Defoe, Wood, D'Avenant, and Burrish were all concerned about England's unfavorable position in the Baltic carrying trade,[5]

---

[1] Robinson, *Account of Sueden*, pp. 148–149, 152–153.

[2] Seaton, *Literary Relations*, p. 43.

[3] Charles Hill, *The Danish Sound Dues and the Command of the Baltic* (Durham, N.C., 1926), pp. 153–210. All countries paid Denmark a toll for the right to pass the Sound. Technically the tax was levied to aid in paying for lights and buoys. Actually it was an out and out toll. Holland and England paid an equal rate. The Swedish exemption dated back to the Treaty of Roskilde, 1651.

[4] Quoted in Eleanor Louisa Lord, *Industrial Experiments in the British Colonies of North America* (Baltimore, 1898), p. 56.

[5] Sir Josiah Child, *New Discourse on Trade* (London, 1696 ed.), pp. 83, 93–94. Gee, *Trade and Navigation*, p. 127; Defoe, *Plan*, p. 75; Wood, *Survey*, pp. 99–100, 116; D'Avenant, *Discourses*, p. 42; and Burrish, *Batavia illustrati*, pp. 569–571.

and well they might have been, for there were two hundred
Baltic ships coming to England yearly, and yet England was
building few ships for that trade. From 1697 to 1700 only half
the Baltic trade was carried in English bottoms. The case of
Norway was even worse. 'From Michaelmas [September 29]
1691 to Mich'as, 1696, there were entered on the Customs
House at London, 1,070 foreign ships from those parts and but
39 English.'[1] Burrish credited the Dutch with being supreme
in the carrying trade, and he considered cheap freight, the
advantages of the German–Baltic trade, and a 'parsimonious
method of living' as the reasons for the Dutch success. He
pessimistically felt that England would never equal them
unless Britain, with her superior fleet destroyed the Dutch
merchant marine, 'which it would be cruelty to think of.'[2]

In peace time, Sweden's trade tactics constituted a hazard
to the economic life of the nation. During war time they were a
peril to the nation itself. In 1715, a year of nominal peace,
Charles Viscount Townshend, the British secretary of state
wrote to the admiral of the British Baltic squadron, 'It being of
the last Consequence to the Nation that the fleet of Merchant
Men who are now upon their Return from the Baltick should
be conducted home in safety, (since if we should miscarry such
a Scarcity of Naval Stores must ensue as would disable
his Maj'ty from fitting out a fleet next Spring upon any
event).'[3]

The Swedish monopolies in the pitch and tar trade offer an
excellent example of the double-barrelled danger, for they
forced the English traders out of business in peace, and in war
so hampered the procurement of naval stores that at times the
safety of the realm was threatened. The Tar Company of
Stockholm was a serious problem for the Admiralty and the
British diplomatic corps in Sweden throughout the War of the
Spanish Succession.

That company was in reality a series of chartered monopolies
with the first, the *Norrlandska Tjäruhandelskompaniet*, going all

[1] Albion, *Forests and Sea Power*, p. 158.
[2] Burrish, *Batavia illustrati*, pp. 569–571.
[3] Townshend to Sir John Norris, August 2, 1715, The Original Letters of Sir
John Norris, BM. Add. MSS., 28,154 and the Letter books of Sir John Norris,
BM. Add. MSS., 28,144.

the way back to March 31, 1648.[1] After a series of complaints, the company was reformed in 1654 and reorganized into the *Förnyade tjäruhandelskompaniet* began a ten year existence to October 31, 1682.[2] High-handed actions[3] and bad management,[4] however, defeated early Swedish attempts at monopoly.

The last chartered company, the *Tjäruhandelssocieteten*, was to have a tremendous influence upon English trade and colonial policies and upon the commercial policy of Sweden. Moreover, it was to have repercussions upon the politics and the diplomacy of the two countries. Organized July 11, 1689,[5] and protected by high-ranking Swedish officials, the new monopoly refused to export pitch and tar except at prices fixed by the company. All nations were to have equal opportunities in the trade except Holland, who labored under the additional restriction that all goods exported to that country had to be sent in Swedish bottoms.[6]

The announcement of the privileges of the new company had been delayed because a treaty existed between Sweden and Holland which was violated in spirit if not in letter by the new restrictions. The weakening of Holland's position as a result of the War of the League of Augsburg and a strengthening of Sweden's diplomatic status in European affairs led to the issuing of the new terms. When the Dutch resident, Van Haaren, complained in 1690 over his country's unfair treatment, he received the bold answer that the new rule was neither a violation of the treaty nor a monopoly, but only a measure that Sweden was forced to take in order to prevent its own economic ruin. In retaliation and in self-defense, the Dutch were forced to find new vendors, and soon, under Dutch encouragement, pitch and

[1] Fyhrvall, 'Tjärhandelskompanierna,' p. 293.
[2] *Ibid.*, pp. 293–316.
[3] Heckscher, *Svensk Arbete*, p. 130.
[4] Robert Jackson, 'Memoir on the Swedish Tar Company,' December 29, 1709 (Public Record Office, State Papers, Sweden, 95/18). The errors in this memoir, which was widely circulated, may in part be responsible for the misleading accounts of the Company which appear in Lord, *Industrial Experiments*, p. 56; Herbert L. Osgood, *The American Colonies in the Eighteenth Century* (New York, 1924), p. 495; and Walter Knittle, *Early Eighteenth Century Palatine Emigration* (Philadelphia, 1937), pp. 111–114. A copy of the memoir edited by John J. Murray may be found in 'Robert Jackson's Memoir on the Swedish Tar Company,' *The Huntington Library Quarterly*, X (1947), pp. 419–428.
[5] Jackson, 'Memoir,' P.R.O., State Papers, Sweden, 95/18.
[6] Fyhrvall, *Tjärhandelskompanierna*,' pp. 325–326.

tar were being manufactured in Russia, Norway, and Courland. The company, therefore, had large surplus stocks which were sold to England and other western European nations at no increase in price.[1] In the beginning, then, England had not been effected adversely by company practices.

Two wars that broke out at the start of the eighteenth century altered the economic situation appreciably. England, engaged in the War of the Spanish Succession, increased her demands for naval stores; on the other hand, the Great Northern War and the consequent Russian invasions of Finland, where most of the stores were manufactured,[2] decreased the supply. As a result, prices rose. The company for its part noting the trading trend, endeavored to reap as great a monetary harvest as possible from transpiring events. In 1703, new restrictions were issued, which dealt a hard blow to an England engaged with France in a struggle to maintain naval supremacy.

No longer was pitch and tar to be sold to the foreign merchants in Sweden. Henceforth the sale was to be through the branches of the company stationed in the various European countries. All products were to be transported exclusively on company ships and were to be vended at Swedish prices.[3] England as a result of the new edits was faced with a shortage of naval stores—wares vitally necessary for waging a successful war against Louis XIV. The situation was one calling for immediate action.

Dr. John Robinson, British envoy to Sweden then in Poland, protested to Charles XII, while Robert Jackson, acting resident minister of Stockholm, registered a complaint with the Swedish chancery.[4] Motivated by Robinson's representations, Charles XII wrote to the Swedish College of Commerce on March 20, 1703, requesting them to give all due assistance to the English factors in Stockholm in order that the needs of the British fleet might be realized. Demands for the present year were to be met along with unfulfilled contracts for the past two years. At the same time that Robinson informed Sir Charles Hedges, the Secretary of State, of his action, he pointed out the difficulties

[1] Jackson, 'Memoir,' P.R.O., State Papers, Sweden, 95/18.
[2] Heckscher and Boëthius, *Handelsstatistik*, *passim*.
[3] Jackson, 'Memoir,' P.R.O., State Papers, Sweden, 95/18.
[4] *Ibid.*

of the situation with such cold logic that copies were sent to several merchants by Hedges 'that they might see how much it was in the power of the king of Sweden to forward the fitting out of the Royal Navy of England or to keep it in harbour.'[1]

The company was not yet licked, however, and asked Charles XII not to compel it to deliver pitch and tar at Stockholm for the British navy, when it would be to Sweden's and the company's advantage to carry it to England and to sell it there on their own account. As a result of the bickering, not one barrel of tar was produced for the Navy.[2] Robinson then urged that the company comply with Charles's letter at least for 1703.[3] He was unsuccessful for Charles XII washed his hands of the matter,[4] and Robinson was forced to admit his failure by asserting that the best that England could expect was to receive Swedish pitch and tar in England at prices fixed by the company.[5]

Jackson, in the meantime, had presented his request that England be allowed to buy at company prices in Stockholm. His memorial to the Chancery had been forwarded to the company. Weeks passed. A letter from Charles XII arrived, ordering the College of Commerce to make a decision in the case. The Chancery thereupon informed Jackson that its hands were tied now that the King was in the affair. Jackson then went to the College of Commerce to present the British case, but to no avail, for the company had friends at court; it was favored by important officials in the government. All that Jackson received for his efforts was a reassertion that the company had a right to regulate the sale of naval stores in any manner that it saw fit. A vague promise was added, however, that the needs of the British fleet would receive first consideration.[6] This was a promise that was not always kept. In addition, tar which had sold for £5 15s. per last in 1687 was by September, 1700 up to £11 per last.[7]

---

[1] Quoted in Lord, *Industrial Experiments*, p. 57.
[2] Jackson, 'Memoir,' P.R.O., State Papers, Sweden, 95/18.
[3] Lord, *Industrial Experiments*, p. 57.
[4] Jackson, 'Memoir,' P.R.O., State Papers, Sweden, 95/18.
[5] Lord, *Industrial Experiments*, p. 57.
[6] Jackson, 'Memoir,' P.R.O., State Papers, Sweden, 95/18.
[7] 'Excerpt from the Board of Trade Journal,' *Calendar of State Papers, American and West Indies, 1700* (London, 1910), p. 533. Cited hereafter as *Cal., Am. and W.I.*

It was quite evident in 1703 that England was to receive the same treatment as Holland in the pitch and tar trade. Because of the international situation, the British government was forced either to accede to the company's demands or to seize what the company sent on the high seas or had in British ports, paying for it at a reasonable rate. There were no other available European sources of supply, and the possibility of imposing a high import duty on Swedish tar was too dangerous in view of the current demands of the fleet.[1] There were, however, the plantations in America. They might possibly provide the answer. They might free the fleet from the 'caprices of a few Swedish Merchants.'[2] Robinson advised his countrymen: 'What difficulties there are in making and bringing it [tar] from New England, I am not acquainted with, but take it for granted England had better give one-third more for it from thence, then have it at such uncertanties, and in so precarious a manner from other countries.'[3]

Hedges evidently took cognizance of Robinson's ideas, for in the latter part of the year he ordered the Board of Trade to consider at what prices naval stores could be imported from America and what amounts could be procured there. After deliberation, the Board decided, and so stated in reports to the Privy Council, that the plantations could not furnish all that was needed, and therefore, the government should pay colonial producers bounties to offset the higher cost of freight entailed by importing products from American ports as compared with those nearer in the Baltic.[4] On December 18, 1704, the House of Commons gave permission for the introduction of a bill to that purpose which was passed and went into effect early in 1705.[5]

The 'Act for encouraging the Importation of Naval Stores from America' offered bounties of £4 per ton for tar and pitch, £3 per ton for 'Rosin or Turpentine,' £6 per ton for hemp, and

[1] Sir C. Hedges to the Council of Trade and Plantations, June 2, 1704. *Cal., Am. and W.I.*, 1704–1705, p. 157. 'The raising of the duty on the Swedes or other Forrainers being a dangerous experiment at this time when it is as difficult to gett any Navall Stores."

[2] Jackson, 'Memoir,' P.R.O., State Papers, Sweden, 95/18.

[3] Quoted in Lord, *Industrial Experiments*, p. 58.

[4] Osgood, *American Colonies*, p. 506; and Knittle, *Palatine Emigration*, p. 120. Both accounts closely follow Lord, *Industrial Experiments*, pp. 61–63.

[5] Lord, *Ibid.*, pp. 63–64.

£1 per ton for all masts, yards and bowsprits. The navy was to have preemption of all such articles within twenty days of their arrival in England, and the bounties were to be paid only after sworn statements had been received by the proper officials that the imports were the product of the plantations. An additional clause forbade the cutting of pitch pine and tar trees which were under twelve inches in growth and 'not being within the Fence or actual Inclosure.' Further acts were passed in 1711 and 1713 for the expansion of bounty payments.[1]

Ireland, where some Palatinate refugees had settled, was also looked upon as a source for naval stores. There the British pushed the cultivation of hemp and flax and tried to stimulate the iron industry.[2] At the same time they were destroying the Irish cloth trade.

It is interesting to note that the sums of money expended on bounties varied with the diplomatic situation in the north. In 1706, the company feared English colonial competition and eased up on its restrictions. As a result, trade moved more freely and only £554 were paid out for colonial naval-stores production. In 1709 the problem was especially acute and £5,840 were expended. As the Swedish privateers increased their raids upon English shipping trading with former Swedish provinces now in Russian hands the amounts expended remained high. The first protective convoy for the merchant ships was sent to the Baltic in 1714 when £6,860 were paid out by the Admiralty. The next year saw George I begin a more aggressive policy towards Sweden. A British squadron was employed in the capture of Swedish Stralsund, and £10,135 were spent for naval stores in the plantations.

By 1716, the fleet was prepared to cover an allied expedition against Sweden proper. At the same time Russian trade practices were interfering with the hemp supply. Consequently £27,410 were expended. In the next year, when diplomatic relations were severed with Sweden, and it appeared that Russia might join that country against the other members of the Northern Alliance, bounty payments soared to £40,354. The

---

[1] Osgood, *American Colonies*, pp. 506–507, 511; Knittle, *Palatine Emigration*, pp. 120–121, 123; Lord, *Industrial Experiments*, pp. 64–74, 87–97; and Albion, *Forests and Sea Power*, pp. 231–256.

[2] Åström, *From Stockholm to St. Petersburg*, p. 18–19.

peak was reached in 1718 when most of Europe was of the opinion that a joint Russo-Swedish invasion of England was in the offing. In that year the bounties amounted to £53,011. With the death of Charles XII and the subsequent rapproachment between England and Sweden, the cost of American bounties declined.[1]

In spite of the money laid out for the fostering of colonial production, the wants of the fleet were for the most part still supplied by the Baltic countries. The naval commissioners were bound by their instructions to buy pitch and tar at the cheapest rates which in spite of the monopoly were quoted in Sweden. Moreover, supplies from America were not up to the best Swedish standards.[2] The cost of transportation from the New World was more expensive than from the Baltic and insurance rates were higher.[3] Speculation and production problems in the colonies added to the difficulties.[4] Many British mercantilists were thus disappointed in America as a source for naval stores.

The most that was accomplished through the American effort was a temporary lowering of prices by the tar company at its London factory. The directors of the company had seen the loss of the Dutch trade and had little desire to give an account of their transactions to the Swedish king if American competition should cause the loss of Sweden's pitch and tar market in Britain.[5] Such was not to happen, but political factors soon shot prices upward again.[6] It was not until after the Great Northern War that the American plantations were to help give the *quietus* to the Swedish naval stores trade. Throughout the first quarter of the century, Englishmen continued to grumble about the high-handed trade policies of the company and about the protective tariff levied by the Swedes upon

[1] Albion, *Ibid.*, p. 418. Appendix B is a list given in pounds of the amounts expended for bounties by the British for naval stores. The list is taken from the P.R.O., Navy Board Out Letters, No. 2204 (April 17, 1777).
[2] Council of Trade and Plantations to Lord High Treasurer, December 20, 1706, *Cal., Am. and W.I., 1706–1708*, p. 339. Åström, *From Stockholm to St. Petersburg*, p. 111.
[3] The same to Anne, January 24, 1710, *Cal., Am. and W.I., 1710–1711*, pp. 46–47.
[4] Lord, *Industrial Experiments*, pp. 67–86.
[5] Jackson, 'Memoir,' P.R.O., State Papers, Sweden, 95/18.
[6] Fyhrvall, 'Tjärhandelskompanierna,' p. 333.

English woollens. When at times it was suspected that France, rather than England, was receiving the coveted pitch and tar, English indignation boiled over.[1] By 1704 England was already trying to obtain naval stores from Russia, as the Dutch had been doing for some time. By 1705 the British had broken the Dutch monopoly of the Russian tar trade; but English attempts to use Archangel as a port rather than the newly built St. Petersburg led to difficulties. The Swedish monopoly of the Baltic tar ports ended in 1710 because of Russian military successes. Even after the peace of 1721, Swedish tar factors faced stiff Russian competition from Dutch traders out of Archangel.[2]

A greater danger to British naval security than the tar company developed as the wars in eastern and western Europe continued. One by one Sweden's possessions along the shores of the Baltic fell into Russian hands. The loss of the Baltic provinces was especially significant from an economic viewpoint. The ports of the East Country had long been famous commercially. Courland's annual value to Sweden was estimated by Robinson, to be 1,200,000 crowns.[3] Moreover, England's most vital naval store, hemp, came from that area in the Baltic—a commodity absolutely necessary to keep ships at sea in that day of sails. To facilitate trade in that product, the Eastland Company had in 1672 been thrown open to all traders who would pay a £2 fine. In 1699 the Russia Company let loose its controls on practically the same basis.[4] Peter's conquests gave him a monopoly in hemp exportation, and he could drive a hard bargain with Englishmen whose maritime strength was dependent upon that commodity.[5]

The rising Russian political and economic strength caused misgivings in England as did the earlier attempts of Gustavus

---

[1] Various letters of Robert Jackson, P.R.O., State Papers, Sweden, 95/18' 95/19, and 95/20.

[2] Åström, *From Stockholm to St. Petersburg*, appendix II, p. 122–130.

[3] Robinson to Raby, October 16, 1708, BM. Add. MSS., 22,198.

[4] David Macpherson, *Annals of Commerce, Manufactures, Fisheries, and Navigation* (London and Edinburgh, 1805), II, 563, 706. For an excellent account of the work of these two companies, see William R. Scott, *Constitution and Finance of English, Scottish and Irish Joint Stock Companies to 1710*, 3 vols. (Cambridge, 1910–1912).

[5] Gee, *Trade and Navigation*, p. 18 and Townshend to Walpole, October 3, 1716, William Coxe (ed.), *Memoirs of the Life and Administration of Sir Robert Walpole* (London, 1798), II, 86. Cited hereafter as *Walpole Memoirs*.

Adolphus to make the Baltic a Swedish lake. The shifting economics saw Russia in the first quarter of the eighteenth century replace Sweden as Britain's chief trading partner in the Baltic.[1]

Sweden, however, did not intend to stand idle while its rival reaped an economic harvest. In 1710, all neutral shipping was barred from the captured provinces, for Charles XII decided that his loss should not be Russia's profit.[2] Privateers based in Sweden began to prey upon English and Dutch ships bound for the Baltic provinces. The foes of Louis XIV instructed their diplomats to ease the situation. The price of hemp soared.

As a result, Captain James Jefferyes was sent to Charles XII at Bender. He hoped to gain some relief for the British merchants and win the consent of Charles XII to a neutralization of Swedish possessions in Germany.[3] Jefferyes began his long trip to the possessions of the Turks. In Vienna he purchased a boat and embarked from that city on the twenty-sixth day of March. On April 28 he reached his destination and on the next day had an audience with the Swedish king. This first audience, although pleasant, accomplished little. Charles XII inquired about the state of Anne's gout, asked about Marlborough, and wanted Jefferyes to define the difference between Whig and Tory. To the King's question as to why the British had delayed so long in waiting on him, Jefferyes said that the British had expected him to return home or they would have sent someone sooner. Charles XII soon excused himself from the conference and Jefferyes waited in vain for him to return. It was not until April 30 that Jefferyes was able to present the petition of the British merchants for freedom of trade to the ports which Sweden had lost to the Czar and a neutrality plan.[4]

On May 2, Jefferyes received his answer. Sweden considered the request made by Britain regarding trade to be inconsistent 'With the Treaty of Commerce & the Custom of Nations in

---

[1] Åström, *From Stockholm to St. Petersburg*, p. 106–119

[2] Various letters of Jackson to Boyle, July and August, 1710, P.R.O., State Papers, Sweden, 95/18.

[3] For a more detailed account of the non-commercial aspects of Jefferyes's mission, see Chapter III.

[4] Jefferyes to Queensbury, May 11, 1711, P.R.O., State Papers, Sweden, 95/17.

Amity.' The Swedish king hoped that the Maritime Powers would stop desiring and requesting something 'so prejudicial to him and so beneficial to his Enemies.' Charles XII could 'by no means agree' to the British request 'especially since he had made it known by his Ministers at their Courts that he had given Orders sometime ago to his College of Admiralty to send a Fleet to block up all those Ports which were taken by the Enemy.'[1]

At Stockholm the agents of England and the States were also active on behalf of trade and commerce. Jackson and Willem Rumpf, the Dutch resident there, presented on March 17, 1711, a joint declaration to the Swedish chancery asking that the Maritime Powers be allowed freedom of commerce in the Baltic. Special reference was made to the lost Swedish provinces.[2] Chancellor Arvid Horn informed the two men that no answer could be made available until the Swedish senators had assembled at Arboga. The English and Dutch diplomats, however, were assured that Sweden had nothing but good intentions toward their respective countries.[3] It was not until July that the Senate considered the request of the two men, and disclosed just how far those good intentions went.

At that time it was decided by the Senate that the problem was one outside its power, and fell within the province of the absent king. The Senate's own feelings on the matter were such as to bring little cause for hope that a bettering of England's commercial position was in the offing. According to a statement sent to Jackson and Rumpf, the trade to the East Country was admittedly important and had been stopped for just that reason. It was hoped by the Senate that Rumpf and Jackson would see the 'justice of his [Charles's] proceedings.'[4] It was asserted that lifting the embargo on the ports would constitute

[1] Müllern to Jefferyes, April 28, 1711, P.R.O., Ibid., 95/16. This letter is dated April 28, but it was not delivered to Jefferyes until May 2, 1711.

[2] Jackson and Rumpf to the Swedish Chancery, March 17, 1711, P.R.O., State Papers, Sweden, 95/18. Rumpf to Heinsius, March 3, 1714, Algemeene Rijksarchief, Archief Anthonie Heinsius (A.A.H.), 1864 discusses an early March meeting with Horn wherein the representatives of the Maritime Powers were told about the great losses suffered by Swedish merchants at the hands of the Anglo-Dutch naval vessels 'dans La Guerre de 1690.'

[3] Count Horn to Rumpf and Jackson, March 22, 1711, P.R.O., State Papers, Sweden, 95/18. For the role of Rumpf, see his various letters to Heinsius, Rijksarchief, A.A.H., 1633.

[4] A report of the proceedings of the Swedish Senate sent to Jackson, July 11, 1711, P.R.O., State Papers, Sweden, 95/18.

a threat to Sweden, for English ships were being sent to those ports, and on arrival were being armed by the Czar. England and the States' actions in requesting that the ports be opened were contrary to existing treaties between the nations, which specifically stated that no party should do anything prejudicial to the interests of the others. The Senate considered free trade of neutrals to their lost provinces a dangerous and prejudicial act against Sweden and the Swedish people.[1]

As might be expected neither Jackson nor Rumpf were satisfied with the Swedish answer. The former insisted to Horn that the forbidden trade 'was of high importance, both in respect to her Majesty's particular service, as well as the general interest of all her subjects, that we could never suffer any interruptions of it, where the treaties in existence guaranteed England and Holland access to all ports in the Baltic regardless of who held them.' Disagreeable results would follow if the Senate did not promptly remedy the situation.[2]

Horn tried to pacify the two men by replying that only the King could change Swedish policy towards the provinces. He did not think, however, that Sweden had explained her position satisfactorily. It was suggested by him that the three countries could work together to effect a restoration of the lands to Sweden. Such an action would be to everyone's benefit, and the unfortunate results which were intimated in the protests of the residents of the Maritime Powers would thereby be averted.[3] After the interview, it was apparent to all that the most that Jackson and Rumpf could hope for was that Charles XII would make a speedy decision in favor of England and Holland. The year 1711 was to run out with them still waiting.[4]

[1] *Ibid.*

[2] Jackson to Rowe, July 15, 1711, P.R.O., State Papers, Sweden, 95/18. Jackson and Rumpf to Horn, July 14, 1711, *Ibid.* The treaties of the Maritime Powers 'donnet de trafiquer sur toutes les places dans la Mer Baltique, sans distinction, si elles sont au pouvoir de la Suede ou des Moscovites. Nous nous flattons encore que le Senat selon sa grande prudence, trouvera moyen de prevenir les facheuse suites que cette interruption pourvoit causer, a moins qu'on y remedie promptent.'

[3] Horn to Rumpf and Jackson, July 19, 1711, P.R.O., State Papers, Sweden, 95/18. Some of the correspondence of Rumpf and Jackson with Horn is in Lamberty, *Mémoires*, VII, 816–822. Cf. Various letters of Rumpf to Heinsius, Rijksarchief, A.A.H., 1633.

[4] Jackson to Henry St. John, December 16, 1711, P.R.O., State Papers, Sweden, 95/19.

Jefferyes at Bender was doing no better. In answer to a petition delivered by the English envoy in late October, 1711,[1] the Swedes charged that the Dutch were selling contraband and ships to their enemies. According to the Swedish secretary, Müllern, the Swedish minister at the Hague had requested the Burgomaster of Amsterdam to forbid the sale of contraband in the future and had been met with a negative reply. Anne's offer to give assurance that the British vessels carried nothing detrimental to Sweden's war effort could not be accepted because Charles XII had to treat all nations equally. Sweden, through necessity, had to blockade the ports and Charles XII wished that the Maritime Powers would stop pestering him on the subject of free trade to that area. No matter what action Britain and the States might take Charles XII would not change his mind.[2]

All through the next year the conflict over trade raged in Stockholm, with Jackson and Rumpf on one side, and the Swedish chancery on the other.[3] The former two were extremely indignant when they discovered that some merchants trading to the Baltic provinces were obtaining passports. Rumpf and Jackson had obtained copies of the original passes issued by the chancery. As a result, Jackson accosted Horn, asking him how it was that passports were being issued to merchants at the same time 'his Excellency had notified me [Jackson] that if any of the ships of her Majesty were met with trading to Riga, or any of the ports in the Czar's possessions, the King had commanded them to be made prize.'[4] Horn expressed surprise at Jackson's charge, but was forced to trump up a weak excuse when Jackson showed him an original passport with Horn's signature on it.[5]

Jackson, in reality, was making a great fuss over nothing, for Swedish privateers and naval vessels did not respect any type of passes issued by the chancery. In August, 1712, a sentence was handed down by Admiral Hans Wachmeister of

[1] Petition of Jefferyes to Charles XII for freedom of commerce and redress of commercial grievances, October 26, 1711, *Ibid.*, 95/17.
[2] Müllern to Jefferyes, November 6, 1711, *Ibid.*, 95/17.
[3] Various letters of Jackson and Rumpf, *Ibid.*, 95/19.
[4] Jackson to Henry St. John, June 28, 1712, *Ibid.*, 95/19.
[5] *Ibid.*

47

the Swedish Court of Admiralty decreeing that all ships bound from Riga with naval stores were lawful prizes.[1]

That was not the only time that Jackson misjudged a situation. Early in the next year (1713) he thought that Charles XII might give special consideration to England and Holland on the matter of the closed ports. In one of his dispatches he expressed the optimistic hope that Whitehall had already been informed of such good news. Even though Horn and other high Swedish officials continually denied that any special concessions had been made, Jackson persistently held to his opinion that the ports would soon be opened. English diplomatic pressure on Russia for the return of the Baltic provinces, according to Jackson's reasoning was to be the price paid by the British for favored treatment of their commercial interests.[2]

His wishful thinking was soon due for a rude shock. Charles XII remained adamant on the matter and emphasized his stand by ordering his captains to seize all ships trading with the lost ports regardless of cargo, country, or passport.[3] Rumpf and Jackson could protest loudly and often, but in vain, to the Swedish authorities at Stockholm. The Senate and the Chancery were powerless and had little influence with the naval officers who took their orders directly from the King.[4]

Jackson tired and irritated at the fruitlessness of his task advised William Bromley, Secretary of State,

> I perceive plainly that tho the Ships be given free, yet they will not be suffer'd to go to any Ports in the Czar's possession. Wherefore unless Her Maj'ty be graciously pleased to take some other vigorous measures to protect Her Subject's Commerce, a stop will never be put to these unaccountable proceedings by all that can be said or done here.[5]

[1] Sentence of Swedish Admiralty signed by Admiral Wachmeister, August 15 1712. Copy in *Ibid.*, 95/15.

[2] Jackson to Henry St. John, February 26, 1713, *Ibid.*, 95/19.

[3] Jackson to Bromley, September 5, 1713, *Ibid.*

[4] Various letters of Jackson, 1713, *Ibid.* See also Jackson to Bromley, February 17, 1714, *Ibid.* Bromley evidently hoped that the joint protests might be effective and he sent Robinson to Holland to discuss measures to be used against Sweden. Rumpf early in the year commented on Horn's coldness and was of the opinion that little would be done against the wishes of Charles XII. Rumpf to Heinsius, January, February, and March, 1714. Rijksarchief, A.A.H., 1864.

[5] Jackson to Bromley, May 22, 1714, P.R.O., State Papers, Sweden, 95/19. Rumpf seems to have been calmer in his protests than was Jackson. Moreover, the

Sweden, however, was not the only country molesting British shipping. In April, 1711, the Danes had issued an edict to privateers of such a nature that the British government warned Denmark that it would not agree to any judgements handed down by Danish prize courts operating under a procedure that Britain considered 'arbitrary and unwarrantable.'[1] Britain protested Danish seizures of British shipping but Frederick IV was 'little disposed to give satisfaction to the British merchant.'[2] As George Tilson, a British undersecretary of state remarked in 1717:

> Our Eastland merchants have a very hard time of it between Swede, Dane, and Muscovite, who all take their ships on one pretence or other.[3]

Thus more drastic steps than diplomatic protests were necessary, if England's shipping were to be unmolested in Baltic waters. Consequently, on July 22, 1714, Commodore Archibald Hamilton was ordered to prepare to sail to the Baltic as a naval convoy for British ships trading to those parts. Hamilton was to protect only those British ships having passports from Queen Anne, which guaranteed to Sweden that none of the ships convoyed carried contraband.[4]

Jackson, in the meantime, had been attempting to obtain a statement from the Swedes that they would honor his Queen's passports and refrain from molesting her merchant shipping. The only encouragement that he received from Horn was a hope that the Swedish naval forces would be kind to the English merchantmen.[5] The Swedish chancellor insisted that he could not give Jackson any information on the matter, and

[1] St. John to Pulteney, November 2, 1711, P.R.O., Foreign Entry Book (F.E.B.), State Papers, Foreign, 104/5.

[2] Townshend to Pulteney, January 4, 1715, *Ibid.*

[3] Tilson to Polwarth, 19/30 July, 1717, *Polwarth Papers*, I, 314.

[4] Instructions for Hamilton, July 22, 1714, printed in *British Diplomatic Instructions, Sweden, 1689–1727,* James F. Chance (ed.), Camden 3rd series, Vol. XXXII (London, 1922), pp. 67–69. Cited hereafter as *British Instructions, Sweden.*

[5] Jackson to Bromley, June 5, 1714, P.R.O., State Papers, Sweden, 95/20.

Dutchman maintained a working agreement with Jacques Campredon, the French minister at Stockholm, something which Jackson refused to do. Some of the information used by Rumpf and Jackson came to them through Rumpf's cultivation of Campredon. Various letters to Hensius from Rumpf in 1714, Rijksarchief, A.A.H., 1864.

49

pointedly asserted that it was not the right of any subject to set aside the commands of the Sovereign.[1] Jackson, on July 16, drew up a long memorial defending Britain's legal position, in the light of existing treaties; at the same time he made a list of all English vessels having passports which he presented to the Swedish government with the demand that all English ships in Swedish custody be released. Because of the real or faked illness of Horn, he was not able to deliver his communication until three days later.[2]

Six days later (on the very day that Hamilton received his instructions) Jackson informed Horn of Britain's resolve to send a convoy into the Baltic to protect her commerce. The English diplomatist hoped that all Swedish admirals would be ordered to respect the British warships and merchantmen. At the same time he pressed for an answer to his memorial of the nineteenth. Horn promised Jackson that the Swedish council of regency would consider the matter that very day, but warned Jackson that he could see no change in the Swedish attitude on the matter of the seized ships. Horn himself said that the information on the convoys 'was the most disagreeable news that could be sent them, but it was not in their power here to Command the Admirals what to do on such occasions.'[3]

Jackson was of the opinion that Horn's attitude was that of many in Sweden, and he realized how impotent the regency government was. For that reason he wrote in July, the last month of Anne's reign: 'I find no mannere of ground to expect Her Majesty's Ships will pass without an attack.'[4] His supposition was correct. On July 30, the Senate returned an answer to his memorial with the usual vagaries. It was suggested that the way to win freedom of commerce was for England to guarantee Sweden's lost possessions.[5] Anne died two days later and George I was king. Jackson, ignorant of the Queen's death, could truthfully write words that would be heatedly received by his new master. 'It is now evident that nothing

[1] Jackson to Bromley, June 26, 1714, P.R.O., *Ibid.*

[2] Memorial of Jackson to Swedish Chancery, July 16, 1714 and Jackson to Bromley, July 24, 1714, *Ibid.*

[3] Jackson to Bromley, July 24, 1714, *Ibid.*

[4] *Ibid.*

[5] Swedish Chancery to Jackson, signed by D. A. van Höpken, 30 July, 1714, P.R.O., *Ibid.*

which can be said or done here is able to put a stop to these unjust and violent proceedings.'[1]

Anglo-Swedish trade differences during the reign of Anne had not been one-sided. The Swedes had ample cause to complain over the conduct of their ally. On March 24, 1714, Gyllenborg, the Swedish minister to London, sent a note to the British government wherein he charged that the English up to that time had furnished Russia with nine warships. In the Baltic where the size of naval contingents was relatively small, the nine ships were sufficient to give the Russians a preponderance of naval strength. Thus England, by contributing ships to the Russian Czar, instead of coming to the assistance of Charles XII as she was bound to do under treaty, was in reality contributing to the defeat of Sweden.[2] Not only had the ministry been negligent the year before in allowing Peter to get the ships, but there were to be other ships sent to Russia in 1714. Gyllenborg pointed out that three ships, the *Arundel*, *Ormond*, and *Fortune* had moved down the Thames to Gravesend 'to be out of reach of being stopped in their intended voyage,' and he asked 'that their going further may be prevented, till such a time that yesterday's examination are laid before Her Majesty and her most gracious resolution taken thereon.'[3]

Bromley, the British secretary of state, realized that there was a good deal of justice in the Swedish remonstrances. In a letter to Daniel Pulteney, the British envoy to Denmark, Bromley pointed out that:

complaints have been made by the Minister of Sweden of the Czars buying ships here and it has been considered whether a Stop might not be put to it, but it is the Opinion of those who

[1] Jackson to Bromley, August 7, 1714, P.R.O., *Ibid.*

[2] Gyllenborg to Anne, March 24, 1714, P.R.O., Foreign Ministers in England Book, State Papers, Foreign, Sweden, 100/62. In the memorial Gyllenborg pointed out 'que le Czar de Moscovie devant en tout recevoir neuf vaisseaux de Guerre de ses agens icy, en y comptant, qui furent envoyés l'année passée, ce Renfort n'est que trop considerable dans le Mer Baltique, ou l'on voit rarement des Flottes plus grandes, que de 20 à 30 vaisseaux. La Suede ne pouvant de plus équipper la Sienne, et ayant pas la plus à craindre, parmi toutes ses autres Rebers, Elle aura aussi celui, de voit que ses meilleurs Amis et Alliez ont voulû contribuer si efficacement a sa Ruine.'

[3] Gyllenborg to Bromley, March 2 and 5, 1714, *Ibid.* Gyllenborg had requested that a Will Fry, a mate on one of the ships being fitted out for Peter, be examined as to the true destination of the ships.

have been consulted on this occasion that as the Law stands, Her Maj'ty cannot hinder her subjects selling Ships to any Princes or States in Amity with Her, & I cannot tell whether it will be adviseable to make a law on purpose for it.[1]

While Bromley was trying to make up his mind, Gyllenborg was receiving information from home which stressed the dangers to Sweden if Peter and the Danes gained a naval superiority in the Baltic. Stockholm itself would be open to attack.[2] In May Gyllenborg received information that four ships had been given passports by Anne to sail for the Baltic. As these four ships were destined for the Russian fleet, Gyllenborg said that it would be impossible for Sweden to recognize Anne's passports.[3] By July, he learned about the Hamilton squadron, and on July 21 he delivered a strongly worded protest which sets forth the Swedish side in the commercial differences rather well.

Sweden, according to Gyllenborg could hardly be expected to allow the same freedom of commerce to those ports now in Russian hands as it had allowed when they were in Swedish hands. If Peter received full value from his new conquests, he would be in a position to effect the total ruination of Sweden. Gyllenborg complained that it was Russian aggression that had forced Sweden to throw up a blockade in the Baltic. Thus Russia and not Sweden was responsible for the commercial difficulties of the Maritime Powers. The idea of convoying merchant ships to the disputed Baltic ports was 'malheureaux et facheux,' and could lead to an unfortunate accident. Sweden could not allow the British ships with or without passports to pass through their blockade for to do so would be to commit suicide. The navy of Charles XII under the circumstances would not be able to 'respecter le pavillion de votre Majesté.' Sweden, according to treaty, should be hoping for British assistance, but the policy of Anne's government appeared to give the Swedes no choice but to have England added to their list of

[1] Bromley to Pulteney, April 23, 1714, P.R.O., F.E.B., State Papers Foreign, 104/5.
[2] Görtz to Gyllenborg, April 13, 1714, P.R.O., Foreign Ministers in England Book, State Papers, Foreign Sweden, 100/62.
[3] Gyllenborg to Anne, May 12, 1714, *Ibid.*

enemies of Sweden, or to consent to a policy which could only contribute to the destruction of the country.[1]

Thus when George I ascended to the British throne on August 1, he inherited a pretext for sending naval units into the Baltic. Approximately nine days later, Hamilton cleared Yarmouth roads.[2] That first small force consisted of a mere four ships,[3] and was allowed to return home unharmed only because of the sufferance of the Swedes.[4] Yet the grievances of the British merchants remained. Bigger and more powerful squadrons could be sent. The close of the War of the Spanish Succession had left many ships which could be put to such a use. Perhaps it would be possible for George I to divert naval units from convoy duty in order to push his own ambitions against Sweden. Yet the diplomatic relations between Sweden and England for the past fifteen years would have to be considered. England's foreign policy in the Baltic would have to be re-drawn along Hanoverian lines. Swedish depredations upon British commerce offered the opportunity for which George I sought. He would have to move carefully because British public opinion for the most part favored Sweden over the other belligerents of the war. Yet it was possible for George I to hope that the well-known rashness of Charles XII might cause Britain to become anti-Swedish in sentiment. The commercial picture in late 1714 must have offered considerable encouragement to the Hanoverian Junta, which was preparing to accompany George I to England.

[1] Gyllenborg to Anne, July 21, 1714, *Ibid.* The Swedes would have the choice of 'bientot avoir le maleur de voir votre Majte au nombre de ses enemis, ou etre forcée à consentir à une Chose, qui contribuera tout autant à Sa Destruction.'

[2] Chance, *George I and the Northern War*, p. 48.

[3] Bromley to George I, *British Instructions, Sweden*, p. 69.

[4] Jackson to Townshend, September 25, 1714, P.R.O., State Papers, Sweden, 95/21.

III

SWEDISH POLICY OF ANNE'S GOVERNMENT

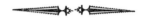

THE foundations of Anglo-Swedish policy throughout the reign of Anne were laid on an alliance concluded in January 1700, between England, the States-General, and Sweden, a treaty which in 1714 still had four more years to run, but one which had suffered various interpretations in its fourteen years of duration.[1] This basic agreement between the Maritime Powers and Sweden had been signed at a time when Europe was slipping into the War of the Spanish Succession and just after the initial hostilities of the Great Northern War had occurred. As the seventeenth century came to a fretful close, William III, then king of England, was laboring mightily to erect a coalition against France and to prevent Sweden from returning to its traditional French alliance. Since the negotiations at Nimwegen in 1674, Bengt Oxenstierna,[2] the Swedish foreign minister acting for Charles XI had consistently maintained an anti-French policy, but one of the initial acts of the government of Charles XII had been to conclude a ten year pact between France and Sweden.[3] Thus William by 1700 was

---

[1] Baron Jean Dumont, *Corps universel diplomatique du droit des gens* (Amsterdam, 1726–1731), VII, pt. ii, 475–477 contains the full text of the treaty along with its separate articles. The same material may be found in Lamberty, *Mémoires*, I, 36–40. Christophe G. de Koch, *Histoire Abrégée des traités de paix entre les puissances de l'Europe depuis la Paix de Westphalie*, expanded by F. Schevell (Paris, 1817–18), XIII, 162–163 has a discussion of the treaty and of northern affairs in general.

[2] Bengt Gabrielsson Oxenstierna (1623–1702) was a well known Swedish diplomat and statesman of the last half of the seventeenth century. His leading political principle was strong friendship with the Maritime Powers and the maintenance of the Holstein connection.

[3] Dumont, *Corps diplomatique*, VII, pt. ii, 441.

more than anxious to make a strong treaty with the 'Boy King,' which would insure Swedish neutrality even though it might not line Sweden actively on the side of England as a member of the Grand Alliance.[1]

The agreement as concluded by William III and Charles XII achieved the latter, for it guaranteed mutual assistance of 6,000 men in case one of the signatories were attacked. Sweden bound herself by a secret article to furnish 10,000 men in place of the stipulated 6,000 if the States-General or Britain were forced to take up arms to uphold the peace of Ryswick.[2] To obtain such stipulations for preserving 'the peace of Europe,' both England and the States were prepared to 'go very far to oblige the King of Sweden and admitt of some inequalities on our side for the ease and benefit of that crown, which could not otherwise in reason be demanded of us.'[3] The price paid was another secret article of more importance to the immediate future, for it bound the Maritime Powers to uphold the treaty of Altona, an agreement signed in 1689 which guaranteed the dukes of Holstein-Gottorp, a cadet branch of the Danish ruling house, certain rights and privileges in Holstein-Gottorp.[4] While the final arrangements were being made, a showdown struggle between the Danish king and the duke of Holstein-Gottorp was already in the skirmishing stage.

The squabble between Duke and King was of long standing and was almost insolvable, for both exercised certain sovereign rights in the Duke's domains. Whenever the situation warranted, one took the opportunity to assert himself against the other. The marriage of Duke Fredrik to Hedvig Sofia, sister of the Swedish king, on June 2, 1698, further complicated affairs between the two, because Holstein could be used by Swedish troops as a springboard against Denmark.

[1] The alliance between Great Britain, Holland, and the Empire, concluded at the Hague, September 7, 1701. The treaty demanded that the Empire be compensated for the loss of Spain and that the security of Holland and England be guaranteed. The allies also demanded that Louis XIV pledge that the Crowns of France and Spain would never be united.

[2] Concluded September 21, 1697. It guaranteed the Protestant Succession in England and the barrier fortresses in the Southern Netherlands to the United Provinces.

[3] William Blathwayt, secretary at war, to Dr. John Robinson, August 15, 1699, *British Instructions, Sweden*, p. 17.

[4] Koch, *Abrégée*, XIII, 138–147.

In fact four days after the wedding Charles XII placed his brother-in-law in command of all troops stationed in Sweden's German provinces.[1] On September 4, 1699, Christian V of Denmark died and the Duke, counting on unsettled conditions in Denmark and the assistance of the Swedish tie, began shortly to construct forts in Holstein in order to gain complete sovereignty in the duchy. Perhaps fear of a Danish invasion of Holstein as an initial move by Frederick IV in the coming Great Northern War prompted the Duke's action. Throughout the fall of 1699, the new Danish king, Frederick IV, assembled troops along the Dano-Holstein border preparatory to making an attack.[2] Frederick William, duke of Würtemberg-Neustadt, was to command these forces, who were awaited by the Duke of Holstein, 'the severest Thorn in the Foot of the King of Denmark.'[3] With an imminent Danish onslaught against Holstein threatening, William did all in his power to avert a rupture which would be detrimental to the alliance he was attempting to forge against France.[4]

The subjects of the English king were divided in their thinking as to who was protagonist and who was antagonist. The anonymous pamphlet, *An Account of the differences between the King of Denmark and the Duke of Holstein-Gottorp* ... pointed out that the Duke was not acting in good faith in constructing forts close to the Danish border, for the presence of Swedish soldiers in those garrisons would allow the King of Sweden to secure a foothold in the 'Heart of the Dominions of the Danish King.'[5] Although Jodicus Crull and other pro-Danish groups set forth the cause of

[1] Defoe, *Charles XII*, p. 16 and Jöran Nordberg, *Konung Carl den XII:tes Historia* (1740), I, 64–65. Rudolf Fåhræus, *Karl XI och Karl XII*, Vol. VIII in *Sveriges Historia till våra dagar*, Emil Hildebrand and Ludvig Stavenow (ed.) (Stockholm, 1923), p. 317. Cited hereafter as Fahräus, *Sveriges Historia*, VIII. Walfrid Holst, *Ulrika Eleonora d.y. Karl XII's Syster* (Stockholm, 1956), p. 27–31. For an up-to-date account of the legal relationships between Denmark and Holstein-Gottorp see Otto Brandt, *Geschichte Schlewsig-Holstein, ein Grundriss* (Kiel, 1957). Pages 158–161 succinctly summarize the position of Holstein-Gottorp during the Great Northern War.
[2] Fåhräus, *Sveriges Historia*, VIII, 329.
[3] Molesworth, *Account of Denmark*, p. 199.
[4] Hugo Larsson, *Grefve Karl Gyllenborg i London åren 1715–1717: Ett Bidrag till Sveriges ytre politik under Karl XII's sista regeringsår* (Göteborg, 1891), p. 5.
[5] *An Account of the differences between the King of Denmark and the Duke of Holstein-Gottorp with some reflections upon the present motions of the Swedes* (London, 1700), pp. 9, 13.

Denmark,[1] Defoe, who was pro-Holstein, insisted that the Duke was within his rights building forts in his own country.[2] William III, ignoring all opinions but his own, remained steadfast to Sweden and decided early to come to the aid of Charles XII should it be necessary.

The Swedish ruler made an initial appeal for help even before March, 1700, when the troops of the Duke of Würtenberg-Neustadt crossed over the border into Holstein. The Maritime Powers were asked to outfit a squadron for Baltic duty which could be used by the Swedes to uphold Holstein sovereignty as outlined at Altona.[3] While Charles XII waited for assistance from his British and Dutch allies, Danish troops rapidly moved through Holstein-Gottorp, capturing and razing the forts of Husum, Eiderstedt, Northditmarsen, and Schwabstedt. Even the Duke's own palace was occupied by enemy soldiers. The town of Tönning was also laid under siege, but an approaching army of Swedes, Hollanders, and Hanoverians under the command of George, Elector of Brunswick-Luneberg, forced the Danes to withdraw from that city.[4]

It is important to note that the future George I of England was actively pro-Swedish during these initial phases of the Great Northern War. In truth it was not until the acquisition of Bremen and Verden by Denmark seemed probable that the Elector abandoned his steadfast friendship toward Charles XII.

In 1700 his loyalty to the Emperor along with his fears of Danish control of Holstein and Danish expansion into Germany outweighed other considerations. Furthermore Hanover's security during the War of the Spanish Succession was in part dependent on the Emperor.[5]

Charles's further expectations for assistance from the Maritime Powers were well founded and were soon realized. Peace in the North was necessary if William III were to receive any effective Swedish aid against France.[6] Peace in Germany

---

[1] Crull, *Denmark Vindicated*, p. 215.

[2] Defoe, *Charles XII*, p. 36, was pro-Holstein and insisted that the Duke of Holstein had a right to build forts in his own country.

[3] Ernst Carlson, 'Sverige och Preussen, 1701–1709,' *Historisk Bibliotek*, VII (Stockholm, 1880), p. 125.

[4] Koch, *Abrégée*, XIII, 165 and Fåhräus, *Sveriges Historia*, VIII, 322.

[5] Mediger, *Moskaus Weg*, p. 10.

[6] Larsson, *Gyllenborg*, p. 5.

was mandatory if German troops were to be released for allied campaigns. To secure those objectives, William, in May, 1700, dispatched a squadron to the Baltic under the command of Admiral Sir George Rooke.[1] This British contingent was reinforced on the twenty-fourth of the month by a group of Dutch naval vessels under Lieutenant-Admiral Phillips van Allemond.[2] The joint naval unit was destined to act as an 'Umpire in the Baltic,'[3] and was to be the weight deciding the balance of Baltic naval power. It was to be the final factor in settling Dano-Swedish differences over Holstein, for the fleets of Denmark and Sweden were 'pretty near an Equality for deciding their frequent differences, but the Preservation of the Peace of Europe, oftentimes obliges *England and Holland* to interpose with their formidable Fleets, and put an end to their Quarrels.'[4] William III having experimented with the more subtle means of diplomatic persuasion to accomplish his aims, committed himself to the use of force for bringing Holstein and Denmark to a peaceful accord.[5]

The Anglo-Dutch squadron when it arrived at the Sound was to 'let the Danes understand' that its reason for being was to contribute 'towards restoring peace and tranquility in those parts and for making good the engagements . . . under . . . the Treaty of Altona.' If the Danes showed fight, the ships of the Maritime Powers were to remain off the Sound awaiting the arrival of the Swedish squadron. If the Danes withdrew to Copenhagen, Rooke's command was to join the Swedes at Karlskrona and to assist them in covering the landing of Swedish soldiers in Denmark. The English admiral was also instructed to do his 'utmost to prevent the Danes from carrying troops from one island, or place to another.' Danish opposition

---

[1] Thomas Lediard, *Naval History of England* (London, 1735), II, 730–732 contains information about the strength of the squadron, as does Burchett, *A Complete History*, p. 583.

[2] Burchett, *A Complete History*, p. 583.

[3] Defoe, *Peter*, p. 103.

[4] Burchett, *A Complete History*, p. 19.

[5] James Vernon to Hugh Greg, British minister at Copenhagen, October 24, and November 3, 1699, *British Diplomatic Instructions, Denmark*, James F. Chance (ed.), Camden third series, XXXVI (London, 1926), p. 19. Cited hereafter as *British Instructions, Denmark*; and Instructions to Sir George Rooke, May 9, 1700, *Journal of Sir George Rooke, Admiral of the Fleet, 1700–1702*, Oscar Browning (ed.), Naval Records Society, IX (1897), pp. 2–3, cited hereafter as *Rooke's Journal*.

was to be met with force; Danish shot with English shot.[1] In the meantime while the Maritime Admirals were en route to the Sound, British diplomats presented an ultimatum to Frederick IV. Denmark was told to abide by the Altona agreement or expect to bear the brunt of Anglo-Dutch naval might.[2]

The squadron arrived off Götenborg June 8 and began its long wait for the juncture with the Swedish fleet.[3] Nearly a month of delay transpired. It appeared at one time that the Maritime naval contingent might not be compelled to make a forceful passage through the Sound. On July 3 Rooke received a letter from Ulrich Gyldenlöve, admiral of the Danish Fleet, informing him and Allemonde that a peace agreement between Frederick IV and the Duke of Holstein had been concluded at the camp of the Danish king in Holstein.[4] However, Rooke, the next day, received dispatches from James Cressett, British envoy extraordinary to Frederick IV, which indicated that the Danes, instead of attempting to settle matters amicably were stalling for time and were making no attempt to face the issues.[5] Undoubtedly hope of assistance from Russia and Saxony-Poland against Sweden and Sweden's allies prompted the Danish delaying tactics. Cressett's information concerning Danish moves prodded Rooke to action. The fleet consequently weighed anchor and began the difficult passage through the Sound. Two days of 'dirty blowing weather' hampered the British maneuver, but by July 6, the ships of the Maritime Powers had effected a rendezvous with the vessels of Charles XII.[6]

Various conferences of Swedish and British naval officers occurred. Rooke also carried on a lengthy exchange of notes with Gyldenlöve. In addition to correspondence and conference, Rooke executed two bombing sweeps against the Danish fleet. On July 24, the allied squadron covered the landing of Charles XII and 5,000 infantry men six English miles from

[1] Instructions to Rooke, *Rooke's Journal*, pp. 1–10.
[2] Declaration to be delivered to Frederick IV by the British minister at Copenhagen, May 17, 1700, *Ibid.*, pp. 10–11.
[3] *Ibid.*, pp. 27–71 and Burchett, *A Complete History*, p. 583.
[4] Gyldenlöve to Rooke, July 3, 1700, *Rooke's Journal*, pp. 67–68.
[5] *Ibid.*, p. 70.
[6] *Ibid.*, pp. 71–72. *Cf.* Burchett, *A Complete History*, p. 584.

Elsinore.[1] Threatened with the siege of Copenhagen, his capital, and with the subsequent bombardment and destruction of his fleet, which lay anchored before the city, Frederick IV sued for peace. At a Chateau in Travendal, August 7, the terms of agreement were drawn up and the final exchange of signatures made.[2] The Altona treaty was reasserted; the Duke was recognized in his rights with certain restrictions; and Denmark promised not to assist the enemies of the Swedish king. The Empire, France, and all other guarantors of the Altona pact were to be invited to play a similar role in the Travendal treaty, which was in reality a victory for Charles XII and his brother-in-law, the Duke of Holstein-Gottorp.[3] William III had reason to be satisfied with his role in the affair. No longer did the Dano-Holstein affair upset Europe and stand in the way of the completion of the diplomatic chains he was forging against France. Sweden was indebted to the Maritime Powers, and William III might call for payment at some future date. His skillful and moderate handling of Swedo-Danish affairs won him the respect of both parties; and on January 20, 1701 Denmark signed the defensive treaty of Odense with England and Holland.[4] The Elector of Hanover, who was later to become King of England, also received considerable prestige from the Travendal treaty, for he had been among the more important mediators of the settlement.

As William III spun his web against her, France endeavored to stay in the good graces of Denmark and Sweden, dependent as the ships of Louis XIV were upon the Baltic for their supply of naval stores. The diplomats of the Grande Monarch were apprehensive less Danish troops fight side by side with those of the members of the Grand Alliance. Both England and France, therefore, had an interest in ending the Great Northern War, which had picked up considerable momentum in the days after

[1] Various letters and minutes of councils of war and other entries in *Rooke's Journal*, pp. 72–92.

[2] *Ibid.*, pp. 100–101. The text of the treaty may be found in Lamberty, *Mémoires*, I, 52–57 and Dumont, *Corps diplomatique*, VII.

[3] Fåhräus, *Sveriges Historia*, VIII, 336 claims that the treaty must be considered 'som en framgång för den dåtida svenska politiken.' Koch, *Abrégée*, XIII, 171, is of the opinion that Denmark was fortunate that Charles XII was moderate in his demands because he wanted to fight Poland, and that the Maritime Powers did not want Denmark's position as a Baltic force destroyed.

[4] Dumont, *Corps diplomatique*, VIII, 1.

Travendal. Their diplomatic overtures made to persuade Peter the Great of Russia to settle his differences were not so successful as Anglo-Dutch representations backed by force had been at Travendal.[1] The Great Northern War and the War of the Spanish Succession were to be concurrent in spite of all endeavors to the contrary made by the rulers and diplomats of the Western European countries. After 1702, when the 'little gentleman in the fur coat' and an open window removed William III from the diplomatic and earthly scene, events in Europe moved at a much more rapid tempo. Almost all of Europe became involved in one of the two great struggles which through thirteen years of combat continued to run their separate courses, although at times they threatened to become merged into one gigantic European conflict.

The Treaty of Travendal was to mark the end of active British assistance to Sweden. Henceforth English efforts so far as Charles XII was concerned would be limited to the role of trying to mediate between Sweden and her enemies.[2] Both Charles XII and the new British queen, Anne, were too involved in their own difficulties and with their own private wars to aid their respective allies. It was important to English interests, however, that the two conflicts did not merge, for such an occurrence might pit Sweden against the Empire, England's long-time ally in arms. There was always a real fear in England that the traditional Franco-Swedish alliance against the Emperor might be resumed. Such apprehensions were further heightened by the death of Oxenstierna in July, 1702, which deprived the English of a valuable friend at the Swedish court.

Events of 1702 definitely indicated that there was ample justification for Britain's concern over Baltic affairs. In the eyes of the British diplomat John Robinson, Sweden seemed to be 'on a precipice,'[3] and the apparent determination of Charles XII to carry the war into Saxony for the purpose of forcing the German elector, Augustus, off the Polish throne could

---

[1] Sir Charles Hedges to Robinson, January 24, 1701, *British Instructions, Sweden*, p. 19; various letters in Lamberty, *Mémoires*, I, 132–135. For comments on French attempts to mediate the Dano-Swedish war see E. Carlson, 'Sverige och Preussen, 1701–1709,' *Historisk Bibliotek*, VII, 23.

[2] Larsson, *Gyllenborg*, p. 5.

[3] Robinson to Hedges, July 12, 1701, P.R.O., State Papers, Sweden, 95/15.

precipitate an avalanche.[1] To avert England's being buried by the events in eastern Europe, Robinson was instructed to go to Prussia, to find out where in Poland Charles XII and Augustus II could be found, and then to go to the two monarchs to bring them to a peaceful settlement of their differences. Robinson was once more to invite Sweden 'to enter into the Grand Alliance' and to contribute 12,000 troops who would aid in eradicating the danger to Europe occasioned 'by the exorbitant power of France and its close conjunction with Spain.' The Saxon troops of Augustus II were also to be solicited to assist in the great cause by serving in the allied armies under the command of John Churchill, Earl of Marlborough.[2]

Robinson's undertaking proved a failure, although the British diplomat's performance was all that might have been expected from any agent. In March, 1703, he had obtained a short open air visit with the King of Sweden. During the five minutes of allotted time, Robinson had not even mentioned to Charles XII the possibility of Sweden making peace with Poland.[3] In addition, Robinson's June conversations with Augustus II, had indicated that the Elector of Saxony was anxious to terminate his war with Charles XII, but would not submit to the loss of his Polish crown, a *sina qua non* demanded by the Swedish ruler. Faced with an apparently hopeless situation,[4] Robinson early in September had withdrawn to Danzig where he could protect British commercial interests there, counteract French influence on Baltic military and diplomatic affairs, and keep a close watch on Franco-Swedish trade relations.[5] While at Danzig, he labored with success to insure that city's neutrality and its safety from the ravages of the Great Northern War.[6]

[1] Larsson, *Gyllenborg*, p. 5.

[2] Instructions to Robinson, December 11, 1702, *British Instructions, Sweden*, pp. 26–29. An account of Robinson's work as a Baltic diplomat written solely from British sources may be found in June Milne, 'The diplomacy of Dr. John Robinson at the court of Charles XII of Sweden, 1697–1709,' *Transactions of the Royal Historical Society*, fourth series, XXX (1948), pp. 75–93. Cited hereafter as Milne, *Robinson*.

[3] Milne, *Robinson*, pp. 80–82 discusses Robinson's efforts in 1703.

[4] Robinson remarked in July: 'even the offers of large sums of money to the Swedish Ministers were as little attended to as our reasons. They knew they could not turn the King from his purpose whatever it was.' Quoted in A. E. Stamp, 'The meeting of the Duke of Marlborough and Charles XII at Alt-Ränstadt, April, 1707,' *Transactions of the Royal Historical Society*, new series, XII (1898), p. 105.

[5] Milne, *Robinson*, pp. 82–83.

[6] Robinson to Harley, September 13, 1704, BM. Add. MSS., 22198.

Robinson was unable, however, to prevent the war from spreading to Saxony. In spite of his efforts the troops of Charles XII, in August, 1706, began to move into the electorate of Augustus II. To meet the new emergency, Robinson and the Hanoverian minister to Charles XII, Count Bodo d'Oberg, both received instructions to prevent the quarrel between Sweden and her enemies from spreading to other parts of the Empire and if possible 'to incline the king of Sweden to retire from Augustus's lands.'[1] 'Because the elector of Hanover hath so great personal interest with the king of Sweden, and his electoral highness having expressed great desire to have these troubles specially pacified and the Swedes got out of Germany,' Robinson was ordered to maintain a close correspondence with various Hanoverian statesmen, among them being George's confidential secretary, Jean de Robethon, who later received much abuse from the English because of Baltic affairs. It should be noted that English diplomats were working in close coöperation with Hanoverians on the problems of northern Europe some years before the elector became George I of England.

The labors of Robinson and Count d'Oberg were complicated by the circumstances occurring in September, 1706. In that month, by the peace of Alt-Ranstädt, Augustus II abdicated the Polish throne in favor of Stanislaus Leszczynski, the Swedish nominee.[2] Charles XII set up his headquarters in the treaty city to await the final fulfillment of the terms of Alt-Ranstädt settlement and Anglo-Swedish relations took a sudden turn for the worse. France attempting to profit from the new situation in Poland immediately recognized Stanislaus as king, while England withheld recognition until March, 1707. England, moreover, never formally ratified the treaty of Alt-Ranstädt, although she had at one time made a binding promise to do so. British delays and vacillation on both counts irritated the impatient Charles XII and it took all of Robinson's consummate skill as a diplomat to allay the easily ruffled

[1] Harley to Robinson, October 1, 1706, *British Instructions, Sweden*, pp. 30–31.
[2] Dumont, *Corps diplomatique*, VIII, pt. i, p. 204, and Lamberty, *Mémoires*, VI, 273–279. The treaty was signed September 13, 1706. Milne, *Robinson*, p. 85, gives November as the month for the renouncing of the throne by Augustus II. See Fåhräus, *Sveriges Historia*, VIII, 384–386 for Charles XII and the Alt-Ranstädt treaty.

feelings of the Swedish monarch. Keeping Charles XII mollified was a full time job for any envoy, or for any foreign office.

The presence of Swedish troops in the Empire and questions as to the use of Saxon troops in the allied armies also presented ticklish problems to the English secretaries of state who walked a diplomatic tightrope in trying to pacify the Emperor, an active ally, and Charles XII, a passive one. Religion, always touchy in Germany, further confused the issues, for the Swedish king and the Emperor began to quibble over the rights of Silesian Calvinists. England consequently was placed in the middle of an embarrassing dispute, which became additionally complicated as the Silesian Calvinists were often not sure, in their own minds, on what rights they were supposed to be insisting. Robinson hoped that some sort of an accord might be reached among the disputants without Charles XII actively intervening as the protector of the Calvinists.[1] Should that have occurred, the entire military situation in the War of the Spanish Succession would have been altered appreciably.

Defoe is perhaps a good weather vane to test the direction of British public opinion toward Sweden. At the opening of the war, he had been pro-Swedish.[2] By 1704, he had shifted:

> The Swede is now Agressor, and as he was Really Injur'd by the Pole in an Unjust Invasion of the Swedish Livonia, yet he ought to be Prevail'd with not to carry his private Resentments on, to affect the present Confederacy of which the king of Poland is a Member.[3]

Augustus II was a member of the Grand Alliance and Swedish action against him was detrimental to British interest. As the British and Dutch had restrained Danish aspirations in Holstein:

> They have the Same Right and as much Reason to Restrain the Swede from kindling a War in the Bowells of the Empire, which will certainly be the Effect of his Dethroning the King of Poland, and Marching a Swedish Army into the Dukedome of Saxony, which appears now to be the Design.[4]

[1] Robinson to Harley, November 11, 1707, BM., Add. MSS., 22198.

[2] See above.

[3] Defoe to Harley, July–August, 1704, George H. Healey (ed.), *The Letters of Daniel Defoe* (Oxford, 1955), p. 48. Cited hereafter as Defoe, *Letters*. Defoe expressed similar sentiments in the *Review*.

[4] *Ibid.*, p. 49.

One way that Charles XII was to be restrained was 'with Sword drawn.' Defoe suggested that Britain 'send a Strong Squadron into the Baltic, not after the Ambassador, but with him.'[1] Defoe even went so far as to advocate British participation in an invasion of Skåne, Sweden's most southern province.[2]

Defoe's articles against the policies of Charles XII, which appeared in the *Review*, brought forth protests from the Swedish envoy to England.[3] Although such Tories as John Dyer, in the *News-letter*, could rally to Sweden's defense,[4] Defoe was read and undoubtedly a considerable portion of the British population reflected Defoe's sentiments. Most populations of warring nations take a dim view on the actions of a neutral, which might react contrary to their own efforts toward victory.

So acute was the state of German affairs in 1707 and in English minds so great the danger that Sweden might join France against the Emperor, that England's ace soldier and diplomat, John Churchill, now duke of Marlborough, decided to go, personally to Alt-Ranstädt to aid Robinson in preventing such a contingency from happening.[5] The British hoped that the military prestige of the victor of Blenheim, coupled with Robinson's knowledge of Baltic diplomacy would provide a combination sufficiently powerful to dissuade Charles from taking any overtly hostile action against the Empire. Marlborough arrived at Alt-Ranstädt on April 27, 1707, and stayed for two days, a duration of time long enough to convince him that Swedish arms were not destined to be used in the War of the Spanish Succession. Nevertheless, the allied general, 'was sorry to observe a great deal of coolness towards the court of Vienna, which may have an ill effect if matters are not accommodated before the Swedes march out of Saxony, otherwise

[1] *Ibid.*, pp. 28, 49 and the *Review*, July 29, 1704.

[2] *Ibid.*, p. 50. See also G. F. Warner, 'An unpublished political paper by Daniel Defoe,' *English Historical Review*, XXII (1907), pp. 132–43.

[3] Luttrell, *Brief Relations*, VI, 215.

[4] See the *Review* for November 6, 1707. In addition to the material in the *Review*, Defoe answered Dyer with *Dyer's News Examined as to His Swedish Memorial Against the Review* (Edinburgh, 1707) and *Defoe's Answer to Dyer's Scandalous News Letter* (Edinburgh, 1707).

[5] Harley to Robinson, April 1, 1707, *British Instructions, Sweden*, p. 33. Marlborough to Harley, April 27, 1707, *The Letters and Dispatches of John Churchill, First Duke of Marlborough from 1702–1712*, Sir George Murray (ed.), (London, 1845), III, 347. Cited hereafter as *Marlborough Dispatches*.

it is more than probable that they will make the Emperor very uneasy in their passage through Silesia'[1] on their way toward Russia.

Marlborough, however, considered Robinson well fitted to accomplish all that could be done in ironing out existing difficulties, and his confidence was not misplaced.[2] On September 1, 1707, an accord was achieved between Sweden and the Empire.[3] England could claim a considerable amount of credit[4] for settling various diplomatic disagreements which had existed between Sweden and the Empire as far back as the Westphalian settlement. Yet England's role in the Swedo-Imperial quarrel did not completely satisfy Charles XII, who was unhappy over the part played by his ally in handling his affairs in Germany. Moreover, the Swedes noticed that England had not guaranteed the Alt-Ranstädt settlement as 'Your Court of Hanover' had done.[5] Robinson, however, continued to act as a trouble-shooter throughout 1707–1708, years in which the entire European diplomatic situation remained ticklish, treaties notwithstanding. Be it the problem of the Holstein succession occasioned by the death of the Duke in 1702 or disorders in the city of Hamburg, Robinson worked diligently to prevent events in northeastern Europe from getting out of hand and to counteract and to circumvent the diplomatic activities of the French envoy to Charles XII, Jean Victor de Besenval. By 1709, the question as to whom was to educate the young duke of Holstein was solved, but the young ducal candidate's claims to the Swedish throne, should Charles XII suddenly die, caused considerable uneasiness, both in Denmark and Germany. Robinson, early in January, 1709, saw the looming complications which might result from a succession

---

[1] Marlborough to Harley, May 10, 1707, *Marlborough Dispatches*, III, 358. Stamp in 'The meeting of Marlborough,' pp. 113–116 reprints three Robinson letters which set forth the details of the conversations of Marlborough with Charles XII better than do those of the great English general.

[2] Marlborough to Harley, May 10, 1707, *Marlborough Dispatches*, III, 359.

[3] Treaty between the Emperor and the King of Sweden, September 1, 1707, Lamberty, *Mémoires*, IV, 473–479. The text of the treaty may also be found in Dumont, *Corps diplomatique*, VIII, 221–222. A discussion of the treaty is in Koch, *Abrégée*, XIII, 203–207. See also Harley to Robinson, September 23, 1707, *British Instructions, Sweden*, p. 37.

[4] Milne, *Robinson*, pp. 87–88.

[5] Robinson to Raby, July 26, 1709, BM., Add. MSS., 22198.

problem and fervently hoped that the Swedish king 'like the Patriarchs' would 'live to begatt Sons and Daughters.'[1] His wishes were not fulfilled and Charles's failure to produce an heir and the consequent results plagued European diplomats throughout the Great Northern War. Robinson nearly lost his life in Hamburg[2] while bringing some order out of the chaos resulting from the presence of Swedish troops there.[3]

Diplomatic labors dangerous and exciting were only a part of his chores, for always matters of trade had to be considered. As Britain and Holland were the leading commercial nations of Europe, it is not surprising that they would try to employ economics in their struggle against France. English diplomats, in 1709, exerted pressure upon Denmark and Sweden to prevent those countries from supplying France and Spain with either corn or naval stores.[4] Parleys achieved some success, but the dispatching of Admiral Sir John Norris to the Sound with six warships proved a much more effective way to prevent the enemy from obtaining adequate war supplies from Baltic lands. The Norris squadron, so far as naval strategy was concerned, performed the same function as had numerous French privateering units in the North Sea, which had raised havoc with British merchantmen returning from the Baltic ports.[5] The high-handed seizures of Swedish corn ships by Norris was deemed harsh, even by Robinson; nevertheless, that British Baltic specialist, well knew that there were times that necessities of war ruled out all other considerations. The cleric-diplomat was hoping in June, 1709 that 'Sir John Norris is so posted, that no ships coming from the East Sea will escape.'[6] Norris performed his tasks well,[7] but experienced difficulties. At one time he was forced into Göteborg with French prizes captured

[1] Robinson to Raby, January 18, 1709, *Ibid.*

[2] Various letters to Boyle, 1708–1709, *Ibid.*, and P.R.O., State Papers, Sweden 82/24.

[3] *Ibid.* For the Swedish attitude on Hamburg affairs see Swedish Chancery to the Swedish minister at Hamburg, April 6, 1709, enclosed in Jackson's dispatches, P.R.O., State Papers, Sweden, 95/18.

[4] Robinson to Raby, May 1, 1709, BM., Add. MSS., 22198 and various letters of Jackson, 1709, P.R.O., State Papers, Sweden, 95/18.

[5] J. H. Owen, *War at Sea under Queen Anne, 1702–1708* (Cambridge, 1938), *passim*, describes the troubles experienced by the Admiralty in bringing its convoys home from the Baltic.

[6] Robinson to Raby, June 14, 1709, BM., Add. MSS., 22198.

[7] For details of Norris in the Baltic see Burchett, *A Complete History*, p. 726.

while sailing under Danish colors, and the Swedish port authorities commandeered the ships and imprisoned the British prize crews.[1] Jackson at Stockholm vigorously protested against the Swedish action, and finally achieved the release of men and vessels.[2]

The Norris squadron was noteworthy on several accounts. First, it introduced Sir John Norris to Baltic waters, where he was later to achieve considerable prestige in the dual role of admiral and diplomat. Secondly, Swedish merchantmen were being stopped under the guise of military necessity by British naval units. Later, when Charles XII's privateers, acting under the same pretext, seized British merchantmen trading to Russian held territory, the Swedish action resulted in British squadrons being sent to the Baltic to protect British trade. In addition, as has been shown in Chapter II, it gave rise to long discussions and to lengthy memoirs drafted by Jackson and other British diplomats, which set forth Swedish treaty obligations and English rights to commercial freedom. It would appear then, that, diplomatically speaking, what was sauce for the goose, was, in the eyes of Englishmen or at least English diplomats, not sauce for the gander. At least such was the way George I and his ministers were later to make their interpretations.

Let us return to 1709. That year saw the entire Baltic picture change as Charles XII began to experience setbacks in Russia which during the summer were to culminate in his disastrous defeat at Poltava. Quickly a reshuffling of the European diplomatic chessmen occurred. Denmark and Poland reëntered the war against Sweden in a jackal-like attempt to realize some of the spoils from the victory of the Russian bear. New faces appeared among the diplomats and old ones disappeared. Against his wishes, Robinson, in August received a call to return to England to assume the duties of an ecclesiastical post. The doctor was of the opinion that the fates had ordained him to a public rather than to a clerical life and he knew that the 'Searcher of Hearts' would substantiate him in his reasoning. He hated to withdraw, because he rightly considered himself

---

[1] Jackson to the Swedish Chancery, July 12, 1709, P.R.O., State Papers, Sweden, 95/18.

[2] Swedish Senate to Baron Siöblad at Göteborg, July 12, 1709, P.R.O., State Papers, Sweden, 95/18.

the person best suited among the British to mediate the Great Northern War.[1] Destiny, the Church and the Tories, however, were to place him at the conference tables at Utrecht rather than those at Stockholm and Nystad.

As a result, Robert Jackson at Stockholm was given expanded powers and shortly, Captain James Jefferyes reëntered the rapidly changing Baltic scene. The Russian victory at Poltava had altered the Eastern European political situation and had rudely upset the balance of power in the Baltic. Sweden no longer was in a position to play a lone hand in eastern and northern Europe. In fact, she would need help from her allies and from other European powers if she were to survive as a first rate nation. Actually, as time continued, there was some who wondered whether Sweden would survive at all.

The return of Denmark and Saxony to active belligerency posed a serious problem to the British foreign office for those two states by renewing hostilities had upset the treaties of Travendal and Alt-Ranstädt with which England was directly linked. She was an outright guarantor of the former settlement and had promised to do the same on the latter 'in the most solemn manner, and in the Queen's name.'[2] Yet Anne of England did nothing to buttress the fading fortunes of Charles XII for it was of immediate concern to her Majesty's government to retain the services of the Danish, Saxon, and Prussian troops who were serving under the allied banner. If hostilities broke out in the Lower Saxon Circle, not only those troops but also others from Holstein and Brunswick stood a chance of being withdrawn from Marlborough's command. Consequently throughout 1709–1711, England pursued a vacillating policy, which in the main was a comedy of blunders and errors. On the other hand, Sweden in her demands for help, ignored the War of the Spanish Succession and failed to recognize that the war in the West completely occupied the resources of the States, Britain, Hanover, and other nations who had solemnly promised to uphold the Travendal and Alt-Ranstädt settlements.[3]

[1] Robinson to Raby, July 3, 1709, BM., Add. MSS., 22198.
[2] Henry St. John to Charles Whitworth, July 12, 1711, *Letters and Correspondence Public and Private of the Right Henry St. John, Lord Visc. Bolingbroke*, Gilbert Parke (ed.) (London, 1798), I, 270. Cited hereafter as *Bolingbroke Letters*.
[3] Fredrik F. Carlson, *Om Fredsunderhandlingarne, Åren, 1709–1718* (Stockholm, 1857), p. 12.

To a point of disgust, self interest dominated British policy. With almost indecent haste, Peter was congratulated on his victory. Anne hypocritically expressed to Augustus II 'Our particular satisfaction on his being happily settled in his Kingdom of Poland with assurances of Our firm friendship for him and Our constant inclination towards advancing his interests.'[1] She, instead of upholding the treaty of Alt-Ranstädt, actually encouraged Augustus II to violate it by overthrowing Charles's candidate Stanislaus, who had been acknowledged Poland's king by England 'after an awkward manner.'[2]

Efforts were made to prevent the spread of the war in Germany. Diplomats assembled at the Hague, who represented the Emperor, the United Provinces, and Britain, drew up on March 31, 1710 a convention declaring that the Swedish provinces were to be considered by all belligerents as neutral territory. The enemies of Charles XII could not invade the sequestered lands, but neither could he use them as a base for operations against Denmark or Saxony.[3] The negotiations resulting from the convention put Charles XII and his allies in an awkward position; for the enemies of Sweden along with Hanover—which did not want the war extended—agreed to the stipulations as drawn up at the Hague.[4] The Swedish ruler, however, considered the treaty of neutrality an insult,[5] and late in the year he repudiated it, notwithstanding that the Swedish Council (Råd) had signified its willingness to comply with convention stipulations. Charles XII in a counter move called upon his allies to live up to their previous treaty agreements and guarantees, rather than impose restrictions upon Sweden which were against his honor to accept.[6] Charles XII pointed out that his enemies were to receive the same treatment

[1] Quoted in Chance, George I and the Northern War, p. 11.
[2] Henry St. John to Whitworth, July 12, 1711, Bolingbroke Letters, I, 270.
[3] Dumont, Corps diplomatique, VIII, pt. i, p. 249; various letters of Jackson written in 1710, P.R.O., State Papers, Sweden, 95/18.
[4] Chance, George I and the Northern War, pp. 12–13. Mediger, Moskaus Weg, p. 11.
[5] Larsson, Gyllenborg, p. 6.
[6] The Swedish minister Müllern wrote July 21, 1710: 'Jag hade gerna önskatt att H. M. conniverat till Haagerconcerten, intilldess man med eftertryck kunde sätte sig deremot, men som Konungens vänner vilja föreskrifva honom vilkor, har konungen för sin gloire ei kunnat annat göra,' quoted in Carlson, Om Fredsunderhandlingarne, p. 11.

from the hands of his allies as himself, and if his friends refused to aid him as bound by treaty, he would trust in Divine help and in the justice of his cause to recoup his losses.[1]

Legally, the Swedish ruler was correct, but the diplomacy of the eighteenth century did not often concern itself with technical niceties. Perhaps a less honorable man than Charles XII—and the one thereby better able to profit diplomatically —would have agreed to the convention with a view towards breaking it at his convenience.[2] Thus, he might have made it feasible for his erstwhile allies to stall for time until a more favorable moment arrived for them to come to Sweden's aid. That time was not long in coming, because shortly Britain and the Empire were faced with the 'danger of having the neutrality broke by the [enemies of Charles XII] rather than by him.'[3] It is possible that Charles XII had repudiated the convention because his diplomatic position had been strengthened in November, 1710, by a renewal of the Russo-Turkish war.

The new Tory government coming into power in 1710 on the wake of the Sacherverell trial, thus inherited many knotty problems so far as northern affairs were concerned. It was adverse to over-interference in continental affairs, for it failed to see how England could profit by a strong diplomatic policy. Yet it did not want to stand by and see Sweden ruined and dismembered by her foes, and the balance of Baltic power upset.[4] Consequently, a trimming game began as England endeavored 'to get out of the present labyrinth, with as few scratches' as possible.[5] Each attempt made by the Tories was as poorly conceived and executed as had been most of the steps

[1] Declaration of Charles XII on the Convention, written at Bender, November 30, 1710, Dumont, *Corps diplomatique*, VIII, pt. i, p. 258.

[2] Werpert Louis de Fabrice, who was with Charles XII at Bender to Baron Friedrich Wilhelm von Görtz, Hanoverian minister, December 15, 1710, *Anecdotes du Roi de Suéde à Bender* (Hambourg, 1760), p. 26: 'J'ai hazardé quoiqu'avec toute la modestie possible d'alleguer toutes la raisons imaginables, pour porter sa majesté à l'accepter (le traité de neutralité) en lui representant l'advantage de son royaume et que du moins il seroit nécessaire de dissimuler quelque tems encore jusqu'à ce que les conjunctures devenant plus favorables, elle put avec succès fair éclater ses desseins.'

[3] Henry St. John to Whitworth, July 12, 1711, *Bolingbroke Letters*, I, 271.

[4] Chance, *George I and the Northern War*, p. 16.

[5] Henry St. John to Whitworth, July 12, 1711, *Bolingbroke Letters*, I, 271. For English hopes see Instructions to James Jefferyes, January 11, 1711, *British, Instructions, Sweden*, pp. 47–50.

taken by the Whigs. Each half-hearted try at interference led to further misunderstanding between the governments of Anne and Charles XII. The gradual progression toward strained relations continued. The change in ministries had at first little effect upon Britain's Baltic diplomacy.

One of the earliest attempts made by the new government to settle Baltic affairs was to send Captain James Jefferyes to Charles XII at Bender for the purpose of winning that monarch to the Act of Neutrality. On April 30, 1711, Jefferyes held a long conversation with the leading Swedish minister, Müllern, and pointed out to him that by the act, Sweden's German provinces had been preserved. Swedish troops were still in Germany, and the Protestant religion was still maintained there. To the Swedish argument that Poland and Jutland should have been exempted from the neutrality, Jefferyes countered that there could have been no neutrality without the inclusion of Jutland and Poland.

Müllern complained that Augustus II had broken his promises regarding the Polish throne. Jefferyes admitted all that, but tried realistically to show that Charles XII was in no position to defend his German possessions, let alone drive Augustus II out of Poland. Anne could hardly be expected to fight for Poland with a major war on her hands and her policy regarding Sweden had been a reasonable one. Müllern said he would do what he could, but he held out little promise, for Charles XII had already taken his position regarding the neutrality proposal.[1] Jefferyes knew too well that once Charles XII had made up his mind, it was nearly impossible for anyone to change it.

On May 2 Jefferyes received a letter from Müllern which summed up the Swedish stand. Actually the letter was dated April 28, two days before he had conferred with the Swedish minister. England and the States were thanked for their endeavors to settle affairs in the North, but Charles XII, however, did not feel that:

> in an affair of such nicety a Verbal Declaration may not be thought sufficient for those Powers who are oblig'd by the

[1] Jefferyes to Queensbury, May 18, 1711, P.R.O., State Papers, Sweden, 95/17; Jefferyes memorial on the Neutrality, May 5, 1715, *Ibid*. See Chapter II for the economic aspects of Jefferyes' mission.

most solemn agreements to assist towards forcing Our Enemies (except the Czar of Muscovy with whom no Friendship can be restor'd but such as must include the Ottoman Port) to just Conditions of Peace, for however Friendly their offices may be in procuring Peace, their Endeavours will be far more service-able if they wou'd threaten the rest of Our Enemies with Force according to the obligations of the Alliance.[1]

As for the Hague convention, Charles XII realized that there was nothing purposely malicious in it,

> but because that Resolution, which was taken without his knowledge and consent is of apparent advantage to his Ene-mies and of great disadvantage to him, he had declar'd twice by his ministers and a Third time under his sign'd manuel that he neither could nor would be ty'd down to obligations of that convention. In which Opinion his Sacred Maj'ty do's still continue.[2]

Jefferyes continued to persuade Charles XII to work out some sort of a solution with his allies, but in the middle of June, had come to the opinion that all arguments with Charles XII would only make him more contrary. The Swedish king re-mained firm in his belief that 'he has been neglected by the Allys, who instead of assisting him in his misfortune, have taken occasion from thence to prescribe him laws.'[3] Charles XII refused to promise not to molest the peace of the Empire for he had 'resolved never to recede from anything that the reasons of Warr or our own Interest require.'[4]

With Charles's refusal to go along with the neutrality conven-tion, the signatories had toyed with the idea of forcibly occupy-ing Sweden's German provinces, but had done nothing tangible in that regard. Sweden's foes, on the other hand, were ready and eager to fall upon those ill-defended territories. It was at this point that Hanover for its own security began to turn towards Russia and its allies. She not only permitted the attack of the allies on Swedish Pomerania; she actually encouraged it.[5]

England still attempting to prevent Sweden's dismemberment opposed the confederated plans of Charles' enemies, but to no

[1] Müllern to Jefferyes, April 28, 1711, *Ibid.*
[2] *Ibid.*
[3] Jefferyes to Queensbury, June 15, 1711, *Ibid.*
[4] Idem to Idem, July 13, 1711; and Charles XII to Palmquist, *Ibid.*
[5] Mediger, *Moskaus Weg*, p. 11.

avail. Saxon troops were withdrawn from the Netherlands, and in August, 1711, the occupation of Swedish Germany began. Charles XII could blame his British ally for not taking a firm stand against his foes; still his own action of refusing the neutrality convention had made it difficult for them to act on his behalf.

In November, 1711, Jefferyes and Müllern held a long discussion over the state of affairs in the Empire. By that time, there was a good deal more sharpness in the conversation. Trade difficulties[1] as well as the diplomatic impasse made the conducting of negotiations difficult. Müllern, while admitting a willingness to allow Britain to mediate the Great Northern War, said that Charles XII 'had reason to look upon them as words of course and compliments rather than anything in reality.' If the Maritime Powers had been really sincere, they would have prevented Sweden's foes from invading her provinces in Germany; to which Jefferyes sharply retorted that if Sweden had consented to the Act of Neutrality, the invasion of his possessions in the Empire would never have happened.[2]

Existing animosities between England and Sweden heightened late in 1711 and early in the next year. Sir Robert Sutton, acting without instructions and directly contrary to the wishes of the home secretaries of state, helped to mediate a peace between Peter and the Sultan, which drastically dashed Charles's hopes for a clear-cut victory over the Russian Czar.[3] The Swedish sovereign, by 1712, had many reasons to be dissatisfied with his British ally, and there was some justification for the erroneous fear in England that France and Sweden might arrive at some sort of an agreement directed against Britain. On March 16, 1711, Bolingbroke commented on French hopes for Swedish alliance:

> It is my opinion, that their expectations from the King of Sweden are too well grounded; and that he has a better under-

[1] See Chapter II.

[2] Jefferyes to St. John, November 10, 1711, P.R.O., State Papers, Sweden, 95/17.

[3] Charles XII was of the opinion that many of his current troubles with the Porte could be traced directly to Britain. Gyllenborg to Townshend, November 13, 1714, Letters of Foreign Ministers in England, Sweden, 1714–1716, P.R.O., State Papers, Foreign, 100/62; various letters of Jefferyes to St. John in 1712, and various letters of Müllern to Jefferyes in May, 1712, P.R.O., State Papers, Sweden, 95/17. *Cf.* Chance, *George I and the Northern War*, p. 27.

standing with France than we seem to apprehend, ever since his protestation against the neutrality.[1]

What Bolingbroke failed to apprehend was the mentality of Charles XII, who refused to unbend and become receptive to French overtures until it was too late for either country to profit by a Franco-Swedish alliance. Nevertheless diplomatic bungling, misunderstandings, stubbornness, and trade disputes were by 1712, seriously undermining, if not breaking, the Anglo-Swedish entente, which had been the cornerstone of William III's Baltic diplomacy.

In spite of the existing tension between the two nations, British diplomats persistently continued their endeavors to mediate the Great Northern War, but the despoilers of Sweden's German possessions were now increasingly less anxious for peace than they had been even as late as 1711. Shifting alliances and friendships on the diplomatic front further complicated the situation for the Tories. The Elector of Hanover, in 1712, moved his troops into the Swedish principality of Verden. From that time onward, a definite change is perceptible in the Elector's policy towards Sweden. His hesitation to act was overcome by Bernstorff who persuaded the Elector as to the dangers of Danish expansion. This is the first decisive step and all others followed as a matter of course.[2] From being Charles's staunchest friend among the German princes, George became at first neutral towards the Great Northern War, and later, strictly hostile to Sweden.[3] Hanover, well on the road to war with Sweden, gradually became determined to drive Sweden out of the Empire for the benefit of the German princes, especially the Elector of Hanover. At the same time Bolingbroke's future sovereign was perpetrating a rift with Sweden, the Britisher was writing:

> The allies are going too far in Pomerania. First they assure us that they only want to drive out the Swedish regiments there, but now it is obvious that their intentions are to expel the Swedish king from German territory. This is too much.[4]

[1] Bolingbroke to Drummond, March 16, 1711, *Bolingbroke Letters*, I, 108.
[2] Mediger, *Moskaus Weg*, p. 13.
[3] Chance, *George I and the Northern War*, p. 29.
[4] Reading, *Anglo-Russian Commercial Treaty*, p. 70.

Tory foreign policy by the end of 1712 was clearly at odds with that of the designated heir to the English throne. The more George veered towards Sweden's foes, the more Bolingbroke leaned towards Sweden. The poor quality of Saxon troops serving in the allied armies[1] and Danish depredations upon British commerce[2] added to Britain's strained relations with the enemies of Charles XII.

Peace loomed upon the European horizon in 1713 so far as the War of the Spanish Succession was concerned. It was hoped by many of the war-weary that the settlement being drawn up at Utrecht could be expanded to a general peace congress which would include the war in eastern Europe as well. Such hopes were rudely dashed by Charles XII who met the mediation proposals with the demand that his allies assist him with the military means as stipulated in their treaty commitments.[3] As the Swedish ruler spurned the olive branch and Robinson assisted at Utrecht, Charles's diplomatic position was worsened by his temporary imprisonment in Turkey and by the occupation by Prussia of Swedish holdings in eastern Pomerania.

All Swedes, however, were not in accord with the proud unyielding sentiments of their monarch. Maurits Vellingk, to some extent the Swedish voice in Germany, and many of his countrymen at home, were in favor of French and English diplomats at Utrecht mediating the northern crisis.[4] Political power in the last analysis, however, resided in the King, who would concede nothing to friend or to foe and who viewed all mediation offers with considerable mistrust and suspicion.[5] The complete ruination of his country was less important to Charles XII than the loss of what he pervertedly considered to be his honor.

Nevertheless, in England in March, 1713, Bolingbroke wrote to the Duke of Shrewsbury: 'The true state of the King of Sweden's affairs is much worse ... it is high time to think of saving him,

---

[1] Henry St. John to Strafford, October 30, 1711, *Bolingbroke Letters*, I, 450.

[2] Idem to Idem, November 9, 1711, *Ibid.*, p. 427–474.

[3] Carlson, *Om Fredsunderhandlingarne*, p. 26. For an up to date account of these negotiations see Jerker Rosén, 'Det engelska anbudet om fredsmedling, 1713,' *Lunds Universitets Årskrift*, 43 (Lund, 1946).

[4] *Ibid.*, pp. 35, 58.

[5] Larsson, *Gyllenborg*, p. 7.

in spite of himself.'[1] His prophecy of 1711, 'we are apt to fear that if Pomerania is once invaded with success, it will not be in the power of the Elector of Hanover nor perhaps of all the Allies, to say to the princes engaged in that war, thus far shall you go and no further,'[2] was proving itself correct. Hanover's unforeseen disaffection from Sweden was more than even the brilliant St. John had bargained for. Yet he would not use force to bring about peace although he could complain that Sweden's foes 'have profited too much already of their enemies misfortunes and obstinacy, and who have carried their success farther than is consistent with the general interest of Europe.'[3] His only solution was shopworn. It was to give diplomacy another chance and once more to offer England's mediation to Charles XII.

Jackson at Stockholm on May 30, 1713, duly received orders to communicate to the Swedish Chancery Bolingbroke's desire to help end the Northern War.[4] The overtures of the British diplomat were well received, and on July 21, he was approached by Count Avid Horn, the Swedish chancellor and leader of a peace party in Sweden. Horn expressed keen interest in the British proposal and indicated that he thought that Sweden's sole salvation lay in the forceful intervention of the Maritime Powers in the Great Northern War. The chancellor admitted that peace could not be obtained without some concessions on the part of Sweden, but felt that Sweden could afford to trust in English and Dutch good offices because both those powers would labor to preserve the balance of power in the North.

It is apparent that Horn had gathered around him a group less foolhardy than the King, who had flatly stated that he preferred to perish sword in hand rather than yield a single

[1] Henry St. John to Shrewsbury, March 24, 1713, *Bolingbroke Letters*, III, 515. Bolingbroke to Breton, March 3, 1713, P.R.O., F.E.B., State Papers, Foreign, 104/9. 'Her Maj'ty is seriously bending her thoughts to enter more determinately into the affairs of the North than she has hitherto been able to do.'

[2] Henry St. John to D'Elias, July 17, 1711, P.R.O., F.E.B., State Papers, Foreign, 104/48. Also quoted in Chance, *George I and the Northern War*, p. 25.

[3] St. John to Shrewsbury, April 19, 1713, *Bolingbroke Letters*, IV, 63.

[4] Jackson to Bromley, August 18, 1713; Swedish Chancery to Jackson, July 31, 1713, P.R.O., State Papers, Sweden, 95/20. This negotiation is discussed in John J. Murray, 'Robert Jackson's mission to Sweden (1709–1717),' *Journal of Modern History*, XXI (1949), pp. 6–8.

inch of Swedish soil. Horn and his adherents were statesmen and were closer to the stark realities of the situation. Faced with economic and political ruin, the Swedes at home could see little sense in sacrificing the entire country for the honor of the King.[1] Yet the shadow of Charles XII covered Sweden like a black cloud of doom. Horn and other Swedish malcontents feared that the sentiments they had expressed could send them to the block, and consequently asked Jackson to be careful and circumspect about the information they had given him. They especially requested that the news of their yearnings for peace be withheld from Count Karl Gyllenborg, the Swedish minister in London, 'whose late conduct towards the Senate hath much lost him their confidence.'[2]

Ten days after his conversation with Horn on July 21, Jackson received a reply from the Swedish Chancery to his May proposal.[3] The Swedish answer written out of protocol was indefinite, rambling, and hedging, and it well illustrated the fear of the sovereign held by the members of the Senate. The Chancery note claimed Sweden had been sold out at conferences so many times that the Swedes did not dare trust the destinies of their country to a general peace assembly as had been suggested by Jackson. They thanked the British minister for the 'pious design' offered by his sovereign and informed him that Gyllenborg had been instructed to do likewise in London. Although glib promises were made to facilitate peace, the Swedes made no additional commitments.[4] Jackson correctly summed up the Senate's attitude in a letter to Bromley dated August 6, wherein he pointed out that the majority of the Swedish people and senators would jump at the English offer if their hands were not tied by Charles XII. An absent king present in spirit cast a dread of frightful vengeance over an entire nation, over a country and a people moving stolidly, hopelessly, and helplessly towards complete disaster.[5] By mid-August, Horn admitted to Jackson that there was

[1] Jackson to Bolingbroke, July 21, 1714, P.R.O., State Papers, Sweden, 95/20.
[2] Idem to Idem, August 6, 1713, Ibid. For Gyllenborg's troubles in London at this time see Larsson, Gyllenborg, pp. 8–10. Vellingk was for peace, Carlson, Om Fredsunderhandlingarne, p. 25.
[3] Jackson to Bromley, August 6, 1713, P.R.O., State Papers, Sweden, 95/20.
[4] Swedish Chancery to Jackson, July 31, 1713, Ibid.
[5] Jackson to Bromley, August 6, 1713, Ibid.

little chance that Charles XII would even consider the English mediation proposal. As for the Senate, it was impotent and could do nothing. As Horn pointed out, it was so far as the Senate was concerned 'useless to send any orders at all from hence to any of their ministers abroad.'[1]

Those Swedish ministers who were at foreign posts must have been constantly confused by conflicting instructions, which came to them from the Senate, the King, and from Vellingk, the man empowered by the King, but with restrictions, to handle Swedish affairs in Germany. Gyllenborg in London, for example, had no letters of credence throughout this critical period, with Charles XII delaying the sending of necessary credentials until September, 1715. The procrastination on the part of the King may have been motivated by the animosity Charles XII had towards England, but it was poor tactics to tie diplomatically the hands of his ministers. Valuable time which might have been spent in allaying misunderstandings between England and Sweden was therefore lost.[2] The stubborn silences of Charles XII and his constant gagging of his agents in England and elsewhere did irreparable harm to Sweden during the days immediately following the conclusion of the War of the Spanish Succession. They also made it difficult for his allies, now free of the French War to figure out ways and means by which they might come to his assistance. Swedish diplomacy, became bogged down, for no one dared act without the King, whose absence and conduct placed his subjects in the awkward position that 'if some other expedient could not be contriv'd by their friends to rescue them, they must fall sacrifice to their enemies.'[3]

Expedients St. John had. Yet none of them were able to accomplish a pacification of the North or to reach an accord with the Swedish king, whose sole refrain was for his allies to send troops and money to enable him to defeat his enemies. Anne's government was not willing to take any aggressive steps without Holland, who seemed reluctant to pursue an active Baltic policy. At one time St. John hoped that France by

[1] Idem to Idem, August 18, 1713, *Ibid.*
[2] Larsson, *Gyllenborg*, pp. 9–11.
[3] Jackson to Bromley, November 9, 1713, P.R.O., State Papers, Sweden, 95/20.

appearing ready 'to interest herself in the Northern quarrel, as guaranty of the treaty of Westphalia' would push the Dutch to intervene.[1] Coöperation from the Dutch would have been difficult to come by, for:

> They seem to be conceived in nothing so much as the Settling their Barrier, and therefore are so apprehensive of Displeasing the Emperor, that they will not do anything without his consent and concurrence.[2]

Even if the States had coöperated, a pro-Swedish policy might have been difficult for St. John to sell to England, for a mounting anti-Swedish sentiment was growing in British commercial circles because of the increasing depredations of Swedish privateers upon British Baltic shipping.

In the meantime, attempts had been made by the Emperor to terminate the northern crisis. Late in December, 1712, he had tried to arrange for the convening of a congress at Brunswick to end the German phases of the Great Northern War, but Sweden's refusal to consider such a meeting prevented deliberations from getting under way. Charles's enemies by way of contrast professed an interest in such a gathering—that is under certain stipulations. Another try was made the next year to hold a Brunswick congress, but little of a substantial nature was accomplished.[3] Jackson at Stockholm worked to include the northern war as a topic for discussion at Baden, where diplomats were winding up the differences still existing between the Empire and France as a result of the War of the Spanish Succession.[4] The inertia or stubbornness of Charles XII prevented the Great Northern War from being mediated at a general congress, be it at Utrecht, Baden, or Brunswick, but throughout the remainder of the northern conflict, the idea of a Brunswick meeting remained. Charles XII eventually did send

---

[1] Bolingbroke to Shrewsbury, July 4, 1713, *Bolingbroke Letters*, IV, 179.
[2] Bromley to Pulteney, April 23, 1714, P.R.O., F.E.B., State Papers, Foreign, 104/5.
[3] Koch, *Abrégée*, XIII, 237–238; 249–250. Chance, *George I and the Northern War*, p. 31 is of the opinion that Lamberty, *Mémoires*, VIII, 295, 324 has confused the dating, but Chance has apparently lumped the two meetings of the Congress into one. Carlson, *Om Fredsunderhandlingarne*, p. 59 refers to the second meeting.
[4] Jackson to the Foreign Office, May 22 and July 3, 1714, P.R.O., State Papers, Sweden, 95/20.

a delegate to Brunswick, but by that time, Swedish tactics had caused all hopes of action at that place to wane.[1]

Britain tried to split Sweden's enemies by using both propaganda and diplomacy.[2] Bolingbroke was of the opinion that Augustus II, who at first welcomed his Russian treaty because it assured him of the Polish Throne, was becoming increasingly aware of an impatient pressure from Peter and of the consequences 'which must naturally follow if *That Prince* succeeds in all the views which is very apparent that he had.'[3] Should Augustus II gain Livonia, Peter's presence in Esthonia would be a heavy price to pay for the acquisition.[4] James Scott, the British envoy to Augustus, on July 31, 1713 was instructed to find out on what terms the Polish king would settle with Sweden '*and the possibility of detaching his Maj'ty from the Confederacy he is now engaged in.*' Scott was told to use his 'utmost skill and attention to pursue that aim and to commit England's efforts to guarantee the Polish crown for the Saxon elector.'[5]

The British hoped that the low ebb that Charles's fortunes had reached at Pruth would soon change. As the Czar became more formidable, '*the jealousy of this Prince's ally becomes much more strong.*'[6] Threats were added to cajoling. Scott was instructed in June, 1714 to assure Augustus II 'how earnestly the Queen desired to see peace and the balance of power restored in the North' and to intimate that England would have taken a different stand in Baltic affairs if she had not been tied up with the French war.[7] Neither British method of mediation or negotiation achieved the desired result.

Yet all through 1714, England 'continued its useless expostu-

---

[1] Daniel Defoe, *Some Account of the life and most remarkable Actions of George Henry Baron de Goertz* (London, 1719), p. 13 is of the opinion that Görtz by insisting on French mediation and that the Peace of Münster be the basis of a settlement purposely made it impossible for the Congress of Brunswick to accomplish anything. *Cf.* Chapter V for additional details on the Brunswick Congress.

[2] For the most balanced account of England's attempt to mediate the Great Northern War and the resulting propaganda see Jerker Rosén, *Det Engelska Ambudet om Fredsmedling 1713, en Studie i Politisk Propaganda*, in *Lunds Universitets Årsskrift*, N.F Ard. I, Bd. 43, Nr. 6 (Lund, 1946).

[3] Bolingbroke to Scott, July 24, 1713, P.R.O., F.E.B., State Papers, Foreign, 104/123.

[4] *Ibid.*

[5] Idem to Idem, July 31, 1713, *Ibid.*

[6] *Ibid.*

[7] Bromley to Scott, June 4, 1714, *Ibid.*

lations in favour of Sweden.'[1] British Tories meanwhile were becoming more cognizant of the possible domestic political ramifications which could result between the developing rupture of Swedo-Hanoverian relations. As George I, the darling of the Whigs, began to gobble up Bremen and Verden and to pay the price for them by joining forces with the foes of his erstwhile ally, the Tories continually favored Sweden. To the die-hard supporters of Bolingbroke and the Stuarts, the preservation of Charles XII became a vital matter, for he might be the very person to assist them in staving off the Hanoverian succession and perhaps to bring about a Stuart restoration.[2] Those people in England who believed in a balance of power for the Baltic also desired Sweden's rescue, for they preferred a strong Sweden to a strong Denmark or Russia. The interests of the different groups commingled in the Bolingbroke administration, which was more and more dominating British foreign and domestic policy. Thus 1714 was a year of much diplomatic activity. Unfortunately for Sweden, there were few tangible results.

David Pulteney, the English minister to Copenhagen, was instructed by Bromley in May to point out to the Danish Court that unhappy and unfortunate circumstances would result in Europe should Russia become the all-powerful force in the Baltic. The British minister called upon Frederick IV of Denmark to settle his differences with Sweden and threatened to use force against him if he did not comply with the English request.[3]

The Danes understandably, highly resented the British action as they did British attempts to pressure Prussia into an attack upon Denmark. Especially galling to Frederick IV were the British attempts to neutralize Holstein now that the Swedes had evacuated the city of Tönning.[4] Britain then was opposed to Danish designs on Schleswig-Holstein and to Danish plans to reduce Sweden by force. Pulteney was to insist that Britain had no deep schemes or plans but just wanted to medi-

---

[1] Chance, *George I and the Northern War*, p. 45.

[2] Michael, *England under George I*, I, 286.

[3] Bromley to Pulteney, May 4, 1714, P.R.O., F.E.B., State Papers, Foreign, 104/5 and *British Instructions, Denmark*, p. 44.

[4] Idem to Idem, November 13, 1713, P.R.O., F.E.B., State Papers, Foreign, 104/5.

ate a peace satisfactory to all. Anne was 'a common Friend' to all the belligerents and intended to conduct herself as such. Yet the role of the peacemaker was difficult, as Bolingbroke well knew:

> I have, I believe, formerly told you that the Northern Troubles are becoming such a Maze of Errors and the Characters of the Parties are so bizarre that the Queen hardly sees a way thro them, and will therefore proceed very cautiously, and not without the Concurrence of those who are equally concerned by treatys and perhaps more so by Interest, in all measures relating to them.[1]

In the autumn of 1713, England had become deeply concerned over the fate of Holstein. Because she was unable to send troops herself to aid the House of Holstein-Gottorp, and because Hanover and the States refused to send any, the only solution that Britain could see was for Prussia to take the place in sequestration. Bromley instructed William Breton, the English minister at Berlin, to do all in his power to persuade Prussia to act before the capture of Tönning sealed the fate of Holstein. He was to point out that it was against Prussian interests to allow Denmark to win the Duchy and that there was a good deal of honor in saving a territory for a prince who was a minor.[2] Britain, herself, however, was to do nothing. Breton was to take 'care (as you have hitherto very prudently done it) not to engage Her Majesty in any part of the Expense necessary for these Expeditions'[3] and in addition, he was to see that he made no diplomatic commitments 'least Her Majesty should be hereafter brought under Difficulties to perform it, from his Swedish Majesty's intractable Temper.'[4]

One commitment that England might have made was to guarantee to Prussia, the Swedish city of Stetten and its environs, which Prussia, along with Holstein had sequestrated, June 22, 1713, under the terms of the Treaty of Schwedt.[5] This

[1] Bolingbroke to Pulteney, May 5, 1714, *Ibid.*
[2] Bromley to Breton, September 26, 1713, P.R.O., F.E.B., State Papers, Foreign, 104/9.
[3] Idem to Idem, November 6, 1713, *Ibid.*
[4] Idem to Idem, November 27, 1713, *Ibid.*
[5] Dumont, *Corps diplomatique*, VIII, pt. i, p. 47 has the text of this treaty. See below for a fuller account of events leading up to the sequestration and for Swedo-Prussian relations in general.

Britain refused to do.[1] In 1714, Swedo-Prussian relations deteriorated from bad to worse. Still Britain hoped for Prussian intervention on behalf of Sweden. Breton was to point out the fatal consequences that would result from the complete defeat of Charles XII. If Sweden were attacked in Skåne or in Finland, Britain asked Frederick William I to threaten Denmark with an invasion of Holstein. If the Danish King or the Russian Czar retaliated against Prussia, England promised to support Frederick William I and was 'now taking measures to make good this Promise.'[2] By the middle of 1714, however, Breton's expostulations were of no consequence, nor were those that Bolingbroke delivered to Louis-Frederic Bonet de St. Germain, the Prussian resident in London. By that time, Prussia was preparing to enter into an alliance with Russia against Sweden, wherein the two powers would mutually guarantee the possessions they had taken from Sweden.[3]

Bolingbroke was determined that Britain did 'not sit still on one hand to see Sweden subdued and the Balance of the North destroyed.' Yet he did not intend to drag England into the conflict as a belligerent. In 1713, he had informed the Swedish minister that the Swedes could not expect the old treaties to draw England into a war and 'to be a partner in all the new designs grafted upon the original quarrell.' Anne was willing 'to enter into all reasonable measures to preserve Sweden from that ruin' which threatened her, but Sweden had to make some moves which could be interpreted as preludes to peace.[4]

Bolingbroke not only conversed with the Swedish minister, but also with the ministers of Sweden's opponents. On his agenda for May, 1713, were appointments with Rosenkrantz, Baron von Schack and a M. d'Elorine, the representatives of Denmark, Russia and Poland respectively. They were informed that the plans of the Northern Alliance to reduce Sweden to nothing forced England to intervene for the Maritime Powers could not on any account 'be tame Spectators of the destruction of Sweden.' He asked that Danish soldiers be withdrawn from

[1] Bromley to Bonet, November, 1713, P.R.O., F.E.B., State Papers, Foreign, 104/9.
[2] Bromley to Breton, May 15, 1714, *Ibid.*
[3] Chance, *George I and the Northern War*, p. 45. See also below.
[4] Bolingbroke to Breton, May 26, 1713, P.R.O., F.E.B., State Papers, Foreign, 104/5.

Holstein. Perhaps 'there was a plausible pretence that the Neutrality was not broken by Denmark; but now the Swedes are gone, that pretence is at the same time removed.'[1]

Bolingbroke hoped that France as a guarantor of the Treaty of Westphalia would 'take some share in the problems of Northern Europe.'[2] Consequently, Matthew Prior, the English minister to France, was told to remind the French court of the long friendship that had existed between Versailles and Stockholm, and was to ask the French:

> to take all the ways which are in their power to divert the Storm at this time ready to fall on their ancient Northern Ally; to detach if possible some of the Princes confederated against him, or at least to slaken their efforts, to gain time during which some effectual measure may be concerted for restoring the Peace of the North, which the circumstances of France as well as those of Great Britain, will put us now every day more and more in a condition of doing.[3]

Time, however, was not on Bolingbroke's side, either in foreign or in domestic affairs. Yet it is to be doubted if his Baltic policy would have been more successful could he have remained in power longer. His criticism of the Whigs for a pointless policy of expediency in northern diplomacy[4] might just as well have been directed against himself. In spite of his hopes for an accord with Sweden, he was forced to use the abortive Hamilton squadron against Sweden rather than to aid her. Swedish privateers had so raised havoc with British commerce. Bolingbroke did insist in his letters that British trade had to be protected by the squadron from both Swedish and Danish naval units. Yet there can be little doubt that Swedish capers hurt England more painfully than did those of Denmark.

Thus when Anne died, Sweden and England were drifting apart in spite of British efforts to maintain the traditional friendship. Precedents for British naval action to bring about peace as in the case of Rooke's squadron and to protect trade as in the case of Hamilton's ships were established before

[1] *Ibid.*

[2] *Ibid.*

[3] Bolingbroke to Matthew Prior, May 6, 1714, *British Diplomatic Instructions, France*, L. G. Wickham-Legg (ed.), Camden third series, XXXV (1925), p. 69. Cited hereafter as *British Instructions, France*.

[4] Various letters of Bolingbroke from 1710–1713, *Bolingbroke Letters*, I–IV.

George I mounted the British throne. Yet the British had stopped Swedish ships for military reasons as exemplified by the Norris action of 1709. Thus precedents could be juggled to suit the situation. They could justify or condemn Swedish privateering activities. Moreover, late Tory friendships could be converted with little difficulty into Whig enmities. George I, working through strong Whig leaders who catered to the merchant groups, could perhaps direct British policy in a way to serve Hanoverian ends. Trade differences and the impatience of war-weary Britons with Charles's irrational attitude towards peace could be exploited to open further the wedge between England and Sweden. Even Bolingbroke despaired of Charles XII ever coming to terms with his enemies 'since in that case he would have no Enemy left at all; and to have one seems to be an article very essential to his happiness.'[1]

New actors and new events in 1715 would supply the answer to the future of northern affairs. England's role was bound to be more active under the elector-king. It was evident that the new ruler would attempt to use his new kingdom to aid his old electorate. His problem was to get around the Act of Settlement and to commit openly his English resources to forceful measures in the Baltic. After all Bremen and Verden were doomed so far as Sweden was concerned, and there was a considerable segment of the English people who felt that Great Britain stood to profit if Hanover took over those principalities.[2]

Swedish leadership through 1715 played directly into George's hands. As Elector of Hanover, he joined the Northern Alliance against Charles XII, who in that year was to increase the number of his opponents. Swedish diplomacy—or lack of diplomacy—was to influence considerably the Hanoverian plans of the British king.

[1] Chance, *George I and the Northern War*, p. 20.
[2] L. A. Nikiforov, *Russische-Englische Beziehungen unter Peter I*, translated from the Russian by Wolfgang Müller N. (Weimer, 1954), p. 169.

IV

EARLY MOVES OF THE NEW GOVERNMENT

SWEDISH diplomats received the news of George's accession to the British throne with misgivings, fearing that 'Swedish Interest might suffer by the late Queen's Death.'[1] Yet there was the hope that George I might continue to be a friend to Sweden and that the rumored return of Charles XII from Turkey might lead to the solving of the commercial differences that existed between England and Sweden.[2] Swedish expectations, however, were to be dashed. George becoming King linked the destinies of England with the Baltic. Even though one need not agree with the statement that the 'coronation gift of George I was a new sea in which the English maritime power must assert itself or be insecure from attack,'[3] it was apparent from the beginning of the new reign that for at least while the succession was in danger, the foreign policies of Hanover and England would run side by side even if they did not actually unite.

Even before George I left for England, he commanded Christoph Schreiber, the Hanoverian resident secretary at Stockholm since 1705, that he should acquaint the Regency with the fact that George had 'already receiv'd very great Complaints of the violences done his subjects trading in the Baltick, by bringing up and making prize of their Ships and cargoes, thô they carry nothing contraband.' The representative

---

[1] Jackson to the Secretary of State, August 22, 1714, P.R.O., State Papers, Sweden, 95/20.

[2] *Ibid.*

[3] Frederick W. Head, *The Fallen Stuarts* (Cambridge, 1901), p. 183.

of the house of Brunswick was to request that such actions stop and that the seized ships be restored or George I would 'not be able to refuse when he comes over to his Kingdoms to grant His Subjects the assistance they may desire in order to obtain satisfaction for the Losses they have unjustly suffer'd.' At the same time, Schreiber assured the Swedish Government that George I, now being King would be in a better position to work for a suitable peace in the North.[1]

Schreiber's proclamation caused considerable speculation and no little alarm in Stockholm where the Swedish people, ignoring George's protestations of friendship towards Sweden, wondered just how much the Elector could borrow from his office as King. Among the perturbed was the non-Swede, Jackson, who wondered if Schreiber would be the person primarily responsible for handling British affairs at the Swedish capital. Schreiber mollified his British colleague by informing Jackson that it would have been a joint declaration if George I had had time to approve someone in England to draft the dispatches. Thus it was made to appear that Hanoverian influence would not predominate at Stockholm. Nevertheless, Schreiber confidentially told Rumpf that Jackson was to be kept ignorant of the fact that the Hanoverian representative was to send one copy of his dispatches to Hanover and another one to the German advisers of the King in London.[2]

Sweden was not the only place where Hollanders were between the British and the Hanoverians. At the Hague, in September, 1714, George I and his German cortege conferred with British and other diplomats. An early opportunity was at that time presented for the Hanoverians to embark Britain upon a new system of foreign policy. An alliance (as had existed in the days of William III) was suggested between the Maritime Powers and the Empire. Eleven days of conversation at the Hague laid the basis for Britain's new policy which was to

[1] Jackson to the Secretary of State, September 25, 1714, P.R.O., State Papers, Sweden, 95/21. Cf. Michael, *England under George I*, I, 72 for the considerations held by George I on the Northern War while he was making preparations to go to London.

[2] Rumpf to Heinsius, September 22, 1714, Rijksarchief, A.A.H., 1864. Schreiber was of the opinion that Jackson would take offense if he knew about the double dispatches.

include, in addition to a triple alliance, the settlement of the Barrier between the States and the Empire.[1]

Appearing on the diplomatic scene were new names and new men who were drastically to affect British diplomacy with the Baltic and the Continent. Four men—two native Englishmen and two foreigners—were to exercise an undue influence on British foreign affairs especially as they concerned Northern Europe during the critical years 1715–1716. A brief sketch and character summary of these four officials would not be amiss at this point in the narrative.

The most important British office, that of Secretary of State for Northern Affairs, went to Charles Viscount Townshend, whose claim to fame rests more on the agricultural experiments that he performed later in life than on his activities in the foreign office. Brother-in-law to Robert and Horatio Walpole, Townshend had had little experience in foreign affairs up to the time of his appointment by George I to Britain's most important secretaryship. He had been a negotiator at Gertruydenberg[2] and was also partially responsible for the unfortunate Barrier treaty of 1709.[3] While at the Hague, in 1709, he had come in contact with various high-ranking Hanoverians, but other factors in addition to the acquaintances he had made at the Hague were responsible for his elevation to the highest post in the British Government.[4] Undoubtedly his politics and his character contributed much to his success.

Townshend was a Whig of moderate views with important political and family connections. Close ties with the two Walpoles were of value to any politico in the early eighteenth century. Notwithstanding his political and family alliances, Townshend was in no position to dominate the King or his

---

[1] Michael, *England under George I*, I, 73–73. One of the best accounts of British policy with the States and with the Empire is Hatton, *Diplomatic Relations*. Cf. also Thomas Bussemaker, 'De Triple Alliantie,' pp. 158–271.

[2] Williams, *The Whig Supremacy*, p. 148. The negotiations at Gertruydenberg were for the purpose of ending the War of the Spanish Succession, but they failed and it was not until 1713 that peace between France and the Maritime Powers was resolved at Utrecht.

[3] Murray, *Honest Diplomat at the Hague*, pp. 41–42. Cf. Hatton, *Diplomatic Relations*, and Geikie and Montgomery, *The Dutch Barrier* for full accounts of the Barrier Treaty of 1709 which had set up a string of Barrier forts on terms much to the advantage of the Dutch.

[4] Chance, *George I and the Northern War*, p. 51.

advisers. He was, however, well known to Hanoverian officials, both in and outside England. With a reputation for uprightness and consistency, Townshend was an excellent choice for a ruler who 'required from his servants fidelity and trustworthiness.' George I was to discover that his new secretary did not always defer to the wishes of his German advisers, and that Townshend's loyalty to England sometimes overruled his loyalty to his sovereign. That same loyalty to country, caused him, at times, to be underhanded in dealing with some of his friends.[1]

Some of Townshend's virtues, which might have been admirable in the abstract, proved to be detriments in the diplomatic and political spheres. His consistency for example could and did occasionally degenerate into stubbornness and small-mindedness. At times Townshend was 'proud, impatient of contradiction, wanting in complaisance; faults of a just man.'[2] His quarrels with trusted and proved friends, his tactlessness, and his inability to mend his political fences eventually opened him to attacks from his enemies. After two and a half years, his enemies gained the upper hand and he lost the direction of Northern affairs to General James Stanhope, a man who in 1714 had been made Secretary of State for Southern Affairs.

Stanhope was a relative newcomer to the political scene. His appointment to the Southern Department had been a surprise not only to the politicians of the day, but also to the General, who heretofore had been known for his heroic actions at Almenara, Saragossa, and Port Mahon. The luster of his military fame was not dimmed by his defeat and capture at Brihuega, and his ambition up to 1714 had been to attain supreme military rank.[3] After his return from captivity in Spain, Stanhope had distinguished himself as a leading Whig debater in a Tory parliament, and during the last years of Anne's reign had done much in organizing support for the Hanoverian succession.[4] He became one of the 'self-appointed guardians' of Hanoverian rights to the British throne.

Like Townshend, Stanhope owed his appointment in part

[1] See Chapter VI for his treatment of the Dutch minister Duivenvoorde on the matter of the Baltic squadron of 1715.

[2] Chance, *George I and the Northern War*, p. 51.

[3] Williams, *The Whig Supremacy*, p. 148.

[4] Basil Williams, *Stanhope, a Study in Eighteenth century War and Diplomacy* (Oxford, 1932) treats in detail Stanhope's activities during this period.

to his friendship with the leading foreigners around the King, especially to Jean Robethon, the King's private secretary. On the other hand, he differed from his colleague, Townshend in that he had a broader conception of foreign policy and was no 'insular politician.'[1] His biographer, Basil Williams, who is prone to draw a trifle too laudatory a portrait of Stanhope, rightly points out that Stanhope was as adept at the conference table as he was on the field of battle.[2] In some respects, he was a Marlborough, but definitely a Marlborough of a much smaller statue.

Trained by education and experience, and endowed with a tongue facile with languages, Stanhope personally conducted British negotiations at various foreign courts, even while Townshend nominally was head of the ministry. Tolerant of foreigners and lacking the provincialism of Townshend and the more able Robert Walpole, Stanhope fitted in well with the Hanoverian conception of diplomacy. More than any other Englishman, he directed British foreign policy towards the same objectives as those desired by the Hanoverians. His diplomacy has been a subject of considerable controversy, and it is constantly argued by many of the Whig historians that he channelled British diplomacy to that of Hanover because he thought that the electorate and the kingdom could mutually benefit each other. On the other hand, it is probable that at times he was unduly influenced by the Germans. There is a third possibility, and that is that he used the Germans to oust Townshend and to gain control of affairs and once he had obtained those objectives he became increasingly less amenable to pressure from the Germans around the King and less concerned about the petty politics of the Germanies.

There is no doubt that Stanhope, while in the Southern Department was much more open to Hanoverian influence than was Townshend, and that he did some rather shabby tricks to gain control of the Northern Department and thus become the head of the Government. After he had achieved his ambition in 1717, he became, at times, openly hostile to some of the Germans around the King. During the span covered by this study, however, he was definitely pro-Hanoverian, and

[1] Chance, *George I and the Northern War*, p. 51.
[2] Williams, *The Whig Supremacy*, p. 171.

his closeness to the ear of George I definitely influenced the diplomacy of the Baltic and of Europe.

During the six and a half years he controlled British foreign affairs, Stanhope paved the way for Walpole's great ministry of peace and reconstruction.[1] The close coöperation of England and France, which after 1721 was the keystone of Walpole's twenty-year rule, was the issue which in 1717 was to drive Townshend and Walpole from office and cause a split in the Whig ministry. Townshend and Walpole were not so opposed to Stanhope in principle as they were to his methods and those methods were often dictated by the Hanoverians. Up to 1717, the Germans became increasingly pro-Stanhope, for they thought that through him they could obtain what they wanted. Later they were in part to be disillusioned, but up to the rupture of diplomatic relations between England and Sweden, Stanhope was working to foster Hanoverian aims along with his own.

The two non-British servants of George I who were the most significant were Baron Andreas Gottlieb von Bernstorff, the first minister of Hanover, and Jean Robethon, an exiled son of a French advocate. The former was a member of the landed nobility of Mecklenburg-Schwerin and played a leading role in the long quarrel existing between his order and Charles Lewis, the ducal ruler, a struggle that was to be highly meaningful for Baltic diplomacy in 1716. As a young man, Bernstorff had fallen in love with the Duke's first consort,[2] and consequently had quitted his native habitat taking service under Duke George William of Zell, an uncle of George I. After the death of Duke George William, Bernstorff had transferred his services to Hanover. Notwithstanding his changed loyalties, Bernstorff possessed large estates and interests in Mecklenburg and his thinking was often influenced by his Mecklenburg holdings.[3]

By 1709, Bernstorff had become the chief minister of George I, and henceforth devoted his tremendous energies and industry

[1] *Ibid.*

[2] Sir Adolphus Ward, *Great Britain and Hanover, some aspects of the Union* (Oxford, 1899), p. 72. *Cf.* Adolph Kocker (ed.), *Selbstbiographie des Ministers Andreas Gottlieb von Bernstorff*, in *Jahresbericht des Kaiser Wilhelms-Gymnasium zu Hanover* (Hanover, 1877), II.

[3] Nikiforov, *Russich-Englische Beziehungen*, passim.

to the aggrandizement of Hanover and the management of his own great estates.[1] That he had a strong voice in the councils of George I cannot be denied. Michael's statement that 'In dealing with Dutch and foreign ministers and ambassadors, he acted the part of a British minister'[2] is highly over-drawn. On the other hand, there is little doubt that although he was an alien, 'he cheerfully meddled in British affairs.'[3] Still it must be remembered that he was a hard working 'conscientious minister with a great grasp of German politics,'[4] and his knowledge of German affairs and Imperial diplomacy was undoubtedly greater than that of anyone around the King. Furthermore both he and George I realized the danger to German trade and commerce should Denmark already in control of the Sound expand that control over the mouths of the Elbe and Weser rivers.[5]

Thus it was only natural that George I would heed the admonitions of such a tried and trusted servant whether his advice dealt with British or non-British matters on the continent. In the last years of his power he became more stubborn and his attitude toward his estates in Mecklenburg-Schwerin and his private land dispute with the King of Prussia caused him to clash violently with Stanhope. In the final analysis, it was Stanhope, rather than the German minister, who persevered. Up to the split in the Whig ministry, however, he and Stanhope worked harmoniously with each other.

Bernstorff's foreign policy was in keeping with the traditions of Hanover: strong and fast friendship with the Emperor and suspicion and distrust toward Brandenburg-Prussia and Denmark. Against the former, he cherished an 'unextinguishable aversion.'[6] He justified the Hanoverian purchase of Swedish Bremen and Verden on the grounds that whereas Sweden could not hold those possessions, it was necessary for Hanover to take them, for it was not to the interest of Hanover to have Denmark on one side of her and Prussia on the other.[7]

[1] Chance, *George I and the Northern War*, p. 83.
[2] Michael, *England under George I*, I, 74.
[3] *Ibid.*
[4] Williams, *Stanhope*, p. 152.
[5] Mediger, *Moskaus Weg*, p. 13.
[6] Ward, *Great Britain and Hanover*, p. 73.
[7] Gyllenborg to Sparre, November 4, 1715, *Handlingar*, X, 270.

Thirty years earlier Bernstorff had proposed a plan whereby Prussia was to receive Stettin, Hanover, Bremen and Verden, Denmark Schlesing and West Holstein, and the House of Gottarp East Holstein and other compensations in the Empire. Thus a buffer would be raised between Denmark and the Empire. This plan blocked by the Great Elector was in substance, the plan revised by Bernstorff in 1712.[1]

The other foreigner, Robethon, was a French Huguenot refugee,[2] who had faithfully served many masters, among them being William III, and George William of Zell. As George I's private secretary, he influenced policy, but his tendency to remain in the background[3] makes it difficult to weigh his importance so far as British diplomacy was concerned. James F. Chance, who based his conclusions on the Robethon Papers in the British Museum,[4] considered Robethon to be extremely able and was of the opinion that he remained in power as long as did Bernstorff, and he shared the fate of his patron[5] when he sought to execute Bernstorff's master plan.[6] Thus up through the limits of this study, he would appear to be a person of real weight in the royal councils. There can be no doubt that he was adept in deciphering enemy dispatches and in the employment of spies and agents.[7]

Robethon's position was indefinite, but one in which he enjoyed a good deal of trust. Confidential secretary to the King, he perhaps exercised on foreign policy a more lasting influence than did any of the other Germans around George I. 'This influence was all the greater from the fact that in his vast correspondence with English ministers and English ambassadors he was apt to leave it uncertain whether he was writing to them on behalf of the Elector or the King of England.'[8] In a day and age when the sovereign played a dominant role in the conducting of foreign relations, it was a brave diplomat indeed

[1] Mediger, *Moskaus Weg*, p. 14–15.

[2] David Agnew, *Protestant Exiles from France in the Reign of Louis XIV* (London, 1866), p. 194.

[3] Williams, *The Whig Supremacy*, p. 147.

[4] James F. Chance, 'John de Robethon and the Robethon Papers,' *English Historical Review*, XIII (1898), pp. 55–70.

[5] *Ibid.*, p. 55.

[6] Mediger, *Moskaus Weg*, p. 17.

[7] Murray, 'Whitebook,' pp. 376–377.

[8] Williams, *Stanhope*, p. 152.

who distinguished or even tried to distinguish between the offices of King and the Elector. Often Robethon would enclose a personal note in his British dispatches, which would include a list of George's desires as Elector.

As is so often the case with men who play behind-the-scene roles, there was a tendency during his ascendancy to overestimate his influence. Usually such men arouse a good deal of animosity, for the manipulator who remains in the background pulling the strings comes to assume, in the mind of the public, the role of a Mephistopheles. Robethon was no exception. He aroused a great deal of unjustified animosity in the British public who hated him not only for his position, but also because he was a foreigner. Historians also have been prone to overstress the importance of Robethon, albeit, he is a highly significant figure. James MacPherson, for example, goes so far as to say that 'The Elector would never have been King of England, but for him.'[1] While Mahon, taking at face value the criticisms of Robethon, labels him 'a prying, impertinent, venomous creature, forever crawling in some slimy intrigue.'[2] Sir Richard Lodge, who based his stand upon the Polwarth papers, also attaches more significance to Robethon than is perhaps justified, yet

> there can be no doubt that Robethon held for a few years a unique position in England, that he enjoyed a confidence not only of Bernstorff, the resident Hanoverian minister, but also of Sunderland and Stanhope, and that he had a hand both on the rudder of British foreign policy and in the bestowal of British patronage.[3]

A study of the Robethon papers and the Polwarth papers, along with other diplomatic dispatches of the day, makes it apparent that Robethon was best able to exert pressure upon those Britishers who had a high regard for royal power. Polwarth at Copenhagen, for example, took the personal letters of

[1] Quoted in Lewis Melville, *The First George in Hanover and England* (London, 1908), I, 242. Much of the correspondence between Robethon and the Whig leaders may be found in James MacPherson, *Original Papers; Containing the Secret History of Great Britain, from the Restoration to the Accession of the House of Hanover,* 2 vols. (London, 1775).

[2] Lord Mahon, *History of England*, I, 316.

[3] Sir Richard Lodge, 'The Polwarth Papers,' *The Transactions of the Royal Historical Society*, fourth series, XV (1932), p. 247.

advice from Robethon at face value and tried to carry out the Hanoverian policies outlined by the King's confidential secretary. Stanhope often disregarded Robethon's postscripts and when he did follow them he may have been carrying out a policy upon which he had already decided without any assistance from the distrusted Huguenot refugee. Sir John Norris, the British commander of naval squadrons which were sent to the Baltic in 1715 and 1716, usually became confused by the Robethon notes, which to Norris appeared to be contradictory orders. As a result, Norris constantly had to have points in his instructions cleared up because of statements in the letters he received from Robethon which conflicted with his orders.

After 1717 as Stanhope gained in power, the influence of Robethon and Bernstorff waned. Yet between 1714–1717 both Hanoverians were in a position to guide and direct British diplomacy because of their influence with the King. Using the power of the throne, they were able to exert pressures upon British diplomats in the field. Usually their efforts pushed British foreign policy to greater extremes than it would perhaps have gone. Only on rare occasions were they able to change the directions of British foreign policy so their influence was more of degree than of kind. Yet they were factors in George's plans to win British support for his German policies.

The four new men at the helm of British diplomacy moved rapidly to involve Britain in George's foreign policy. There can be little doubt that Whig circles were united on the subject of foreign relations and hoped that England would play as strong a role in European affairs as she had done under the rule of William III and the government of Marlborough.[1] It was not until the Hanoverians were firmly established upon the throne and the Tories were completely discredited that a split between the followers of Townshend and Stanhope becomes noticeable, with the latter standing for a close tie-up of Hanoverian and British diplomacy and the former opposing it.

The British people were for some time kept in ignorance of their new ruler's designs upon Bremen and Verden,[2] and when the news did leak out there was considerable difference of opinion as to the desirability of the King's having the duchies.

[1] Michael, *England under George I*, I, 64.
[2] Croissy instructions, *Recueil, Suède*, II, 270.

Pros and cons on the question were bruited about throughout
1715 and 1716. Those defending the royal action could point
out that Cromwell, in 1657 had solely 'as a means of access to
the Protestant states of north Germany'[1] toyed with the idea
of adding Bremen and Verden to England. The areas also were
strategically located so far as trade was concerned. For that
reason George I was following a line just as English as Hanoverian. The fact that George I was joint ruler of the two
countries, made it even more necessary that those two places
be in his hands rather than those of Sweden in order to facilitate
passage between England and Hanover. Without a ready
access between his two countries, the liberties of England and
British freedom might be endangered.[2] Thus Bremen and
Verden had important economic and military significance
because of their location.[3]

Another argument advanced by the friends of the King, was
that Bremen and Verden both had at one time belonged to the
House of Brunswick. Even though the possessions had been his
own, George I had not tried to get them back from Sweden.
However, when he saw that Sweden was to lose them anyway,
he stepped in and brought back what was his own. The safety
of his own dominions and of the Protestant succession dictated
his actions rather than any personal desires for aggrandizement.[4]

The Tories, on the other hand, saw the acquisition of
Bremen and Verden as a peril which menaced the liberties of
Englishmen. If George I intended to rule England as he did his
electorate, the control of Bremen and Verden, with the port of
Stade would make it easy for him to bring Hanoverian troops
to England and to establish a military rule.[5] It was such a fear
that caused England to call upon Dutch aid in the Jacobite
rising of 1715, rather than to employ soldiers from Hanover.[6]
Some enemies of the new king pointed out that Britain ought
not to embark upon Hanoverian projects of aggrandizement

[1] Godfrey Davies, *The Early Stuarts, 1603–1660* (Oxford, 1937), p. 225.
[2] Gyllenborg to Sparre, February 7, 1715, *Handlingar*, X, 118.
[3] Jägerskiöld, *Sverige och Europa*, p. 13.
[4] *An Account of the Swedish and Jacobite Plot and a postscript relating to the Post-Boy of Saturday, February 23* (London, 1717), p. 14.
[5] Gyllenborg to Sparre, June 11, 1715, *Handlingar*, X, 334. *Cf.* G. Syveton, "L'erreur de Görtz," *Revue d'Histoire diplomatique*, IX (1895), p. 429.
[6] Michael, *England under George I*, I, 299–300.

until the succession was more firmly established at home and until disorders in Scotland were quieted.[1]

Yet many Englishmen believed that Bremen and Verden would be of considerable value to British trade. Townshend and the two Walpoles who broke in 1717 with Stanhope over foreign policy disagreed over method rather than objective so far as the two former Swedish principalities were concerned. In answer to a letter by Simon van Slingelandt, the Secretary of the Council of State of the United Provinces, and later Pensionary of Holland, wherein the Hollander had written 'As much as the crown of Great Britain is superior to the electoral cap, so much is the king interested to sacrifice Bremen and Verden for a peace rather than continue any longer in a war,' Townshend reported, March, 1717:

> I am of opinion, that every attempt should be made to induce the king of Sweden to make peace, without depriving him of any of his dominions situated out of the empire, for in regard to his German provinces, I must tell you frankly, without any partiality to the pretensions of the king, but simply with a view to the interests of Great Britain and Holland, that we must not suffer Sweden to retain any longer those gates of the empire which, since the peace of Westphalia, she has never made use of but for the purpose of introducing confusion and disorder, or of turning Germany from the pursuit of its true interests against France. . . . I lay it down as a principle, that for the advantage and tranquility of Europe, the king of Sweden ought to be deprived of those provinces which have supplied him with the means of doing so much mischief.[2]

It is of significance that the above was written after Townshend had been deprived of his office of secretary of state. Townshend's brother-in-law, Horatio Walpole defended the purchase of Bremen and Verden by Hanover in a pamphlet entitled, *The Interest of Great Britain Steadily Pursued,* stating:

---

[1] Philip D. Stanhope, Earl of Chesterfield and Edmund Waller, *The Case of the Hanover Forces in the Pay of Great Britain Impartially and freely examined; with some Seasonable Reflections on the Present Conjuncture of Affairs* (London, 1743), p. 3. Although written later than the events described above, this pamphlet contains some of the arguments used in 1715–1716.

[2] Townshend to Slingelandt, March, 1717, Brievan van Lord Townshend aan Simon van Slingelandt, 1714–1717, Rijksarchief, Archief Slingelandt, 118. A copy of this letter may be found in Coxe, *Walpole Memoirs,* I, 87.

Now, whether it be most for the Interest of *Great Britain*, that those Countries which command the Navigation of the *Elbe* and *Weser*, the only inlets from the *British Seas* in *Germany*, and which in case of any Disturbance in the *North* are most capable of protecting, or interrupting the *British* trade to *Hamburgh*, should remain in the Hands of Denmark, who had frequently formed Pretensions on that City; or of Sweden, who molested our Commerce in the Baltick, rather than be annex'd for ever to the King's Electoral Dominions, is a Question which can easily be decided by a bare Inspection into the Map of *Europe*.[1]

As for the Hanoverians who accompanied the King to England, any pretext or excuse was sufficient so long as the House of Brunswick obtained the sought after possessions. Count Andreas Bernstorff, George's first minister for Hanover, said that if Hanover did not take Bremen and Verden, Denmark or Prussia would. Thus it was better for everyone concerned that Hanover purchase the places from Denmark. To which Count Karl Gyllenborg, the Swedish minister at London, commented sarcastically, 'Y-a-t-il jamais eu une excuse ou plus injuste plus ridicule.'[2]

The push against Sweden was on, however, before the majority of Englishmen were cognizant of what the new directors of British foreign policy were doing.[3] George I was not one to sit idly by without grabbing from Sweden while his neighbors enriched themselves at the expense of Charles XII.[4] The need for quick decisive action was heightened by the return of the Swedish ruler to Stralsund late in 1714. Trade and the precedent of the Hamilton squadron were to be used to facilitate Hanoverian aims and to justify George's policy to his British subjects and to Europe in general.

[1] Horatio Walpole, *The Interest of Great Britain Steadily pursued; In Answer to a Pamphlet entitl'd the Case of the Hanover Forces impartially examined*, third edition (London, 1743), pp. 12–13. This pamphlet went through three editions in an equal number of weeks, William Coxe (ed.), *The Memoirs of Horatio, Lord Walpole, selected from his correspondence and connected with the history of the times from 1678 to 1757*, 2 vols. (London, 1898), II, 5. Cited hereafter as Coxe, *Memoirs of Horatio Walpole*.

[2] Gyllenborg to Sparre, November 4, 1714, *Handlingar*, X, 270.

[3] Croissy Instructions, *Recueil, Suède*, II, 270. *Cf.* Michael, *England under George I*, I, 287.

[4] Louis Wiesener, *Le Régent, l'Abbé Dubois et les Anglais (d'après les sources Britanniques)*, 3 vols. (Paris, 1891–1899), II, 3. Cited hereafter as Wiesener, *Le Régent et les Anglais*.

The Schreiber note then introduced a new diplomatic offensive against Sweden that obtained a considerable momentum before many English were cognizant that their foreign policy was taking a new direction. On the tenth of December, the new secretary of state, Townshend, instructed Jackson at Stockholm and Captain James Jefferyes, who was accredited to Charles XII at Stralsund, to issue demands that England receive compensation for the losses she had suffered at the hands of Sweden.[1] Detailed accounts of British maritime losses which were valued at £65,449,909 were presented by the two agents with an insistence that the ships seized had carried British passports certifying that they carried no contraband.[2] In British eyes, Sweden's action had been 'violent and unfriendly' and violated not only freedom of commerce, but also the existing treaties between the two countries.

In London a similar policy was pursued. Gyllenborg received copies of the dispatches sent Jackson and Jefferyes along with a demand that from henceforth there should be no molesting of British trade by Swedish naval units.[3] The British government hoped that Charles with his 'usual regard to Equity and Justice' would redress the grievances of the British merchants so that England and Sweden could live together 'upon that amicable Foot that—had flourished so long to the mutual Satisfaction and Advantage of both.'[4]

It was not until January 14 that Jackson was able to present his memorial to the Swedish Chancery.[5] Although Horn promised an answer within a few days, Jackson had little expectation that anything tangible would be accomplished. Those Swedish government officials with whom he talked offered him little encouragement, and Jackson knew that in all probability his memorial would be forwarded to Stralsund as the regency did

---

[1] Townshend to Jackson and Jefferyes, December 10, 1714, *British Instructions, Sweden*, pp. 70–71. See also BM., Add. MSS., 28154.

[2] *Ibid.*, and Jackson's statement of losses as presented to the Swedish Chancery, January 14, 1715, P.R.O., State Papers, Sweden, 95/21.

[3] Jackson to Swedish Chancery, January 14, 1715, P.R.O., State Papers, Sweden, 95/21 and Townshend to Jackson, December 10, 1714, copy in BM., Add. MSS., 28,154.

[4] Townshend to Gyllenborg, December 10, 1714, copy BM., Add. MSS., 28,157.

[5] Jackson to Swedish Chancery, January 14, 1715, P.R.O., State Papers, Sweden, 95/21.

not dare act without the King.[1] Thus he was not disappointed on the twenty-ninth when the news came that his representation had been sent for action to the camp of Charles XII.[2]

The Swedish answer followed the usual pattern. The British ships were trading to prohibitive ports, and it was useless to reiterate the Swedish reasons for closing those ports. British traders were not being discriminated against 'as Mr. Resident seems to think hath been done' because the prohibition applied 'likewise to His Swedish Majesty's own Subjects.' Moreover it was suggested that since Charles XII had returned to Stralsund and 'was in the neighborhood,' it would be better if all important diplomatic notes be sent directly to him.[3] The regency was doing its best to avoid the issue. Its suggestion that the British use a direct approach to the King was hardly a fruitful one because Jefferyes had to wait until May 31 before Charles XII came around to giving him an answer.[4]

One did not have to wait until late spring, however, to ascertain the intentions and the policy of the Swedish king regarding Baltic trade. On February 18, 1715, he had issued a new edict of privateering which practically precluded all Baltic commerce.[5] Not only were the new trade restrictions as set forth in the proclamation a direct violation of existing treaties between Sweden and the maritime countries, but its high-handed manner of enforcement could only create additional friction between Sweden and her one-time friends. Moreover the blockade as set up was a paper one to be enforced by privateers rather than by regular fleet units.[6] Many Swedish merchants soon turned their attention to privateering, for the new regulations dealt Sweden's already badly shaken economy a cruel blow with 'the Merchants of this City [Stockholm] finding that this New Edict is like to be as ruinous to them and their own trade as to those it seems more particularly design'd to injure.'[7] Even worse for Sweden, Charles XII by his conduct

[1] Jackson to Townshend, January 22, 1715, *Ibid*.

[2] Idem to Idem, February 5, 1715, *Ibid*.

[3] Swedish Senate by Ehrenstrahl to Jackson, January 29, 1715, *Ibid*.

[4] Charles XII to Jefferyes, May 31, 1715, Lamberty, *Mémoires*, IX, 255–256.

[5] Edict of Privateering, February 8, 1715. Among a number of places a copy can be found in P.R.O., State Papers, Sweden, 95/21.

[6] Michael, *England under George I*, I, 288.

[7] Jackson to Townshend, March 19, 1715, P.R.O., State Papers, Sweden, 95/21.

played directly into the hands of the Hanoverians who desired British naval forces to assist them in dismembering Sweden.

The Swedish edict provided a real impetus to plans already underway for dispatching an Anglo-Dutch squadron to cover Anglo-Dutch Baltic commerce. The German historian Michael makes much of the fact that plans to send a squadron were formulated even before Charles XII issued the privateering decree; and more perfidious in Michael's eyes is the fact that a decision to send such a squadron was reached in January even before a new parliament was elected. The whole plan seems to Michael to be some deep seated and dark scheme that originated in the mind of Bernstorff.[1] According to the latter, however, the plan originated with the Dutch, or at least the Hanoverian minister so stated to Petkum, the Holstein minister in London who was handling Swedish affairs until Gyllenborg received the proper credentials.[2]

Michael is quite right; the original formal proposal for a joint squadron was presented on January 21 by the English ambassador to the Hague, William, Lord Cadogan, but the timing had little to do with any attempt to circumvent the parliamentary process. Already the Dutch had under discussion a plan to send twenty-four warships to the Baltic to protect their own vital commerce in that area.[3] What Michael did not know or ignored was the fact that informal discussions for a joint undertaking had been in progress throughout November and December by British and Dutch leaders. Even before Cadogan offered his formal proposal, the size of the squadron and the number of ships to be contributed by each country had been pretty well fixed. The Dutch admirals considered that a combined fleet of thirty-two warships (twelve to be provided by the States) would be sufficient to convey the merchant ships to their respective Baltic destinations and back home again. The proportion decided upon for each country followed Anglo-Dutch practice in the War of the Spanish Succession.[4] The origination of the idea of the joint venture goes at least back to discussions held by the Dutch and the Tories over the

[1] Michael, *England under George I*, I, 287–288.
[2] Gyllenborg to Charles XII, February 4, 1715, *Handlingar*, X, 123.
[3] Bussemaker, 'De Republiek,' p. 335.
[4] Hatton, *Diplomatic Relations*, p. 75.

Hamilton squadron, and can hardly be considered to be of Hanoverian or even of Whig conception.

If two Germans, one a modern historian and the other an eighteenth century statesman, are in disagreement as to who originated the squadron, the same thing might be said for two Swedes occupying a similar status so far as the main reason for the sending of the squadron is concerned. The historian, Stig Jägerskiold, makes quite a point over the fact that the squadron was stronger and entailed a greater expense than England's own trade warranted, and he thereby intimates that considerations other than trade were paramount.[1] Gyllenborg, however, who had no love for the Hanoverian Whigs, as late as July, 1715, said that the main purpose of the squadron was to bring the materials necessary for keeping naval and merchant vessels at sea, no matter what the cost.[2] Again it should be pointed out that the size of the squadron needed was pretty well determined by Dutch admirals. Moreover it should be remembered that so far as military and naval supplies are concerned, that necessity factors always outweigh those of cost. Admittedly Gyllenborg altered his opinions about the squadron as the summer progressed, but his views pretty well followed changes in policy as the Hanoverians more and more attempted to implicate the fleet in the Great Northern War.

Thus it is quite apparent that the original and the chief *raison d'être* for sending the squadron was the protection of trade, that is so far as the majority of Englishmen and all the Dutchmen were concerned. The reading of the various British and Dutch sources substantiates such a supposition. The Hanoverians and their Whig supporters, however, had other plans for it. They hoped to use trade discontentments to effect an open rupture between Sweden and the Maritime Powers, and to bring about the abrogation of the Anglo-Swedish treaty. That might be accomplished by diverting the squadron from its true objective. The Hanoverians and such English ministers who went along with the King so toned down discussions about the annexation of Bremen and Verden that the Dutch plenipotentiary to England, Arent Wassanaer van Duivenvoorde

---

[1] Jägerskiöld, *Sverige och Europa*, p. 13; Michael, *England Under George I*, I, 287 makes the same observation.
[2] Gyllenborg to Sparre, July 28, 1715, *Handlingar*, X, 187–188.

remarked: 'For their part the English ministers lie and deceive and wish to appear to know nothing about northern affairs which have so great a relationship to the Elector of Hanover. When a certain minister this morning asked Townshend something concerning Bremen and Sleswig, he claimed to know nothing.'[1] So ably did George I and his advisers mask their motives in 1715 that England, a neutral state, was able to support effectively a belligerent without abandoning its neutrality and without incurring a declaration of war from Sweden, the state against which it acted and the state to which it was solemnly allied by treaty.[2]

The British policy or perhaps one should say the Hanoverian policy of deception is best illustrated by the diplomacy behind the fitting out of the Baltic squadron. France had at first attempted to talk the Dutch out of agreeing to the Cadogan proposal, but after seeing that Amsterdam, the seat of French strength in the United Provinces, was the city with greatest interest in Baltic commerce,[3] the French changed tactics and offered to participate in the undertaking.[4] Not only did the Hanoverians fear that the French offer would, if accepted by the Dutch, tie their hands so far as operating against Sweden was concerned, but many of the British thought that France was throwing up a smoke screen which would prevent the Dutch from participating in the squadron until the season was too far advanced for effective action.[5] Thus began a series of prevarications by those Englishmen who loyally followed George I regardless of what the cost might be to England. Stanhope, the second secretary of state and perhaps one of the

---

[1] Duivenvoorde to Heinsius, May 31, 1715, Rijksarchief, A.A.H., 1930: 'en op sijn beurs liegen en bedriegen, d'englese ministers willen niets termoignere te wete van de saeke van het Noorde voor so veel de relatie hebbe met de Ceurforst van Hanover; dese morgen als seeker minister den Lrd. Townshend nog vroeg wat omtrent Bremen en Sleswijk was gereguleert verclaerde hij daer van niets te weten.'

[2] Michael, *England under George I*, I, 289.

[3] Bussemaker, 'De Republiek,' pp. 365–366.

[4] Walpole to Townshend, February 4, 1716, MSS. Letters of Horatio Walpole to Townshend, 1714–1716 now on deposit at the Indiana University Library, Bloomington, Indiana. Cited hereafter as Walpole Letters, Indiana. These have been edited by the author under the title *An Honest Diplomat at the Hague*.

[5] Townshend to Walpole, February 11, 1715, P.R.O., F.E.B., State Papers, Foreign, 104/81; Walpole to Townshend, February 4, 1715, P.R.O., State Papers, Holland, 84/252.

most ardent supporters of George I at this time, wrote Stair, the British minister to France that the Dutch by February 2 had agreed to Cadogan's proposal but what was even more important had 'settled a fund for equipping a Squadron to joyn with ours in the Baltick.'[1] Perhaps he by so doing hoped to have Stair impress France with a *fait accompli* so far as Dutch decisions regarding the squadron were concerned. Whatever the motive he deliberately deceived Stair, for the States at this point (as Stanhope well knew) were far from reaching any kind of a formal agreement to commit their ships to the Baltic trade. It was not until March 18 that the States settled the problem of paying for the Squadron and agreed to coöperate with the English. Even then two provinces, Zealand and Utrecht, refused to go along with the others and firmly insisted that the French offer for joining the British and Dutch ships be accepted.[2]

To frustrate French plans and to forestall any possibility of Holland withdrawing from the undertaking the government in London duped the Dutch ambassadors there, and treated them in a most deceitful manner. Townshend himself, was the worst culprit as he used his friendship with Duivenvoorde to deceive him. So far as the states were concerned, the squadron was to confine itself to the protection of commerce. As the ships were being prepared for sea, rumor after rumor came into Holland indicating that Britain intended that her ships should have other tasks beyond convoy duty. Consequently, Heinsius, who was having a great deal of trouble with the pro-French party in the States, asked his joint plenipotentiaries at London, Duivenvoorde and Phillip van Borssele van der Hooge, to send him a copy of the instructions which were to be given to the Baltic commander, Admiral Sir John Norris.[3]

The request of the Pensionary was not so easy to carry out as

[1] Stanhope to Stair, February 2, 1715, *British Instructions, France*, p. 89.

[2] Resolutiën, Staten Generaal, March 7, 1715, Rijksarchief; Walpole to Townshend, March 8, 1715, Walpole Letters, Indiana; and Walpole to Townshend, March 8, 1715, P.R.O., State Papers, Holland, 84/252. The letters on deposit at Indiana were personal and often contain much more information than do the official ones written on the same day.

[3] Much of the foregoing and following material dealing with the Dutch and the squadron is discussed at a much greater length and in more detail in the author's article, 'The United Provinces and the Anglo-Dutch Squadron of 1715,' *Bijdragen voor de Geschiedenis der Nederlanden* (1953), pp. 20–45.

it might appear on the surface to have been. Historians have for a long time differed over the contents of the Norris instructions, and it is quite evident that few people in 1715 knew exactly what the Norris instructions entailed. A careful reading of the sources clearly indicates that there were many times that the admiral himself was not completely clear as to what exactly was expected from him. Actually Norris was provided with two sets of instructions, one formal and written and the other informal and oral. As Townshend was undoubtedly familiar with the plans of the King, there can be no doubt that he lied to Duivenvoorde for over a period of three months. Constantly and consistently he attempted to conceal the fact that Norris would take reprisals for British losses suffered at the hands of Sweden.[1] It must be admitted that Townshend succeeded very well, aided appreciably by the trust that Duivenvoorde placed in their long friendship. In spite of tangible evidence to the contrary[2] Duivenvoorde, who in March considered Townshend to be as peace-loving as an Amsterdam burgomaster,[3] continued to believe, until information from de Veth himself proved otherwise,[4] that the instructions to Norris and those to the Dutch commander, Lucas de Veth, would correspond 'word for word.'[5]

While English diplomats deceived their Dutch colleagues and did everything possible to expedite Dutch naval preparations, Gyllenborg ruefully watched the Thames fill with armed ships being equipped for the Baltic.[6] During the same period, Anglo-Swedish diplomacy moved at a more rapid tempo. Jefferyes was ordered by Townshend to continue working for reparations and satisfaction and to restress to the Swedish king that his new edict of privateering was a direct 'infraction of ye treaties between the two nations.'[7] Charles by his action had

---

[1] Various letters of Duivenvoorde to Heinsius, March to June, 1715, Rijksarchief, A.A.H., 1930.

[2] Ibid.

[3] Duivenvoorde to Heinsius, March 1, 1715, Ibid.

[4] De Veth to States General, May 31, 1715, copy in Secrete Resolutiën, Staten Generaal, June 7, 1715, and Heinsius to Duivenvoorde, June 7, 1715 (minutes), Rijksarchief, A.A.H., 1943.

[5] Heinsius to Duivenvoorde, May 3, 1715 (minutes), Rijksarchief, A.A.H., 1943.

[6] Gyllenborg to Sparre, February 25, 1715, Handlingar, X, 137–140.

[7] Townshend to Jefferyes, March 1, 1715, copy BM., Add. MSS., 28,154.

added new fuel to existing flames of English discontent. Both maritime nations considered the new edict piratical.[1] As the disappointed and bitter Townshend put it:

> The Swedes continue to heap new hardships upon them [merchants] by this late Edict, which contains several Innovations that No Treaty, Law, or Reason can justify. We can look upon such Proceedings as Piratical only, and Commissions founded upon such Orders can be calculated for no other purpose, but to set the neutral Powers at Defiance, who are concerned in the Commerce of the Baltick.[2]

Admittedly the language of Townshend was strong, but one must remember that Dutch protests were in a similar vein. Moreover some terms of the new edict were impossible for ships already in the Baltic to comply with. For example, the Swedes insisted that all ship masters carry birth certificates signed by the magistrates of their home towns, a custom unusual in Britain. In addition, all ships that had sailed before the publishing of the edict would be liable to seizure. Thus ships at Danzig waiting for warmer weather before they began their homeward passage did not dare to sail without the proper credentials; and if they waited until such papers could come from England, the delay would ruin the masters and the shipowners alike.[3]

Both Jackson and Jefferyes protested against the Swedish edict and the refusal of the Swedes to make any allowances for the ships stranded at Danzig.[4] As spring moved towards summer, the latter became involved in a series of bitter arguments with Swedish officials at Stralsund. He had become especially disgusted with Baron Kasten Feif, Swedish minister in charge of such affairs at Stralsund, to whom he had presented at least two long memorials during the last days of March.[5]

Although Feif promised to procure Jefferyes an answer, he did not live up to his oral engagements, and the Englishman

---

[1] Various letters between the States and Sweden, Lamberty, *Mémoires*, IX, *passim.*

[2] Townshend to Jefferyes, March 8, 1715, copy BM., Add. MSS., 28,154.

[3] Jefferyes to Feif, March 21, 1715, *Ibid.*

[4] Jefferyes to Townshend, April 12, 1715, *Ibid.*; and Jackson to the Swedish Chancery and Jackson to Townshend, March 31, 1715, P.R.O., State Papers, Sweden, 95/21.

[5] Jefferyes to Townshend, March 22 and 29, 1715, copies BM., Add. MSS., 28,154.

had to prod him constantly for action. Time and time again Feif put the English envoy off with 'excuses, either that he has not found opportunities to lay it [the memorial of March 29] before the King, or that he himself has been hurried with Business.' Jefferyes' questions regarding the fate of the stranded merchantships received similar treatment. As a result, Jefferyes concluded:

> I am now apt to look upon the delay he makes as a refusal to my request, and therefore resolve (unless a positive answer can soon be procured) to advise the Merchants thereof, to the end that they may take the best precautions for their safety they are capable of.[1]

On April 11 the Feif-Jefferyes talks degenerated into angry recriminations, name calling, and threats, which were not far removed from war ultimatums. At that time Jefferyes forced Feif to admit that he had not as yet presented the British memorial to Charles XII. At bay, Feif offered reasons for his procrastinating 'so very frivolous, as plainly shew this Court has no mind to give his Maj'ty satisfaction either for the loss of his Subjects' Ships and Effects, or regulate matters relating to trade upon the foot of the Treatys.'[2] The angry Englishman threatened that George I might look upon the long delay as a rejection 'of his just Demands, and consequently such Measures might be taken for the Security of our Commerce in the Baltick as would be disagreeable to them.'[3] Feif could only insist that the delay was not his fault, and he promised to lay the British memorial before the Swedish king just as soon as possible.

The Swedish minister, however, was a great deal more specific on the matter of the ships at Danzig. His answer irritated Jefferyes just as much as his vagueness on the memorial, because he said that unless the ships received the proper passes from home they could not count upon Charles XII to issue special ones. They could 'expect no Mercy at the hands of the Swedish privateers.' This 'unfriendly answer' destroyed 'the little hopes' Jefferyes still had that Sweden might recognize

[1] Jefferyes to Townshend, April 5, 1715, *Ibid.*
[2] Idem to Idem, April 12, 1715, *Ibid.*
[3] *Ibid.*

British commercial difficulties. By late April he was 'plainly' convinced that Charles had 'no mind to favor' Britain with 'any Resolution.'[1] Thus Charles played directly into George's hands by making it absolutely mandatory that Britain send naval units into the Baltic. His refusal to recognize diplomatic procedure until it was too late hurt him in this instance as it had in many others and would continue to do so until his death.

Jackson as might be expected had no better success than Jefferyes. On March 31 he presented a long memorial to Horn, which in addition to the usual complaints and arguments contained a heated protest against the seizing of five British ships at Göteborg. Those vessels had put into that port expecting to be treated as friends, but instead—at least in English eyes— they had been accorded a reception reserved for enemies. Although the ships carried British passports and no contraband, the ships' masters were persecuted before the Swedish admiralty court and their ships threatened with confiscation. Jackson therefore asked that the ships be released and that the Swedish chancery intervene on behalf of the British shipmasters.[2] So far as Jackson was concerned, the entire affair illustrated 'at what a violent rate these people are driving; and that they are resolv'd to ruin and destroy the whole trade of these parts.'[3] The British minister was especially perturbed over an earlier intervention of the Swedish Senate on behalf of some Dutch ships taken by the Swedes at Göteborg, for he saw in the action favored treatment for Dutch merchants over the traders from Britain.[4]

Although Horn gave Jackson no encouragement to expect change in Swedish policy, he did inform the British minister that Admiral Leuwenhaupt, the commander at Göteborg, refused to comply with the Senate's order to release the Dutch ships. The port authorities had specific instructions from Charles XII which 'made it too evident . . . that no further respect be had to any orders of the Senate in these cases.'[5] The

[1] *Ibid.*, and Idem to Idem, April 19, 1715, *Ibid.*
[2] Jackson to the Swedish Chancery, March 31, 1715, P.R.O., State Papers, Sweden, 95/21.
[3] Jackson to Townshend, March 31, 1715, *Ibid.*
[4] Idem to Idem, March 19, 1715, *Ibid.*
[5] Idem to Idem, April 2, 1715, *Ibid.*

future of the Baltic trader was indeed a bleak one no matter from what country he came.[1]

It was not until the squadron had sailed from England that Charles XII answered the English memorials. The Swedish king was extremely indignant over the representations made by Jackson and Jefferyes in late March and early April. He was especially incensed with the conduct of Jefferyes whose threats and heated words had at times bordered upon a declaration of war. Sweden considered that certain expressions used in the British notes—and in the Dutch notes too for that matter— were contrary to the good friendship that existed between England and Sweden, and it was hoped that Jefferyes was exceeding his instructions.

Point by point the Swedish stand was explained. Admittedly there was much that was valid in the Swedish arguments, but Charles XII should have realized that the present circumstances compelled him to do all in his power to avoid giving George I any opportunity for implicating England in the Baltic struggle. For Charles XII to expect Britain to fight for his Baltic provinces was of course juvenile and perhaps far too much in keeping with his character. To insist that England first enter the war on his side and then promise all the trade privileges that could 'reasonably' be expected could make little appeal to an England who had received no help from Charles XII at the height of his power and to an English mercantile group who could remember that the trade concessions resulting from assistance leading to Travendal had been a series of monopolistic regulations designed to exclude Britain from the Baltic carrying trade. Diplomats and statesmen who could remember naval shortages resulting from Tar Company policies were still alive and in many cases they were now in positions of responsibility. In addition, Charles XII had hardly the reputation for being a reasonable man.

Some arguments used by Sweden, however, were just and make an excellent case for those historians who charge that George I and the English Hanoverians had no interest in trade, but were just groping for pretexts to circumvent the Act of Settlement. For example, England was asking for immediate damages and as yet Britain had not paid for the Swedish ships

[1] *Ibid.*

she had seized during the wars between England and France which had raged with a few truces from 1689 to 1713. The Swedish ships taken, like those of the British, had been engaged in trading with the enemy even though they had not been carrying contraband. England was also reminded that Sweden had not taken reprisals upon British merchant ships as the Danes had done in retaliation for losses suffered at English hands. In order to contrast the situation of Sweden in 1689 and that of England in 1715 and to shed light on English high-handedness a mild Swedish protest letter of 1689 was included with the Swedish answer. It was hoped by the Swedes that the British would compare the more gentlemanly conduct of the Swedes with their own actions.[1] Unfortunately the Swedish king, himself, became in his arguments a little high-handed and peremptory by asking that those British ministers who advised Britain to violate the existing Anglo-Swedish treaties be punished. Charles XII might cower his own ministers into supporting a hopeless war, but Britain was hardly Sweden. Moreover British statesmen were apt to be a great deal more independent than their Swedish counterparts, many of whom actually dreaded the possibility of Charles XII returning to Sweden.

The Swedish note suggested, and rightly so, that George I had designs for his Baltic ships which went beyond the protection of commerce. Yet again the attempt to establish proofs fell flat. For example, the main argument used was the fact that Anne had sent a small number of ships to the Sound in the previous year in comparison to the large numbers destined for Baltic service in 1715. What the comparison failed to mention, however, was that the squadron of the previous year because of its ludicrously small size had been unable to achieve its purpose. There can be no doubt that Dutch estimates as to the size necessary to do the job were a basic minimum. Actually, as will be shown later, when the Dutch would not coöperate with the English, the latter did not have sufficient ships to accomplish anything by themselves.

Excusing the delay in answering the English memorials on the ground that previous replies in reality covered the situation,

[1] Charles XI to Leyoncrona, October 12, 1689, *Handlingar*, X, 223–226 and extract of Charles XII to George I, May 15, 1715, *Ibid.*, X, 219–223.

the Swedish memorial had some charges of its own to make. The privateering edict had been found necessary to circumvent the ruses of foreign neutral merchants who were sneaking into the prohibited ports and aiding Russia in its war against Sweden. Both England and Holland were accused of furnishing Peter the Great with war supplies. The Swedes claimed that it was the Maritime Powers they were fighting on the sea rather than the forces of the Russian czar.[1]

This last charge had considerable truth in it. Throughout May, Gyllenborg in London had labored to prevent the sailing of three armed ships, which were being fitted out in England and were destined for Russian service. If the ships did sail in spite of Swedish sensibilities, Gyllenborg asked that they not be placed in the convoy and thus have immunity from attacks by Swedish privateers. If such occurred, Gyllenborg pointed out that England would not only be violating its treaty agreements,[2] but also would be committing fraud under the guise of neutrality.[3]

Of more importance than the three Russian ships and their neutrality is the position of the squadron itself. Certain important questions must be considered. What was the sole purpose of the squadron? Did the squadron violate British neutrality and if so what were the subsequent effects?

The instructions to Norris give an excellent insight into the problems involved. The British commander was armed with two sets of instructions: one set oral and the other written. The latter was the most important and definitely shows that protection of commerce was the main *raison d'être* so far as most Englishmen were concerned. Yet they were drafted in such a way that Norris would have great latitude of action. Moreover they included the taking of reprisals,[4] a fact which was concealed from the Dutch until the two units rendezvoused in the Sound. One of the chief reasons that the Dutch were not informed of the reprisal clause was that a large peace party in

[1] Extract of Charles XII to George I, May 15, 1715, *Ibid.*, X, 219–223.
[2] Gyllenborg to Townshend, May 18, 1715, *Ibid.*, p. 158. The ships in question were the *London*, the *Richmond*, and the *Allen*.
[3] Idem to Idem, May 21, 1715, *Ibid.*, p. 159.
[4] List of English and Dutch ships bound for the Baltic, BM., Add. MSS., 28,154; Chance, *George I and the Northern War*, p. 86 sets the number of ships higher.

the States would interpret reprisals to mean the involvement of the States in the northern conflict. Under ordinary circumstances one might consider the reprisal clause in the instructions as nothing but an attempt by the British to use the fleet to open the Baltic trade. Other factors, however, make one wonder. Norris was to begin seizing Swedish ships immediately after he sent the Swedes an ultimatum through Jackson and Jefferyes. Like Pontius Pilate, he was not to wait for an answer. In addition, his oral instructions were nothing but a series of suggestions as to how he might by exploiting the reprisal clause aid Sweden's enemies as much as possible and still stay within the letter if not the intent of his written instructions.[1] These oral instructions were given to Norris privately at a conference with the King during which Bernstorff made him take notes on the main points which concerned the King as Elector.[2] Norris, moreover, in addition to his instructions and his detailed commands from the admiralty was to obey such orders he would receive from the King, Townshend, or some other principal secretary of state.[3]

The role of the Hanoverian ministers in the diplomacy behind the squadron was a powerful one and definitely proves that George I planned to use the squadron to pull his own chestnuts out of the Baltic fires. Gottlieb Justus Püchler, George's resident at the Danish court, was a far more important pawn than his English colleague, F. Hanneken. Jean Robethon, the royal secretary, constantly included the King's wishes as Elector in his dispatches to the fleet commander. If one remembers that all George's orders came through his Huguenot secretary, one can appreciate Norris's difficulties. It was a 'bold man in those days who refused to obey royal orders even by such an irregular channel.'[4] Robethon also needled Norris through his father-in-law, Admiral Matthew Aylmer, 'who was much at court,'[5] and to whom Norris wrote long letters

---

[1] Queries of the Baltic commander and answers given by George I and Bernstorff, BM., Add. MSS., 28,154. Cited hereafter as Queries and Answers.

[2] Michael, *England under George I*, I, 291. Mediger, *Moskaus Weg*, p. 18.

[3] Admiralty to Norris, May 10, 1715, Order Book of Sir John Norris, BM., Add. MSS., 28,144.

[4] Williams, *Stanhope*, p. 232.

[5] Chance, *George I and the Northern War*, p. 85.

discussing Baltic problems.[1] Moreover, George had promised his allies British naval support, and it was these allies and his Hanoverian ministers who spread reports in London and at the Hague that Norris would act offensively against Sweden.[2] George's allies as Bernstorff told the Prussian Bonet were not to tell the Admiral 'Please help us in this or that operation,' but simply to say 'We know of the presence of Swedish ships. Please come and attack them.'[3]

If Bernstorff used double talk to Bonet, the same can also be said of his directions to Norris as shown in the 'queries and answers' as found in the Norris papers. Some dealing with basic issues have little innuendo and left the Admiral in little doubt as to what he should do. He was to coöperate with the Danes as much as possible even to using their ammunition and hospital facilities. While the store ships were loading, he was to be off Bornholm or Karlscrona to intercept ships which might be going to Stralsund even though such a station was hazardous to the fleet in bad weather. Moreover he was to protect the ships of George's Danish, Prussian, and Russian allies.[4] As Bernstorff informed the Russian diplomat Kurakin, Norris had been sent not just for trade protection and reprisals but to prevent Sweden from sending reinforcements to the hard-pressed Swedish troops in Pomerania.[5]

The extent of Townshend's involvement in George's personal schemes is more difficult to assess than is that of the Hanoverian ministers. The late Basil Williams, one of the great authorities on this period, is of the opinion that Norris had no written hint from Townshend in the original instructions or by private correspondence to go beyond his detailed orders,[6] yet the Admiralty orders of May 10 and a letter from Norris to Townshend, May 18, indicate that Norris had received some indication from the Secretary that duties beyond the protection of

[1] Various letters of Norris to Aylmer, 1715, BM., Add. MSS., 28,143 and 28,154.
[2] Heinsius to Duivenvoorde, May 3, 1715 (minutes), Rijksarchief, A.A.H., 1943, and Duivenvoorde to Heinsius, May 31, 1715, Rijksarchief, A.A.H., 1930.
[3] Quoted in Michael, *England under George I*, I, 291.
[4] Queries and Answers, BM., Add. MSS., 28,154.
[5] Nikiforov, *Russiche-Englische Beziehungen*, p. 168, and Mediger, *Moskaus Weg*, p. 18.
[6] Williams, *Stanhope*, p. 232.

commerce might be expected from the squadron. Townshend probably omitted putting anything definite in writing purposely in order to forestall any parliamentary investigation as to the use of British naval units and how the employment of the same coincided with the Act of Settlement.[1] His subterfuge with the Dutch shows that he was quite willing to compromise his honesty so far as the Baltic squadron and reprisals were concerned. Townshend wanted the instructions to both Baltic commanders to be 'fairly general so that affairs could be worked out on the spot.'[2]

Well might Townshend have been careful of Parliament and government, for some of his colleagues wanted a strict interpretation of Britain's relation with Hanover. Among others, the First Lord of the Admiralty, Edward Russell, Earl of Orford, strongly opposed the fleet's taking any offensive action against Sweden in coöperation with George's electoral allies, and he 'was pleased to express himself in the presence of Townshend' on that score.[3] Moreover, Orford saw that the amount of ammunition supplied the squadron was limited to peace time requirements. It took a special request to increase, from forty to sixty, the number of rounds on Norris's flagship, the *Cumberland*.[4]

The members of the Northern Alliance were as interested in what action Norris would take and how far he would go, as were the English and Dutch admiralty boards. The verbal and oral instructions that Norris received linked him with the allies of Hanover and with the Baltic diplomacy of 1715, which, in that year, was extremely active. Norris personally was to play an important role in that diplomacy for Bernstorff intended to use the British fleet as bait to lure the members of the Northern Alliance into his plans to drive Sweden from the Empire. Events had caused Bernstorff to alter his diplomacy, especially Denmark's position in Germany.[5] Thus the subsequent

---

[1] Line of Battle, enclosed in Admiralty to Norris, May 10, 1715 and Norris to Townshend, May 18, 1715, BM., Add. MSS., 28,144.

[2] Duivenvoorde and Borssele to Fagel, May 30, 1715, extract in Rijksarchief, Secrete Resolutiën, Staten Generaal, May 3, 1715.

[3] Norris to Aylmer, June 30, 1715, BM., Add. MSS., 28,143.

[4] Norris to Burchett, April 14, 1715, and Burchett to Norris, April 16, 1715, BM., Add. MSS., 28,135.

[5] Mediger, *Moskaus Weg*, p. 19.

diplomatic maneuvering was to influence Norris and exert many divergent pressures upon him. Consequently some understanding of Baltic diplomacy in 1715 is necessary before taking up the saga of the Anglo-Dutch Baltic squadron of that year.

V

BALTIC DIPLOMACY IN 1715

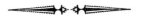

THE advent of the Elector of Hanover to the thrones of England, Ireland, and Scotland was only one of two dramatic events which highlighted the diplomacy of the Great Northern War during the last half of 1714. The second happening saw Charles XII once more playing an active role in northern European affairs. On the night of November 21, the Swedish king, half dead from exhaustion and with the wound in his foot reopened, arrived before Stralsund, the most important of his remaining possessions in the Empire.[1] With the Swedish king's return to his own dominions from Turkish-Europe and with the accession of George I to the British throne, a new phase in the diplomacy of the Great Northern War began.

New ministers and new advisers came into prominence in Sweden as they had in Britain. Sweden embarked upon her last great adventures in the field of international politics while England came to assume a more active role in Baltic affairs. Gradually she drifted toward open enmity with Sweden. With Sweden's failure during the subsequent years to divide her enemies and to defeat them, a new balance of power arose in the North. Russia became the dominant country. Romanoff supplanted Vasa as the leading dynasty. England by attempting to aid Hanoverian politics within the Empire was to contribute

---

[1] Charles XII to the Queen Mother, Hedvig Eleanora, November 11, 1714, *Konung Karl XII's Egenhändiga Bref*, E. Carlson (ed.) (Stockholm, 1893), p. 7, and Idem to Ulrika Eleanora, *Ibid.*, pp. 136–137. Charles XII had traveled the nine hundred miles from Wallachia to Stralsund in fourteen days. As the King had stated in the letter to his mother, he had 'gick medh posten fort.'

to this changing diplomatic situation which brought about a new balance of power opposed in many ways to British interests.

Sweden at the time of Charles's return was as exhausted as her ruler.[1] To be sure, the arrival of the leader in his own lands did momentarily raise the sunken hopes and courage of the Swedes,[2] but these hopes, false to begin with, were soon dashed. Beset on all sides by her enemies and soon to add two more, the ruin of the kingdom seemed imminent. Finland had succumbed to the Czar, who was contemplating a march into Sweden proper from the East in collaboration with a Danish invasion of Skåne, Sweden's southern province. It appeared in late 1714, that Sweden could not muster sufficient forces to repel one invasion, let alone cope with two. A single smashing defeat would have knocked Sweden completely off her feet, yet many victories would have been necessary to effect a restoration of Sweden's former greatness. Manpower was lacking and what naval and land forces that Sweden could muster were poorly equipped. The loss of the Baltic provinces had been aggravated by famine in Sweden and starvation stalked through the land.[3] Only by most heroic efforts had the Swedish people been able to continue the war. To some these efforts were misplaced. According to Bolingbroke the heroism of the Swedish king and the absolute resignation of his subjects to the royal will had brought Sweden to the brink of disaster: 'the inflexible obstinacy which this prince has shewn and the high terms he has insisted upon, even at the lowest ebb of his fortune, have made it impossible for his true friends to speak and act on his behalf, as they on several occasions have done with great probability of success, and do still continue to furnish those who are avowedly his Enemys with very plausible pretences, the former to do nothing for him, the latter to do everything against him.'[4]

The finances of the kingdom were sadly depleted and there was no money to pay what soldiers Charles XII was able to levy. Swedish credit was at such a low ebb that the bank of

[1] Fåhräus, *Sveriges Historia*, VIII, 461.

[2] Carl Gustav Malmström, *Sveriges politiska historia från Konung Karl XII's död till Statshvalfningen, 1772*, 6 vols. (Stockholm 1893), I, 34. Cited hereafter as Malmström, *Sveriges politiska historia*.

[3] Fåhräus, *Sveriges historia*, VIII, 461.

[4] Bolingbroke to Prior, 6 May, 1714, *British Instructions, France*, pp. 68-69.

Hamburg would not advance the Swedes money even at one hundred percent interest.[1] Not only were the troops in want, but the diplomatic representatives of the nation had hardly enough money to carry out the routine duties of their offices.[2] Gyllenborg at London for example was in constant financial embarrassment, a predicament from which he could not escape. Throughout all of 1714, a critical year in Anglo-Swedish relations, he did not receive any money at all from Sweden. He was so shabby that he could not even show himself at the English Court to congratulate George I on his birthday. Without privilege and credit,[3] Gyllenborg was harassed and insulted by his creditors who threatened to sue him for non-payment of his obligations. Without means he could not follow the example of other foreign diplomats in London and hire newswriters (*aviseskrifare*) to help present his country's case, but had to watch passively as Sweden's enemies misled the British public 'through false and bitter accounts.'[4] Whenever the Swedish minister wished to insert corrections in the newspapers, the printers refused to accept them without a stipend.[5] Thus, without money, Gyllenborg could neither correct nor control the mounting public opinion against Sweden, which was so artfully fostered in both England and Europe by the enemies of Charles XII.

What meager funds that were in Sweden were not always available to the government. Many of the richer families who lacked the courage and patriotism of the King and his gallant, weary, and over-matched troops made no contributions at all to the war effort. Some such as the Count Wrede feared that the government, to fulfill its military needs would confiscate their money and property. Consequently they exported specie to foreign banks.[6] The various restrictions laid upon trade by Charles XII had also contributed to the diminishing money

---

[1] Müllern to Sparre, 10 April, 1715, quoted in Carlson, *Om Fredsunderhandlingarne*, p. 77. *cf.* Nordmann, *La Crise du Nord*, p. 18.

[2] Sparre to Gyllenborg, May 6, 1715, *Handlingar*, X, 527.

[3] Quoted in Larsson, *Gyllenborg*, p. 9: 'Frammande ministrar hafva här ingen förmän och ingen kredit.'

[4] *Ibid.*, p. 10: 'Genom osanna och bittra berättelser."

[5] *Ibid.*, p. 10.

[6] Campredon to Orléans, February 9 and March 2, 1715, *Handlingar rörande Sveriges historia åren 1715-1720*, Carl Gustav Malmström (ed.) (Uppsala, 1845), pp. 33–34. Cited hereafter as *H.R.S.H.*

supply of the nation. His commercial edicts had brought trade almost to a standstill and had thereby prevented the burghers of Stockholm from using the only means at their disposal to refill their emptied purses.[1] The activities of privateers who sailed under Swedish and other letters of marque prevented wares from either entering or leaving the country. Tolls therefore were almost non-existent and work in the mines had nearly stopped. Iron, once valued at forty dollars *kopparmynt*[2] had fallen in value during 1714 to twenty dollars.[3] With famine threatening the country, tax collecting was extremely difficult. Charles XII had been able to farm out the taxes in the south and west of the country, but no one would accept the responsibility in Stockholm. Consequently, the capital was threatened with economic ruin. Observers noted that toll collectors in other ports would lower revenues in order to divert Stockholm trade to their wharves.[4] To enforce the various and sundry exactions, Charles XII had to resort to law suits,[5] which were hardly conducive to a united Sweden. Furthermore, excessive litigation acted as a restraint upon the flow of goods and upon the economic well-being of the country.

The government of the country was in as chaotic a state as were its economic resources. When the Swedish king had embarked upon his great military adventure, he had left his country in the hands of a regency, just as his illustrious predecessor Gustavus Adolphus had done a century earlier.[6] So long as the gods of war had smiled upon the Swedish cause, all had run smoothly, but when Swedish arms began to suffer adversities, Senate and Regency had become less amenable to the wishes of the sovereign.[7] Jackson was of the opinion that a

---

[1] Chance, *George I and the Northern War*, p. 75.

[2] One *kopparmynt* equalled one *silvermynt*, which equalled between one-third and one-fourth of a *riksdaler*.

[3] Carlson, *Om Fredsunderhandlingarne*, p. 78. The author cites a quotation from Hopkins to Görtz, n.d. For a highly detailed account of Sweden's economic position at this time see Gustav Edward Axelson, *Bidrag til kännedom om Sveriges tillstånd på Karl XII's tid* (Visby, 1888).

[4] A résumé of a letter from Campredon in *H.R.S.H.*, pp. 35–37, and various letters of Jackson, September and November, 1714, P.R.O., State Papers, Sweden, 95/21.

[5] Campredon to Orléans, April 27, 1715, *H.R.S.H.*, p. 27.

[6] Croissy instructions, *Recueil, Suède*, p. 256.

[7] *Ibid.*

revolution was pending in Sweden. The British minister at Stockholm was not sure what the course of the revolt might be, but he was sure that it was coming. The dismal setbacks on the battlefield and at the conference tables and the constant drainage of men and money from Sweden had affected all classes.[1]

Friction and distrust worked in both directions. Jacques de Campredon, the French resident at Stockholm, wrote in 1715, that the officers and the governors of the Swedish provinces no longer obeyed the command of the King's council.[2] To make matters more complicated—at least from a diplomatic standpoint—Charles XII while at Stralsund, ordered that no one from Sweden visit him without permission.[3] Since it was impossible to carry out the levies of the King for troops and money, the Senate decided to disobey the King's command and sent him a protest regarding his requirements of them. Count Johan August Meyerfield, the governor-general of Pomerania carried out the decision of the Senate. The Count took with him a peace offering of 100,000 *riksdalers*, which had been squeezed with a good deal of difficulty from the burghers of Stockholm.[4] The subjects of Charles XII who resided in Sweden proper felt that such a financial sop was necessary for 'As much as the generality of this Nation will certainly rejoyce at the King's return, as much his resentments are apprehended by most of those who had the chief direction of affairs during his absence.'[5]

Those who feared the King did so with reason. Shortly after the arrival of Charles XII at Stockholm there were wholesale removals from office which were 'fatal to many of the first Rank,'[6] and which hampered Swedish efficiency. The new bureaucracy was for the most part ignorant of its duties, and consequently there were additional troubles and confusion in the administration of the government.[7] Throughout the last

[1] Jackson to Bromley, January 2, 1714, P.R.O., State Papers, Sweden, 95/21.

[2] Résumé of a Campredon letter, *H.R.S.H.*, p. 38.

[3] Jackson to Townshend, November 20, 1714, P.R.O., State Papers, Sweden, 95/21.

[4] Chance, *George I and the Northern War*, p. 60. For the various quarrels that Charles XII had with the Swedish Senate, see And. Fryxell, *Berättelser ur Svenska Historia*, 46 vols. (Stockholm, 1903), XXVI.

[5] Jackson to Townshend, November 20, 1714, P.R.O., State Papers, Sweden, 95/21.

[6] *Ibid.*

[7] *H.R.S.H.*, p. 38.

part of the seventeenth century and during the first two decades of the eighteenth century, there was a keen rivalry between the old aristocratic nobility and the more democratic nobles who owed their being to service rather than birth. During his last years, Charles XII turned more and more to the new men. Among them were Müllern in foreign affairs, Feif in the war department, Fahlström in finance, and Cronhielm in religious affairs.[1]

All were under the presidency of Baron Georg Heinrich von Görtz von Schlitz who came to be an economic czar controlling finance, commerce and the navy and who continually increased his voice in foreign affairs. As the siege of Stralsund progressed, Görtz, of a noble Franconian family, gradually gained considerable influence over the Swedish king.[2] Unlike the other members of the new civil service, the Baron was an experienced and capable diplomat and a statesman of no small parts. While in the employ of the Duke of Holstein-Gottorp, Görtz first became acquainted with Charles XII, and in a short time rose to be the leading Swedish secretary of state. His position in the Swedish state system was a unique one and in some ways was enviable. As a Holsteiner, he was not subject to Swedish laws and customs.[3] Thus he was able to execute his plans and carry out the functions of his office extra-legally. He was accountable to the King and to the King alone for what he did. Consequently his fortune was inextricably linked with that of the King. That chance bullet before the fort at Frederikshald which sent Charles XII to his grave sent Görtz indirectly to the scaffold, but he went boasting that at least he died in good company.

The Whig historian, Lord Mahon, in his *History of England* has made much of the Baron's avoidance of two duels with General Friedrich Wilhelm von Grumbkow, a minister of the King of Prussia. Mahon charges Görtz with cowardice and wonders how Charles XII, a man of great bravery and fortitude,

---

[1] Nordmann, La Crise du Nord, p. 31, and Hugo Valentin, *Frihetstidens Riddarhus Någrå bigrag till dess Karakteristik*, Akademisk Afhandling (Stockholm, 1915), p. 16.

[2] James F. Chance, 'The Swedish Plot of 1716–1717,' *English Historical Review*, XVIII (1903), pp. 81–82. Cited hereafter as Chance, 'Swedish Plot.' Cf. H. J. Lindeberg, *Görtz, ett offer för enväldet* (Stockholm, 1925), pp. 25 ff.

[3] Malmström, *Sveriges politiska historia*, I, 37.

could tolerate a craven in his service.[1] Actually, Görtz had lost one eye upon the 'field of honor,'[2] and he was a person of great audacity, whose many exploits in diplomacy well rival the military feats of his adopted sovereign. The keen and penetrating Voltaire in his *Histoire de Charles XII* more accurately described him:

> Never was a man at once so bold and so artful, so full of expedients amid misfortunes, so unbounded in his designs, or so active in the prosecution of them; no project was too great for his daring genius to attempt, no means too difficult for his sagacity and penetration to discover; in pursuing his favorite schemes he was equally prodigal of presents and promises, of oaths, of truths, and of falsehoods.[3]

With the advent of this man to power, Swedish diplomacy was revitalized,

> and he rather seem'd to act in all Places where he came as an Instructor to Ambassadors than an Ambassador himself: In this Capacity we find him transacting the most intricate Affairs between the Ambassadors of Sweden, at sundry Courts of which in their Order: Today we found the *Baron* in *Holland*, tomorrow in *France*, anon in the Court of *Prussia*; now *here*, now *there*, as the King's Affairs requir'd.[4]

Görtz, however, was more than a traveling diplomat. Charles XII singled him out for 'the most important Trusts' and began

> to communicate to him his most secret Councils, and first or last, engage him in Matters of the greatest Consequence in his Kingdom; not only relating to Alliances, Peace and War, and the like, but even in the Civil Administration of his Government, his Treasury, the Commerce of his Subjects, the Execution of Treaties Abroad, and of Justice at Home, and in a Word, he became especially in the latter Part of his Majesty's

[1] Lord Mahon, *History of England*, I, 257.
[2] Schuyler, *Peter the Great*, II, 238–39. Defoe, *Göertz*, p. 2 considered Charles XII to be an excellent judge of men and used his selection of Görtz for important tasks as an example.
[3] Voltaire (François Marie Arouet), *Histoire de Charles XII* (Paris, 1882), p. 429. Cf. Lindeberg, *Görtz*, p. 17: 'I sin politiska gärning var Görtz sålunda utan skrupler, en mästare i den smidiga intrigens konst.'
[4] Defoe, *Goertz*, p. 6.

life, not only his particular favorite, but even his Prime Minister in the great Transactions of War, Peace, Trade, and Government.[1]

To a man less adventurous than Görtz, the task of preserving a portion of the Swedish Empire would have seemed impossible to accomplish. Görtz knew Sweden's weaknesses and realized that necessity compelled Sweden to remain on the defensive. Her solution lay in participating in all negotiations, putting on a good front, stalling for time, and hoping for a split among her enemies. Görtz had no illusions about his financial schemes. They existed for the moment and were not designed for the long haul.[2]

Yet in spite of the bleak prospects lying ahead, there was some possibility for success. The spirits of the Swedish people, depressed almost to despair, soared upward with the return of their beloved leader to his own provinces.[3] Not only were the hopes and the courage of the Swedish people enhanced, but the diplomatic position of the country was appreciably bettered. The enemies pressing in upon the nation knew through long and hard experience the character of Charles XII, and they understood only too well what the Swedish king could undertake and accomplish with only a few soldiers.[4] With the prestige and impetus resulting from the King's homecoming, it appeared that Swedish diplomacy under the magic hand of Görtz might extricate the nation from the worst of its troubles. Unfortunately for the country, its ruler was more apt to heed councils of war rather than those of peace,[5] and he was prone to rely too much upon Swedish arms and too little upon diplomacy as the medium by which his enemies might be brought to terms.[6]

Sweden in the year 1715 diplomatically stood at the crossroads. One road stretched toward a settlement of the war by a general peace congress and the other path went to individual and separate treaties with her sundry enemies. The former seemed the most logical way out of the international wilderness,

[1] *Ibid.*, pp. 2–3.
[2] Nordmann, *La Crise du Nord*, p. 33.
[3] Malmström, *Sveriges politiska historia*, I, 34.
[4] Croissy instructions, *Recueil, Suède*, II, 260.
[5] Carlson, *Om Fredsunderhandlingarne*, p. 77.
[6] Vellingk to Müllern, August 30, 1715, *Ibid.*, p. 86.

because it was only through a general peace congress that an armistice would be achieved;[1] and an immediate suspension of hostilities appeared almost mandatory for the Swedes. Moreover the congresses that had brought a conclusion to the War of the Spanish Succession could have served as examples for a settlement in the North. Indeed attempts had been made to include the Baltic conflict among the topics of the Utrecht deliberations.[2] In order for Sweden to profit from an international congress, it was important for her to win both Austria and France to her standard.[3] France was traditionally pro-Swedish, but the relations between Austria and Sweden during the past century had been far from pleasant. In addition, the problem of effecting a working union between the rival houses of Bourbon and Hapsburg complicated matters for the Swedish diplomats.[4]

As stated above, the relations between Sweden and Austria left much to be desired. When Charles XII had stood at the height of his power and military glory, he had entertained ideas which had caused a great deal of friction between Vienna and Stockholm. Especially galling to the Emperor had been the Swedish king's meddling in Imperial affairs which had gone so far as to give aid to Silesian Protestants who were revolting against the Empire. The result of Swedish interference had been the achieving of religious toleration for Silesian Calvinists.[5] Charles XII had also set up a plan with the House of Hohenzollern by which the Imperial title would alternate between a Catholic and a Protestant prince.[6] The reception by the Hapsburgs at Vienna to such a scheme may well be imagined. So far as the war in the North was concerned, the Empire as far back as 1706 had offered to mediate, and at that time had attempted to gain a promise from Charles XII not to extend the conflagration into the Empire.[7] The answer of the Swedish monarch had been the invasion of Saxony.

Notwithstanding these difficulties there was a possibility that

[1] *Ibid.*, p. 82.
[2] See Chapter III.
[3] Gyllenborg to Sparre, February 7, 1715, *Handlingar*, X, 119.
[4] *Ibid.*
[5] A convention to this effect had been signed by the Emperor, September, 1707.
[6] Croissy instructions, *Recueil, Suède*, II, 253.
[7] *Ibid.*

Austria might be won over to espouse Sweden. In the first place, the idea of a general peace congress to end the strife and bloodshed in the North was not a new one. In 1712, when the Swedish armies under Count Magnus, Marshall Stenbock were in the Empire, the Emperor Charles VI had summoned a congress of neutral German princes to deal with the problem of Stenbock's troops. A meeting had been held at Brunswick about the middle of December, under the leadership of the Austrian representative, Count Damian Schönborn. Attending were envoys from Prussia, Hanover, Wolfenbuttel, Hesse-Cassel, and Münster. It was decided that the attending powers in concert with the Elector of the Palatinate should raise a force of 20,000 men to enforce peace in the Germanies.

All belligerents of the Great Northern War who did not pull back their troops beyond the Imperial boundaries were to be declared enemies of the Empire, and Swedish troops were not to enter Poland. In other words, all the soldiers of Charles XII excepting those required to garrison Swedish possessions in the Empire were to withdraw to Sweden. Those areas in Bremen and Swedish Pomerania already occupied by the enemies of the Swedish king were to be sequestered to the Emperor for the duration of the war. If one of the belligerents in that conflict suffered total defeat, the neutrals pledged themselves to employ their forces against the victor. The German princes, however, could not agree upon the execution of their plan, and consequently no definite action was taken. In March, 1713, the Congress of Brunswick, having accomplished nothing, was prorogued.[1]

The Congress was scheduled to convene again in 1714, and it was apparent to many that such a meeting would find no favor with the Swedish king. Charles XII had reason to suppose he would not receive a fair deal from the Empire. As Bolingbroke wrote:

> The Emperor has old quarrells to the House of Gustavus, the treatys of Westphalia are an Eyesore to him, the danger he ran when this King was in Saxony is hardly forgot, and in a word the aggrandizing of the Czar, and the bringing of that prince into the neighbourhood and affairs of these parts of Europe

[1] Chance, *George I and the Northern War*, p. 31. See also above.

seems to be a principle of policy taken up at Vienna within these few years.[1]

The British Secretary of State also was of the opinion that the princes and states of the Empire were quite a bit under Imperial influence and would therefore back Charles VI at a general peace congress. In fact Charles XII could not even count upon the aid of his ally Holland because of the Barrier Treaty that the Dutch were negotiating with the Empire. Concerning that negotiation, Bolingbroke scathingly said that the Dutch would rather risk their friends, religion, and trade 'than expose themselves to the danger of having a Bicoque the less in the Spanish Netherlands.'[2] Actually the States fared poorly in the Barrier negotiations because George I in order to obtain Imperial support for his designs against Bremen and Verden backed the claims of Charles VI, the new owner of the Spanish Netherlands, against those of the United Provinces.[3]

By 1715, however, the trend of Austro-Swedish affairs took a decided turn for the better. When those two greed-motivated German princes, the King of Prussia and the Elector of Hanover, decided to join the ranks of Sweden's foes, an excellent opportunity presented itself for a rapprochement between Charles VI and Charles XII. Especially was such a move to the interest of the Emperor who had much to fear from a powerful Prussia and a strong Hanover. Even though he might be persuaded to allow Bremen and Verden to go to Hanover in return for George's aid as King of England in the Barrier negotiations, he was jealous of any extension of Prussia and was opposed to the contemplated expansion of Denmark into the Empire.[4] Thus Sweden might have a chance to win Charles VI over to her side. To accomplish this, Swedish envoys had to be sent immediately to both Brunswick and Vienna. Charles XII temporized and short-sightedly refused to act unless the Emperor would absolutely guarantee that Sweden would receive

[1] Bolingbroke to Prior, May 6, 1714, *British Instructions, France*, pp. 68–69.
[2] *Ibid.*
[3] For an excellent account of Anglo-Dutch diplomacy and its relation to the Baltic, see Hatton, *Diplomatic Relations, passim*. See also Murray, *An Honest Diplomat*.
[4] Gyllenborg to Sparre, June 11, 1715, *Handlingar*, X, 338–339. Görtz wanted Sparre to persuade Louis XIV to use his influence to induce Charles XII to send an envoy to a general peace congress. See Görtz to Sparre, February 8, 1715, *Handlingar*, VIII, 233. Cf. Chance, *George I and the Northern War*, p. 80.

as the result of a general peace congress not only all of the places she had previously held in Europe, but an indemnity as well.[1] Charles XII moreover wanted the meeting held in some place other than Brunswick, and suggested as alternatives Danzig, Breslau, or Königsberg.[2] The Swedish monarch in addition refused to address the Emperor by the title 'King of Spain.'[3]

On June 6, Charles XII was persuaded to write the Emperor in the desired form.[4] On the above date he sent two letters to the Imperial Court, one with the proper title and one without. The second of these contained some vague proposals concerning a peace negotiation.[5] These two letters arrived at Vienna along with two additional letters about the end of July. Although the fourth letter recognized the Emperor as the sole arbiter of affairs in Northern Germany and offered submission to his decision,[6] there were no attempts made by Sweden to send envoys either to Brunswick or to Vienna. The Emperor, for his part, did not dare give the guarantees for the return of Sweden's lost provinces as requested by Charles XII. He did not have sufficient military resources to enforce such a promise even though he might have desired to make it. With an exhausted treasury, the Emperor said that it was impossible for him to make any moves on Sweden's behalf.[7] Actually, Charles XII had acted too belatedly. His foes meanwhile had won the Emperor over to neutrality. They could continue the siege of Stralsund and Wismar without worrying about Imperial interference.[8] Despite efforts made by the French envoy at Vienna, Count de Luc, the two Charleses drifted apart.[9] Swedish

[1] Memoir of Sparre, February 1, 1715, *Handlingar*, VIII, 184. *Cf*. Carlson, *Om Fredsunderhandlingarne*, p. 85.

[2] Croissy instructions, *Recueil, Suède*, II, 266; Charles XII to Strahlenheim, March 24, 1715, in Carlson, *Om Fredsunderhandlingarne*, pp. 82–83n.

[3] Carlson, *Om Fredsunderhandlingarne*, p. 84.

[4] Görtz to Sparre, June 18, 1715, *Handlingar*, VIII, 245.

[5] Carlson, *Om Fredsunderhandlingarne*, p. 85. Chance, *George I and the Northern War*, p. 81 claims that Charles XII did not address the Emperor by his titles until late in July.

[6] Luke Schaub to the Foreign Office, July 24, 1715, P.R.O., State Papers, Foreign, German Empire and Hungary, 80/32.

[7] Carlson, *Om Fredsunderhandlingarne*, p. 85.

[8] Chance, *George I and the Northern War*, p. 81.

[9] Sparre to Gyllenborg, July 11 and August 5, 1715, *Handlingar*, X, 342, 345–346.

negotiations with the Emperor were soon broken off; the enemies of Charles XII had successfully wooed the head of the Hapsburgs.[1]

The conduct of Prussia and Hanover toward the Emperor contrasted sharply with that of Sweden. Frederick William I of Prussia took care to send representatives to Brunswick where they professed to have every regard for the constitutional over-lordship of the Empire. At Vienna the Prussian ministers were especially active in presenting flattering professions of submission, and they were aped in this by the envoys of George I. Both the King of Prussia and the Elector of Hanover realized that Imperial assent was necessary for any permanent change of ownership in Sweden's German provinces.[2]

Hanover had more to offer the Emperor than did Prussia. George I as King of England was important to Austria as a counter-balance against the Dutch in the Low Countries. The English navy, moreover, was necessary if Charles VI was to carry out his aims in Italy. It also could be used to frustrate Spanish ambitions on the Italian peninsula. Mutual aspirations led to the signing on June 6, 1716, of the treaty of Westminster. The English sovereign assented to Imperial designs upon Italy in return for Imperial aid for his Electoral plans in the North.[3] Thus did Sweden lose Charles VI, the one man in the Empire who might have been her logical supporter.

So far as Russia was concerned, the Emperor could have accomplished little toward arranging a Russo-Swedish peace settlement, because Russia, outside the Empire, was beyond the Imperial jurisdiction. The French Court was of the opinion that the best policy for Sweden was first to settle affairs in the Empire and then to turn the full force of Swedish arms against the Muscovites.[4] The thinking of Görtz followed a similar pattern. Nevertheless, there were rumors bruited about Europe in January, 1715, that Sweden would make a separate peace

---

[1] Carlson, *Om Fredsunderhandlingarne*, p. 85.

[2] Chance, *George I and the Northern War*, pp. 80–81.

[3] Gyllenborg to Sparre, November 25, 1715, *Handlingar*, X, 275. The various letters of Horatio Walpole, Walpole Letters, MSS., Indiana. *Cf.* Verbal van der Heeren Borssele en Duivenvoorde, Envoyen aan Hof van Engeland, 1715, Rijks-archief, Legatie Archief, 820.

[4] Croissy instructions, *Recueil*, *Suède*, II, 272–273.

with Russia.[1] Giving credence to the diplomatic gossiping was the well-known fact that Russia feared a reopening of her war with Turkey and was taking every precaution to protect herself from a Turkish invasion through Poland.[2] Russia mistrusted Augustus II of Poland. Peter feared that the King of Poland might come to terms with Charles XII, terms that might be to the disadvantage of Russia.[3] Peter also suspected that Poland had designs upon Livonia, a one-time Swedish province currently in Russian hands.[4]

Steps were taken to resolve Swedo-Russian differences. The first moves came through the efforts of Karl, Landgrave of Hesse-Cassel. Hoping to persuade Russia to adjust her differences with Sweden, that Prince had sent an envoy to St. Petersburg, who proposed that one of the sons of the Landgrave marry the Czar's niece, Anna, Duchess of Courland. As the Landgrave was a friend of Sweden and closely tied to that country, such a marriage might have been the means to affect a rapprochement between Peter and Charles XII. At first the Czar was in favor of the union but later decided that the marital knot should not be tied until after a general treaty had been effected, rather than before as had been suggested by the Hesse-Cassel envoy.[5] Any settlement between Russia and Sweden would have necessitated concessions by both sides and neither country during the first few months of 1715 would consider yielding any territory to the other.[6] Peter, moreover, expected great things from the accession of Prussia and Hanover to the Northern Alliance. Consequently the negotiations bore little immediate fruit, but from late 1716 on Peter turned away from his allies and became more open to Swedish overtures.

From Poland, Sweden in 1715 had hopes for great success. Internal affairs in that country were in a wretched condition. The Poles regarded the Saxon troops of Augustus II with a

---

[1] Mackensie to Townshend, January 21, 1715, *Sbornik Imperatorskago Russkago Istorisheskago Obschestva* (St. Petersburg, 1867–1916), LXI, 339. Cited hereafter as *Sbornik*.

[2] Mackensie to Tilson, April 12, 1715, *Ibid.*, LXI, 353.

[3] Mackensie to Townshend, February 4, 1715, *Ibid.*, LXI, 340.

[4] *Ibid.* These rumors and fears were exploited by Görtz late in 1716. Cf. Defoe, *Goertz*, pp. 33–34.

[5] Mackensie to Townshend, February 18, 1715, *Sbornik*, LXI, 353.

[6] Sparre to Gyllenborg, March 11, 1715, *Handligar*, X, 324.

great deal of fear and no little jealousy. Augustus II was maintaining his electoral troops along the Polish frontiers to frustrate any invasion of Poland from Sweden or Turkey, but his Slavic subjects resented the proximity of German soldiers. Later in the year (October 10, 1715) this policy of Augustus II caused a war to break out between Poland's malcontents and the Saxon soldiers of the Polish king.[1] Augustus II in 1715 had failed to reach an agreement with Russia,[2] although on January 1, 1715, he had signed an agreement with George I as Elector of Hanover. This pact was a defensive alliance which protected the provinces of both rulers from the belligerents of the Great Northern War.[3]

Despite this agreement with a prince soon to become an active enemy of Sweden, Augustus II was not adverse to making some sort of an arrangement with Charles XII, especially if he could profit thereby. Early in 1715, Marshal Count Jakob Heinrich von Fleming, the first minister of Augustus II as Elector of Saxony, intimated to Görtz that Augustus II was willing to place Swedo-Polish differences under French mediation. Fleming also said that he would be willing to meet with Görtz so that they might work out terms that might be the basis for a negotiation. Charles XII contrary to his customary policy allowed the Swedish diplomats to make arrangements for such a meeting.[4] It was suggested by some Swedes that the Landgrave of Hesse-Cassel act as a mediator, but little could be expected from that quarter because that prince was of the opinion that Charles XII should achieve an accord with the Danes before undertaking any other negotiations.[5]

During the last days of January, 1715, Görtz and Fleming conferred at Hamburg. The Swedish representative assumed

---

[1] The manifesto of Vardislau Grundzinski, the Marshal of the Polish malcontents, who called themselves the Confederates, *The Historical Register*, III, 18–22.

[2] Mackensie to Townshend, January 28, 1715, *Sbornik*, LXI, 346.

[3] Görtz to Sparre, February 4, 1715, *Handlingar*, VIII, 235. Cf. Chance, *George I and the Northern War*, p. 64.

[4] Görtz to Sparre, January 28, 1715, *Handlingar*, VIII, 232–233. General Stanislaus Poniatowski was sent to Stanislaus Leszczynski to discover what terms the latter would make with Augustus II. Leszczynski had been made King of Poland by the peace of Alt-Ranstädt in 1709, a peace made possible by the soldiers of Charles XII.

[5] Sparre memoir, February 1, 1715, *Handlingar*, VIII, 184.

the position that the Hanoverian-Polish pact was merely defensive,[1] and consequently requested that Saxony not only refrain from overt hostilities against Sweden, but allow Charles XII freedom of action to bring his enemies to terms.[2] Fleming insisted that before anything could be accomplished, Charles XII would have to declare his stand on a general peace. Görtz felt that he could not make any declarations toward a general peace until he had found out French sentiments on the matter.[3] Both the Swedish and Saxon ministers agreed to make a draft of their objectives. On February 4, 1715, Baron Görtz returned to Stralsund.[4]

The concessions that Augustus II was willing to grant were under the circumstances generous. Stanislaus Leszczynski, who had been made King of Poland in 1709 by Charles XII was to be allowed to retain the title of King, but Augustus II refused to accord it to him by a formal act. The Elector of Saxony was willing to pay off all debts connected with the lands of Stanislaus and was even willing to augment the revenues of those lands. The arrangement would have given Charles's puppet king an annual income falling just short of 100,000 écus. Görtz thought that Charles XII would be satisfied with the financial stipulations, but that he would never agree to Fleming's suggestion regarding the Polish succession. Consequently, the proposals went unacted upon. On March 26, the Baron wrote that 'the project had gone up in smoke.'[5]

The failure of Görtz to work out a pacification with Augustus II was not a heavy blow to Swedish diplomacy. By June, 1715, the Saxons were no longer masters of their own fate. If anything happened to separate them from Hanover, they would be forced to accede to Sweden's demands. If Sweden collapsed, they would have had to espouse the Northern Alliance.[6] In the middle of 1715, France tried to

---

[1] Görtz to Sparre, February 4, 1715, Handlingar, VIII, 235: 'L'alliance qu'il [Fleming] vient de conclure avec la cour d'Hanover n'est simplement que defensive'.
[2] *Ibid.*
[3] Görtz to Sparre, January 28, 1715, *Ibid.*, VIII, 232.
[4] Idem to Idem, February 4, 1715, *Ibid.*, VIII, 235.
[5] Görtz to Sparre, March 26, 1715, *Ibid.*, VIII, p. 238. 'Le project dont j'ai fait mention est allé en Fumée puisque les ingrédiens qui m'ont été fournis n'étoient convenable.'
[6] Idem to Idem, June 18, 1715, *Ibid.*, VIII, 247.

arrange a settlement between the two countries. Once more nothing tangible was accomplished.[1]

Swedish diplomatic setbacks in Prussia and England, however, were of much more serious consequence. Anglo-Swedish diplomacy is described in subsequent chapters, but a full treatment of Sweden's diplomacy with Prussia is necessary for an understanding of George's policy toward Sweden. Prussia since the Treaty of Westphalia (1648) had always wanted to possess Swedish Pomerania, especially the city of Stettin. Notwithstanding that desire Prussia—as stated above—did not join the initial plan for the dismembering of Sweden. When those places of interest to Prussia were threatened by the adversaries of Charles XII, the House of Hohenzollern began to consider ways and means to annex the long sought after territories. If Sweden were to lose Pomerania and its urban jewel, Stettin, Prussia did not intend that any nation other than Prussia, should wear it.

The initial acts of the Prussians had been pro-Swedish. In 1713, Frederick I, the old king of Prussia, had endeavored to effect a settlement between Sweden and Saxony, whereby the two countries, having resolved their own differences, would form a coalition designed to drive Peter and his Russian soldiers from the Empire. Charles XII had refused to consider the Prussian proposition because it demanded as a *sine qua non* that the Swedish king leave the Empire and recognize Augustus II as King of Poland.[2] An excellent opportunity was thus lost by Charles XII to unite his country with Prussia.

Görtz himself while working as the minister of the Duke of Holstein-Gottorp, had paved the way for the entrance of Prussia into the Northern imbroglio.[3] On June 10, 1713, a convention had been signed at Hamburg between Count Maurits Vellingk, a Swedish minister, and the Duke Administrator of Holstein, in which the Swedes agreed to place the towns of Wismar and Stettin in the hands of Holstein-Gottorp and some other neutral power for the duration of the war.[4] It was only after he had been assured that Sweden would assent

[1] Croissy to Count Fleming, June 9, 1715, Lamberty, *Mémoires*, IX, 280.
[2] Chance, *George I and the Northern War*, pp. 35–36.
[3] Schuyler, *Peter the Great*, II, 241.
[4] *The Historical Register*, III, 8–14.

to a sequestration of the two towns that the new king of Prussia, Frederick William I, had considered coöperating with Holstein.[1] On June 22, a formal treaty was drawn up by Görtz and Vellingk. This agreement provided that Stettin and Wismar should be garrisoned with an equal number of Prussian and Holstein troops for the duration of the war. When hostilities had ended the two places would be returned to Sweden.[2] In addition, the King of Prussia was to join himself with Great Britain, Hanover, and the United Provinces for the purpose of saving Tönning[3] and other domains of the Duke of Holstein from the Danes. If Hanover and the States delayed, Prussia promised to act with England and to use all possible means to raise the siege of Tönning and restore the lands of the Gottorp house.[4] A secret article in the treaty recognized the succession of the Duke of Holstein to the Swedish throne and promised in return a cession of a part of Swedish Pomerania, which consisted of the City of Stettin and all its dependencies up to the Peene River.[5] Expenses incurred in garrisoning the sequestered regions were to be paid for by Sweden at the end of the war.[6]

The sections dealing with Wismar and Stettin failed to materialize because Count Johan Meyerfield, the commander of the Swedish forces in Pomerania refused to turn over the fortresses.[7] The Duke-Administrator of Holstein suggested taking the places by force, but Frederick William I did not wish to make any moves that could be interpreted by the Swedes as overt acts of aggression.[8] The result was a temporary stalemate.

Such was the state of affairs at the time that Russian and

---

[1] Manifesto of the King of Prussia, Lamberty, *Mémoires*, IX, 284–295. Cf. Dumont, *Corps diplomatique*, VIII, 452–456.

[2] *The Historical Register*, III, 8–14; Lamberty, *Mémoires*, IX, 284–295; Dumont, *Corps diplomatique*, VIII, 456, 552.

[3] Tönning was a town in Holstein which had harbored the army of Marshal Stenbock, a Swedish general. Because of the aid rendered Sweden (Tönning actually had little choice in the matter), Denmark invaded Holstein. For the treaty made between Stenbock and Holstein-Gottorp on January 21, 1713, see Dumont, *Corps diplomatique*, VIII, 318–320.

[4] *Ibid.*, VIII, 392.

[5] Chance, *George I and the Northern War*, p. 36; Schuyler, *Peter the Great*, II, 242n.

[6] Croissy instructions, *Recueil, Suède*, II, 257.

[7] *The Historical Register*, III, 8–14.

[8] Prussian Manifesto, Lamberty, *Mémoires*, IX, 284–295.

Saxon troops burst into Swedish Pomerania. Görtz prevailed upon Meyerfield, who was besieged in the citadel of Stralsund, to accept those arrangements which had been drafted on June 22.[1] At Schwedt, a Brandenburg village on the Oder River, a treaty was drawn up by Count Fleming, the representative of Augustus II, Prince Alexander Menshikov, the commander of the Russian forces in Pomerania, and Frederick William I. Stettin and that portion of Swedish Pomerania situated between the Oder and the Peene Rivers were given in sequestration to Prussia and Holstein-Gottorp. A similar disposition was to be made of Wismar and Stralsund after they had capitulated to the Russian and Saxon armies. After all of Swedish Pomerania had been conquered, Peter and Augustus II promised to withdraw their troops from the area.

Frederick William I on the other hand took it upon himself to prevent Charles XII from utilizing Swedish Pomerania as a base to conduct military campaigns against Poland, Saxony, or Schleswig-Holstein. If force were necessary to fulfill this portion of the treaty, the other signatories pledged themselves to come to the assistance of the Prussian ruler. Chasing the Swedes from Pomerania had been a costly undertaking. Consequently, Frederick William I—always loath to part with money—was forced to advance Russia and Saxony 400,000 *riksdalers*. Thus the latter two countries were reimbursed for their campaign expenditures.[2] Having doled out such a considerable sum of money, the King of Prussia asked Charles XII to allow him to have control of Stettin's revenues.[3]

Prussia, then, acquired Stettin and its dependencies not from Sweden, but from the enemies of Charles XII, and as the result of a payment of 400,000 *riksdalers*. By this expenditure, Frederick William I had taken over a mortgage upon the territory. Because Charles XII refused to refund the money and meet what was in Prussian eyes a just obligation, the creditor held on to the title. In 1720, the ruler of Prussia foreclosed and the territory was formally ceded to him. The Prussian historian, Droysen, considers the treaty of Schwedt one of the most important ever concluded by Prussia. After a long series of setbacks,

---

[1] Schuyler, *Peter the Great*, II, 241ff.; *The Historical Register*, III, 8–14.
[2] Dumont, *Corps diplomatique*, VIII, 407.
[3] Lamberty, *Mémoires*, IX, 284–285.

it represented a decisive step forward. Moreover it laid the basis for the future development of Prussia's northern policy.[1]

The originator of the sequestration plan, the Duke Administrator of Holstein-Gottorp, fared poorly by its results. Prussia was unable to persuade Hanover and England to participate in any joint undertaking to save Tönning from the Danes. Frederick IV of Denmark was furious at the Schwedt negotiations. Faced by a threat of an attack from Prussia, he did agree to refer Danish differences with Holstein-Gottorp to the Congress of Brunswick. In the last analysis it was Russia who called the tune. Peter the Great refused to ratify the treaty of Schwedt if Prussia committed any overt acts against Denmark, with whom Russia was allied. Consequently, Frederick William I abandoned Holstein, although his secretary of state, Rüdiger Heinrich von Ilgen, advocated at the time that the houses of Hohenzollern and Vasa unite to suppress the rising power of the Romanoffs. Sustained by Russia, Frederick IV disregarded his promises concerning Holstein and continued the siege of Tönning, which capitulated on February 7, 1714.[2]

Holstein-Gottorp also was short-changed on the matter of the sequestered area. Frederick William I refused to allow Holstein to furnish Stettin with a garrison equal to that of Prussia on the grounds that the Holstein troops were pro-Swedish.[3] The Prussian king also pointed out that it had been Prussia who had put up the 400,000 *riksdalers* which had made the sequestration possible.[4] Holstein being much the weaker of the two powers had to bow to Prussian wishes. Frederick William I was thus left the sole master of the city.

Charles XII for his part never recognized the Treaty of Schwedt. As soon as he heard about it, he began making representations against it through his ministers at Vienna. Consequently Frederick William I became uneasy and feared that the Swedish monarch would by means of force expel him from the sequestrated areas before he had been reimbursed for his expenditures.[5] The Prussian ruler had exerted a great deal

[1] Johan Gustav Droysen, *Geschichte der Preussischen Politik*, 5 parts in 14 vols. (Leipzig, 1885–1886), part IV, Vol. III, 59. Cited hereafter as Droysen, *Geschichte*.
[2] Chance, *George I and the Northern War*, p. 39.
[3] Croissy instructions, *Recueil, Suède*, II, 258; Lamberty, *Mémoires*, IX, 284–295.
[4] Croissy instructions, *Recueil, Suède*, II, 258.
[5] *The Historical Register*, III, 8–14.

of effort in obtaining the Stettin region. It was only under-
standable that he would take equal measures to keep it. If he
had to lose it, a man as parsimonious as Frederick William I
would make doubly sure that he would not lose his investment
also. Consequently he appealed to Louis XIV in the hope that
French pressure might bring Sweden to an amicable settlement
of the problem. To pacify Charles XII, the Prussian ruler
agreed to help Sweden recover her lost provinces in return for
a cession of Stettin and its environs to the Hohenzollern
domains.[1]

In March, 1714, Louis XIV in response to the Prussian pro-
posal sent to Berlin Count Conrad Alexander de Rottembourg,
a general of Brandenburg descent who was in French service.[2]
At the time French policy was directed to courting Prussia
against Austria and Hanover. Consequently, French support of
Prussian pretensions in Swedish Pomerania was dictated by
diplomacy. Rottembourg, therefore, was instructed to win
Charles XII over to an agreement of the Schwedt settlement.
If Rottembourg succeeded, Versailles was ready to guarantee
Stettin and its contingent territory to Prussia. Fully cognizant
of the economic and strategic value of Stettin, the French
Ministry for Foreign Affairs hoped that Sweden could be
reconciled to its loss by the promise of Prussian aid in the
restoration of other lost Swedish provinces. In exchange for
Stettin, Prussia would exert pressure upon Peter the Great and
persuade him to relinquish St. Petersburg and the Baltic Provinces. The French hoped that the growing Prussian distrust of
Russia would lead to Prussian acquiescence in such a plan.
Prussia had to commence negotiating with Russia before
France would sign a guarantee of Stettin with Frederick William I. Nevertheless Rottembourg was empowered to work for
such an alliance even though Prussian diplomacy might be
unable to move Peter the Great to surrender his conquests. In
order to grease the diplomatic wheels, Rottembourg was permitted to offer pensions to the different Prussian ministers.[3] As

---

[1] Croissy instructions, *Recueil, Suède*, II, 258.

[2] Chance, *George I and the Northern War*, p. 44.

[3] Rottembourg instructions, March 11, 1714, *Recueil des instructions données aux
ambassadeurs et ministres de France depuis les traités de Westphalie jusqu'a la revolution
française*, A. Waddington (ed.), vol. XVI, *Prusse* (1901), 292ff. Cited hereafter as
Recueil, Prusse.

an additional means of insuring success, Louis XIV suggested that Baron Erik Sparre, the Swedish minister at Paris, go with Rottembourg to Berlin. Sparre after the conclusion of the negotiations in Prussia would then continue on to Turkey to enlighten Charles XII as to what had transpired.[1]

Like so many efforts to extricate Charles XII, the Rottembourg mission of mediation came too late. By the time that he arrived in Berlin, Frederick William I had been forced by events to adopt an anti-Swedish policy. Peter the Great meanwhile had been caressing 'Oberschenck' von Schlippenbach, the Prussian minister at St. Petersburg. After the representative of Frederick William I had been sufficiently softened up, Peter proposed a treaty in which Prussia and Russia would mutually guarantee the lands they had taken from Sweden. On June 12, 1714, a treaty was drafted which assured Ingria, Carelia, and Esthonia with the ports of Viborg, Narva, and Reval to the Czar and Stettin and its dependencies to Prussia. The combined efforts of Görtz, Sparre, and the British, French and Swedish ministers at Berlin to block the consummation of the treaty proved fruitless.[2] Görtz was expelled with contempt from the Prussian court, and all hopes of Prussian intervention in the Dano-Holstein dispute were dashed to the ground.[3] Frederick William I had joined Sweden's foes saying, 'I may fare ill. I don't mind; the Swedes must clear out of Germany.'[4]

The return of Charles XII to Stralsund complicated the machinations of the Prussian king, as it did all of the despoilers of Sweden.[5] Prussia was so located that should Charles XII have decided to thrust his army into Saxony, the domains of Frederick William I stood to become a theater of military operations. To prevent such a circumstance from happening, the Prussian ruler mobilized his armed forces.[6] Charles on the other hand demanded the immediate return of Stettin and insisted that Prussia by holding the area was violating sundry treaties of alliance that Prussia and Sweden in the past had concluded

[1] Croissy instructions, *Recueil, Suède*, II, 259.
[2] Chance, *George I and the Northern War*, p. 45.
[3] Droysen, *Geschichte*, Part IV, vol. II, 94.
[4] Michael, *England under George I*, I, 287.
[5] Croissy instructions, *Recueil, Suède*, II, 260: 'Les affaires dans le Nord pirirent une nouvelle face.'
[6] *Ibid.*, p. 259.

with each other.[1] The Prussian king refused to heed the remonstrances of Charles XII and claimed that his hands were tied by his treaty obligations with Peter and Augustus II. To afford Sweden Pomerania as a base for Charles XII to wage war in the Empire was in Prussian eyes a direct violation of the Schwedt agreement. The one condition always necessary before Pomerania could be returned to Sweden—the repayment of the 400,000 *riksdalers*—was always ignored by Sweden.[2]

During the first few months of 1715, negotiations between Prussia and Sweden made no progress whatsoever. Charles XII complicated the situation by maintaining an absolute silence on all diplomatic matters revolving around Sweden's relations with Prussia or with the Empire.[3] Görtz was quite sure that Sweden could make no moves without French aid and hopefully thought that Charles XII would accede to French and Austrian mediation if only to reaffirm Franco-Swedish friendship.[4] Prussia too was sanguine and counted upon French mediation to settle the northern question at least so far as Frederick William I was implicated in it.[5]

The friends of Sweden although sorely tried by the conduct of Charles XII continued to work on Sweden's behalf. The Landgrave of Hesse-Cassel and Count Rottembourg pooled their energies and resources and attempted to find a way by which the diplomatic impasse might be broken. The former suggested that Prussia turn Stettin over to him, and promised to reimburse Prussia for the sum that it had advanced at Schwedt. Charles XII for his part was to promise to refrain from using the controversial city as a base of operation.[6] Prussia rejected the Landgrave's proposal on the ground that to accept it would be to break faith with Russia and Poland. Such an act in Hohenzollern eyes would have been the same as returning Stettin to Sweden for the son of the Landgrave was betrothed to the sister of the Swedish king. If Stettin were in

[1] *Ibid.*, pp. 260–261.
[2] Prussian Manifesto, Lamberty, *Mémoires*, IX, 284–295.
[3] Görtz to Sparre, February 4, 1715, *Handlingar*, VIII, 236: 'Pour moi je crois qu'il s'est propose de ne faire absolument rien sans conference avec la France.'
[4] *Ibid.*
[5] Sehestedt to Westphal, March 26, 1715, Correspondence of George von Westphal, Danish Rigsarkiv, Copenhagen, T.K.U.A., Russland C 122. Hereafter cited as Westphal Correspondence.
[6] Lamberty, *Mémoires*, IX, 268.

the custody of Hesse-Cassel, Charles XII would be sure to employ the strategic location of the city in his military ventures against Russia and Poland. The only concession that Prussia made toward the Hesse-Cassel overture was to make an offer to mediate a general northern pacification.[1]

The French government well knew that Prussia would endeavor to retain Stettin as long as possible. It also felt that any compromise between Frederick William I and Charles XII would be impossible to achieve. Something more drastic had to be hazarded. The French proposed that Stettin after Frederick William I had received a refund of his outlay be turned over to some neutral power not so suspect to Sweden as Prussia was.[2] Prussia, however, did not deem this proposition from France worth answering. Louis XIV, therefore, decided to send Henri Francois, comte de Croissy to Frederick William I in a desperate attempt to compass some sort of a settlement.

Charles XII by refusing to undertake any sort of negotiation with Prussia lost an excellent opportunity to preserve the bulk of his German possessions and to decrease the number of his enemies.[3] Some small concessions on the part of Sweden might have resulted in the preservation of much Swedish territory. Droysen, however, defends the policy of the Swedish king by pointing out that the most valuable asset of Sweden was the prestige of her sovereign. By bowing to Frederick William I that prestige would have been seriously impaired. Droysen was of the opinion that a bold stroke by Swedish arms could still save the situation for Charles XII.[4] There can be little doubt that Droysen like many of the contemporaries of Charles XII overestimated the striking capacity of the Swedish forces. Yet Charles XII did control the Baltic until the advent of the British squadron in 1715. Moreover the Swedish ruler was a gambler at heart and had—and justifiably so—great faith in his own abilities as a general. Consequently the advice of his diplomats went unheeded. On February 23, 1715, he took a step which later proved to be disastrous. He ejected a handful of Prussian troops from the island of Wolgast.[5]

[1] Croissy instructions, *Recueil, Suède,* II, 261–262.
[2] *Ibid.,* II, 262.
[3] Chance, *George I and the Northern War,* p. 64.
[4] Droysen, *Geschichte,* Part IV, Vol. II, 113.
[5] Lamberty, *Mémoires,* IX, 269. An officer and twelve soldiers were ejected.

Frederick William I was furious when he was informed about the Wolgast affair. Furthermore he was in a position to give vent to his passion, for he had just signed a treaty with Augustus II which militarily strengthened his hand.[1] There was talk in Prussia of an immediate declaration of war, and Rottembourg had his hands full trying to ease the tension that existed. Prussia's ruler refused to even consider French mediation until Wolgast was returned to him. Such a condition on the surface was a flat rejection of French good offices, but the Prussian court informed all foreign ministers that it had accepted the good offices of France, provided of course that the Emperor approved. There was little likelihood, however, of Imperial complaisance. Charles VI categorically stated that he disliked foreigners concerning themselves in affairs relating to the Empire, and that he had the sole prerogative to be arbiter of all Imperial disputes.[2]

After Rottembourg's attempts at appeasing Prussia and Sweden, events moved rapidly. Prussian troops moved into Usedom, and on April 21, Charles XII invaded the island and made himself master of it.[3] Thereupon Frederick William's soldiers at Stettin disarmed everyone who was not a Prussian and the Prussian ruler expelled Baron Karl Gustav von Frisendorff, the Swedish minister to Berlin. The dismissal of Frisendorff from the Hohenzollern capital on April 26 marked the formal commencement of hostilities between Prussia and Sweden.[4] The Prussian ruler in his war manifesto accused his Swedish brother monarch of assaulting Wolgast and Usedom and employing Swedish armed vessels on the Peene River in order to blockade Stettin.[5] On the next day (April 27, 1715) Prussia and Hanover concluded a treaty directed against Sweden.[6] This pact was ratified by Prussia on May 17, the month in which Prussian troops recaptured Usedom Island.[7] By that time Frederick William I had become firmly convinced that

[1] Chance, *George I and the Northern War*, p. 64. The treaty was made February 3, 1715. On the same day, Frederick William I signed a treaty with Russia.
[2] Lamberty, *Mémoires*, IX, 269.
[3] Charles XII to Hedvig Eleanora, April 30, 1715, *Egenhändiga Bref*, p. 9.
[4] *The Historical Register*, III, 8–14.
[5] Prussian Manifesto, Lamberty, *Mémoires*, IX, 284–295.
[6] Chance, *George I and the Northern War*, p. 69.
[7] Syveton, 'L'erreur de Görtz,' IX, 433.

only through military pressure could Charles XII be brought to make any concessions or be forced to make peace within the Empire.[1] Such was the situation when Croissy arrived at Berlin to mediate Swedo-Prussian differences. The French envoy made his diplomatic entry at a time when the animosities long smoldering had burst forth into a full scale conflagration.

Croissy, brother to the Marquis de Torcy,[2] was a man after the heart of the Swedish king.[3] In this respect, he was very similar to Jefferyes, the English minister who had accompanied Charles XII through much of his campaigning in Central and Eastern Europe.[4] Versailles had figured that a soldier could perhaps accomplish more with Charles XII than could a professional diplomatist. For this reason Croissy had been selected for the post. The new mediator was the type who could accompany the Swedish ruler on his long madcap rides and his strenuous and hazardous military adventures.

Croissy's instructions were dated April 23, 1715. While en route to Berlin, he was to visit the Landgrave of Hesse-Cassel and inform him as to the tenor of the French plans concerning Stettin. Sweden could not allow the number of her enemies to increase. Charles XII had to be convinced that he could not enter the Empire. Such an act on his part would cause the Great Northern War to break out with renewed vigor. Croissy, however, was to remain silent on the matter of subsidies for Sweden.

From Hesse-Cassel, Croissy was to continue his journey to Berlin. There he was to persuade Frederick William I that it was contrary to Prussia's interest for him to throw in his lot with the enemies of Charles XII. Such a step could only lead to Prussia's becoming a war theater, something that Prussia

[1] Frederick William I to the Emperor Charles VI, July 29, 1715, *Handlingar*, VIII, 240.

[2] Jean Baptiste Colbert, Marquis de Torcy (1665–1746), after a varied career in foreign affairs had become French secretary of state and grand treasurer of state. He served at that post from the beginning of the War of the Spanish Succession up to the death of Louis XIV. See Michaud, *Biographie Universelle*, VIII, 561–562.

[3] See the note by Carl Bågenholm in *H.R.S.H.*, p. 53 and Görtz to Sparre, June 18, 1715, *Handligar*, VIII, 247.

[4] For a lucid and fascinating account of the adventures of Jefferyes with Charles XII see Ragnhild Hatton (ed.), *Captain James Jefferyes' Letters from the Swedish Army, 1707–1709*, in *Historiska Handlingar*, Del. 35:1 (Stockholm, 1954).

should avert at all costs. What spoils that Prussia might realize by joining the Northern Alliance, would be but poor compensation if the Mark of Brandenburg became despoiled by warring armies before Charles XII could be brought to terms. The French minister was to emphasize this latter point by pointing out that Brandenburg would be the first place invaded by the Swedish king, for Charles had a well-known custom of dealing first with those enemies who had once been his allies. If Prussia adopted the propositions that had been advanced by the Landgrave of Hesse-Cassel, Prussia would show herself to be extremely generous and could perhaps expect an opportunity to mediate the conflict between Poland and Sweden. Croissy was also to hint that the object of his mission was to effect a peace between Poland, Sweden and Prussia.

Having won Prussia over, Croissy was to continue on to the camp of the Swedish king at Stralsund. There he was to complete the circle of this ambitious French mediation scheme. Croissy was to explain that the best expedient to prevent Bremen and Verden from becoming a possession of either Denmark or Hanover was to reach an agreement with the King of Prussia. To effect such a settlement, the French minister was to suggest that Charles XII allow some prince other than Frederick William I to occupy Stettin in sequestration until a final pacification of the North was achieved. Under such a plan, Prussia was to be paid the money that she had given to Russia and Saxony.[1]

The French plan involved a good deal of wishful thinking on the part of Versailles. The men around Louis XIV were of the opinion that Charles XII, although apparently highly incensed at Prussia, could be induced to listen to peace overtures, which could only place him in a better position to resist his enemies.[2] This anticipation of false hope had been strengthened at Hamburg where Croissy had been informed by a high ranking Swedish officer that the cession of Stettin would not stand in the way of a general peace settlement.[3] Thus it was with great expectations that the Count de Croissy arrived at Berlin. He entered the city on May 2, 1715, accompanied by

---

[1] Croissy instructions, *Recueil, Suède*, II, 266–277.
[2] *Ibid.*
[3] D'Huxelles to Tessé, May 20, 1717, *Sbornik*, XXXIV, 540.

Poussin the French Minister to Hamburg.[1] The two diplomats were to coöperate with Count Rottembourg to forestall any hostile action on the part of Frederick William I that might be directed against the Swedish king.[2] Not only was Croissy too late to assist Sweden, but the hopes that he entertained and his character actually acted to the detriment of Charles XII.

Croissy, who disliked ceremony, on the day after his arrival had an interview with Frederick William's privy-councillor, Marquis Ludwig von Printz. On May 5 he left with Poussin and Rottembourg to see the Prussian king who was with his army. The French delegation reached the Prussian camp on the seventh but it was not until the tenth that they were granted an audience with Frederick William. In honor of his guests the Prussian ruler typically paraded his soldiers.[3] In the course of conversation, Croissy discovered that Prussia would make peace with Sweden only if Charles XII returned Usedom, Wolgast, and the territory at the mouth of the Peene river. Frederick William I pointed out to his French visitors that Prussia could easily obtain all her aims from Russia, because Russia would rather have anyone but Sweden in possession of Swedish Pomerania.[4]

After his interview with the Prussian ruler, Croissy took himself to Stralsund where he soon became an enthusiastic admirer of the Swedish king. So pro-Swedish did he become because of his hero-worship of Charles XII that he began to bend his efforts not towards mediating the Prusso-Swedish quarrel, but rather to assisting Charles XII in his plans to revenge himself upon his enemies.[5] He began to neglect his diplomatic duties, preferring to spend his time riding with the Swedish king and inspecting the elaborate preparations that Charles had devised to protect Stralsund.[6] His fertile imagination worked overtime in conjuring up schemes by which Charles XII and Sweden might be saved. Among other projects, he tried to interest Charles XII in the cause of James Stuart, the pretender to the English throne. For the moment, however, the Swedish ruler

---

[1] Lamberty, *Mémoires*, IX, 274.
[2] Croissy instructions, *Recueil, Suède*, II, 266–277.
[3] Lamberty, *Mémoires*, IX, 274.
[4] *Ibid.*
[5] Chance, *George I and the Northern War*, p. 78.
[6] Lamberty, *Mémoires*, IX, 275–276.

was not interested in assisting a Catholic pretender to the throne of Britain. Eventually, however, Swedo-Jacobite negotiations were to play an important role in Anglo-Swedish relations.

While Croissy was royally being entertained by his Swedish host, Prussian and Swedish troops were making sorties against one another.[1] Prodded by events, the French diplomat bestirred himself and wrote Ilgen, asking him to help arrange a peaceful settlement. In his note to promote peace, Croissy, with little subtlety and less tact, informed the Prussian minister as to the impregnability of the Stralsund defenses.[2] On May 24, he received his answer. Frederick William I sarcastically thanked Croissy for his information concerning the strength of Stralsund's fortifications, and claimed that Charles's thoughts constantly tended toward war rather than peace. Consequently, the Prussian king considered it impossible to reach any accord with Sweden. If Charles XII promised to abide by the stipulations of the Treaty of Schwedt, Prussia would be willing to come to terms with him. The articles signed at Schwedt and only those articles were the conditions upon which Prussia would consent to negotiate.[3]

After an exchange of letters, Croissy on June 9 drafted a most interesting letter. He insisted that Prussia could not oppose Swedish seizure of Usedom because the Schwedt agreement had already been abrogated by the Prussian refusal to allow Holstein to maintain a garrison in the area equal to that of Prussia. Prussia, moreover, had no right to place troops in the open country surrounding the city. The Schwedt convention limited the Prussian garrison to Stettin proper. Because of Prussian violations of the Schwedt treaty Charles XII had been forced to act. Croissy, therefore, accused Prussia of opening hostilities between Sweden and Prussia, a crime that heretofore Frederick William I had leveled against Charles XII.[4]

Ilgen replied to the Croissy note on the thirteenth. He informed Croissy that Wolgast and Usedom had been included in the original sequestration, and that the relative strength of

---

[1] *Ibid.*, IX, 275.
[2] Croissy to Ilgen, May 22, 1715, *The Historical Register*, II, 245–250.
[3] Ilgen to Croissy, May 24, 1715, *Ibid.*
[4] Croissy to Ilgen, June 13, 1715, Lamberty, *Mémoires*, IX, 279.

Holstein and Prussian troops in the Stettin garrison had been arrived at with Holstein's approval.[1] The Prussian minister furthermore wrote that Stettin could not be returned even if Charles XII promised not to enter Saxony or Poland because the word of the Swedish king was not to be depended on. The latter statement showed the true hand of Prussia, because Charles XII had the reputation of being the most trustworthy monarch in Europe. Not only did it make Croissy's blood boil, but it made any peaceful settlement between Charles and Frederick William I impossible.[2] The Swedish monarch would stand no insults so far as his personal honor was concerned. The negotiations between Croissy and Ilgen dragged on throughout the last part of 1715, but Sweden and Prussia had drifted widely apart.[3] Charles's policy toward Prussia and his stubbornness had added another adversary to Sweden's already large list of foes. Croissy had failed completely in his mission and the death of Louis XIV in September, 1715, would bring into power in France a group of ministers who were less pro-Swedish.[4]

The next enemy that Sweden added was Hanover. This in itself would have been detrimental to Sweden because Hanover was one of the more important states in the Empire. In the present state of affairs, it was disastrous because George Augustus, Elector of Hanover, was also King of England. Once that George became embroiled in the northern conflict, it became a matter of conjecture as to whether Charles XII could keep his supply lanes open to Stralsund, because George I as King of England might bring the resources of the British fleet to aid him in his German politics. To accomplish that, George I would have to win his subjects around to his way of thinking. As Hanoverian and British policy toward Sweden was so closely interwoven, it will be considered more carefully in a later chapter. Suffice to say, that Hanover signed a series of treaties with Poland, Denmark, Prussia, and Russia and by early May had become a full-fledged member of the Northern

---

[1] Ilgen to Croissy, June 13, 1715, *Ibid.*, IX, 281–282.
[2] Croissy to Ilgen, June 19, 1715, *The Historical Register*, II, 259ff.
[3] Various letters between Croissy and Ilgen, Lamberty, *Mémoires*, IX, 309–311. See also Frederick William I to the Emperor, July 29, 1715, *Handlingar*, VIII, 240.
[4] Syveton, 'L'erreur de Görtz,' IX, 433.

Alliance. By these treaties George I committed himself as Elector to contribute ground troops to assist in expelling Sweden from the Empire, and secretly promised as King of England that the British navy would be employed to cut Stralsund off from Sweden.[1]

Swedish diplomacy in 1715 did win some victories although they were shallow if one compares them with the losses. The small diplomatic gains that Sweden made with France and Spain were poor compensation for the addition of two new enemies. Baron Eric Sparre had returned to France in December, 1714, with instructions to float a loan of two million *riksdalers* from France. The sum to be solicited was to be a subsidy with Charles XII mortgaging the Duchy of Zweibrücken. Sweden needed the money to raise a war force of 70,000 men which could be hired from the various German princes. At the time that Sparre requested the loan, he also asked France to guarantee the treaties of Nimwegen and Westphalia. Thus France would assure Sweden of her Imperial holdings.[2]

During the early months of 1715, France and Sweden had much in common. They were both struggling to maintain possessions in the Empire and thus had a mutual interest in the preservation of each other's territory. Louis XIV and his foreign minister, the Marquis de Torcy, were as one in the opinion that a strong Sweden was absolutely necessary if French influence in the North were to be continued. The two French leaders, however, also felt that it would be impossible to reconstruct the Baltic empire of Charles XII as it had existed at the turn of the century. The Russian victories had been a too serious blow to Swedish prestige to make a return to the status quo possible. As the French viewed the situation, the great problem was to determine what Sweden would have to sacrifice in order to hold the rest of her possessions. French interests dictated that Sweden be persuaded to cede her Baltic provinces to Russia and continue her footholds in the Germanies. Sweden then, as had been true since the time of Gustavus Adolphus and Richelieu, could be utilized by France to counterbalance

---

[1] Dumont, *Corps diplomatique*, VII has the texts of the treaties. Cf. Chance, *George I, and the Northern War*, pp. 58–73 for a more detailed discussion of these negotiations.

[2] Instructions to Sparre, December 14, 1714, Lamberty, *Mémoires*, IX, 79.

Austria.[1] Sweden too had great hopes from France. After all, France had bailed Sweden out after Sweden had lost Pomerania to Prussia during the wars of Louis XIV. The importance that Sweden placed upon Sparre's mission was well shown in a letter from Görtz to Sparre dated January 28, 1715, in which the former informed the Swedish minister to France that he had an excellent opportunity to play the role of saviour to the Swedish nation.[2]

A week earlier (January 21, 1715) Sparre had presented a memoir to the French government asking for 200,000 *écus* to aid Swedish troops in Pomerania and for the money offered to mortgage the Duchy of Zweibrücken and the County of Veldentz. Sparre pointed out that the money would enable Charles XII to hire mercenaries, and asserted that Charles XII was willing to make a treaty with France which would guarantee the treaties of Westphalia and Ryswick. De Torcy inquired as to the war objectives of Sweden and requested information about the possibilities of Swedish peace negotiations with Denmark, Russia, Poland, and the Empire. Sparre said that Charles XII would demand a restoration of the House of Holstein before he would negotiate with Denmark and demanded as a *sine qua non* the return of his Baltic provinces before any accord could be reached with Russia. Charles XII, so Sparre insisted, had expressed a willingness to have all of his troubles considered at a general peace congress at which France and the Empire would be the mediators. Charles XII, however, remained firm in his determination that the meeting be held at some place other than Brunswick.[3]

The Swedish envoy on February 2 gave the French Court additional reasons why assisting Sweden would be to the advantage of France. If Charles XII could have the money, he could recruit at once, 23,000 troops from various German princes.[4] With such a force it would be a simple task for Charles

---

[1] Syveton, 'L'erreur de Görtz,' IX, 421–422.
[2] Görtz to Sparre, January 28, 1715, *Handlingar*, VIII, 232. Cf. Görtz to Sparre, February 4, 1715, *Ibid.*, p. 237. 'Enfin Mon cher Baron, le salut de votre patrie de la notre est entre nos mains.'
[3] Sparre mémoire, January 21, 1715, *Ibid.*, VIII, 178–184.
[4] Sparre mémoire, February 2, 1715, *Ibid.*, VIII, 186–187. In this document Sparre drew up a list of the various German princes who would furnish Sweden with troops and gave the expected size of each contingent. He set the number at

to terminate the Great Northern War. If Louis XIV did not come to the support of Sweden, Charles XII would through necessity be forced to turn to the enemies of France. Thus Louis XIV would lose the best means at his disposal to curb the power of the Emperor. Sparre intimated that if Sweden collapsed she would drag her friends down with her. If compelled to capitulate, Sweden would be forced to grant the Maritime Nations favorable trade concessions, and as a result the commerce of France and other nations would suffer. He reiterated that Charles XII, because of the great esteem he had for Louis XIV, would consent to French and Imperial mediation.[1]

By the end of the month, Sparre despaired of reaching any agreement with France. A primary reason for his difficulties was the delay he experienced in his communications. Every time that he wrote Stralsund asking for additional information on French affairs, the time of usefulness for the reply was past before the ministers around the King at Stralsund answered. Lack of information on such matters as Prussia's attitude toward Sweden and conversely, the terms on which Sweden would negotiate with Poland, etc., made it almost impossible for Sparre to reply to De Torcy's repeated questions.[2] Also impatiently awaited by Sparre, was an answer to the French demand that Sweden effect a rapprochement with Austria.[3] Sparre had other troubles in addition to lack of coöperation from home. Baron Friedrich Ernst von Kniphausen, the Prussian agent at Paris, was untiring in his efforts to place obstacles in the way of Sparre's attempts to bring about a Franco-Swedish agreement.[4]

In spite of the heavy odds against him, Sparre in part accomplished his ends. On April 3, 1715, a treaty was signed between France and Sweden which promised Sweden a yearly

[1] *Ibid.*
[2] Sparre to Vellingk, March 15, 1715, *Ibid.*, VIII, 198.
[3] *Ibid.*
[4] Idem to idem, February 2, 1715, *Ibid.*, VIII, 195.

less than one-half of the first hopes and thus shows that he realized Sweden's worsening position.

subsidy of 600,000 *riksdalers*.[1] Each party guaranteed the other's possessions on the basis of former treaties; namely those of Westphalia, Nimwegen, Ryswick, Baden, and Oliva. The agreement is significant in the fact that there were specific clauses as to what would transpire in the Empire (especially on the matter of Holstein). Yet nothing specific was mentioned regarding peace between Sweden and Russia and Poland.[2] Sparre was most happy with the outcome of his labors and was of the opinion that Sweden had gained a great deal by the treaty. There were no articles in it that were detrimental to Sweden. He also thought that French mediation of the Northern War would give occasion for France to promote the Swedish retention of Swedish Pomerania.[3] France throughout the remainder of 1715 attempted to mediate between Sweden and Prussia. As Sweden added more enemies, the treaty became somewhat embarrassing to France, who received nothing from the treaty except a promise that should France be attacked, Sweden would make a diversion on her behalf in the Empire, or by rendering direct military assistance.[4] Sweden by increasing the number of her opponents rendered negatory those clauses in the treaty relating to Swedish aid for France. She could not help herself, let alone help others.

Such was the background of Swedish diplomacy as George I attempted to implicate England in his Baltic adventure. Charles XII hurt his country terribly in 1715 by his deficiencies in diplomacy, his refusal to cede parts of his territory in order to save other portions, and his long periods of silence. His diplomatic bunglings were even more serious when he antagonized England into an anti-Swedish policy. As England moved against Sweden, her ally, the States General, would in part at least reluctantly follow suit. Before the story of Anglo-Swedish relations can be continued, a brief survey of Danish diplomacy in

---

[1] Sparre to Gyllenborg, Palmquist, *et al.*, May 6, 1715, *Ibid.*, X, 525–526. Carlson, *Om Fredsunderhandlingarne*, p. 80. Axelson, *Bidrag till kännedom om Sveriges tillstånd*, p. 169 points out that by 1719 only 450,000 *riksdaler* had been paid to Sweden by France. See also Nordmann, *La Crise du Nord*, p. 28–29.

[2] Syveton, 'L'erreur de Görtz,' IX, 424.

[3] *Ibid.*

[4] Sparre to Palmquist, May 6, 1715, *Handlingar*, X, 525–526. Sweden was to supply 5,000 infantry and 2,700 horse or eight warships if she did not make a diversion.

the period is perhaps necessary; for it was from Denmark that George I received Bremen and Verden.

The return of Charles XII had placed the Danes in an extremely precarious position.[1] Denmark had suffered heavily because of the long drawn out war, and her finances in 1715, were so unstable that Frederick IV, King of Denmark, considered pawning his Swedish conquests in order to raise sufficient funds to outfit his fleet for sea.[2] He offered the island of Rügen and Stralsund after their capture to Prussia if Frederick William I would advance him a sum adequate to meet Danish naval expenditures. The Danes felt that if a speedy termination of the Northern War were not forthcoming, Denmark would be unable to continue the struggle.[3] The heavy weight of the war burden was taxing the Danish people beyond their ability to pay.[4]

Denmark had more to fear from the returning military genius than did the other members of the Northern Alliance, because of the proximity of Denmark to Sweden,[5] and undoubtedly the inhabitants of Zealand remembered only too well the Swedish invasion of that island in 1700.[6] Consequently, it was of utmost importance for Denmark to bring Charles XII to terms as soon as possible.[7] To prevent Denmark from being attacked from two sides it was vitally necessary for Denmark to have all Swedish troops expelled from the Empire.[8] To accomplish such objectives, Frederick IV had a fleet barely strong enough to oppose the naval units of Sweden,[9] and an army of fifty-six battalions, which, unfortunately for Denmark, consisted

---

[1] Edward Holm, 'Studier til den Nordiske Krigs Historie,' (Dansk) *Historisk Tidsskrift*, Series V, Vols. 3, 7 (Copenhagen, 1881–1882), *passim*. Cited hereafter as Holm 'Studier.'

[2] Syveton, 'L'erreur de Görtz,' IX, 429; Droysen, *Geschichte*, Part IV, Vol. II, 147.

[3] *Ibid.*

[4] Wibe to Sehestedt, March 7, 1715, Westphal Correspondence, Rigsarkiv, T.K.U.A., Russland C 122.

[5] Croissy Instructions, *Recueil, Suède*, II, 269.

[6] *Danmarks Riges Historie*, John Steenstrup, Kr. Erslev, A. Heise, V. Mollerup, J. A. Fredericia, E. Holm, et A. Jörgenson authors, 8 vols. in 6 (Copenhagen, 1896–1907), V, 14. Hereafter cited as *D.R.H.*

[7] Holm, 'Studier,' Series V, Vol. III, 7.

[8] Wibe to Sehestedt, March 7, 1715, Westphal Correspondence, Rigsarkiv, T.K.U.A., Russland C 122.

[9] *Ibid.*

mostly of inexperienced militia.¹ Although this army was stronger than the Danish army had been in 1712 when it had successfully withstood the Swedish in Pomerania, the return of the Swedish monarch altered the situation. In all of Denmark there was no general of sufficient military skill to pit himself against the military genius of Charles XII.²

Unable to cope with the Swedes without assistance, the Danes throughout 1715 directed their diplomacy with a view toward winning new and active allies. Their diplomatic policy not astute in itself, was aided and abetted by the blunders of Charles XII. As has been stated above, it was due more to the diplomatic *faux pas* of Sweden's king than to any statesmanlike coups by Danish diplomats, that Prussia and Hanover were in 1715 won over to the side of Frederick IV.

As the year opened, Denmark had two allies, Russia and Saxony. On June 28, 1709, Frederick IV had concluded an alliance with Augustus II of Saxony, which was directed against Sweden³ although Denmark at the time was not at war with that country. On October 22 of the same year an alliance had been signed between the Czar of all the Russias and the King of the Danes. That pact had brought Denmark back into the northern conflagration⁴ as an active participant. Jackal-like, the Danes hoped to feed off the Swedish carcass that the Russian Bear had laid low.

The first new ally that the Danes acquired after Charles's return was Brandenburg-Prussia. Up to 1715, the relations between Denmark and Prussia had been anything but friendly because of the pro-Swedish attitude that had been maintained by the Prussian court. Moreover, Frederick William I and Frederick IV had disagreed over the sequestration of Stettin. The latter was especially incensed over the clause in the treaty of Schwedt which had guaranteed the political and territorial integrity of the House of Holstein.⁵ It will be recalled that only pressure from Russia had prevented the Prussian foreign secretary Ilgen from persuading Frederick William I to employ force in order to expel the Danish troops from the city of

¹ Syveton, 'L'erreur de Görtz,' IX, 428.
² Holm, 'Studier,' Series V, Vol. III, 7.
³ *D.R.H.*, V, 29.
⁴ *Ibid.*, p. 35.
⁵ See above.

Tönning. The Danish king refused to consider the Holstein question on any other footing than it be settled only after the culmination of a general peace with Sweden and insisted upon his right to retain possession of the duchy until a final settlement of the Northern War had been achieved. The Danes defended this *sine qua non* by claiming that it would be impossible for them to continue the war against Sweden without control of the duchy. With some justification, they explained their entire policy toward Holstein by charging that the House of Holstein-Gottorp throughout the entire Northern War had been hostile and faithless to Denmark and that they had no alternative but to consider the Gottorp House as an open enemy.[1]

In March, General Franz Joachim Dewitz, the Danish plenipotentiary in charge of the Prussian negotiations, despaired of reaching any agreement with the Prussian court,[2] which insisted that Denmark make an alliance with England-Hanover before it attempted to reach an accord with Prussia.[3] The rapid deterioration of Swedish-Prussian relations by the next month had appreciably altered the situation. Two months later, May 17, 1715, a treaty was concluded between the crowns of Denmark and Prussia,[4] and on Thursday morning, May 23, Dewitz arrived at the Danish camp before Stralsund with the treaty. On the next day, Councillor of Justice von Holtz left for Berlin to assist General Bendix Meyer in making the exchange of ratifications.[5] This was accomplished on May 30.[6]

The agreement guaranteed to Prussia, Usedom, Wolgast, and the Stettin district up to the Peene River, and the Danish king bound himself to enforce this guarantee by a fighting force of 6,000 soldiers plus 2,000 calvarymen or dragoons. Denmark also pledged to assist Prussia if she were attacked by Sweden or by Sweden's ally, France. In return Frederick William I

---

[1] Frederick IV to Westphal, April 2, 1716; Sehestedt to Westphal, March 30, 1715, Westphal Correspondence, Rigsarkiv, T.K.U.A., Russland C 122.

[2] Dewitz to Frederick IV, March 21, 1715, *Ibid.*

[3] Frederick IV to Peter, March 16, 1715, *Ibid.*

[4] Chance, *George I and the Northern War*, p. 69; cf. Droysen, *Geschichte*, Part IV, Vol. II, 130.

[5] Holstein to Westphal, May 27, 1715, Westphal Correspondence, Rigsarkiv, T.K.U.A., Russland C 122. Holm claims that General Dewitz was the one who made the exchange of ratifications with Meyer, Holm, 'Studier,' Series V, Vol. III, 150.

[6] Holm, 'Studier,' Series V, Vol. III, 150.

guaranteed to Denmark Hither Pomerania (*Vor-Pommern*) includ-ing the island of Rügen from the Baltic to the Peene. Prussia promised to assist Frederick IV with 6,000 men if Denmark were attacked by the Swedes in Schleswig, Holstein, Jylland, Oldenborg and Delmenhorst. Both signatories agreed to have twenty battalions in the field by June in order to attack the Swedes at Stralsund and Rügen. Prussia in addition, promised to furnish at her own cost transport ships for the projected attack. Denmark won her point as to the Holstein question, which was to be referred to the Congress of Brunswick. Under no conditions whatsoever was the head of the Gottorp house to be left with his dominions in Holstein if he succeeded to the Swedish crown.[1]

The treaty with Prussia did not significantly better the diplo-matic position of Denmark, because Frederick William I was not an ally to be implicitly trusted. Her Russian ally also left much to be desired. Peter was a dangerous military bedfellow because his disorderly soldiers caused considerable difficulties in those areas in which they were billeted. As a result, Frederick IV turned to the King of England. Frederick needed help, and George I in his capacity of Elector of Hanover wanted to possess Bremen, Verden and the port of Stade.[2]

In January, 1715, George I sent a preliminary draft of a treaty to Copenhagen. These proposals carried by the Russian minister, Baron von Schack, who was returning from London, provided that Frederick IV should evacuate Bremen and Stade within fourteen days after he was requested to do so by George I. As soon as Hanover was in possession of the places, George I as Elector would declare war upon Sweden, and bound himself to contribute 30,000 crowns toward defraying war expenditures. George I refused to participate in the siege of Stralsund, but did pledge himself to contribute 6,000 men to Denmark should her German provinces be attacked. George I also promised to pre-vent troops coming from southern Germany from going to the aid of Sweden. Frederick IV, however, demanded that the declaration of war precede the evacuation and that the subsidy be 50,000 crowns quarterly. The Danish king, further insisted that George as Elector had to play an active role in the Stral-

[1] Treaty between the two countries, printed in *Ibid.*, pp. 150–151.
[2] Croissy Instructions, *Recueil, Suède*, II, 269.

sund war operations. According to Danish thinking, those provisions which dealt with auxiliary aid could more properly be embodied in a defensive treaty.[1]

The Danes by March, however, were willing to make sacrifices and to tone down their demands until they agreed in essentials with the Hanoverian proposals.[2] Undoubtedly, the demand made by Prussia that Denmark reach an accord with Hanover before there could be a Dano-Prussian treaty significantly influenced the Danish decision.[3] Before George I could have his way, a month passed, and the pendulum swung back in favor of the Danes. By April it was apparent that the estrangement between Prussia and Sweden had become irreconcilable, and that a Dano-Prussian treaty would be consummated regardless of the Dano-Hanoverian one. Consequently, when George I, on May 2, 1715, signed in London, a treaty with the Danes, Frederick IV was in a position to refuse ratification until the Elector of Hanover promised to contribute equally with the King of Denmark as to any compensation that might be arranged for the Duke of Holstein-Gottorp.[4] On July 28, the treaty which had been signed on May 2 was ratified by Denmark and the clause treating satisfaction for Holstein-Gottorp was included as a separate article.

In addition to the separate article, the terms of the alliance between Hanover and Denmark were as follows: Bremen and Verden were ceded *in perpetuum* to the Electors of Hanover for the sum of 300,000 *reichsthaler* and the Duchy of Bremen was to be turned over to Hanover fourteen days after the treaty ratification. If, by May 1, 1716, the war with Sweden were still in progress, Hanover—unless by that time she were an active belligerent—promised to make a quarterly payment of 50,000 *thalers* for one year. If the war ended before the allotted time, Hanover's payments were to be proportional to the war's duration. The initial payment was to be made on May 13, 1716. George I also promised to bring pressure as King upon Parliament in order to persuade that body to pay a subsidy that

---

[1] Chance, *George I and the Northern War*, p. 70.
[2] Frederick IV to Peter the Great, March 21, 1715, Westphal Correspondence, Rigsarkiv, T.K.U.A., Russland C 122.
[3] Idem to Idem, March 26, 1715, *Ibid.*
[4] Chance, *George I and the Northern War*, p. 69.

England had owed Denmark since the Anglo-Dano treaty of 1701. In addition, George I was to aid Denmark in receiving arrears that England owed to those soldiers from Denmark, who had fought against Louis XIV.[1]

As in the Dano-Prusso alliance, the treaty between Hanover and Denmark provided for the redistribution of Sweden's provinces in Germany. The northern half of Swedish Pomerania with the island of Rügen was to go to Denmark. Prussia was to receive Stettin and the area up to the Peene, which included Demmin, Loitz, Anklam, Wolgast, and the islands of Usedom and Wollin. Wismar with the island of Poel added was to become a free imperial city after its fortifications had been razed. The country (*Amt*) of Neukloster was to be ceded to the Duke of Mecklenburg, provided that Mecklenburg remained neutral, and satisfaction was given to the estates of Mecklenburg for forage with which they had supplied the Danish army.[2] In addition, the tolls at Warnemünde were to be abolished. Frederick IV moreover was to retain possession of Schleswig on the ground that Denmark had sustained great damages when the Duke of Holstein-Gottorp had allowed Stenbock's army to take refuge within the walls of the city of Tönning.[3] Any compensation that the House of Gottorp might receive for the loss of Schleswig was to be arranged at the Congress of Brunswick. As in the Dano-Prussian treaty there was a clause barring the King of Sweden from holding territory in Holstein. Should the Duke of Holstein-Gottorp succeed to the throne of the Vasas, he would be compelled to resign his titles in Germany to the next agnate.

Both contracting parties promised to guarantee the possessions of the other with a force of 8,000 men of which 3,000 had to be either horse or dragoons.[4] The circle of alliances was closed on October 26, 1715, by the treaty of Greiswald between Hanover and Russia. In this treaty Russia guaranteed Bremen and Verden to Hanover in return for a guarantee of Ingria,

---

[1] The amount due was 413,000 *thalers. Ibid.*, p. 71 and Frederick IV to Söhlenthal, April 18, 1716, Söhlenthal Correspondence, Rigsarkiv, T.K.U.A.

[2] This clause well illustrates the fact that certain individuals high in Danish and Hanoverian official circles were Mecklenburgers. Dewitz and Bernstorff are good examples.

[3] See above.

[4] Holm, 'Studier,' Series V, Vol. III, 3.

Carelia and Esthonia, including the city of Reval. This alliance, according to Douglas Reading, was one of the worst of Peter's blunders because it embroiled him in German affairs.[1] Especially influential on subsequent diplomacy were the affairs of Mecklenburg in which Peter increasingly became involved. About the marriage of Peter's niece to the Duke of Mecklenburg more will be said later.

For Denmark her diplomatic relations with Russia throughout 1715 were of primary importance. The bulk of these negotiations concerned plans for a joint Dano-Russian invasion of the Swedish mainland. As far back as 1709, Peter had promised 6,000 Russian soldiers who would act as an auxiliary body in any war operations against Sweden proper.[2] Nothing had come of the Russian proposal because stormy weather had prevented the Russian troops from being transported from Danzig to Denmark. Conversations of a similar vein had continued throughout 1710 with Russia making plans to invade Finland while a joint Dano-Russian force poured into Skåne. The Turkish declaration of war upon Russia had put all such schemes to bed for a while.[3]

Once relieved of the Turkish danger, Russia continued to apply diplomatic pressure upon Denmark to bring to maturity the early and abortive plans for a Swedish invasion. On March 6, 1716, the Danish chancery on the one side and the Russian ambassador, Prince Dolgoruky, and Peter's Adjutant-General, Jagousinsky, on the other had concluded a convention at Copenhagen for the invasion of Sweden. Denmark was to supply the fleet while Peter was to furnish transport craft and a landing force of 15,000 soldiers. This expeditionary force was to capture and demolish the Swedish harbor of Carlskrona so that it militarily would be rendered useless. That being accomplished, Frederick IV promised to participate in an attack upon the Swedish interior and pledged 24,000 men to the undertaking. Before the Danish king would move so great a force from his own territory, he had to be assured that there would be no attacks upon his southern boundaries while he was away on foreign fields. Consequently, Russia had to promise Prussian

[1] Reading, *Anglo-Russian Commercial Treaty*, p. 72.
[2] Holm, 'Studier,' Series V, Vol. III, 3.
[3] *Ibid.*, p. 4.

neutrality and to see that the Swedish garrison at Wismar did not harm the Danish forces in Pomerania.

Consequently nothing was accomplished. The ratification of the Prussian guarantee of neutrality had not been forthcoming until June 12. That date had been too late for Frederick IV to participate in a Swedish invasion. The Danish king asserted that inclement winter weather would hit the task force before it could accomplish its mission. The elements were probably just one factor contributing to Danish inaction. Frederick IV feared any invasion of Sweden while Anne was on the British throne. The pro-Swedish sentiments of Anne and her advisers in 1714 made any overseas attack upon Sweden quite danger-ous. Frederick IV, moreover, at that time was expanding the greater portion of his energies toward effecting a settlement of the Holstein-Gottorp question and the expulsion of the Swedes from the Empire.[1]

In 1715, the Danes sent Hans Georg von Westphal to Russia as ambassador. The new envoy arrived at St. Petersburg on March 4, 1715.[2] For the most part Westphal was pro-Russian and adhered closely to the policies of Count Ditlev Wibe, who although Home Secretary of Denmark had assumed control of foreign affairs.[3] Westphal was also anti-English and his senti-ments were reciprocated by the British who held Westphal in low esteem. Alexander, Lord Polwarth, the British envoy at Copenhagen described Westphal as follows: 'You guessed extremely right of our friend Mr. Westphal; a greater rogue never was.'[4]

One of the first duties of the new ambassador to Russia was to press for the payment of a subsidy valued at 16,000 rubles, which the Russians at one time had promised to Denmark.[5] Westphal, who held his first audience with Peter the day after

[1] *Ibid.*, pp. 4–5.

[2] Mackensie to Townshend, March 5, 1715, *Sbornik*, LXI, 357.

[3] Fleming's account of the Danish Court, *Polwarth Papers*, I, 413: 'Of all the ministers, he [Wibe] is the most clear-headed.' Robethon memorial to Polwarth, June 1, 1716, *Ibid.*, I, 32: 'Mr. de Wibe is the most able and energetic of all, and has presently the principal direction of affairs, and chief credit with the King. He is to be regarded with suspicion as he is not friendly to us.'

[4] Polwarth to Robethon, January 5, 1716, *Ibid.*, I, 159.

[5] Sehestedt to Westphal, February 2, 1715, Westphal Correspondence, Rigs-arkiv, T.K.U.A., Russland, C 122.

his arrival,[1] met with little success in raising money from the Czar, and by the end of March he had abandoned all hope of accomplishing the financial part of his mission.[2] Frederick IV might give weighty reasons and detailed arguments why Peter should pay the delinquent subsidy, but the Russian Czar could not be persuaded to give pecuniary assistance to his Danish ally.[3]

On the matter of Holstein, Westphal fared considerably better in his endeavors to solicit Russian help. Early in 1715, the Imperial Court had desired to consider the Holstein-Gottorp question separately from the Northern War.[4] At this stage of developments, Peter at the request of Westphal,[5] took a hand, and instructed all Russian ministers at foreign courts to refrain from interesting themselves in the question. At the same time they stated that Holstein had to be considered by Russia as an enemy of the Northern Alliance, and that the restitution of the Duke of Holstein-Gottorp to his possessions before the conclusion of the Northern War would be prejudicial to Peter and to his allies.[6] On March 22, Westphal was able to inform his sovereign that if Charles XII attacked Holstein, Russia would support the Danish pretensions to Holstein. Peter, moreover, offered his army to Frederick IV—a force which the Danish ruler could use in any operation he so desired just so long as it was directed against Sweden. The sole responsibility that Denmark had to assume for the Russian troops was to see that they were adequately supplied with bread, meat, and forage.[7]

The generous offer from the Russian Czar did not long go unheeded. On May 7, 1715, Wibe wrote to Kristian Schestedt, the Danish Foreign Secretary, and set forth the advantages that

---

[1] Mackensie to Townshend, March 5, 1715, *Sbornik*, LXI, 357.

[2] Frederick IV to Westphal, April 20, 1715, Westphal Correspondence, Rigsarkiv, T.K.U.A., Russland, C 122: 'Wie du [Westphal] hast alle Hofnung verlohren, fur uns von des Czaren Lbd: einige subsidien zu erhalten.'

[3] Holm, 'Studier,' Series V, Vol. III, 13.

[4] Rosenkrantz, the Danish envoy to the Congress of Brunswick, to Frederick IV, March 22, 1715, Westphal Correspondence, Rigsarkiv, T.K.U.A., Russland, C 122.

[5] Sehestedt to Westphal, April 2, 1715, *Ibid*. The Danes claimed that without Holstein they would be unable to continue the war ('ohne welchen wir den Krig zu continuiren nicht in Stande seyn würden').

[6] Sehestedt to Westphal, March 30, 1715, *Ibid*.

[7] Frederick IV to Westphal, April 20, 1715, *Ibid*.

might be derived from employing Russian troops in the Danish campaigns against Stralsund and Wismar.[1] Wibe pointed out that Denmark straining under the war burden might effect a speedy termination to the German phase of the conflict by utilizing Russian manpower.[2] These proposals were thus being considered by Denmark at the same time that she was negotiating with Hanover and Prussia for offensive and defensive alliances against Sweden.[3] To bring the Russian troops to the scene of operations required control of the sea. Consequently, Russia and Denmark were vitally concerned with the activities of the British fleet in 1715. The Baltic squadron of Sir John Norris figured largely in the plans of the Northern Alliance which had committed itself to expel the Swedes from the Empire.

[1] Wibe and Sehestedt to Westphal, May 7, 1715, *Ibid.*
[2] *Ibid.*
[3] See above.

VI

THE BALTIC SQUADRON
OF 1715

SUCH was the background against which the Baltic squadron
of 1715 operated. After the delays usual in outfitting an
eighteenth-century naval force, Norris cleared the Nore in the
Cumberland on May 29, 1715.[1] With him were fifteen other ships
of the line, two frigates, and sixty merchantmen. Seven days
later, they all arrived at Fleckerö, a small island off the Norwegian coast.

Here a rendezvous was made with an east coast contingent
consisting of two more ships of the line and twenty-eight additional traders. The British group now totalled one hundred and
six sail. After a two day delay because of contrary winds, the
contingent proceeded to Elsinore, arriving there on June 10.
The Dutch admiral, De Veth, had arrived on the sixth with
twelve warships and over two hundred merchant vessels.[2]

[1] Norris to Townshend, May 29, 1715, BM., Add. MSS., 28,144. The dates
advanced for Norris's sailing are horribly garbled. Michael, throughout his
account, becomes very confused by the different styles of dating in the various
countries. A. P. Tuxen and C. L. With-Seidelin, *Erobringen af Sveriges Tyske
Provensen, 1715–1716*, vol. VII of *Bidrag til den Storre Nordiske Krigs Historia* (Odense,
1922), p. 89 claims the squadron sailed the twenty-second. Hereafter this work
will be cited *Bidrag . . . Nordiske Krigs*, VII. Chance, *George I and the Northern War*,
p. 82 uses the general dating 'at the end of May,' while William Laird Clowes,
The Royal Navy from the earliest Times to the Present (London, 1898), II, 7 is accurate.
Robethon to Norris, May 31, 1715, BM., Add. MSS., 28,154: 'Your Father-in-
Law was at Court Yesterday to inform the King that you were sail'd the day
before with all the Ships.'

[2] De Veth to Heinsius, June 8, 1715, Rijksarchief, A.A.H., 1928. List of ships
bound for the Baltic, BM., Add. MSS., 28,154; Norris to Robethon and to
Orford, June 10, 1715, BM. Add. MSS., 28,143. There is some doubt as to whether
Norris arrived late on the night of the ninth of June or early in the morning of
the tenth.

Almost at once a council of flag officers was held to decide how coöperative measures would be taken against Sweden. Quickly, those present were brought to the realization that the British and Dutch orders did not coincide 'van woort tot woort' as the Dutch had been led to believe. De Veth had in contrast to Norris been instructed to avoid all hostilities with Sweden, and under no circumstances was he to take reprisals. Only if the charges under his care were set upon by Charles's privateers was he 'to meet force with force.'[1] The Dutch admiral admitted knowing about Norris's instructions, and said that he had been told 'from a private hand' to act with his British colleague; but he also insisted that he was compelled to abide by his written orders.[2] The English thus learned that trade protection and Hanoverian power politics were in Dutch eyes two distinct goals. Although Dutch treasure might be expended for trade, neither ships nor money were to be employed by De Veth to assist in political adventures. The most the Dutch leader promised was to write home for orders which might correspond more closely with those of the English, and perhaps allow him to go beyond just protecting the merchantmen.

While hopefully waiting for the diplomatic mills of the States to grind out new orders for their commander, Norris started his own diplomatic wheels turning. Letters were sent to the Danish court informing it of the arrival of the English fleet along with a British request to use Danish port facilities. The Danish government was informed that the British admiral would 'not lose any opportunity in endeavors to promote harmonious relations between the English and the Danish crowns.'[3] The British and Hanoverian ministers in Denmark, F. Hanneken and Püchler received similar notifications.[4] On June 11, Cap-

[1] Instructions to De Veth, May 18, 1715, Rijksarchief, Secrete Resolutiën, Staten Generaal: 'sal hij gewelt met gewelt keeren.'
[2] Minutes of the council of war, June 10, 1715, BM., Add. MSS., 28,154; Norris to Townshend, June 17, 1715, BM., Add. MSS., 28,144; Norris to Robethon and to Orford, June 10, 1715, B.M., Add. MSS., 28,143. See also extract of De Veth to the States General, June 11, 1715 in Rijksarchief, Secrete Resolutiën, Staten Generaal, June 18, 1715.
[3] Norris to the Danish Regency, June 10, 1715, BM., Add. MSS., 28,144. The Danish government was under a regency because Frederick IV was with his troops in Germany.
[4] Norris to Hanneken, June 10, 1715, Ibid.

tain N. J. Fÿnboe was sent with dispatches to Jefferyes,[1] who was to acquaint Charles XII with the news that the British squadron intended to stop all Swedish ships until Sweden made reparations for British losses and promised to let English commerce move 'without any Interruption or Molestation whatsoever.'[2] Two days later Jackson was sent a similar letter with the added stipulation that if he knew of any additional damages that Britain could claim against Sweden, he was to include them in his representation.[3]

Püchler's actions give an excellent insight as to what Hanoverians expected from the Norris squadron. Two letters from the Hanoverian minister awaited Norris at Elsinore, letters filled with misunderstanding as to the true nature of Norris's orders and reeking with Electoral optimism. The Hanoverian, who knew Norris was to work through him, ordered the Admiral to station the main body of the fleet off Hanö, and send the vast number of merchantmen into the Baltic covered by just the frigates. Between fourteen and sixteen Danish ships stood ready to assist Norris, and the combined squadron would be more than sufficient to deal with Sweden's fleet totalling somewhere between eighteen and twenty ships of the line. So happy was Püchler about the rosy future in store for the confederates of the Northern Alliance that he thought the Danish king was taking unnecessary precautions equipping additional warships.[4]

Norris's answer to Püchler, dated June 11 must have considerably toned down the king's Hanoverian agent. The Admiral gave Püchler the bad news that Dutch coöperation could not be counted upon beyond the protection of trade and commerce although Norris hoped that De Veth's orders might be changed. The idea that the Danes should stop equipping warships was unthinkable, especially if the Swedes put all their vessels into one group, and the Danes continued their practice of splitting their ships into different squadrons—a practice that the battle-wise English admiral considered extremely bad as it continually gave the enemy local naval superiority

[1] Norris to Fÿnboe, June 12, 1715, BM., Add. MSS., 28,135.
[2] Norris to Jefferyes, June 12, 1715, BM. Add. MSS., 28,144.
[3] Norris to Jackson, June 14, 1715, *Ibid.*
[4] Püchler to Norris, June 11 and 16, 1715, *Ibid.* and BM., Add. MSS., 28,154.

in spite of Sweden's having an inferior number of ships. Norris continued:

> Having acquainted you with the State of the Dutch and our affairs, you'll give me leave also to acquaint you that what you propose of my quitting the Protection of the Merchant Ships of our Country and blocking up Carlscrone, seems impracticable, since my Orders are in the first place to protect our Trade, and then, so far as that will admit, to pursue the other Ends you will see in my letter to Mr. Jefferys . . .[1]

Thus Norris could not be persuaded to join the Danes in spite of inducements that ran from free hospitalization for English sailors to a weekly supply of venison for the Admiral's table.[2] Trade considerations were paramount; and Norris's plans for implicating the Dutch in British plans received a serious setback when De Veth informed him that if the British instigated an attack upon a superior Swedish force, they would have to go it alone.[3] Thus with his hands tied because he could neither join with the Danes nor persuade the Dutch to join him, Norris bowed to circumstances. On June 14, a meeting of the war council worked out detailed plans for convoying the merchantships to their destination.[4] Norris needed the Dutch ships on two counts. One to prove that the squadron was not a Hanoverian pawn; the other because the Dutch ships provided the balance of power which gave the squadron its naval superiority.

Norris evidently expected to be set upon by the Swedish fleet. As he informed Townshend on June 13, 1715: 'I have from all hands in these parts that the King of Sweden has directed his Naval Force to attack us.' He received additional information as to the strength of the Swedish naval units. Thus

---

[1] Norris to Püchler, June 12, 1715, BM., Add. MSS., 28,144.

[2] Püchler to Norris, June 12, 1715, BM., Add. MSS., 28,154 and Kristian Sehestedt to Norris, June 11, 1715, BM., Add. MSS., 28,144. Cf. Geheimeregistratur der Anno 1715, Vol. 275, Rigsarkiv, T.K.U.A. especially the entries for June 11 and 12. The latter material was microfilmed by Professor Waldemar Westergaard, U.C.L.A., who kindly allowed the author to use this and other materials in his possession.

[3] Vlootvoogden . . . , Rijksarchief, Archief Staten Generaal, June 4, 1715, No. 7176; and De Veth to Fagel, Rijksarchief, Secrete Resolutiën, Staten Generaal, June 11, 1715.

[4] Minutes of council of war, June 14, 1715, BM., Add. MSS., 28,154; Norris to Townshend, June 13 and 14, BM., Add. MSS., 28,144; and De Veth to Heinsius, June 14, 1715, Rijksarchief, A.A.H., 1928.

he had to defer to Dutch wishes as he needed their coöperation. If the Swedes did contest the passage of the merchantships, Norris was prepared to 'maintain the Honour of our Nation so far as our Force will admit.'[1]

He could only hope that the taking of reprisals would sting Charles XII into action. Norris therefore informed his captains that they were to start taking Swedish ships until 'the Abrogation of an unjustifiable Edict, relating to the privateers published by the King of Sweden 8/19 February last.' The English ship masters were to take special care that nothing be taken from the Swedish ships because when the English received the 'Reparations and Satisfaction' that was their due, the Swedish ships were to be set at liberty. As for the Swedish crews, they were to be treated 'in a civil and friendly manner.'[2] Norris intended to keep his fleet in the Bay of Ruyk until the post of June 14 arrived 'in Hopes that the Dutch Rear Adml. may thereby receive further Orders to Act in Conformity with his English allies.'[3] With the failure of the post to make for any changes in the situation, the joint squadron began to put into operation the complicated plans which the commanders had drawn up to convoy the merchant ships to their destinations.[4]

The news of the decisions taken by Norris and De Veth was received in London with mixed feelings. The Admiralty ever prudent was pleased with the cautious policy of Norris and considered him to be the best judge of affairs, as he was on the spot. They also wanted the squadron to be kept as intact as possible.[5] Townshend expressing the King's feelings, indulged in his usual double talk, and his reaction is difficult to assess from the official papers. Yet it is quite apparent that Townshend and his sovereign were working in complete accord in 1715. For example, the Secretary of State wanted Norris to meet the desires of the Admiralty and the traders, but also to apply himself as soon as he could and 'with all the dilligence and earnestness' possible to carrying out that part of his instructions

[1] Norris to Townshend, June 13, 1715, BM., Add. MSS., 28,144.
[2] Norris to his Captains, June 14, 1715, BM., Add. MSS., 28,154.
[3] Minutes of the council of war, June 14, 1715, *Ibid.*
[4] *Ibid.*
[5] Admiralty to Townshend, July 2, 1715, P.R.O., Secretary's Letter Book, State Papers, Foreign, 104/155 and Burchett to Norris, July 1, 1715, BM., Add. MSS., 28,154.

relating to reprisals. Again Norris was told that the best way to prevent Swedish designs upon the merchantmen was to hinder the Swedish squadron at Karlscrona from joining the Swedish ships at Stockholm. Yet the King thought 'it best to leave that point' along with others to the Admiral's prudent management, although Bornholm where British fleet units could participate in the siege of Stralsund was again suggested as the best station for the British ships.[1]

When Norris's father-in-law, Aylmer, told Robethon what had transpired, the Royal Secretary along with Bernstorff expressed considerable regrets that Norris had weakened his squadron to protect the trade, and hoped he would shortly return to Bornholm 'to pursue the further Ends' of his instructions. Bernstorff also hoped that Norris might find himself strong enough to fight the Swedes without having to rely upon De Veth for assistance.[2] At the same time Townshend was doing all that he could to move the Dutch to act with Norris,[3] while Hendrik Frederik von Söhlenthal, the Danish ambassador to London, was striving mightily to have the English court order Norris into action against the Swedes.[4]

The Danes were also busy at home. Sehestedt and Krabbe informed Püchler, the Hanoverian minister to Copenhagen, that the best place for the squadron to anchor was near the island of Hanö which was close to Karlscrona.[5] The fleet could be protected from the weather while it blockaded the Swedish port by Bornholm 'turning about that Island according to the Several Winds.' Although Norris had not coöperated, he did advise the Danes to keep their fleet intact and thus they could prevent the Swedes making any 'Descent in Holstein.' He also warned them that to divide their forces might be to flirt with disaster.[6]

---

[1] Townshend to Norris, June 25, 1715, P.R.O., F.E.B., State Papers, Foreign, 104/155. Copies of this letter are in BM., Add. MSS., 28,144 and 28,154. In the letter book of Norris (28,144) this letter is erroneously dated one month later. A printed copy is in *British Instructions, Sweden*, pp. 78–79.

[2] Robethon to Norris, July 1, 1715, BM., Add. MSS., 28,143.

[3] Borssele and Duivenvoorde to the States General, June 28, 1715, Rijksarchief, Secrete Resolutiën, Staten Generaal, July 21 and 22, 1715.

[4] Danish Chancery to Söhlenthal, June 27, 1715, Rigsarkiv, T.K.U.A., Geheimeregistratur, Vol. 257.

[5] Robethon to Norris, May 21, 1715, BM., Add. MSS., 28,143.

[6] Norris to Robethon, June 23, 1715, *Ibid.*

The arrival of the squadron in the Sound saw the speeding up of the diplomatic offensive against Sweden. On June 22, Jackson received letters from Townshend and Norris which informed him as to the type of representation that he should make to the Swedish Government at Stockholm.[1] Accordingly, on June 25, Jackson presented a note to the Swedish Chancery asking for satisfaction and reparations. Damages this time were placed at £69,024 2s. 9d., plus the value of some ships that had been seized at Göteborg under the new privateering edict operating as an *ex post facto* law. The English resident claimed that the losses to British merchants had been so great that they had been forced to discontinue trading in the Baltic. The Edict of February had given England's Baltic trade its final blow, for now even those ships bound for Sweden might be taken as lawful prizes. From the British point of view the situation was intolerable and could not be allowed to continue. George I, therefore, had sent his fleet into the Baltic to protect British commerce and to make reprisals until Charles XII came to his senses and notified Norris that Britain had obtained the trading liberties for which it sought.[2]

The news of the arrival of Norris in the Baltic had a great effect upon Swedish public opinion. Horn was very dejected[3] at the news, and a wave of bitterness arose against Jackson which was heightened by his memorial of June 14/25. For a while there was wild talk of throwing him in prison.[4] The British diplomat naturally was quite concerned as to what might happen to him should Norris instigate an aggressive action against Swedish fleet units, for 'as they [the Swedes] now esteem us their most mortal enemy, so I am already shun'd as an infectious person. But I thank God I am entirely easy since happen what will, I never doubt, that care will be taken of me.'[5]

The Dutch minister at Stockholm, Willem Rumpf, was not able to enjoy such comforting thoughts or such peace of mind. If the Jackson memorial made a 'grand bruit' in the Swedish

[1] Jackson to Townshend, June 17, 1715, P.R.O.; State Papers, Sweden, 95/21.
[2] Jackson to the Swedish Chancery, June 14, 1715, *Ibid.* A French translation of this letter may be found in Lamberty, *Mémoires*, IX, 256–258.
[3] Jackson to Townshend, June 28, 1715, P.R.O., State Papers, Sweden, 95/21.
[4] Rumpf to Heinsius, June 29, 1715, Rijksarchief, A.A.H., 1923.
[5] Jackson to Townshend, July 4, 1715, P.R.O., State Papers, Sweden, 95/21.

capital, it also stirred up the diplomat from the United Provinces.[1] After years of mutual trust and coöperation, Jackson and
Rumpf began to go their separate ways. The former must bear
the brunt of the blame for the falling out because he presented
the memorial of June 14/25 without consulting Rumpf. Up to
that time the two diplomats had kept each other informed as
to their movements and usually all such representations had
been given jointly.

Thus Rumpf under ordinary circumstances would have been
disturbed by Jackson's action. A note that was little more than
an ultimatum naturally excited him even more. By demanding
immediate payment, Jackson was insisting upon a point that
the Swedes would not have been able to fulfill even had they
so desired.[2] The unilateral action on the part of the British
minister had placed Rumpf in a very awkward position, especially if the Swedes began to ask him embarrassing questions
about the squadron. After all the two countries were united in
the Baltic affair and what one did reflected upon the other.
Jackson might not mind being 'shun'd as an infectious person,'
but it is quite evident that his Dutch colleague did not want to
expose himself to similar treatment, but desired at all costs to
forestall an open rupture between the States and Sweden.

Consequently Rumpf called Jackson to task for the way that
he had acted. Jackson passed off the matter by telling Rumpf
that he had simply forgotten to tell him about the letters he had
received from Norris containing new orders from the King.
Such an obvious deception was bad enough, but Jackson added
insult to injury when he informed Rumpf about his surprise
over the Dutch excitement, and added that he could see no
reason to pay any attention to Dutch interests because the Dutch
in the Baltic affair could only be considered as auxiliaries.[3]
Consequently they had nothing to do with the formulation of

---

[1] Rumpf to Heinsius, June 29, 1715, Rijksarchief, A.A.H., 1923.

[2] Jackson to the Chancery, June 25, 1715, P.R.O., State Papers, Sweden,
95/21.

[3] Rumpf to Heinsius, June 29, 1715, Rijksarchief, A.A.H., 1923. Jackson's
memoir made a 'grand bruit.' Rumpf sent the States a copy of it in August, for he
did not have time to make a translation: 'il [Jackson] vint chez moi pour com-
muniquer son Memoir, après l'avoir deja presenté au Comte de Horn; Parcequ'-
étoit de *La Lettre de L'Admiral Norris, il fil semblant de l'avoir oubliée*, et se contenta
de me *dire qu'il m'y* etoit fait mention en aucune *manniere* de nos Interets, et
qu'il regardoit L'Escadre des Provinces Unies, dans cett'affaire come auxiliare.'

policy. Jackson, up to that point, was correct, because the Dutch did not know what had been going on, but Norris was soon to find that the States would have considerable to say about Baltic policy. They had no intention, if they could help it, to allow Hanoverian politics to run Anglo-Dutch diplomacy in the Baltic. The attempts of Townshend, Jackson and others to cozen them placed a strain upon Anglo-Dutch relations.

At Stralsund, there was also much bitterness displayed because of the Baltic squadron. Jefferyes presented his memorial on June 12/23 which contained all the usual demands, including the one for immediate payment of damages. At Sweden's behest, Jefferyes altered the use of the expression 'Brigandages' in referring to Sweden's privateering activities, an action for which Townshend later commended him. The British secretary did not want to give 'any handle of Cavil to the Swedish Ministers' even though many of the acts of the privateers could 'properly fall under no other denomination.'[1] As at Stockholm, there was considerable apprehension as to what the English squadron might do. Such a state of mind was according to the English king 'very natural for those who have given such severe Provocations . . . frame to themselves strange Schemes, such as their fears may suggest.'[2]

Norris hoped for an early reply to his representations and demonstrations,[3] but such was not forthcoming. As was to be expected, Jackson had accomplished nothing at Stockholm. He received a letter from the Regent and the Senate on June 29, which informed him that his memorial had been of such consequence that it had been forwarded to Charles XII at Stralsund. As soon as they had received an answer from the Swedish king, they would instantly inform him.[4] To obtain any kind of commitment or acknowledgment from Charles XII was a task of major proportion as Jefferyes was finding out. Soon he was to inform Townshend 'that I find my Self after 3 weeks expectation

[1] Townshend to Jefferyes, June 30, 1715, P.R.O., F.E.B., State Papers Foreign, 104/155, and Jefferyes to Charles XII, June 23, 1715, copy in BM., Add MSS., 28,154.
[2] Townsend to Jefferyes, June 11, 1715, P.R.O., F.E.B., State Papers, Foreign, 104/155.
[3] Norris to Captain Gordon, June 19, 1715, BM., Add. MSS., 28,135.
[4] Ehrenstrahl for the Senate and Regency, June 29, 1715, P.R.O., State Papers, Sweden, 95/21.

as far from an answer to the Memorial I presented the 12th past as the first moment I solicited one.' The British envoy had learned that the Swedish ruler evidently had read the note but claimed that he was too busy to answer it. Such temporizing was about all that Jefferyes expected even if he waited '3 months longer; for in my humble opinion, if this be a feigned excuse, they may make use of it to the end of the chapter; and if a true one 'tis not likely that the King of Sweden, who was so taken up with Business when the Enemy was at a distance, will be less employ'd now he is at the City Gates.'[1]

Jefferyes also knew that Norris was waiting for an answer. Consequently he kept Fÿnboe staying around for one. Jefferyes 'Left no Stone unturn'd' and as the forces of Prussia and Denmark approached to within three miles of Stralsund, he thought that he had better get Fÿnboe out of the city, answer or no. The Swedes refused to grant permission for Fÿnboe or Jefferyes to leave through the enemy lines under a flag of truce, and said that if they wished to leave, they could leave by boat through Sweden. Jefferyes argued that the Swedes could drop them off just as easily at Wismar or Lübeck rather than Ystedt in Sweden, but the Swedes refused.[2]

Unable to learn anything officially, Jefferyes relied upon hearsay. The rumor that was most prevalent in the Swedish camp was that Sweden was going to propose a 'Liquidation with his Majesty for Losses they pretend to have sustain'd in the former Warr.' The Swedes were pretty united in their belief that the revoking of the privateering edict would work a great hardship upon Charles XII. Being of the opinion that rumor was better than no information at all, Jefferyes decided to get Fÿnboe secretly out of the city, especially after he heard that a Swedish squadron of twenty-two to twenty-five ships would soon be ready and which would perhaps be joined by a squadron from France. Of such are the hopes and conversations of men in beleagured cities that are about to fall.

Sneaking Fÿnboe out of the city would be bound to have repercussions;

> I doubt not but the Swedes will make a great noise about this, and perhaps give out, that the Captn is going to inform the

[1] Jefferyes to Townshend, July 10, 1715, BM., Add. MSS., 28,154.
[2] *Ibid.*

Danes of what passes here. But since I look upon it to be as much for the Interest of his Majesty that the Admirall be appriz'd of the State of affairs here, as the Swedes think it for their advantage that he be kept in ignorance, so I humbly hope his Maj't will not take this Step amiss but will graciously please to Support me in case these people make their complaints of it.[1]

Left to his own devices, without orders and without hope of obtaining any, Jefferyes could only follow his 'reason and judgement.' He himself had hoped to withdraw to some neutral place during the storming of Stralsund, but felt that if he left, the Swedes would interpet his 'retreat as a Token that his Majesty's Fleet has some design against them.' To prevent ugly talk he decided to remain at Stralsund while the city was under attack: 'My Station being near the King of Sweden. I have Judg'd it more advisable, to endure the inconveniencys of a Siege than to quitt my post without his Maj'tys positive orders.'[2]

Fÿnboe escaped from Stralsund by water having first made his way to the Danish lines. On his way through the Danish camp he had an interview with the King of Denmark who was wondering where Norris and the English fleet were and who informed Fÿnboe that he expected them some time ago to put in their appearance before Stralsund. Fÿnboe was to ask Norris if he were to aid them and then to return to the Danes with Norris's answer so that they could prepare their affairs accordingly.[3] Thus the month of July ran out before Norris heard any news from Stralsund and even then the information that he received was not definite.

The most immediate and most tangible result of the coming of the British-Dutch squadron was the freeing of the Baltic of privateers. As Jackson commented 'Upon the news of Sir John Norris's arrival at the Sound, all the Swedish capers that belong to this place are return'd to the River.'[4] Thus the convoying of the merchantmen to their destinations went without incident. By July 4 the task was done, and the warships, lacking only

---

[1] *Ibid.*
[2] *Ibid.*
[3] J. Fÿnboe to Norris, August 1, 1715, *Ibid.*
[4] Jackson to Townshend, June 28, 1715, P.R.O., State Papers, Sweden, 95/21.

four ships rendezvoused at Reval.[1] English hopes that Sweden might provoke De Veth to action had not materialized. Unbeknown to both commanders, Charles XII had given his seamen specific orders to avoid all engagements with the Anglo-Dutch warships.[2] With the trade safe, Norris was now bound to put into operation those parts of his instructions dealing with reprisals and the blockading of Stralsund. The Hanoverians and their allies were expecting Norris to act.[3] Still no further orders awaited De Veth or Norris at Reval and there was as yet nothing from Jefferyes. The only news to be had was that a strong Swedish squadron had been off Reval fourteen days before the arrival there of the Anglo-Dutch ships.[4] The British thus had to have Dutch help to carry out any additional plans that Norris might want to place in execution. The situation at Reval was about the same as the one that had existed when the first rendezvous had been effected in the Sound.

Events repeated themselves. Norris called for a series of councils of war.[5] All depended upon De Veth. Throughout June the British admiral had clung to the thought that the Schout-bij-Nacht was 'a good man' who would go 'as far as he' could 'to act with' the British units.[6] After the councils of early July, De Veth became 'a very good man and deserves a better Character than I am able to write.'[7] The Dutchman by then had agreed to join in a cruise off Courland and off Bornholm in order to obtain information about a Swedish squadron that was supposedly 'at Sea.'[8] Although the projected manoeuver was nothing more than a reconnaissance sweep in force and at most would place the squadron before Bornholm for a few days only, Norris clearly expected better things. On July 4, he happily but discreetly wrote Townshend:

[1] Norris to Püchler, July 4, 1715, BM., Add. MSS., 28,144.
[2] Charles XII to Lt. General Liewen, June 6, 1715, *Konung Karl XII's Egenhändiga Bref*, pp. 407–498.
[3] Norris to Robethon, July 7, 1715 and Robethon to Norris, July 30, 1715, BM., Add. MSS., 28,143.
[4] Norris to Townshend, Püchler, and to Burchett, July 1, 1715, BM., Add. MSS., 28,144; De Veth to Norris ca., 29 June, 1715, BM. Add. MSS., 28,154.
[5] Minutes of council of war, June 30 and July 4, 1715, BM., Add. MSS., 28,154.
[6] Norris to Aylmer, June 23, 1715, BM., Add. MSS., 28,143.
[7] Norris to Robethon, July 7, 1715, *Ibid.*
[8] Minutes of council of war, July 4, 1715, BM., Add. MSS., 28,154.

I have had the good Fortune to prevail with the Dutch Adml: to join with me in such a Cruise as will not only serve for the security of our Commerce, but also enable me to answer the other purposes of his Maj'ty so far as the time will allow by which the season of the Year and the Weather incident to these Countries will oblige us to return homeward.[1]

According to De Veth, who had no need for innuendoes, the purpose of the cruise was to prevent Swedish transports from reaching Stralsund.[2]

The question at once arises as to whether Norris persuaded De Veth to disobey his instructions. The historians Chance and Michael, who make no allowances for Norris's optimism, are inclined to the affirmative and imply that De Veth did not know the true nature of the British plans. Hatton, who read the Dutch sources, is of the opinion that De Veth knew about the purpose of the cruise but was pressured by Norris into taking the offensive.[3] All three make much out of little. If the minutes of the council of war are interpreted literally—and they should be to discover as to what was agreed—it will quickly be noted that De Veth promised practically nothing. First the cruise could not begin until four ships convoying trade to Houghland had rejoined the squadron. Secondly, the squadron on its way to Bornholm was to put in at Danzig to discover if any new orders had arrived to regulate the conduct of the two commanders. While at Danzig, another council of war was to be held to consider the proper time to return to Reval to begin gathering the homeward-bound merchantmen.[4] The best that Norris could expect—and even that was remote or at least tentative—was that the squadron after it left Danzig might lay a few days before Bornholm before it returned up the Baltic to pick up the traders. By being a few days before Bornholm, however, Norris perhaps hoped to fill George's commitments to the Northern Alliance by token if not by

[1] Norris to Townshend, July 5, 1715, BM., Add. MSS., 28,144. Norris wrote in a similar vein to Püchler and promised that soon the squadron would make the Danish king happy.
[2] De Veth to the States, July 7, 1715, Vlootvoogden . . . , Rijksarchief, Archief Staten Generaal, No. 7176 and De Veth to Heinsius, July 7, 1715, A.A.H., 1928.
[3] Chance, *George I and the Northern War*, p. 80; Hatton, *Diplomatic Relations*, pp. 78–80.
[4] Minutes of council of war, July 4, 1715, BM., Add. MSS., 28,154.

action; and perhaps by going to Bornholm he might relieve
some of the pressure that was being put on him not only by
the Hanoverians but also by the rulers of Denmark, Prussia,
and Russia.[1]

Even to take advantage of this slight opportunity, time was
of the essence. Norris turned down an offer by Peter the Great
to confer, because 'considering what we have to do and the
length of Ground we have to sail, a moment ought not be lost
in Compliments.'[2] Such precautions were to no avail. Time
ran out on the British admiral as De Veth probably expected
that it would. The four ships were late returning. The elements
were not favorable. It was not until July 21 that the fleet
dropped anchor at Danzig where they discovered that the long
overdue mails had been forwarded by land to Reval.
The Dutch refused to go on before they received the
dispatches from home. De Veth informed Norris that as his
orders were to observe a strict neutrality, he could not continue
the cruise.[3]

Three days later Norris sadly wrote Townshend that his
'hopes of an Opportunity to have answer'd all the Expectations
your Ldsp, could have imagined of us' had been blasted by the
Dutch refusal to supersede their instructions.[4] The only chance
for action was that there were new orders in the awaited post.
That possibility vanished with the mails of July 27, which contained another resolution of the States which reaffirmed the
Dutch intention to avoid aggressive action.[5] Norris toyed with
the idea of engaging the Swedes on his own, but he could only
do so at a great risk to his own ships and to the merchantmen
with which he had been entrusted. The outcry that would
arise in London from failure was more than Norris dared risk.[6]
Consequently, the fleet hoisted sail and headed back to Reval

[1] Various letters to Norris from Peter the Great, Frederick William I of Prussia,
and Frederick IV of Denmark, *Ibid*.

[2] Norris to Aylmer, July 6, 1715, BM., Add. MSS., 28,143.

[3] Minutes of council of war, July 21, 1715, BM., Add. MSS., 28,144 and
28,154; Norris to Townshend, July 24, 1715, BM., Add. MSS., 28,144; and
De Veth to Heinsius, July 24, 1715, Rijksarchief, A.A.H., 1923.

[4] Norris to Townshend, July 24, 1715, B.M., Add. MSS., 28,144.

[5] Instructions to De Veth from Fagel, June 22, 1715, Rijksarchief, Resolutiën
Staten Generaal, June 22, 1715. There is a copy in BM., Add. MSS., 28,154.

[6] De Veth to the States, July 27, 1715, Vlootvoogden . . . , Rijksarchief, Archief
Staten Generaal, No. 7176 and De Veth to Heinsius, same date, A.A.H., 1928.

to begin gathering the merchant fleet. Norris admitted that he had been 'prevented of doing what I thought to have done . . . when I writ . . . from Reval' by Dutch non-coöperation.[1]

Norris arrived at Reval on August 3 where a new headache awaited him in the form of a Danish frigate which carried urgent dispatches from Denmark. At that court there was a good deal of unhappiness with Norris's conduct, which in Danish eyes was directly contrary to 'la promesse faite.' The farther east that Norris went the more useless he was in assisting in the blockade of Karlscrona.[2] Danish pressure upon Püchler had caused him to promise that Norris in good time would take his station as the Danes desired.[3] Consequently, the Danish privy councillors Sehestedt and Krabbe had written Norris in the early part of July requesting his return immediately.[4] Norris, who when he received the letter was going in the opposite direction, could only repeat his own personal desires to assist the Danes and promise to expedite the gathering of the merchantmen in order to free his hands for other projects.[5] To achieve that end as rapidly as possible, a joint council of war was held on August 9 to consider a course of action.[6]

Norris in addition attempted to persuade De Veth to 'enterprise a venture for a few days,' but all to no avail.[7] The post which arrived on August 10 offered him some encouragement for it brought him news as to what was transpiring in London. At Whitehall constant pressure upon the Dutch diplomats, Duivenvoorde and Borssele, had brought the States around to promising that they would ask Charles XII for damages sustained at the hands of Swedish privateers. The new resolution of the States was actually an empty gesture so far as the Hanoverians were concerned, because it did not even threaten reprisals. Only after the Dutch envoy to Prussia, Christiaan

---

[1] Norris to Püchler, July 27, 1715, BM., Add. MSS., 28,144.
[2] Wibe to Püchler, July 8, 1715, Rigsarkiv, T.K.U.A., Geheimeregistratur, Vol. 257.
[3] *Bidrag . . . Nordiske Krigs*, VII, 91.
[4] Sehestedt to Norris, June 28, 1715, Krabbe and Sehestedt to Norris, July 8, 1715, BM., Add. MSS., 28,154.
[5] Norris to Krabbe and to Sehestedt, August 6, 1715, and to Raben, August 8, 1715, BM., Add. MSS., 28,144.
[6] Minutes of council of war, August 9, 1715, BM., Add. MSS., 28,144 and 28,154.
[7] Norris to Aylmer, August 10, 1715, BM., Add. MSS., 28,143.

Karel, Baron van Lintelo, requested damages and received a negative answer from the Swedes would the States reconsider the possibility of aggressive action.[1] By that time, winter would suspend all naval operations in the Baltic. Time was running out on the Baltic commander, and De Veth could do nothing until he heard from Lintelo or from the Hague.[2]

Like the hour glass measuring the time, Norris's patience was becoming exhausted. Literally bombarded by conflicting orders, pleas, and complaints from Dane, Hanoverian, Prussian, Russian and Briton, Norris was caught in the middle. He could do nothing, but yet was blamed for his inactivity. Even the Admiralty, relying on misinformation was becoming harder to handle. The Dutch would not aid him, he could not join the Danes, and Orford had limited his supply of munitions. He could not act alone. He complained bitterly: 'my Reputation is much more valuable than my being; and since my Youth I never avoided a Warlike action that was in my Power so I will preserve that Character till I am no more. . . . As I have all the Duty to our Royal Master, and a Thirst to shew him my Life is at his Service, if be possible for me to shew it, I will do it with great pleasure, and let my L. Orford's Conscience answer himself for the hardships he has put on . . .'[3]

He might console himself to some extent, however, with the success that he was having in cultivating a personal friendship between himself and Peter the Great. He was to fare better in that regard than most Englishmen did during the next five years. The day after the arrival of the Anglo-Dutch fleet at Reval, Admiral Apraxen and his command of nineteen men-of-war anchored in the same harbor. The Czar himself was serving in his own fleet with the rank of vice-admiral. Norris at once was invited to visit the Russian ships. Later the Czar returned the compliment,[4] and congratulated his host on being the first British officer to conduct a fleet to Russian dominions by way of the Baltic.[5]

[1] Rijksarchief, Secrete Resolutiën, Staten Generaal, July 8, 1715.
[2] Norris to Aylmer, August 10, 1715, BM., Add. MSS., 28,143. This is not the same letter as the one cited in footnote 7 on page 175 .
[3] *Ibid.*
[4] Norris to Townshend, August 4, 1715, BM., Add. MSS., 28,144 and Norris to Robethon, August 10, 1715, BM., Add. MSS., 28,143.
[5] Norris to Aylmer, September 2, 1715, BM., Add. MSS., 28,143.

Both admiral and Czar achieved a healthy respect for each other. The latter displayed his well known curiosity and insisted on inspecting all parts of the ship 'even to the Powder Room.'[1] Norris during the visit was extremely impressed with his royal visitor. 'The Improvement he has made by the help of the English Builders, are such as a Sea Man would almost think impossible for a Nation so lately used to the Sea; they have built three 60 Gun Ships which are every way equal to the best of that Rank in our Country.'[2] Norris sounded a word of warning to his countrymen by predicting that Peter would soon be equal to his neighbors in shipping. Russia's only want was seamen, and Peter was doing all that he could to change soldiers into sailors.[3]

His discussions with and impressions of Georg von Westphal, the Danish minister who was with Peter, were not so favorable. Westphal constantly reminded Norris of his inactivity and how little Britain was contributing to the Northern Alliance. To the Dane it appeared that George I would obtain Bremen and Verden and do nothing in return. Norris blamed De Veth for his own passive performance; and said that if Charles XII had acted in his usual rash manner, England would have had a provocation to take the offensive. Furthermore George I had signed the treaty with Denmark over Bremen and Verden in his capacity as Elector and not as King of England. Admittedly Britain might profit by the transactions, but neither admiral nor king could use the British fleet in the manner that they and the Danish king wished.[4]

Norris also had his troubles with Frederick William I, King of Prussia, although it must be admitted that Norris succeeded somewhat better in mollifying that dour monarch than did George I. Throughout his reign the English king had nearly as much trouble with his son-in-law, the Prussian ruler, as he did with his own son, the Prince of Wales. Baltic affairs did not increase domestic harmony between the in-laws. Frederick William—always suspicious and perhaps rightly so, if he judged

---

[1] Idem to Idem, August 10, 1715, *Ibid.*
[2] Norris to Townshend, August 10, 1715, BM., Add. MSS., 28,144.
[3] Norris to Robethon, August 10, 1715, BM., Add. MSS., 28,143.
[4] Rigsarkiv, T.K.U.A., Geheimeregistratur, Vol. 257. Westphal was commended for his conduct by Wibe. Wibe to Westphal, September 15, 1715, Westphal Correspondence, Rigsarkiv, T.K.U.A., Russland, C 122.

others by himself—had attempted even before the departure of the Norris squadron to hold George I to a definite promise of British naval assistance in confederate military ventures. Always he had been answered through Johann Wilhelm Heusch, the Hanoverian minister at Berlin, rather than through any of George's representatives as king. What assurances he obtained were always vague and uncertain and quite unsatisfactory to the Prussian ruler who like his more famous son could never distinguish between the offices of King and Elector.

George's attempts to circumvent the dilemma caused by his dual role indicates to a considerable extent the fine line diplomatically speaking that George I had to draw, a line that caused embarrassments to his British subjects and also to many of the statesmen and chanceries of Europe. His explanation as to the way that Heusch was to explain the existing situation must have sounded phony to his partners in the Northern Alliance.

> We promise the King of Prussia on Our faith and troth that the said squadron shall in every way second operations in Pomerania against Sweden, and hope his Prussian Majesty will believe Our word, that there will be no want in the fulfilling of this promise. But we could not give a written engagement, since the providing of the squadron pertains to us as King, and if We gave a written engagement We could not use Our German Ministers, but We should have to give it by the hands of English ministers.[1]

Furthermore George hoped 'that We shall not be urged to have superfluous and unnecessary demonstrations of hostility made against Sweden . . . since this would only cause Us *embarrassment* here and would do no good there.'[2] To Frederick William I, however, George's embarrassments meant little or nothing. The Prussian king saw only an urgent need for British naval aid if the operation against Stralsund were to be expedited. Time was money to the parsimonious king. He did not care nor know about British party politics and did not realize that his outspoken comments often played into the hands of the British Tories and thus made it even more difficult for

[1] Quoted in Williams, *Stanhope*, p. 232. A slightly different translation with the same meaning can be found in Michael, *England under George I*, I, 289.
[2] Quoted in Williams, *Stanhope*, p. 232.

George to assist his allies.[1] Failing at Whitehall, he turned directly to the *Cumberland* and the British admiral.

The first Prussian overture made to the admiral was on July 27 when the latter was at Danzig. At that time Frederick asked Norris to cover a number of corn ships which were at Königsberg, but were destined for the Prussian soldiers participating in the Stralsund siege. According to the Prussian ruler his request was in accord with the 'strict alliances in which I have the Hon. to find myself with the King your Master and in consequence of the Orders of his Maj'ty.'[2] Norris readily agreed to the Prussian proposal if the ships were ready to join his convoy as he came back down the Baltic with the merchantmen, but refused to give the ships special coverage because such would mean that they would 'suffer some Insult from the Swedes, which they cannot do when with me.'[3]

Prussian plans for the British squadron, however, went beyond the convoying of corn ships. Consequently Norris on August 17 received a letter from Frederick William dated August 7 which summed up the military situation before Stralsund. A superior Swedish force had caused the Danish fleet to withdraw to more shallow water and as a result the attack upon Usedom had been delayed. That island had to be taken before Charles XII could be dislodged from Pomerania. The time then had come for Norris to execute the design that 'they had in England in sending you with the squadron that you command into the Baltic.' Now must the British admiral act according to the 'intentions de sa Majesté Britannique et conforme au veritable Interest de Ses Royaumes.' Norris was to work with the Danes to bring about the withdrawal of the Swedish fleet so that it could do nothing against 'la liberté du Commerce ny autrement.'[4]

Norris of course could do nothing. As he pointed out, he was obeying his master's commands by refusing to separate from

[1] Michael, *England under George I*, I, 296.

[2] Frederick William I (by Ilgen) to Norris, July 27, 1715, BM., Add. MSS., 28,144; 'étroites Alliances dans lesquelles j'ay l'honneure de me trouver avec le Roy vôtre maître et en consequences des Ordres desa Majesté.'

[3] Norris to Frederick William I, July 28, 1715, BM., Add. MSS., 28,144 and Norris to Captain Gordon, July 28, 1715, BM., Add. MSS., 28,135.

[4] Frederick William I to Norris, August 7, 1715, BM., Add MSS., 28,154. Püchler to Norris, July 31, 1715, BM., Add. MSS., 28,144 contains an excellent account of the naval engagement as it happened before Stralsund.

the Dutch. As soon as De Veth received instructions from Lintelo, which would allow the Dutch commander to take the offensive, Norris said he would be most happy to do as Frederick William I desired. Anything that the latter could do to expedite Lintelo's mission to Charles XII would be to the advantage of all concerned.[1]

Harassed by the monarchs in the Northern Alliance and ignored by the British ministers at home,[2] Norris watched as the seasons changed on the Baltic station and the cold weather approached. Provisions dwindled and the beer ration sank dangerously low. 'When our Men be reduced to drink water in these parts and are at short Allowance of other Provisions, it will soon introduce a Sickness among them.'[3] Violent storms, which battered the ships and caused one Dutch ship of forty-four guns to founder added to the troubles of De Veth and Norris.[4] As the commanders came down the Baltic they found that the Prussian corn ships were not ready. Instead at Danzig Road there was another terse invitation from Frederick William for the squadron to deliver Rügen from the Swedish fleet. That was 'le vray Moyens' for Norris to cover the merchantmen from the Swedish pirates and to add to his reputation.[5]

Norris, by way of contrast was happy to hear from Püchler who informed him of the Danish victory over the Swedes off Jasmund on August 8. The Danish victory had forced the Swedes to withdraw to Bornholm,[6] and Norris could thus happily write Frederick William I that British aid was not necessary so far as the confederate plans against Stralsund were

[1] Norris to Frederick William I, August 19, 1715, BM., Add. MSS., 28,144.

[2] Norris to Townshend, August 19, 1715, BM., Add. MSS., 28,144. Although Townshend had written Norris about the Dutch decision to send Lintelo to Stralsund, he evaded the Admiral's questions as to what should be done if De Veth failed to coöperate.

[3] Norris to Townshend, August 19, 1715, *Ibid.*

[4] Idem to Idem, September 2, 1715, *Ibid.* Cf. various letters of Norris to his captains throughout August, BM., Add. MSS., 28,135, and various letters of De Veth to the Admiralty at Amsterdam throughout September–November, Rijksarchief, Archieven der Admiraliteitscolleges, No. 1656.

[5] Norris to Hobman on the *Beaumont*, September 1, 1715, BM., Add. MSS., 28,135; and Frederick William I to Norris, August 31, 1715, BM., Add. MSS., 28,144.

[6] Püchler to Norris, August 14, 1715, BM., Add. MSS., 28,144 and 28,154. For details of the battle see *Bidrag . . . Nordiske Krigs*, VII, 107–118 and Thyra Sehested, *Admiral C. T. Sehesteds Saga* (Copenhagen, 1904), pp. 97–109.

concerned.[1] Furthermore, it must have been of considerable satisfaction for Norris to be able to point out to Püchler and the Danes that Jasmund had been possible because the Danes had followed British advice and met the enemy with all the force that they could muster.[2] Yet there was more naval work to be done. The Danish king wanted Norris to force the Swedes all the way back to Karlscrona so that Prussian artillery could safely be transported from Stettin to Stralsund.[3]

When Norris arrived in Köge Bay, September 13,[4] he received news that made it possible for him in part at least to carry out the desires of the Danish king. There at Köge Bay, he was met by a Danish Frigate, which carried a dispatch from Townshend dated August 13, a dispatch, which altered to a considerable extent the purpose of the British Baltic expedition. The mask of neutrality so long used by George I was partially discarded. The expostulations of his allies were in part to be answered. Cloaking his changed policy with the charge that Sweden had not answered British representations on commerce, George I announced his intention to leave eight ships in the Baltic after the bulk of the squadron returned to England. These vessels according to George were 'to support the Right of his People, and the just demands he has made on their behalf.' As eight ships were too small a number to act alone, they were to be placed under the command of a 'discreet' officer but not a flag officer and were to join the Danish fleet and to work with it to prevent Swedish domination of the Baltic. Frederick IV on his side was to supply the detached vessels.[5] Thus George I still talking about the ships being left for reprisals would as King be partially fulfilling the commitments he had made as Elector. Commercial interests had no bearing on the decision to leave the eight ships for the season was over sofar as trade was concerned. Any privateers at sea at that time would have found slim pickings indeed.

[1] Norris to Frederick William I, September 2, 1715 and Norris to Püchler, same date, BM., Add. MSS., 28,144.
[2] Norris to his various captains, August and September, 1715, BM., Add. MSS., 28,135.
[3] Püchler to Norris August 14, 1715, BM., Add. MSS., 28,144.
[4] Norris to his various captains, August and September, 1715, BM., Add. MSS., 28,135.
[5] Townshend to Norris, August 13, 1715, BM., Add. MSS., 28,154.

The change in British policy was a direct result of pressure put upon George I as Elector by his allies. Both Chance and Michael, the former relying too heavily upon the latter, over-emphasize the effect of the Prussian protests upon George I.[1] To be sure Frederick William I had written George I twice on the subject of leaving British ships in the Baltic to prevent the Swedes from endangering military operations against Stralsund. In one letter dated July 27 he naïvely stated that 'surely those must not prove to have been right' who maintained that Norris had come to the Baltic exclusively for the protection of British trade.[2] Yet it was Denmark, not Prussia who held the necessary cards to force the English king's hand. His ace of trumps was Bremen, which Denmark absolutely refused to turn over to Hanover until the promised naval aid was realized. Moreover, it was Denmark who had the most to profit should George I leave British ships of war in the Baltic because Denmark was bearing the brunt of the task in blockading Karlscrona. Thus when the Danes added their peremptory demands to Prussia's more vehement ones, George I was forced to pressure his British ministers into following his Hanoverian diplomacy.

Practical considerations prevented George I from leaving the entire squadron. First, the traders had to cross the North Sea where they might be set upon by Swedish privateers or those belonging to George's rebellious Jacobite subjects who did not recognize the Hanoverian succession. Second, as stated above, munitions and provisions were low and Denmark, having trouble meeting the demands of its own ships, could supply only a limited number of English vessels.[3] An entire fleet joined with the Danes would make the reprisal excuse seem even weaker than it actually was. Townshend would go along with the Hanoverians only if he could rationalize his stand. Men such as Orford would definitely resist such an overt act of hostility as joining the entire Baltic contingent to the Danes. Actually they opposed any British aid to the fleet of Frederick IV.[4]

[1] Chance, *George I and the Northern War*, p. 90, and Michael, *England under George I*, I, 294.

[2] Michael, *England under George I*, I, 294.

[3] Queries and Answers, BM., Add. MSS., 28,154.

[4] Chance, *George I and the Northern War*, pp. 90–91, and Michael, *England under George I*, I, 294–297.

Thus George I caught between the cross fire of his subjects and his allies arrived at the compromise plan of leaving the eight vessels, which are usually referred to collectively as the Hopson squadron.

How George I came to arrive at this command decision is extremely significant. It provides an excellent example of how George I as Elector was able to work his will upon his British ministers. Moreover, it offers tangible evidence that George I was violating his coronation agreement and the laws of Parliament and allowing Hanoverian considerations to dominate English affairs. For these reasons, the diplomacy behind the Hopson squadron is worth tracing in detail.

On July 27, the same day that the King of Prussia had written George I, his Danish colleague had followed suit. Frederick IV admitted that the Danish victory had eased the naval situation somewhat, but went on to point out that Danish losses and overall insufficiencies had brought the operation before Stralsund to a standstill. Thus Norris had to take action soon. When he did, he should operate in conjunction with the Danish fleet to destroy Swedish sea power. Frederick IV pointed out that any misfortune to the Danish fleet would be a loss to and a direct blow against the King of England. When Norris joined the Danes and aided in cutting off the Swedes from Pomerania, Bremen would be ceded to Hanover. George I would also have to promise that Norris would remain before Stralsund until all danger of Swedish naval relief to that city was removed.[1]

George I, as might be expected, at first tried to temporize. His defense for his vacillating conduct must have appeared weak in the eyes of his allies. Winds and unforeseen incidents were all blamed for Norris's long absence in the Baltic. George I said that Denmark could count upon Norris moving at the right time and upon Hanover abiding by her treaty stipulations. George I cautioned the Danish king against setting his expectations too high, and charged that Frederick's failure to live up to his own obligations had prevented him from

---

[1] Rigsarkiv, T.K.U.A., Geheimeregistratur, Vol. 257. See also various letters from the Danish chancery to Söhlenthal throughout June and July, 1715, Rigsarkiv, Söhlenthal Correspondence, T.K.U.A., England C.

carrying out Hanoverian promises; the Danish failure undoubtedly was a refusal to give him Bremen without assurances of naval
support. 'It was old history; lack of mutual confidence and the
King of England's lack of power to uphold what the Elector of
Hanover had promised.'[1]

The dispatches of Söhlenthal, the Danish ambassador to
London, must have plunged the Danish court even further into
the depths of gloom. Late in July Bernstorff had given Söhlenthal all sorts of conflicting statements. First the proposed treaty
between Russia and Hanover had to be adjusted before Norris
could be ordered to act. Hanover was against Denmark's
guarantee of certain of the Baltic provinces to Russia. Norris
would lie off Bornholm as soon as the trade was secure, but
George I could make no definite commitments. Bernstorff
climaxed his double talk by saying that he understood that
Norris already had orders to join the Danes. The last was
too much for the Danish envoy who reminded Bernstorff
of the decisions taken by De Veth and Norris, and the out
and out refusal of Norris either to join the Danes or to act
alone.

The Söhlenthal-Bernstorff conversation made it quite apparent to the latter that until the Danes were certain of naval aid
they would not let go of Bremen. Consequently, Bernstorff and
the other Hanoverian advisers of the King along with George I
persuaded the British ministers to allow ten British ships to join
the Danes in order to strengthen the sea power of Frederick IV.[2]
The compromise agreed upon was satisfactory to Söhlenthal,
even after the number of ships promised was reduced from ten
to eight.[3] Thus on August 13 orders to Norris to detach the
ships were drawn up. On the next day, they were sent to
Püchler, who was to forward them to Frederick IV for trans-
mittal to Norris.

Ten days later Püchler, George's Hanoverian minister to
Denmark, received the new instructions. To Püchler whose
sole interest was the acquisition of Bremen and Verden for
Hanover, the new orders were the best news possible. Norris's
inactivity had made his work nearly impossible to achieve, and

[1] *Bidrag . . . Nordiske Krigs*, VII, 140.
[2] Mediger, *Moskaus Weg*, p. 17, 20.
[3] *Bidrag . . . Nordiske Krigs*, VII, 140.

he had begun to fear that Prussia and Denmark, drawn more closely together by the Danish naval victory at Jasmund, might work to exclude Hanover from the Swedish spoils. He hurried to deliver the good news to Ditlev Wibe, the Danish councillor, but could not do so because of Wibe's illness. Then Püchler himself became stricken.[1] The honor of showing Frederick IV the new commands for Norris and its covering letter went then to Heusch, who was stationed at the confederate camp before Stralsund.

Thus orders for an English admiral were transported to a Danish king through two Hanoverian diplomats, with the British diplomats on the scene playing no role whatsoever. Püchler did inform Norris that he could expect new commands on arrival at Copenhagen, which for the moment could not be sent because of important reasons.[2] The 'grand reason' why the dispatches could not be moved through regular channels was a simple one. Heusch refused to forward a copy of the instructions to Norris until he was absolutely certain that Bremen was in the possession of Hanover. Frederick IV refused to turn that place over to George I until Norris was actually sent the orders to join his ships.

Püchler arose from his sick bed to confer with the Danish councillors, Wibe, Holstein, and Dewitz. His initial attempt to circumvent the diplomatic impassé that had arisen back-fired on him, for he carried with him unopened dispatches from Hanover, which when he presented them to the Danes, complicated matters considerably. They contained in addition to complaints about fleet inactivity, snide remarks about the insanity of the Danish government. Püchler, burned by his own carelessness at not reading the dispatches before presenting them, tried unsuccessfully to defend his government. He was badly pressed for time, as news came to him that Norris was already on his way to the Sound.[3] He knew that Norris would be inconvenienced by any long delays, and therefore decided to act on his own.[4] On September 13, by means of the Danish

[1] Püchler to Norris, August 18, 1715, BM., Add. MSS., 28,144.

[2] *Ibid.*: 'Il y a une grande Raison pour que je ne dois pas encore vous envoyer cet Ordre, ni l'addresser à present à Copenhagen.'

[3] *Bidrag . . . Nordiske Krigs*, VII, 144–145.

[4] Püchler to Norris, August 28, 1715, BM., Add. MSS., 28,144 and 28,154.

frigate *Hvit Orn*, he sent Norris the orders to leave the eight ships after the admiral had worked out details with the Danish admiralty.[1] To Townshend's detailed instructions to Norris, Püchler added one of his own. He requested that the ships to be detached not be 'des plus petits de vôtre escadre.'[2]

Norris took his advice literally and prepared to leave behind 'the best Ships of my Squadron,'[3] which were to be under the command of Captain Edward Hopson, 'a discret Person as far as I am able to make judgement.' Hopson was of non-flag rank, the eldest captain in the squadron, and had been the only British captain who had been present at Anglo-Dutch joint war councils. Moreover, all eight captains chosen to remain had been appointed to their present commands by an admiralty board that had come into existence since George I came to the English throne. Consequently, Norris was of the opinion that they would go out of their way to make George I and the men around him happy. So far as Norris could see there was no reason for the ships to remain in the Baltic after October 21, because by that time the 'Affair of Rügen should be completed,' and the Baltic weather would make it impossible for the ships to do any additional service for Denmark until spring.[4] Although Michael presses the point a little too far, it must be re-stressed that Norris was thinking in a different vein than that outlined by his written instructions, which stated that the eight ships were to act in concert with the Danes 'to compel the Swedes to make Reparation for the damages done to his Maj'ty's Subjects, and to revoke the said unjustifiable Edict lately publish'd.'[5] To the men on the scene, such as Norris and Hopson, Britain was leaving the eight ships to aid an ally of George I as Elector against another ally of George I as King. Naval thinking was in terms of direct British naval assistance in the siege operation against the German possessions of Charles XII, no matter what words the ministry at home might be using to circumvent the Act of Succession and to dupe, or at least to pacify, the

[1] *Bidrag . . . Nordiske Krigs*, VII, 144–145.

[2] Püchler to Norris, September 10, 1715, BM., Add. MSS., 28,144.

[3] Norris to Raben, to Krabbe and to Sehestedt, September 14, 1715, BM., Add. MSS., 28,144.

[4] Norris to Townshend, September 16, 1715, *Ibid*. Cf. Norris to Aylmer, September 17, 1715, BM., Add. MSS., 28,143.

[5] Instructions to Hopson, September 14, 1715, BM., Add. MSS., 28,144.

Parliament.[1] After working out details for detaching the eight ships, Norris weighed anchor for home. A run of bad weather kept him for days in the Sound. Finally he was able to clear for England, landing near the mouth of the Thames on October 28 after a battle with the elements which more than justified his nickname 'Foul-Weather Jack.'[2] By leaving some of his ships serving under Danish command, Norris made it possible for George I to occupy on October 14, 1715, Bremen. At long last he had control of the mouths of the Elbe and Weser rivers.[3]

The effect of Hopson's squadron upon Baltic military affairs is difficult to assess. One early and measurable result was that the Danes were able to call three of their badly battered vessels into port 'which . . . would not have been done if we had not join'd them.'[4] On the matter of the role of Hopson in the capture of Stralsund, the Teutonic historians, Droysen and Michael hold opposite views. The former, ardent nationalist that he is, insists that the eight British ships made no difference to the outcome of the campaign. Inclement weather kept the Swedes from leaving port while Danish and Prussian troops brought the fortress to its knees.[5] Michael on the other hand credited the eight ships with giving the Danes naval supremacy in the battle for Baltic sea power. Consequently the Swedish fleet under Vice-Admiral Evert Taube did not dare run the Blockade,[6] an interpretation with which an English authority on this period, Basil Williams, agrees.[7]

There is no doubt that the months of October and November were exceptionally stormy ones, and that during that period the combined Anglo-Danish naval forces spent some time in port. Nevertheless during the crucial moments of the campaign for Rügen the blockading squadron kept at sea, notwithstanding the storms and the damage that it suffered from the wintry

[1] Michael, *England under George I*, I, 297–298 makes much of this point to substantiate his thesis that the Hanoverians dominated British foreign policy at this time.

[2] Norris to Burchett, October 28, 1715, and to Townshend, October 28, 1715, BM., Add. MSS., 28,144.

[3] Mediger, *Moskaus Weg*, p. 20.

[4] Norris to Townshend, September 16, 1715, *Ibid.*

[5] Droysen, *Geschichte*, Vol. IV, Pt. ii, 140–142.

[6] Michael, *England under George I*, I, 298.

[7] Williams, *Stanhope*, p. 233.

blasts.[1] If the ships covering the landing could be at sea, there seems little reason to believe that storms alone prevented the Swedes from strengthening their garrisons in Germany. Moreover, if the tempests did not deter the confederates from braving the storms and landing troops on a hostile shore, they should not have prevented Taube from landing supplies at friendly ports. We should remember that amphibious operations were not the science they are today and that in the days of sailing ships inclement skies made the work of the blockade runner easier and that of the blockading force much more difficult. Thus it is quite probable that the Hopson squadron did assist in the capture of Rügen, which fell on November 16 to a combined Danish-Prussian force.[2] Even though they may not have fired at a single Swedish warship, their presence caused Taube to delay attempting to relieve beleaguered Stralsund. The eight British ships along with those of the Danes provide an excellent example of a 'fleet in being' having a significant effect upon military operations.

There are some historians who in their attempts to minimize the influence of Hopson exploit two factors which occurred in the later phases of the Stralsund siege: one that in spite of Danish pleas[3] Hopson withdrew his ships from the scene of active operations before the city capitulated; and two that Admiral Taube was able to break out of his containment and carry supplies to Stralsund while Hopson was still in the Baltic. If one ignores certain obvious contradictions, the two arguments can be used to buttress or to belittle the significance of Hopson. Half-truths always can be so employed. To be sure Hopson was not in the immediate waters before Stralsund, but his absence does not necessarily imply that British naval demonstrations had not contributed to the final surrender of the Swedish citadel. Moreover, Rügen was the key to Stralsund's defenses and to its ability to withstand a long siege. Norris earlier had predicted that the work of the eight ships would be

---

[1] Frederick IV to Admiral Gyldenlöve, November 22, 1715, Rigsarkiv, T.K.U.A., Geheimeregistratur, Vol. 257.

[2] Frederick IV to George I, Peter I, and Augustus II, November 23, 1715, *Ibid.*

[3] Frederick IV to George I, December 22, 1715, Rigsarkiv, T.K.U.A., Geheimeregistratur, Vol. 257.

completed with the capture of that island,[1] and Hopson had been at sea and had been very much in evidence when Rügen surrendered.

Taube's movements also bear consideration. Admittedly he did run the blockade while Hopson was in the Baltic, but he did it at a time when the English naval officer had retired from active operations and was only waiting for favorable wind to take his contingent to England. The reasoning that Taube failed to move because of the weather and that he took the first opportunity with clear skies to sail to Stralsund is without historical foundation. The ease with which Taube moved can in part be traced to Hopson's withdrawal, but more important to the fact that most of the Danish ships were away on convoy duty instead of being on their station before Stralsund. The Danes gambled that Taube would not try to relieve Charles XII and lost.[2] Thus when Taube made his bid to assist Stralsund the principle of the 'fleet in being' had been violated by the Danes. The Swedish admiral was astute enough to take full advantage of the opportunity presented to him. The Danes once more had dispersed their ships and once more paid a price, for Taube coming too late to help Stralsund sailed with 700 men and four months supply to Wismar, Sweden's last possession on the continent. If the Danes had not been off their post, the capture of that city would have been less costly to them and to the other members of the Northern Alliance.

As is well known, Charles XII escaped to Sweden to continue his battles with his enemies. As 1715 came to an end, Hopson and his contingent arrived back in England, but already plans were being made by the Hanoverians to send a squadron the next year which was to place trade and commerce second to naval and diplomatic considerations.[3] While the naval units prepared for another season of campaigning, the diplomats scurried about in their attempts to capture any advantages that might facilitate the approaching action in the field.

[1] Norris to Townshend, September 16, 1715, BM., Add. MSS., 28,144.
[2] Frederick IV to Gabel, December 13, 1715, Rigsarkiv, T.K.U.A., Geheime-registratur, Vol. 257.
[3] Instructions to Norris, May 21, 1716, BM., Add. MSS., 28,128.

VII

ANGLO-SWEDISH INTER-SQUADRON DIPLOMACY, 1715-1716

THE diplomacy of George I and British overt acts of hostility toward Sweden cloaked under the guise of pseudo-neutrality could not continue unchallenged by Charles XII. His character dictated otherwise. So far as England was concerned, George I changed the Great Northern War from:

> Distant Battles of the Pole and Swede
> Which frugal Citizens o'er Coffee read,
> Careless for who shall fail or who succeed[1]

to a conflict which threatened to involve not only English ships, treasure, and seamen, but even Britain itself. The threat of Britain's security reached all the way to the Hanoverian succession. For a considerable length of time, George's propaganda had accused Charles XII and his countrymen of aiding the Jacobites. George I, by such tactics was making a Stuart restoration more and more advantageous for Sweden. By August of 1715, Gyllenborg was of the opinion that Sweden in July, 1715, should have sent three or four thousand troops to England to dethrone the Hanoverian elector,[2] who had departed from the traditional friendship with Sweden long maintained by Britain and the Electorate.

---

[1] Nicholas Rowe, *The Fair Penitent* (1703), prologue.
[2] Thomas Westrin (ed.), 'En förklaring af Grefve Carl Gyllenborg agående hans förhallande till Pretendenter" (Svenska), *Historisk Tidskrift* (1903), XXIII, 288. Cited hereafter as Gyllenborg's, 'Förklaring.'

Whatever influence the events of 1715 had upon Swedish-Jacobite relations, there was noticeable in Swedish diplomatic circles a growing anti-British and anti-Hanoverian sentiment. The Hopson squadron caused the Swedish cup of bitterness to overflow. Various types of rumors filled Stockholm, none of them to the advantage of English subjects and traders. Jackson reported from Sweden's capital city that the Senate had received orders from Charles XII:

> To arrest all English merchants and seize all the ships and effects of the British Nation, the very moment they get intelligence of any hostility being begun by any of the ships Sir John Norris left with the Danes, and as they conclude that an encounter will unavoidably happen whenever their fleet gets to the Coast of Pomerania, I am also informed that dispositions are already made for putting the King's order in execution upon the first notice of any action.[1]

The British minister also noted that the Swedish people were following the fortunes of the Stuarts in Scotland with greater interest. For the most part, the Swedish populace was in sympathy with the Pretender and was chagrined that the majority of Englishmen were standing firmly behind the House of Brunswick-Luneberg.[2] Such information as the Swedes received concerning the rising of the '15' reached Stockholm through Gyllenborg, whose 'relations of late have savour'd strongly of malice and party animosity.'[3]

Jackson, who hoped that the news concerning James's landing in strength in Scotland was false, was of the opinion that Gyllenborg's continued protests against British naval activity was prompted 'by other motives than the interest of his country.' Yet, he was forced to admit that the 'very impertinent' Swedish minister to London was much applauded at home, and that there was little doubt that Gyllenborg's anti-Hanoverian conduct would 'be justified by his master.'[4] The British diplomat, however, took heart in the thought that the death of Louis XIV

---

[1] Jackson to Townshend, October 17, 1715, P.R.O., State Papers, Sweden, 95/21.
[2] Idem to Idem, August 9 and September 3, 1715, *Ibid.*
[3] Idem to Idem, October 29, 1715, *Ibid.*
[4] *Ibid.*

would be detrimental to any schemes that Swede or Jacobite might entertain against England.[1]

According to Jackson, Gyllenborg should have sat tight and accepted Britain's stand in the Baltic without protest, a view to which Larsson, one of Gyllenborg's biographers concurs. The latter charges the Swedish minister with being overly suspicious, with over-estimating England's negotiations with his country's foes, and with the error of considering that Norris's squadron intended to force Sweden to make peace and to prevent the relief of Stralsund. Larsson is of the opinion that the Pretender and trade were the sole motives for dispatching Norris to the Baltic.[2] Larsson unfortunately ignored the fact that Gyllenborg himself, up to the time that diplomatic and military events proved otherwise, had considered trade the paramount reason for sending the squadron into the Baltic. The Hopson contingent's role before Stralsund can conveniently be considered as the watershed not only for England's commitment to the Northern Alliance, but also in the thinking of the Swedish minister at London. It must be admitted, however, that even before Gyllenborg heard about Hopson, his distrust of George I had assumed rather large proportions. After he found out about the eight ships he became almost an irreconcilable foe of the Hanoverian succession.

Just before he learned of Hopson's activities, however, he presented Charles's answer to the British demands which had been made by Jefferyes and Jackson the previous June, and which the Swedish ruler considered to be little short of an overt declaration of war. It was only because Charles XII had wanted Britain's friendship and because of the moderation of the Swedish ministers that an open rupture between the two countries had been prevented, at least so the Swedish note asserted. Expressing surprise at the size of the Norris squadron, Charles XII declared a ready willingness to give all reasonable satisfaction for damages committed by Swedish privateers contrary to the tenor and meaning of the privateering ordinances. There was nothing in the Swedish actions which did not have a precedent in a prohibition made in 1684 by the Maritime Powers against Swedish trade with France. One difference was

[1] Jackson to Townshend, September 3 and 13, 1715, *Ibid.*
[2] Larsson, *Gyllenborg*, pp. 11-15.

that Charles XII was stopping trade to only a few towns as compared with the British and Dutch whose edicts had been leveled against Swedish commerce with an entire country.

To substantiate the point that Sweden was acting under law and treaties, Gyllenborg enclosed with the Swedish reply a memoir delivered by Sweden in 1689 protesting British restrictive action on Swedish shipping. That memoir and one delivered in 1697 by Kristofer Leyoncrona [Lejoncrona] to the Lords Justices of England had been couched in the language of friends and of diplomats rather than in blustering threats as had been the note delivered by Jefferyes. According to Sweden, Charles XII had the right to expect similar treatment rather than the 'mémoire menacant de Monsr. Jefferyes.'

Sweden took the position that the subjects of Great Britain were the ones at fault, for by furnishing Russia with war materials, the British were directly violating the intent if not the letter of the treaties of 1661 and 1700. Peter had been furnished by the Maritime Powers with ships of war complete even to crews and officers. That practice had continued to such an extent that it might be said that the Russian fleet was more Anglo-Dutch than Muscovite. If the British wished to re-establish complete freedom of trade, the logical way would be for George I to live up to his treaty promises and assist Charles XII to reconquer his lost provinces. If such were done, the Swedish king would be most happy to give the British all the commercial privileges that they reasonably could expect.

Charles XII had some complaints of his own to make against Great Britain. Former injuries to Swedish shipping still remained without compensation. England still refused to fulfill her engagements wherein she had promised to maintain the Protestant religion and the balance of power in the Baltic. Whereas Britain was supplying arms to Sweden's enemies, Sweden to the contrary had up to the peace of Ryswick furnished William with a contingent of 6,000 men and helped bring about that peace. The Norris squadron should have come to the Baltic to save Sweden rather than to convoy a few merchantmen, and it would be well for England to beware of the rising power of the Czar, who would monopolize all Baltic trade.[1]

[1] Gyllenborg to Townshend, September 12, 1715 with enclosures, *Handlingar*, X, 210-213.

Thus the Swedish king based his cause upon pleas of precedent and justice and failed to reckon how little his chance for success was in view of the changing state of affairs in the Baltic.[1] The political aspirations of George I and the Hanoverian Junto made no allowance for what was right or what had been done. Aggrandizement outweighed justice. To obtain Bremen and Verden active coöperation with an ally's foes was necessary. Hopson had to be left in the Baltic. Power and greed outweighed precedent.

By the end of September a courier brought Gyllenborg the news that some British ships were to winter in the Baltic, and he forthwith hastily drafted a protest to Townshend. That individual answered the Swedish minister with the terse reply that British vessels would stay in northern waters until Sweden had given ample satisfactions for the privateering depredations of her subjects. The English secretary, however, did attempt to mollify Gyllenborg by assuring him that the Hopson squadron would not act militarily in concert with the Danes against Sweden.[2]

Although not at all pacified by Townshend's perverted or at least misleading statement, Gyllenborg could do little. Additional information continued to come into the Swedish minister's hands, who appears to have had excellent news sources close to the highest offices of the British government. On October 3, he delivered a vehement note to Townshend, which laid bare Swedish thinking on the basic facts of the Hopson squadron and on the importance of Bremen and Verden in British diplomatic thinking.[3] That protest should be considered in detail because it shows the influence that the Hopson squadron had upon the diplomacy of 1716, and almost represents the 'point of no return' for Britain's underwriting the seizure by George I of the two former principalities of the Swedish king.

Gyllenborg charged that Hopson had effected a junction with the Danes and had aided the allied attack against Stralsund by preventing Sweden from sending assistance to the

[1] Chance, *George I and the Northern War*, p. 94.
[2] Gyllenborg to Sparre, September 30, 1715, *Handlingar*, X, 230; Gyllenborg to Müllern, October 1, 1715, *Ibid.*, X, 232.
[3] Gyllenborg to Townshend, October 3, 1715, *Ibid.*, X, 243-245.

hard pressed Stralsund garrison. Pointing out that British action was tantamount to a declaration of war, Gyllenborg wondered if Sweden was to consider that open hostilities now existed between the two countries; at the same time he expressed the hope that George I would not violate his treaty obligations to Sweden and aid in the partition of that land by the enemies of Charles XII. Nevertheless it was apparent to Gyllenborg that the Swedish interruption of British commerce could not be considered in the same light as Hopson's joining the Danes in open hostilities against Sweden.

Reiterating that Charles XII had answered all of England's demands in a satisfactory manner, the Swedish minister pointed out that winter had arrived in the Baltic and that the season for commercial activity had passed. He hoped that the winter could be used to eradicate differences between England and Sweden so that the former could conform to the friendship and the agreements that had once governed relations between the two countries. The present course of events pushed by the German advisers of George I could only be harmful to British commercial interests, which should be considered over and above Hanoverian territorial aspirations. It was well known in diplomatic circles that Hanover had promised British naval assistance to the Northern Alliance in exchange for Bremen and Verden. Gyllenborg pointed out that such commitments were contrary to various sacred acts of the British parliament, to which neither the Hanoverian king nor his ministers were paying the slightest attention.[1]

Townshend answered the Gyllenborg note a week later, and expressed surprise at its tenor and wording. Again he stressed the fact that Swedish privateering was contrary, not only to international law, but also to the specific existing treaties and added that no comparison could be made between the action of Charles XII and that of Britain and Holland during the wars with Louis XIV. In the second instance only contraband was being seized instead of all ships as was the case in the Baltic conflict. Moreover, as Townshend so piously and self-righteously put it, Sweden had gained by England's seizure of her vessels in spite of the fact that certain indemnities

---

[1] *Ibid.* The same letter may be found in Lamberty, *Mémoires*, IX, 297–298.

were still due because the victories over Louis XIV had preserved the liberties of all Europe from French aggression. Bemoaning a forty percent rise in the cost of naval stores, the English secretary claimed that his countries losses to Swedish privateers were exceedingly high, and to those losses should be added £163,584 19s. 4d., the cost of outfitting the Baltic convoy. Before the latter could be recalled, reparations had to be made, and Townshend concluded his note by sarcastically complimenting the Swede on the knowledge and zeal that he possessed concerning English statutes relating to the Protestant Succession.[1]

Such heated proposals and counter proposals show that the situation was rapidly getting out of hand, and that the upshot of Anglo-Swedish diplomacy during 1715 illustrates the gradual but constantly growing estrangement between the two countries. The gap widened with the Hanoverian declaration of war coincident with the cession of Bremen and Verden. Well might Townshend insist that no convention existed between Denmark and England concerning the eight ships, the war declaration, or the cession of the provinces, but Gyllenborg could not be so convinced.[2] He became so bitter that for a time he avoided showing himself at the Hanoverian court where Swedish reverses were celebrated and his sovereign ridiculed. In debt, dejected, and downhearted, he requested in vain that he be relieved of his post.[3]

Chance is of the opinion that one can 'quibble' over the point whether the eight vessels were left in obedience to the terms of a treaty concluded between Hanover and Denmark for the cession of Bremen and Verden as was charged by Gyllenborg.[4] Townshend, says Chance, was legally correct in his denial because the events leading up to the Hopson squadron show conclusively that at least a meeting of the minds existed

---

[1] Townshend to Gyllenborg, October 11, 1715, *Handlinger*, X, 250–255: 'Le Roy sans doute ne peut qu'estre fort rederable à un Ministre Etranger que le fait ressouvenir des Lois de Son Royaume et je dois vous remercier de le peine que vous aves prise sur ce chaptre.'

[2] Townshend to Gyllenborg, October 11, 1715, *Handlingar*, X, 250–255.

[3] Larsson, *Gyllenborg*, p. 17. Perhaps Larsson was a little cautious in stating that George's declaration of war had little immediate influence on Anglo-Swedish relations. Cf. Chance, *George I and the Northern War*, p. 95 for a contrary opinion.

[4] Chance, *George I and the Northern War*, p. 95.

among the British, Hanoverians and Danes at Copenhagen regarding the eight ships, the cession, and the war declaration, and that any quibbling on Townshend's part was as shallow as his master's reasons for opening hostilities against his one time ally.

George I insisted that he as Elector of Hanover had declared war upon Charles XII to bring about peace in the upper and lower Saxon Circles and because Charles XII refused to take part in the Congress of Brunswick. Moreover, he maintained that Charles XII was contemplating an attack upon Brunswick in the same manner that he had made an 'unjustifiable' assault upon the king of Prussia at Wolgast. The statement by Charles XII wherein he threatened that he would avenge himself upon his false friends could only be directed at Hanover, and his attempts to use force to win back what he had lost through his own fault was equivalent to a declaration of war.[1] To this obvious rationalizing, Gyllenborg commented: 'Y-at-il Jamais eu une excuse ou plus injuste ou plus ridicule?'[2] As Wiesener so aptly stated, the real reason for George's declaration was that he could not sit idly by and see his fellow sovereigns gobble up portions of Sweden without Hanover having its place at the trough.[3] The pros and cons of his action summarized by Chance illustrate the importance of the Hanoverian war declaration to future events in the Baltic.

The action was certain to worsen already strained relations between England and Sweden, for Charles XII well known for his abhorrence of alienating any portion of his patrimony could hardly be expected to distinguish between England and Hanover. The next three years carried a constant threat of a Swedish invasion of Scotland as retaliation by Charles XII for the action of George I against him. Moreover the possibility that Spain and Russia might also assist in such an undertaking increased the difficulties under which British foreign policy labored. The rise of Russia in the Baltic instead of restoring the balance of power in that area upset it more than it had been

[1] War Manifesto of George I, October 4, 1715, *The Historical Register*, III, 15–18, and Idem, November 13, 1715, Lamberty, *Mémoires*, IX, 299–307.

[2] Gyllenborg to Sparre, November 7, 1715, *Handlingar*, X, 270.

[3] Wiesener, *Le Régent et les Anglais*, II, 3: 'À la ruine de la grandeur suèdoise en allemayne, George s'était attribué les duchés de Brême et de Verden sans autre motif que de ne pas rester les mains vides, alois que tous ses voisins se garnissaient.'

previously, and in reality brought into existence an Anglo-Russian animosity that was to last for the next twenty years.

Chance admitting these drawbacks inherent in Hanoverian policy was of the opinion that 'no government in 1715 could have found arguments to oppose the wishes of the sovereign' in view of the overall picture facing European diplomats at the time. Sweden was doomed and refused to resolve her commercial difficulties with Britain. Naval stores had to be procured, and Peter was in possession of the chief ports from which they were supplied. He could be counted on for a more liberal trade policy than could be won from the Swedes. Moreover, with a pacification of Germany imminent, it was better 'to court the victor than the vanquished.' 'No one could have foretold the improbable course of events, have reckoned with the personality of Görtz, or have suspected the difficulties that were to arise with yet nascent Russia.'[1]

That Charles XII might be captured at Stralsund or killed was undoubtedly a possibility, but not to have seen the possibility of Russia's rise is something else again, for as has been shown in previous chapters, many pamphleteers and statesmen had called attention to the dangers apparent in the changing balance of power in the Baltic. What many had seen in 1715 before Hopson's squadron and the Hanoverian war declaration surely must have been noticeable to some in the fall of that same year. Perhaps Englishmen could not have reckoned with the personality of Görtz, but one wonders whether the Hanoverians in October, 1715, were ignorant of his talents. The Danes held him to be a source of great danger to Denmark at that time, even though it might not have been possible to have predicted then the great influence he would soon have in the councils of Charles XII. It is also difficult to agree completely with Chance's ideas on Russian trade policies as opposed to those of Sweden. Surely British merchants saw the danger from both sides, and Russian unpredictability had always hampered Anglo-Russian trade. In fact the Communist historian Nikiforov asserted that it was British trade interests desiring to exploit Russia which drove George I into an anti-Russian policy in 1716.[2]

[1] Chance, *George I and the Northern War*, pp. 96–97.
[2] Nikiforov, *Russische-Englische Beziehungen*, pp. 15–17.

George I on October 28, 1715, at Greisfswald entered into an alliance with Russia. Thus the last link was finally forged in a chain of alliances designed to bring Sweden to terms.[1] This act was to influence greatly the future of Anglo-Baltic relations. More and more did Britain become implicated in the complicated diplomacy resulting from the escape of Charles XII from Stralsund, and the subsequent advent of Görtz to a position of responsibility acted as a stimulus to Swedish efforts on both the diplomatic and the military fronts. 1716 was the critical year for the Northern Alliance and for British diplomacy in general. Neither the members of the Northern Alliance nor the Whig ministers of George I could stand the strain of that year without schisms developing.

The Hanoverians, however, guessed wrong, as to the end of the war, as did many of the Swedes, for Charles XII did not go down with the fall of Stralsund. For a hectic three days Charles XII, a page, and two Swedes waged a battle with nature and Danish cruisers, and on December 13, 1715, their small six oared boat landed at Träleborg on the coast of Skåne.[2] A thirty hour battle against ice floes on the flats before Stralsund, close escapes from Danish naval vessels, and innumerable other adventures had not daunted the Swedish king. He immediately began to make plans to punish his enemies for their unjustified attacks upon Sweden. His return home after fifteen years of wandering marks the last phase of the great Swedish warrior's attempts to prevent the dismembering of his country. One week before Charles XII reached Träleborg, Baron Görtz, now the most important of his ministers, had already arrived in Sweden. With the coming of the Baron and the King, the Regency came to an end.[3] New influences, new negotiations, and in some places new men saw the war increase in tempo as Charles XII after contemplating an invasion of Denmark[4] settled for an

---

[1] Nordmann, *La Crise du Nord*, p. 27.

[2] Jackson to Townshend, December 20, 1715, P.R.O., State Papers, Sweden, 95/21. For accounts of Charles' escape see Bain, *Charles XII*, p. 267; Fåhräus, *Sveriges Historia*, VII, 450-451; Samuel E. Bring (ed.), *Karl XII till 200 årsdagen af hans död* (Stockholm, 1918), p. 420; and Oscar Browning, *Charles XII* (London, 1899), pp. 319-320.

[3] Malmström, *Sveriges politiska historia*, I, 35.

[4] For Charles XII's new council see Rumpf to Heinsius, February 4, 1716, Rijksarchief, A.A.H., 1969.

attack upon the Danish king's most important province, Norway. Not all people in Sweden were happy over the King's home-coming, especially those Swedes who still had money, for they feared that Charles XII would take their wealth from them as soon as he found out about it.[1] Others not so economically minded thought that the return of Charles XII would forecast the 'total destruction of the kingdom,'[2] 'it being forseen that nothing but his death will put an end to the war whatsoever catastrophes should still befall the nation before that happens.'[3] In fact, Jackson reported that many of the Swedes worried more over the probability of Charles's escape from Stralsund than they did over the loss of Bremen and Verden and informed Townshend that 'everyone hopes the king will be killed.'[4] Jacques Campredon, the French minister to Sweden, opined that the subjects of Charles XII considered royal stubbornness to be the cause of their misfortunes; and the English and Dutch ministers continually confirmed such thinking, informing the Swedes that there could be no hope for peace as long as Charles XII had some means for carrying on the war. Con-sequently nobles and commoners alike yearned for an end to hostilities and resisted all attempts to forward the war effort.[5] As the Swede Müllern wrote: 'All the people long only for peace.'[6]

In spite of the opposition, Görtz by superhuman efforts which employed all sorts of financial schemes, was able to raise funds, troops, and vessels so that his master could keep fighting. New tariffs, embargoes, and taxes were levied upon the long suffering Swedish people throughout the spring of 1716, as Görtz daily made himself more powerful in financial affairs.[7]

---

[1] Jackson to Townshend, December 20, 1715, P.R.O., State Papers, Sweden, 95/21
[2] Ibid.
[3] Idem to Idem, October 29, 1715, Ibid.
[4] Idem to Idem, November 12, 1715, Ibid.
[5] Letters of Campredon in April and May, 1716, H.R.S.H., pp. 38–39.
[6] Müllern to Vellingk, January 9, 1716: 'Alla menniskor längta här blott efter fred, och jag är in sanning ofvertygad, att det är enda medlet at få ett slut på våre lidanden.' Quoted in Carlson, Om Fredsunderhandlingarne, p. 88.
[7] Various letters and inclosures of Jackson, Spring, 1716, P.R.O., State Papers, Sweden, 95/22. Cf. Sigurd Schartau, 'Om Sveriges inre tillstand under Karl XII's tid," in Bring, Karl XII, p. 510; Syveton, "L'erreur de Görtz," IX, 434; B. von Beskow, Friherre Georg Henrik von Görtz, statsman och statsoffer, XLIII in Svenska Akademiens Handlingar ifrön år 1796 (Stockholm, 1868), pp. 187–296. One of the better studies of Görtz's financial policy is G. Lindeberg, Svensk Economisk Politik under der Görtzka Period, pp. 94ff.

By the arrival of Spring and good weather, Charles XII had sufficient forces mustered to make the capture of Sweden a long and costly undertaking for any would-be invader. Yet Sweden would have to be captured or the King killed before peace could reign in the north; a scheme 'to accommodate matters' might have been found by the diplomats 'if one had to do with any other prince but the King of Sweden.'[1]

While the military was active, the chancery was accomplishing little; at one time it appeared that it might not be able to send out letters to Swedish agents because it lacked writing materials.[2] The King was evidently able to operate for an indefinite period of time without any diplomatic dispatches, for he maintained a complete silence in his correspondence with Swedish envoys from the middle of February to the fifth of June.[3] In addition to royal negligence, the elements also prevented diplomatic intercourse. Although the winter of 1715–1716 was not cold enough for Charles XII to invade Denmark across the ice over the Sound, it was sufficient to tie up all mail to and from Sweden for the first quarter of 1716. Jackson considered the winter to be as rigorous as the one of 1708 had been, and in early January, 1716, he gave up hope of receiving much mail from home until April.[4] Swedish couriers not only had to contend with King and nature, but also with the privateers of the Northern Alliance. The lack of instructions and information must have been a great burden to diplomats such as Gyllenborg, especially when one remembers that Charles XII had been too preoccupied during the long siege of Stralsund to do more than carry on spotty negotiations with the outside world.

Yet Gyllenborg to the best of his ability tried to accomplish something by way of diplomatic channels. He was aided by the royal silence in one respect, for Townshend was ever anxious to ascertain what the next action of the unpredictable Swedish king might be. Evidently not being in possession of dispatches

---

[1] Stairs to Polwarth, November 16/27, 1716, *Polwarth Papers*, I, 133.

[2] Müllern to von Kocken, June 23, 1716: 'Jag kan icke lemna oanmarkt, att man med snaraste icke mera kan skrifva något af brist på papper ock lack,' quoted in Carlson, *Om Fredsunderhandlingarne*, p. 88.

[3] *Ibid.*, p. 87.

[4] Jackson to Townshend, January 7, 1716, P.R.O., State Papers, Sweden, 95/22.

sent by Jackson with the information that Sweden contemplated an attack upon Norway,[1] Townshend on February 8 attempted to pump Gyllenborg as to the size of the Swedish armies and as to whether Denmark might not be attacked. Gyllenborg ignored the ill-concealed ruse, but did state that in all probability, Denmark would be invaded unless she gave back all that she had taken from Sweden. The British minister undoubtedly thinking of Bremen and Verden retorted that it would be difficult for Frederick IV to return all his conquests without some sort of preliminary peace articles being drafted first. Gyllenborg showed Townshend how impossible such a step would be. Charles XII would not be pleased with any preliminary peace drafts with Denmark, because that country had unrighteously begun an unjust war. Townshend terminated the conversation by turning away from the Swedish diplomat without saying a word.[2]

By March, information from Sweden began to seep through to England. Whatever there was lacking in intelligence was more than compensated for by rumor. Coffee houses throughout London hummed with the news that Charles XII was to send 12,000 soldiers to France to work for a Stuart restoration with the Duke of Orleans, Regent of that country. The Hanoverian court spread and more or less substantiated news to that effect, which supposedly had come to London from Lord Stairs, the British minister at Paris. Such purposeful gossip was according to Gyllenborg, aimed at ruining the Tories and at giving the Hanoverians an opportunity and pretext to follow out George I's program of European expansion which was in direct violation of the British constitution. With many of the 'lesser people' in England either demanding the total destruction of Sweden or making other similar threats, Gyllenborg, who knew the importance of British public opinion, went to Townshend to register a strong protest against the spreading of rumors linking Sweden with the Jacobites. He considered it both odd and amazing that Lord Stairs knew more about the plans of Charles XII than did that monarch's own ministers. At the same time he took the opportunity to express his low opinion of Admiral George

[1] Idem to Idem, February 24, 1716, *Ibid.*
[2] Gyllenborg to Charles XII, February 8, 1716, *Handlingar*, X, 125–126.

Byng, 'a violent man,' who was said to be destined to command the Baltic squadron in place of Norris. The sole satisfaction that Gyllenborg obtained from Townshend was that Stairs had only suspected that Sweden was implicated in Jacobite plotting and that he had made no definite accusation. Small help such a concession with the rumor agencies insisting to the contrary. All that Gyllenborg could hope for was that Norris rather than Byng would be the squadron commander. No matter who the admiral, events were such by March that the Swedish diplomat was found to be referring to his country as 'poor Sweden.'[1]

The stories of March, 1716, concerning Swedo-Jacobite relations were not the first of that sort to appear in Europe by any manner of means. Baron Erik Sparre, Swedish minister at Paris, had complained in October the year before about newspaper accounts linking him with Jacobite activities and playing up the fact that he had given a dinner to the exiled Jacobite lords, Ormond and Bolingbroke.[2] Such smoke would indicate at least some fire, and it would perhaps be well to trace Swedish relations with the Stuart adherents from early 1715 to March, 1716, because the Stuart-Swedish negotiations were to play a significant role in Anglo-Swedish diplomacy throughout 1716 and into early 1717 when the actual rupture of relations between the two countries took place.

The father of the idea of Swedish assistance to James must always remain a mystery. Perhaps Gyllenborg in England along with his pro-Jacobite friends and wife first thought of Charles XII's making an invasion of England. Perhaps it grew out of the exiled Jacobite court in Paris.[3] The Duke of Berwick, illegitimate son of James II by Arrabella Churchill, claimed in his *Memoirs* to have originated the plan, because Louis XIV refused to help further the Jacobites and because the interests of Charles XII were 'entirely opposite to those of King George.'[4]

---

[1] Gyllenborg to Sparre, March 30, 1716, *Ibid.*, X, 284-288.
[2] Sparre to Gyllenborg, October 7, 1715, *Ibid.*, X, 354.
[3] For various interpretations as to the origin of the plan see Syveton, 'L'erreur de Görtz,' IX, 430; Fryxell, *Berättelser*, XXIX, 43; Th. Westrin, 'Friherre Georg Henrich von Görtz Brefur fängelset i Arnhem 1717, med en inledning,' (Svensk) *Historisk Tidskrift* (1898), XVII, 91; and James Fitzjames, Duke of Berwick, *Memoirs of the Marshall Duke of Berwick*, L. J. Jooke (ed.) (London, 1779), II, 210.
[4] Berwick, *Memoirs*, II, 210.

The project of a Swedish invasion of England was not so far-fetched as it might first appear, although the final result of such action is definitely debatable. Most historians of the various and sundry Jacobite risings are of the opinion that the '15' had the best chance for success, and it is quite possible that additional veteran Swedish troops lead by the incomparable Charles XII might have changed Sherrifmuir and Prestonpans from defeats to victories. Charles XII had everything to gain by a Stuart restoration and little to lose. Many Englishmen opposed George's foreign policy and (as has been stated above) feared that Bremen and Verden as a part of Hanover would pose a direct threat to British liberties.[1] Moreover a traditional connection had existed between Scotland and Sweden which dated back to the days of Gustavus Adolphus. General Hugo Hamilton, the commander of Göteborg, had come to Sweden from Ireland and was of an old Scottish family. His nephew, General Hugo Johann Hamilton was one of the more famous *Karolinen* captured at Poltava, and his brother Jacob had been killed fighting in Ireland in 1692. The two nephews were Swedish born, for their father had also come over to Sweden from Ireland and with his brother, General Hugo Hamilton had been raised to the Swedish peerage.[2] Other family alliances between Swede, Scot, and Tory also existed, and it was feasible to many that General Hugo Hamilton, aided by Swedish soldiers, might be the Monck of a second restoration.

For lack of a better starting place, let us open Jacobite-Swedish conversations at the French court with Berwick making a proposal that was at first considered by the 'Sun King' and the men around him 'as Chimerical.'[3] Yet the French court kept the matter open and after it had held some conversations with Sparre and had discovered that the Swedish minister was not averse to a Swedish diversion against Scotland the negotiations began to advance more rapidly. The old king, Louis XIV, approved of the project[4] and gave Berwick permission to

---

[1] Westrin, 'Friherre . . . Görtz Bref,' XVII, 92

[2] *Nordisk Familjebok*, X, 1211ff. and H. E. Uddyren, *Karolinen Hugo Johans Hamilton en Lefnadsteckning*, in *Skrifter utgifning af Hamiltonska Slaktforeningen* (Stockholm, 1916), II, 1–3.

[3] Berwick, *Memoirs*, II, 212–213.

[4] Westrin, 'Friherre . . . Görtz Bref,' XVII, 95, Syveton, 'L'erreur de Görtz,' IX, 416–432.

negotiate with Sparre and the French minister, Jean Baptiste Colbert, Marquis de Torcy.[1] These three worked out a plan wherein France was to give the Swedes a subsidy long overdue, and the Pretender was to contribute 50,000 crowns to cover the cost of embarking a Swedish force from Göteborg to Scotland. This contingent of between 6,000 to 8,000 men had already been assembled at that Swedish port under the command of Hamilton, evidently intended for the relief of Stralsund. The plotters were of the opinion that forty-eight hours and a good wind could see the Swedish troops safely landed in Scotland.[2]

Unfortunately, Berwick's *Memoirs* give no indication as to when these preliminary overtures took place, but if he were the originator of the plan—and it is quite possible that he was not— he would have had to have made his initial moves sometime before mid-April, 1715. By that time, Versailles was definitely considering the possibility of Swedish aid for James Edward Stuart. When Croissy set out for the camp of Charles XII at Stralsund, he carried with him instructions dated April 12, 1715, which commanded him to sound out Charles XII on the matter of Jacobite assistance and to find out what the attitude of the Swedish king might be regarding an invasion of Scotland by his soldiers. The French diplomat was cautioned to treat the matter as delicately as possible because Louis XIV well knew that failure to live up to his promises to withhold aid from the Jacobites could embroil him in a war with England, a contingency the French ruler wanted at all costs to avoid.[3]

The Count de Croissy was hardly the man for delicate assignments, and it has already been illustrated how he soon

[1] Berwick, *Memoirs*, II, 212-213.
[2] *Ibid.* Cf. Syveton, 'L'erreur de Görtz,' IX, 430ff., and Wiesener, *Le Régent et les Anglais*, II, 3.
[3] Croissy Instructions, Recueil, Suède, 75, 276; 'Avant que de le finir, le Roi juge à propos d'instuire le Comte de Croissy des vues que plusieurs Anglois mécontens de gouvernement de leur pays forment pour sa garantir des périls dont ils se croient menacés par la vengeance de leurs adversaires. Ils regardent le Roi de Suède comme leur liberateur, et persuadés des mauvaises intentions de roi leur maître à l'égard de ce prince, ils jugent que le salut de la Suède est de faire un joui une Angleterre, en y appuyant et de troupes et de vaisseaux les intérêts du Chavalier de Saint-Georges. Cet article est trés délicat à traiter, Sa Majesté S'etant engagée à ne donner à ce prince aucun secours directement, ni indirectement. Mais sans violer sa promisse, Elle peut s'informer de ce que les princes étrangers pensent sur ce sujet, et c'est pendant le cours de son ambassade auprès du roi de Suede.'

became a fiery partisan of Charles XII in that sovereign's quarrel with the King of Prussia. Yet his known friendship with Charles XII and the Jacobites made him an excellent mouthpiece for the latter in their attempts to get Swedish support. He arrived at Stralsund on May 14 and ten days later received from Gyllenborg a fully drawn up proposal for the Scottish invasion.[1] That draft, coming as it did from England, gives considerable credence to the theory that Gyllenborg rather than Berwick actually was the author of what became in 1716 the Swedish-Jacobite plot. As for Croissy, although he was not the originator, he was definitely a collaborator and would-be expediter, and conducted all his conversations with Charles XII on the subject in a way which made Louis XIV appear more enthusiastic about the plot than he actually was.

Charles XII undoubtedly pleased by the subsidy treaty which had been concluded in April between France and Sweden[2] listened patiently to Croissy's proposition, but courteously refused the French overture. He reaffirmed his desire to abide by his English alliance, and pointed out to the French ambassador that George I at that time (May, 1715) had not yet openly placed himself on the list of Sweden's foes. Moreover he could not spare troops for the British venture because every available Swedish soldier was needed for the defense of Stralsund. Charles XII apparently caused Croissy to believe that he considered the plan to have some merit. On the other hand, the French diplomat noted that opinion towards the proposal was divided so far as the ministers of Charles XII were concerned. Müllern opposed the idea because it would alienate Sweden from the good graces of the Protestant princes of Europe, while Vellingk was in favor of it.[3] As for Görtz, already a rising star in Swedish councils, one may be sure that Croissy had many conversations with him over the venture, and that the wily Görtz mentally was filing away for future reference the thought that the Jacobites sometime, somehow, somewhere might be of assistance to Sweden.[4]

---

[1] Westrin, 'Friherre . . . Görtz Bref,' XVII, 94.
[2] *Ibid.* It is rather difficult to adopt Westrin's opinion that the subsidy treaty might indicate an acceptance of the plot by the Swedish king.
[3] Croissy to Louis XIV, May 16, 1715, *H.R.S.H.*, p. 36.
[4] Syveton, 'L'erreur de Görtz,' IX, 433.

Croissy's enthusiasm was not dampened by the answer of Charles XII, and he continued his Jacobite activities to such an extent that in June, Louis XIV, to cool down his ardor, instructed him to desist from his efforts on behalf of the Stuarts. The ageing king told Croissy that he intended to keep his word and abide by the terms of the Utrecht settlement, and that his sole wish as sovereign was to spend his last remaining days in peace.[1] Croissy, however, did not allow a reprimand from his ruler to deter his efforts on behalf of the Chevalier, and it is possible but not probable that by the time he received the rebuke from Louis XIV, Charles XII had already been won over to the idea of the Scottish diversion. At least, an undated letter from Croissy made such claims. Troops numbering 4,000 were to be sent to Scotland under Lieutenant-General Hugo Hamilton, the Swedish Jacobite in command at Göteborg. A certain Captain Christopher was to command the sea forces and Baron Konrad Rank, a general in the service of the Prince of Hesse-Cassel, was to be dispatched to Scotland to win over the Duke of Argyle to the cause.[2]

Whether Croissy was stretching the facts or not is debatable. There is an excellent chance that the French minister was allowing his wishes to become realities, as he so often did. Still a letter from Louis XIV to Croissy, June 4, indicates that Charles XII was giving the diversion idea serious consideration, because in it Louis XIV urged caution in such a way as to imply that Charles XII had just about committed himself to Croissy's viewpoint.[3] But Louis XIV himself may have been relying upon Croissy's misinformation. It hardly seems likely that Charles XII was planning to invade England in view of his predeliction to strike at his closest enemy, which in the spring of 1715 were the rulers whose troops were before the gates of Stralsund.

Back in Paris, however, the negotiations between Sweden and the Jacobites continued with Louis XIV attempting to

[1] Louis XIV to Croissy, June 2, 1715, *H.R.S.H.*, p. 56: 'Réglez votre conduite sur le principe, que je veux observer la paix, et pour satisfaire à ma parole, et pour le bien général de mon royaume; et ne proposer rien, qui puisse tendre au renouvellement d'une guerre, qui serait également contraire à l'une et à l'autre.'
[2] *H.R.S.H.*, p. 56n.
[3] *Recueil, Suède*, II, lxxvii n.

profit from Swedish animosity towards Hanover and the English king, but planning in no way to commit himself to any action which might be considered a cause for war by Britain. On July 7 the King of France arranged for a meeting at Marly between Berwick, Torcy and Sparre. Charles XII was dubbed the 'Liberator of Great Britain' by Berwick, who offered the Swedish minister 50,000 *riksdalers* if Charles would land between 4,000 and 5,000 men at Newcastle.[1] Berwick also wanted to give Sparre a letter to Charles XII from the Pretender, which the Swede refused to accept. Yet four days later in writing to Müllern and Charles XII about the conference with Berwick, Sparre suggested that the plan deserved Swedish attention.[2] Sparre, during the meeting, had told Torcy that the time was ripe for such a move, but that it should be a French venture also and not one confined only to Sweden and the Jacobites.[3]

It is evident that by the time that Norris reached the Baltic with the 1715 Squadron, two Swedish diplomats were in favor of the Scottish plan. Sparre had committed himself as such and was attempting to persuade France to make a diversionary attack upon Prussia at the same time.[4] Gyllenborg claimed to be in favor of the Jacobites as far back as the spring of 1715.[5] In July after hearing about the Dano-Hanoverian treaty regarding Bremen and Verden, he bitterly complained: 'May God forgive them who did not inform the King about the plan which I drew up,' a plan whose successful outcome at least so far as Gyllenborg was concerned was assured.[6] Without France, however, any attempts to unseat the Hanoverians would have been unsuccessful, but any action that Charles XII took so far as his diplomats in Paris and London were concerned would

[1] Westrin, 'Friherre . . . Görtz Bref,' XVII, 94.
[2] *Ibid.*, XVII, 94–95.
[3] Sparre to Gyllenborg, July 11, 1715, *Handlingar*, X, 342.
[4] *Ibid.*
[5] Gyllenborg to Sparre, September 5, 1715, *Ibid.*, X, 204, claims to have given high placed Swedish officials an account of the plan 'six months ago,' and that the Swedes had let an excellent opportunity slip by.
[6] Th. Westrin, 'En förklaring af Carl Gyllenborg angående hans förkållande till Pretendenten' (Svensk), *Historisk Tidskrift*, XXIII (1903), p. 287: 'Gud förlåte dem, som ej förelagt vår herre konungen den plan, som jag uppgjort för att förekomma allt detta och hvars framgång var osviklig.' Also in Gyllenborg to Sparre, August 31, 1715, *Handlingar*, X, 198, 349. In the latter citation Gyllenborg's letter is in French.

be justifiable in view of George's seizure of Bremen and Verden.[1] Yet the desperate always hope and Gyllenborg continued to insinuate to his Tory friends that if France openly declared for the Chevalier, Sweden would do likewise.[2] Müllern, intrigued with the thought of money, had Sparre and Gyllenborg attempt a loan from Berwick or from the British Jacobites, but to no avail.[3] Sparre continued on occasion to meet British exiled Jacobites, but apparently made efforts to shun any close associations after learning that Charles XII did not want to entangle the Vasas with the problems of the Stuarts.[4] As for the King, he doggedly continued the defense of Stralsund. The Swedes at home watched events and hoped for a Jacobite victory in Scotland that could lead to the defeat of the Hanoverians.[5]

There may have been some justification for Gyllenborg's censure against those Swedes who opposed the plan, because it was feasible though risky; and Charles XII might better have used his troops in Scotland than in the heroic but useless defense of Stralsund. It is possible that Charles XII may have allowed to pass by a golden opportunity to oust Hanover. Sir Charles Petrie, the best known of the Jacobite historians, is of the opinion that the Hanoverian succession was threatened more in 1715 than it was thirty years later because of the widespread Jacobite sentiment that was prevalent in England in the first year after George became King.[6] It is apparent that Jacobitism after 1715 ceased to be such a vital factor in English public life.[7]

Yet all was not lost for the Jacobites after they suffered defeat on the edge of the Scottish highlands at Preston and Sherrifmuir. To be sure the Chevalier, unhappy son of an unhappy father, was forced to flee for his life, and much

[1] Gyllenborg to Sparre, July 28, 1715, and Sparre to Gyllenborg, August 30, 1715, *Handlingar*, X, 198, 349.
[2] Gyllenborg to Sparre, July 27, 1715, and September 5, 1715, *Ibid.*, X, 198, 204.
[3] Westrin, 'Friherre . . . Görtz Bref,' XVIII, 94, and Müllern to Gyllenborg, July 14, 1715, *Handlingar*, X, 198–199.
[4] Sparre to Gyllenborg, September 30, 1715, and October 7, 1715, *Handlingar*, X, 353–354.
[5] Rumpf to Heinsius, February 29, 1716, Rijksarchief, A.A.H., 1769.
[6] Sir Charles Petrie, *The Jacobite Movement* (London, 1932), p. 130.
[7] Oliver, *The Endless Adventure*, I, 203.

material and treasure had been squandered in the 'Fifteen.' Yet his position was not impossible. There were still Tories in England willing to declare for James if he would change his religion; the clans in the highlands, hostile to the Act of Union of 1707, were always more than ready to rally to the Stuart tartan. Other highlanders could always be depended upon to 'go out' whenever booty and looting were in the offing. The Catholics in Ireland constituted the majority of the population and could be counted to participate in any anti-Hanoverian uprising. In addition, there were over 2,000 Irish soldiers in the pay of the King of Spain, who might also be employed in an English adventure.[1] Moreover, James had many friends among high French officials, who would do their utmost to bring about a Stuart restoration.

Nevertheless the position of the Pretender was not so favorable as it had been a year earlier. His weakened status is well summed up by Petrie: 'By now it had become clear that James was at the mercy of events; that is to say, he had become a pawn upon the international chessboard. He was no longer in a position to treat with the monarchs of Europe on an equal footing, and they merely made use of him and his supporters when it suited their policy to make themselves unpleasant to the British government.'[2] Yet a pawn played carefully and given proper support can checkmate a king.

With defeat came flight and the need for refuge, and neither James nor his supporters overlooked Sweden as a possible haven. On February 26, 1716, a vessel carrying a French flag was sighted off the coast of Sweden and shortly thereafter landed a number of unknown persons in the domains of the Swedish king. The alert Jackson suspected that the new arrivals might all be Jacobites for they concealed their names; that is all but one, Lord Deffus, who could not assume an alias in Sweden because he was too well known there. That worthy had been in Sweden eight years previously and had married the daughter of the Swedish admiral Siöblad. There was a rumor that James himself was among the dejected refugees,

---

[1] Mar to Oxford, October 2, 1716, *Calendar of Stuart Papers,* Historical Manuscripts Commissions *Reports* (London, 1902), III, 9. Cited hereafter as *Stuart Papers.*

[2] Petrie, *The Jacobite Movement,* p. 149.

but after two days of investigation, Jackson came to the conclusion that the Pretender had gone elsewhere.[1] Yet six important Jacobite commanders were in the group,[2] and Jackson immediately delivered a strongly worded protest to Horn asking that 'men guilty of such detestable Crimes' as Jacobitism be seized by the Swedish authorities and not given any succor. Horn promised to send the memorial to Charles XII from whom there was little possibility of a speedy answer.[3] Such incidents although not significant in themselves provided fuel for the English propaganda mills justifying the conduct of George I in the Baltic.

Although James may not have been on the boat with Lord Deffus, he was considering Swedish territory as a possible place of refuge. He left Scotland on February 5, 1715, and returned to France. He spent eight days in Paris sometime during the month of February, and on March 2 held an interview with Baron Sparre in the Bois de Boulogne.[4] During the conversation, he asked Sparre to forward an autographed letter to Charles XII wherein he requested asylum in Sweden. The Swedish minister refused to send the letter on to Stralsund, although he reported the meeting and James's request to his sovereign.[5]

James apparently did not relish having to apply to Sweden for aid, but the low ebb of his affairs after his defeats in Scotland made such a course of action necessary.[6] He much preferred Lorraine as a sanctuary, but after its duke refused to receive him, he had been compelled to depart to a place near Chalôns on the Marne.[7] Certain of the Pretender's followers such as James Butler, Duke of Ormond, were displeased with their leader's choice, and were of the opinion that he should have gone to Deux Ponts, a possession of Charles XII.[8] Such a

[1] Jackson to Townshend, March 1, 1716, P.R.O., State Papers, Sweden, 95/22.
[2] Idem to Idem, March 12, 1716, *Ibid.*
[3] Jackson to the Swedish Chancery, March 6, 1716, and to Townshend, March 20, 1716, *Ibid.*
[4] Mar to Inese, August 25, 1716; Magny to James, August 22, 1716, *Stuart Papers*, II, 7, 226, 370.
[5] Westrin, 'Friherre . . . Görtz Bref,' XVIII, 97.
[6] James to the Duke of Lorraine, March 13, 1716, *Stuart Papers*, II, 15.
[7] *Ibid.*
[8] Ormond to James, March 17, 1716, *Ibid.*, II, 20.

step would, according to the Marquis of Magny, one of James's followers, have had both advantages and disadvantages.

According to Jacobite reasoning, if James went to Deux Ponts it would appear that he was seeking to wage war against the House of Brunswick, and thereby his prestige would be enhanced throughout Europe. Going to Sweden would be even better, for there he would be near Charles XII and in a position to excite that monarch to a greater interest in Jacobite affairs and to more affection for the Pretender. In addition, if Sweden, long a defender of Protestantism, would espouse the Jacobite cause, the Protestant distrust in England of James's Catholicism, which had been increased by Stuart reliance upon the court of Louis XIV, would be lessened. On the other hand, Sweden was far away and difficult to get to. The forces of the Swedish king were too busy to aid the Stuarts at the moment. With Dutch and British sea power what they were, the only hope for Swede-Jacobite success in Scotland lay in surprise, which of course was impossible should James be in Sweden or in any domain of the Swedish king. Such an exposure of plans would only result in larger naval squadrons being sent to the Baltic by Holland and England.[1] One other difficulty so far as residence of Deux Ponts was concerned was that its location in the Empire entailed permission from the Emperor Charles VI, who daily was becoming more pro-Hanoverian and anti-Swedish.

In spite of the doubtful desirability of a refuge in Sweden or in Swedish possessions for James, his supporters endeavored to have permission for James to enter Swedish territory should it become necessary. On March 17, 1716, John Erskine, Earl of Mar, and Ormond conferred with Sparre to that purpose. The Swedish minister replied that he could not take it upon himself to answer their request, but offered assurances of friendship on the part of Charles XII, and promised to aid the Jacobites by writing his master to find out his pleasure on the matter.[2]

In the meantime French policy was veering away from Jacobitism and falling into line with the Hanoverian succession. Diplomatic pressure upon the French court applied by Lord

[1] Magny to James, March 17, 1716, *Ibid.*, II, 21.
[2] Ormond to James, March 17, 1716, *Ibid.*, II, 20.

Stair was making James's stay in France increasingly difficult. The indefatigable British minister in France also intended to frustrate Swedo-Jacobite negotiations. His machinations led to Sparre's being called before Marshal d'Huxelles to explain his activities with James and with James's agents. The Swede denied all charges and branded British reports concerning a treaty between Charles XII and James as one of the 'dreamt and exaggerated stories that Stair was sending back to lull Parliament and his master to sleep.'[1] Yet Sparre in a letter to Gyllenborg explained his actions and revealed his true feelings by stating that he wished that some sort of an agreement between the Swedish king and the British pretender did exist.[2]

The month of April, 1716, saw Gyllenborg doing yeoman service in an attempt to prevent the embarking of the fleet to the Baltic. Whether he did this to further the cause of Jacobitism is doubtful, for his sole motive appears to have been the keeping of Britain out of the Northern conflict. He hoped that commerce was the reason for British actions and urged his court to relieve its restrictions upon British and Dutch commerce. If Charles XII would ease the burdens of the Baltic traders, he might forestall the intervention of the Maritime Powers in Baltic affairs, or failing in that would make Britain an open aggressor against Sweden and perhaps cause European public opinion to come around to the side of Charles XII.[3]

Gyllenborg's proposal contained much good common sense and showed him to be a diplomatist willing to make concessions and shifts should his country thereby profit. Late April saw in England a rising tide of Russophobia, with one British minister telling the Spanish ambassador that should George I go too far against Sweden for his own private interests, the national welfare of England would cause his British ministers to oppose his policies.[4] As a result Gyllenborg and Townshend had a series of conversations in late April, 1716, in which both ministers conversed freely. The meeting of April 25 is especially interesting and revealing, and may be an early indication of

[1] Sparre to Gyllenborg, March 30, 1716, *Handlingar*, X, 357.
[2] *Ibid.*, X, 358.
[3] Gyllenborg to Sparre, April, 1716, *Ibid.*, X, 298.
[4] Larsson, *Gyllenborg*, p. 22.

the growing split in the Whig party which was to assume major proportions as the year progressed.

Gyllenborg on April 25 evidently went to Townshend to obtain information concerning Norris's instructions, and was told that Sweden was not to aid the Jacobites either directly or indirectly and was to repeal the ordinance of privateers. England would not permit Charles XII to attack the Danish islands, but on the other hand, promised to save Sweden from an attack upon Skåne if Charles XII ordered a cessation of hostilities and demanded the good offices of George I to obtain it. Charles XII furthermore was to name his ministers to take part in a general peace conference and to give up all hope that his German provinces would be saved. Gyllenborg asked if those Jacobites now in Swedish service who promised not to meddle in English affairs might retain their posts, a request that Townshend rejected on the grounds that they would influence Charles XII. Townshend moreover refused to clarify Sweden's compensations for her German losses and said that Norway would not be considered a part of the Danish islands.[1] On the latter point he appears to be at odds with the King who had informed Norris that Norway in Sweden's hands would be a threat to the peace and safety of England.[2] Gyllenborg's request for an embargo upon four ships bound for Russian service was also denied. Townshend at first tried to make the Dutch responsible for the four ships being sold to Russia, but could not refute Gyllenborg's charge that two had been built in England. On the other hand he did agree that if Denmark controlled both sides of the Sound, British commerce would be threatened.[3] Norris's instructions had stressed the dangers to British trade that were apparent if Sweden succeeded in her Norwegian invasion.[4]

It would appear then that Townshend's version of British sentiments on the matter of Norway, differed from the demands that Norris was ordered to lay before the Swedish king. It is also apparent that both the Hanoverians and the Whig anti-Hanoverians in England would have liked to have seen

[1] Gyllenborg to Sparre, April 25, 1716, *Handlingar*, X, 309-314; cf. Larsson, *Gyllenborg*, p. 20.
[2] George I to Norris, May 10, 1716, BM., Add. MSS., 28,145.
[3] Gyllenborg to Sparre, April 25, 1716, *Handlingar*, X, 309-314.
[4] George I to Norris, May 10, 1716, BM., Add. MSS., 28,145.

the Northern War concluded with Charles XII excluded from Germany. Neither group wanted Denmark to have both sides of the Sound, but there was considerable disagreement as to how far England should go to obtain Bremen and Verden for the king. The growing power of Russia and the possibility that Sweden might be completely conquered by a joint Russian and Danish force caused considerable concern in England throughout 1716. If that were to be the price that Britain had to pay for Electoral gains, some in England were beginning to think that the sale should be called off. Plans of Russia and Denmark for an invasion of Sweden were something that diplomatists and naval men had to seriously consider.

VIII

THE PLAN TO INVADE SKÅNE

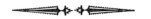

Iₙ the meantime the Allies had taken Stralsund.[1] After many
years of wandering, Charles XII had come home. Almost at
once he began to look around to see how he might harass his
many enemies who had brought him to bay. There was little
doubt in European diplomatic circles that Charles XII would
hit either Denmark or Norway, for those two areas were closest
and Charles had a habit of striking at his nearest foe. Throughout the rest of the winter there was the possibility that Charles
XII might move his troops across the ice against Denmark.[2]
The season, however, was not cold enough for the Swedish king
to hazard the passage from Skåne to Zealand, so consequently
he turned his troops against the Danish province of Norway.
The Norwegian invasion threw the Danes into terror[3] and was
to have far reaching repercussions upon the diplomacy of the
Northern Alliance. Among other things, it revived once more
in Denmark plans for an invasion of Sweden.

As has been stated above, the plan for a Russo-Danish attack
upon Sweden had been discussed by Danish diplomats for
some time, but for one reason or another had never come to
maturity. The fear of Sweden, however, caused Frederick IV
for the time being to tone down his misgivings toward Russia
and to think more seriously about using Russian troops to
administer the *coup de grâce* to the badly wounded 'Lion of the

[1] Frederick IV to Westphal, December 25, 1715, Westphal Correspondence,
Rigsarkiv, T.K.U.A., Russland, C 122.

[2] Holm, 'Studier,' V, iii, 44.

[3] *Ibid.*, p. 14. F. Klagh on March 28, 1715, wrote Frederick IV: 'Gud maa vide
hvad Enden vil blive paa den Elendighed. Kommer der ikke uden Ophold hurtig
Hjaelp af Skibe og Folk, er Norges Rige i største Fare.'

North.'[1] Russian troops had been invited to participate in the siege of Stralsund, but before they arrived on the scene of operations, it had become evident that the city could be captured without Russian assistance. Frederick IV, therefore, requested Peter to leave his troops in Poland, as they would not be needed in Pomerania. Should Peter persist in bringing his troops to Stralsund, Denmark and Prussia would have had to provide for them. In order to meet the cost, they would have been compelled to recall some of the allied troops which had been besieging the city. Such a contingency would have resulted in long and fatiguing marches which at best would have inflicted an extreme hardship upon the soldiers themselves. If the Russians, however, remained in Poland, they could constitute a ready reserve for the next series of military operations should Charles XII escape the noose that was being tightened around him at Stralsund. If such occurred, an allied invasion of Sweden might be mandatory.[2] Thus before Charles XII even made his way back to Sweden, his Danish rival had been considering how he might, if necessary, pursue the Swedish king into his own homeland.

The presence of the Russian troops in Poland made all of the members of the Northern Alliance happy with the exception of Poland herself. From Polish bases the Russian troops could rapidly march into North Germany to take part in any operations that the members of the Northern Alliance might desire. Soon Frederick William I of Prussia renewed a convention with Peter the Great, wherein it was provided that Russian soldiers be used against Swedish Wismar. In the beginning of 1716 the Russian army began to move out of Poland and into Mecklenburg. Wismar, meanwhile, was under siege by a force of 10,000 Danes, 4,000 Prussians and 4,000 Hanoverians. Peter was quite content to have his forces in Mecklenburg. From there with proper naval support he might be able to throw a force of thirty battalions of infantry and 2,000 cavalry into Sweden itself.[3] He also could use those troops to assist the Duke of Mecklenburg against his rebellious nobles.

---

[1] Syveton, 'L'erreur de Görtz,' IX, 437.

[2] Frederick IV to Peter, December 1, 1715, Westphal Correspondence, Rigsarkiv, T.K.U.A., Russland C 122.

[3] Holm, 'Studier,' V, iii, 11–12.

In February, 1716, Peter presented George Westphal with a detailed plan of operation for an attack upon Sweden. The Russian troops were to be covered by a combined fleet and were to be transported to Sjaelland. From there, along with Danish units, the invasion group would move against Sweden. Peter was to furnish forty-five galleys and promised to add to his thirty battalions, three guard regiments which would supply a hard core for his infantry.[1] The Danish king on receipt of the plan had some reservations. He was of the opinion that Russia and Denmark should not operate unilaterally, but that they should include Prussia and England in the plan and thus insure its success.[2]

As Danish reluctance toward the project had to be over-come, Peter suggested a Dano-Russian conference to be held some place in Holstein or at Stralsund. At such a meeting Peter and Frederick IV could work out definite arrangements for the coming campaign.[3] Peter had been ill in December, 1715, and to recuperate had decided to take the waters at Pyrmont. As these waters were not suitable for therapy until July, Frederick IV wanted to know what Peter would do between the time of the interview and the time when the spa opened for the season. Stralsund was not feasible for a meeting so far as the Danish king was concerned, because after the long siege, the city was beset with many diseases which made it dangerous to convene there.[4] Frederick IV in addition wanted the conference expanded to include the kings of England and Prussia. If George I could not be persuaded to attend in person, he should at least be urged to be represented by a diplomat.[5]

The invasion of Norway by Charles XII altered the attitude of Frederick IV toward a conclave with Peter the Great and his entourage. It had become quite apparent that a continuation of war operations was absolutely necessary if Norway were to be saved. Pleading that Denmark was bearing the weight of the war almost alone, Frederick IV asked Peter for fifteen battalions

[1] Project for campaign, February 12, 1716, Söhlenthal Correspondence, Rigsarkiv, T.K.U.A., England C.
[2] Holm, 'Studier,' V, iii, 13.
[3] Peter I to Frederick IV, February 10, 1716; Sehestedt to Westphal, March 21, 1716, Westphal Correspondence, Rigsarkiv, T.K.U.A., Russland, C 122.
[4] Idem to Idem, *Ibid.*
[5] Holm, 'Studier,' V, iii, 17.

of soldiers and 1,000 horsemen plus nine ships which the Russians had already promised him. Frederick IV also wanted 10,000 Russian soldiers transported to Pomerania. Danish naval leaders feared that the Swedish fleet would be at sea first and would either relieve Wismar or join the Swedish squadron at Göteborg and thus be in a position to conquer Norway. Should the latter event take place, the Baltic would be free to the ships of Charles XII. Denmark hoped that Peter would take advantage of the situation and make a diversion upon Northern Sweden and thereby force the Swedish fleet to withdraw to Stockholm and its environs.[1] As Professor Holm has pointed out, the retention of Norway had become of utmost importance in Danish diplomatic thinking, and the Danish court was becoming increasingly pessimistic about the state of affairs there.[2]

Peter answered the Danish pleas by saying that the old idea for an invasion of Skåne would be the most logical way to relieve Norway. As the Romans by attacking Carthage during the Punic Wars had freed the Italian Peninsula from the armies of Hannibal, so could the Danes save Norway by striking directly at Sweden. Once more Peter called for a meeting with Frederick IV but begged off from going to Holstein. By now he wanted to meet at Stralsund or Mecklenburg. Frederick IV, meanwhile, had become set on Holstein, for he did not want to be far away from Denmark, the situation in Norway being what it was.[3] By April, however, the Danes expressed a willingness to meet at Luneburg or Schwerin.[4]

Meanwhile, all was not going smoothly between Frederick IV and Peter the Great. The Danish king was not so enthusiastic about the coming campaign as the Russian czar, who complained that the Danes were not making any preparations for the great adventure. Peter also noted through his ambassador

---

[1] Frederick IV to Peter I, March 21, 1716; Idem to Westphal, March 28, 1716; Sehestedt to Idem, March 24, 1716, Westphal Correspondence, Rigsarkiv, T.K.U.A., Russland, C 122.

[2] Holm, 'Studier,' V, iii, 15: 'Det er klart, at Kong Frederik har set Forholdene i Norge i det sorteste Lys.'

[3] *Ibid.* The Danes suggested Kiel or Gluckstadt in Holstein; Sehestedt to Meyer, March 21, 1716, Westphal Correspondence, Rigsarkiv, T.K.U.A., Russland, C 122.

[4] Frederick IV to Westphal, April 7, 1716, *Ibid.*

Dolgorucky how skittish the Danes were over the Swedish attack upon Norway and he became highly distrustful of the Danes whom he feared would make a separate peace with Sweden in order to prevent Norway from falling to the armies of Charles XII. By April, Peter was quite sure that the Danes had already opened negotiations to that effect with Sweden. Time and time again, Dolgorucky held conversations with the Danish court on the matter—conversations that did little to promote a working arrangement between the two monarchs.[1]

Events transpiring on the Continent in April, 1716, added to the existing ill feelings and animosities. By the beginning of that month it had become apparent that Wismar would soon capitulate. Actually the Danish general, Franz Joachim Dewitz, who was in charge of allied military operations had by April 8 already opened negotiations for surrender with the Swedish garrison in the city.[2] In the meantime, General Prince Nikita Ivanovich Repnin, who was in charge of the Russian forces that were to take part in the siege, was hastening to have his troops on the spot before the city fell. Their arrival had been delayed by a Swedish squadron which had been fitted out through the self-sacrificing efforts and patriotism of the burghers of Karlskrona and Karlshamn.[3] Consequently, the Russian soldiers had had to travel by land and only a few of them reached Wismar before it fell.[4]

Actually Repnin with a mere handful of troops had left the main body of his forces in order to be in on the kill. The reason for Russian haste stemmed from the approaching marriage of Peter's niece Katharine to Charles Leopold, Duke of Mecklenburg-Schwerin. The latter wanted Wismar, and Peter, whose troops had assisted the Duke of Mecklenburg-Schwerin in his troubles with the Mecklenburg nobility, was more than willing to do another favor for his niece's future husband. In the winter of 1715–1716, Duke Charles Leopold, whose pro-Swedish proclivities did not preclude his designs upon Wismar, had made an attempt to get the besieged city into his hands by

[1] Holm, 'Studier,' V, iii, 18.

[2] *The Historical Register*, III, 523–524 contains a good account of the surrender of Wismar.

[3] Chance, *George I and the Northern War*, p. 106.

[4] *Ibid*. Holm, 'Studier,' V, iii, 28–31 has an excellent account of the diplomatic complications arising from the fall of Wismar.

offering the Swedish vice-governor a sum of money if he would turn the city over to him in sequestration as had been done with Stettin. The Prussian commander had been told about the plan, but nothing had come of it. The Danish king had also been approached, but he refused to take the overtures seriously.[1]

The coming nuptials of Katherine and Duke Charles Leopold, however, altered the situation and the Danish king attempted to forestall any attempts by the Duke of Mecklenburg-Schwerin to have Russia intercede on Mecklenburg's behalf in the Wismar affair. Westphal was instructed to work against any moves by Mecklenburg to recover Wismar, and was to state that such an occurrence would not be approved by the kings of England, Prussia, and Denmark. All offensive and defensive alliances concluded by Denmark with Prussia and England had committed Wismar to become a free Imperial town after demilitarization.[2] The idea that the city should go to the Duke of Mecklenburg-Schwerin was unthinkable to the allies for that duke had always been partial to the King of Sweden. Above all things, the King of Denmark would hold true to the treaties that he had made with George I and Frederick William I.[3]

On April 16, George Ernest von Werpup, the son-in-law of Bernstorff and the Hanoverian representative in the Wismar camp, wrote the Duke of Mecklenburg and told him that General Dewitz had instructed him to inform Mecklenburg that Dewitz would not allow any troops to enter Wismar after the city was taken except those belonging to Denmark, Prussia and Hanover, the three powers that had maintained the long blockade and siege. This restriction was especially applicable to Russian and Mecklenburg troops.[4]

Needless to say, the decision of Dewitz was hardly one to make the future bridegroom happy. It was additionally galling to the Duke because both Dewitz and Bernstorff were members of the Mecklenburg nobility and were at odds with Charles

---

[1] Holm, 'Studier,' V, iii, 23, 25.
[2] Frederick IV to Westphal, March 31, 1716, Westphal Correspondence, Rigsarkiv, T.K.U.A., Russland, C 122: 'So bald sothane Stadt und Vestung Wismar eingenommen seyn wird, die fortificationes derselben so forth geschleiffet, und die Stadt dem Keyser zu einer freyen Reichs-Stadt offeret werden solle.'
[3] Ibid.
[4] Werpup to the Mecklenburg Court, April 16, 1716, Ibid.

Leopold. Two days after the Duke's wedding on April 17, the city capitulated and Repnin requested permission to enter the city with his soldiers. Dewitz refused the Russian request on the grounds that he lacked instructions from Denmark, but actually he wrote to his sovereign and advised him to refuse Russian entry. Repnin became enraged at Dewitz's refusal, and on April 20, 1716, when a body of Prussian soldiers were marching into the city, he tried to put 1,000 Russians in with them, hoping that they could sneak into the city as Prussians. The Hanoverian commander, General Pentz, discovered them and said that his orders were to deny them admission. At another portal into the fortress, Dewitz personally stopped other Russians preparing to enter. The forces of Repnin were too small to have recourse to violence, and all that they could do for the moment was to camp outside the city and hope that the channels of diplomacy would succeed better than had the schemes of their commander.[1]

On the same day that Repnin tried to smuggle his men into Wismar, Baron Peter Pavlovich Shafirov, the Russian vice-chancellor, delivered a strongly worded protest to Westphal over the Dewitz exclusion of the Russian troops. Nine days later Peter himself sent another complaint to Frederick IV, with the veiled threat that if Repnin had not been a moderate man an open rupture would have occurred in the Northern Alliance. Asking for satisfaction, the Russian czar demanded that Russian soldiers be included in the Wismar garrison. At the same time the Russians excluded the Danes from the city of Rostock.[2] It is possible that Peter the Great offered the Danish king a large sum of money for Wismar, but Holm aptly points out that Danish sources contain nothing to indicate such a transaction, many historians to the contrary.[3] The Russian czar seized the island of Peel and thus closed the entry to the port of Wismar, excluded Prussians as well as Danes from Rostock and laid a tax upon the Mecklenburg nobility which struck at the purses of Bernstorff and Dewitz as well as other Mecklenburg nobles in foreign service.[4]

[1] Holm, 'Studier,' V, iii, 31–32.
[2] Frederick IV to Westphal, April 30, 1716, and to Peter on the same date, Westphal Correspondence, Rigsarkiv, T.K.U.A., Russland, C 122.
[3] Holm, 'Studier,' V, iii, 34.
[4] Syveton, 'L'erreur de Görtz,' IX, 436–437.

Yet according to Nikifarov, Peter was all sweetness and light during the Wismar affair, because he did not want to offend his allies or hamper future military operations against Sweden.[1] Thus the capture of a city that ended Swedish control of any part of Germany became 'the apple of discord' among her enemies because the presence of Russian troops in lower Germany was highly upsetting to the members of the Northern Alliance.[2]

Frederick IV saw the Russian reaction to the Wismar affair as a serious threat to the proposed invasion of Skåne and even worse as a real danger to the Northern Alliance itself. It is probable that he would have acceded to Peter's wishes if he had been a free agent, but he well knew that a concession on Wismar could only cause him trouble with Hanover and Prussia, who as a result might desert the Northern Alliance and court Sweden.[3] He needed the British fleet to protect not only Norway but Denmark itself.

Thus when Frederick IV answered Peter's note on April 30, 1716, he refused to budge on the matter of Wismar, but was willing to concede Rostock to the Duke of Mecklenburg-Schwerin.[4] The Danish king excused himself by pointing out that along with Prussia and Great Britain he had made treaties as to the final disposition of Wismar, and these treaties could not be broken. They had been made prior to any Dano-Russian agreements. Furthermore, Denmark, Prussia, and Hanover had successfully carried out all the naval and military operations that had led to Wismar's surrender before the Russian troops under Repnin had arrived on the scene. The future of Wismar after demolition of the fortress had to be that of a free Imperial city.

The admittance of Russian soldiers into the city as a part of the garrison could have led only to hard feeling and fierce jealousy because Wismar was a German city and Germans would resent the presence of Slavic troops there. If Peter persisted along the lines of his present conduct, people would be in a position to say judgingly that the Russian czar wanted to

[1] Nikiforov, Russische-Englische Beziehungen, p. 174.
[2] Nordmann, La Crise du Nord, p. 59–60.
[3] Ibid.
[4] Frederick IV to Peter, April 30, 1716, Westphal Correspondence, Rigsarkiv, T.K.U.A., Russland, C 122.

concern himself in Imperial affairs even more so than he was doing at present. Consequently, the position of the Northern Alliance would be weakened. Frederick IV concluded with the hope that the Wismar trouble would not lead to disunity and impede forthcoming military operations, for it was the ardent desire of Denmark to prosecute the war in a vigorous fashion.[1]

Frederick IV was correct. The increasing involvement of Peter in Imperial affairs was looked upon in the Empire with considerable misgivings. With Sweden trying to use the Treaty of Westphalia to cloak its peace feelers, the Danes did not want to irritate the Emperor. Long and furiously the Danes might well argue that the Westphalian settlement had been changed many times by consecutive treaties that were more convenient;[2] nevertheless, any changes in the Empire had to require Imperial sanction, and that sanction might be more difficult to come by if Peter increasingly meddled in German affairs. Russian soldiery, moreover, were following traditional policy and causing great economic hardship every place they were billeted—be it friend or foe, the Russian treatment of the inhabitants varied but slightly.

It was the marriage of Peter's niece with the Duke of Mecklenburg-Schwerin that first brought Peter into Imperial politics. Peter's troops moved into Mecklenburg early in 1716 and shortly thereafter began to aid the Duke in his struggles with the nobility. The Germanies watched Russian moves carefully. They knew that Peter had acted in Poland more like a conqueror than an ally of Augustus II, and that he had established his influence in Courland by means of a family alliance without making himself direct master of the country. It was becoming quite evident that he intended to follow a similar policy in Mecklenburg. To many Germans it appeared that Peter was bent on taking over the incongruous role in the Empire that Sweden had formerly enjoyed. Denmark became uneasy because she feared that Russia would challenge her control of the Sound. Hanover became alarmed at the prospect of having such a dangerous enemy close by, and in England there was the dread that the Baltic might become a Russian lake. The King of Prussia was frightened, and the Emperor

[1] Frederick IV to Westphal, April 30, 1716, *Ibid.*
[2] Sehestedt to Westphal, April 4, 1716; Frederick IV to Weyberg, March 31, 1716, *Ibid.*

always resented outsiders intruding in Imperial affairs. Meanwhile, the Mecklenburgers suffered terribly from the exactions of the Russian soldiers and provided a dire warning as to what might happen to other German territories under Russian control.

The presence of these foreign troops in Mecklenburg dominated the politics of Northern Europe for the next two years. The plight of the Mecklenburg nobility transcended the boundaries of the Duchy because many of the nobles occupied high positions in the service of other princes. Bernstorff 'was heart and soul with his order in its struggle for its rights.' Dewitz and Holstein, high in Danish circles, were also members of that same nobility, while many others were refugees at Copenhagen, Hamburg, and Lübeck. So great was the animosity and fear held by Europe regarding the Mecklenburg marriage, that Kurakin advised Peter against it on the grounds that he would lose allies who were of utmost importance to him. The Russian minister especially warned against giving any offence to Bernstorff, who had rendered a great service on behalf of the Northern Alliance.[1] Kurakin concluded his objections to Peter on the marriage with 'I do not know if the Duke's help is as valuable to us as that which we stand to lose because of him'; and lose Bernstorff, Peter did because of his Mecklenberg policy.[2] Nikiforov claims that Peter planned to build a canal through Mecklenburg connecting the Baltic with the North Sea. Such a plan if ever in the gossip stage would have made the Danes uneasy, especially in light of the Sound dues. Peter did however hope to use Mecklenburg ports and cities to expand his naval and commercial enterprises.[3]

In many ways it appears that the marriage was a political blunder. It cost Russia the help and the good will of Hanover, Prussia, and England and added to Imperial suspicions of the Northern Alliance, because it had been responsible for Russian troops entering North Germany. It frustrated the plans for the invasion of Skåne, and caused Peter's allies to distrust him,

---

[1] Mediger, *Moskaus Weg*, p. 28–32. For a detailed account of Bernstorff's and Hanover's stand on Mecklenburg's internal affairs see Hans-Joachim Ballschmieter, *Andreas Gottlieb von Bernstorff und der Mecklenburgische Ständekampf (1680–1720)*, in *Mitteldeutsche Forschungen*, XXVI (Köln, 1962) also Mediger, *Moskaus Weg*, p. 28.

[2] Nikiforov, *Russische-Englische Beziehungen*, p. 183.

[3] *Ibid* and Mediger, *Moskaus Weg*, p. 28–30.

especially after the Wismar affair. In Europe it erroneously began to be bruited about that Peter had already made a separate peace with Sweden and was using the invasion plan as a mask to cover his designs against Germany.[1] With the Mecklenburg marriage and the Wismar affair, the Northern Alliance began to show weaknesses which were to split it asunder before the year was out and in 1717 was to contribute indirectly to the split in the Whig ministry.

To preserve the Northern Alliance and to carry on operations against Skåne, it became apparent to the Danish king that a conference between the members of the alliance was necessary. Peter on May 2, 1716, suggested that Wismar might be a suitable spot for him to meet Frederick IV, a proposition heartily rejected by the Danes.[2] Peter a day earlier had left Danzig enroute to Prymont. Hoping to assure himself of Prussian aid during an invasion of Sweden, he conferred on May 17 with Frederick William I at Stettin. Peter requested that his Prussian ally contribute the Prussian cavalry to the coming campaign, something which Frederick William I refused to do. The Prussian ruler did agree—for a price—to place a score of transport ships at Peter's disposal and to allow the city of Wismar, after demolition, to be added to the domains of the Duke of Mecklenburg.[3] By May it was evident that the role of Prussia henceforth would consist in making money from the campaigns of her allies engaged in the Great Northern War, rather than in assisting them.[4]

Meanwhile, in Schleswig-Holstein, Frederick IV fumed as he impatiently awaited the czar's arrival. He had been very distrustful of the Stettin conversations and had wanted personally to confer with the Prussian ruler. His hopes had not

[1] Rigsarkiv, T.K.U.A., Geheimeregistratur der Anno 1716 and Westphal Correspondence, T.K.U.A., Russland, C 122. Good secondary accounts of the importance of the Mecklenburg marriage are: Syveton, 'L'erreur de Görtz,' IX, 436ff.; Chance, *George I and the Northern War*, pp. 106–107; and Holm, 'Studier,' V, iii, 22–35.

[2] Frederick IV to Westphal, May 11, 1716, Rigsarkiv, Westphal Correspondence, T.K.U.A., Russland, C 122.

[3] Previous to the Mecklenburg marriage, Prussia had been willing to allow Russian troops to participate in the siege of Wismar. Whereas the Danes had been hurrying to capture the city before the Russians arrived, Frederick William I had been persuaded only after a great deal of pressure to leave his troops before the city walls. Holm, 'Studier,' V, iii, 35.

[4] Chance, *George I and the Northern War*, p. 110.

materialized because Frederick William I refused to make the journey to the domains of his Danish colleague, who in turn could not travel far from Denmark, events in Norway being what they were. The King of Denmark erroneously prided himself on being able to exert considerable influence on Frederick William I, and was of the opinion that if he had been able to confer with the Prussian ruler, Denmark would have received more aid from Prussia than the option to hire transport ships.[1]

On May 28 at Ham-and-Horn, a country place in the vicinity of Hamburg, the long awaited meeting of the heads of the Danish and Russian states took place.[2] Danish counsels were divided. Holstein and Dewitz, both Mecklenburger nobles, were anti-Russian, but the two native-born secretaries of state, Sehestedt and Wibe, were in favor of coöperating with Peter the Great.[3] The latter had their way, and on June 3 a convention was drawn up and signed between the two countries. The final signatures were exchanged at Altona, which was where Frederick IV was staying and which at the time was only a small town outside the city of Hamburg. Consequently, for a long time the Altona Convention was referred to by historians as the 'Convention of Hamburg.'[4]

Whatever the name, the convention set forth the details of the long contemplated assault against the Swedish mainland, the object of which was to force Charles XII to make a peace terminating the drawn-out war. As in the February project, the assault was to be a double-barreled affair, with Russian troops numbering 20,000 crossing the Gulf of Bothnia and attacking Stockholm itself. This was to be done just as soon as the Swedish fleet was safely shut up in Swedish harbors.

The invasion of southern Sweden through the Province of Skåne was, however, to be the principal undertaking. To accomplish this end the Danes were to furnish 10,000 cavalry and twenty battalions of infantry. The Russians for their part

---

[1] Holm, 'Studier,' V, iii, 37. Cf. *The Historical Register*, III, 525.
[2] Holm, 'Studier,' V, iii, 37.
[3] Fleming account of the Danish Court, *Polwarth Papers*, I, 412–413.
[4] Syveton, 'L'erreur de Görtz,' IX, 437. For purposes of simplicity, it is called the Altona Convention throughout this work.

were to contribute 2,000 of the former and forty battalions of infantry. It was possible that an additional 1,000 horse would be added to the Russian contingent if transportation facilities could be made available. Frederick IV in accordance with the convention made at Stralsund on September 6, 1715, was to maintain fifteen of the czar's battalions and 1,000 horse coming from Rostock to Zealand. These troops were to be ready for embarkation by the end of June at the latest. The Russian guards were to be transported in Peter's ships while 1,000 Russian cavalrymen were to travel to Zealand by land in the company of the King of Denmark's horse, the latter sovereign pledging himself to provide for the sustenance of the Russian troops in the same manner as his own from the time that Peter's men arrived in Holstein. All stores which had been accumulated at Rostock were to be brought along with the troops just as soon as the Swedish naval forces were swept from the Baltic. Because the transporting would entail a sizable expenditure, Peter undertook to make the most pressing demands upon the King of Prussia that he hand over the transport ships either gratis or at an extremely low price.[1]

It will be noted that the invasion and the troop movements necessitated maritime superiority, and consequently, the convention dealt to some length with plans destined to provide the Northern allies with the control of the Baltic. A joint fleet was to be put to sea with the Czar providing fourteen ships of the line and the King of Denmark, eighteen. This combined fleet was to remain active as long as the operations required or the season permitted. It was also hoped that the English squadron shortly expected in the Sound would participate in the naval movements and advance the success of the descent by maintaining a strick blockade upon Karlskrona.

The Russo-Danish army was to remain in Skåne or its adjoining provinces as long as the war continued and were to be withdrawn only after mutual consent had been given. All places conquered along with their artillery and magazines were to be handed over to Denmark. There were, however, some exceptions to this clause. Until the Russian troops could withdraw and in case of necessity, half of them might be garrisoned

---

[1] The Convention of Altona. Holm, 'Studier,' V, iii, 152–158 prints the convention in full. Cf. Chance, *George I and the Northern War*, pp. 111–112.

in some conquered places. The supreme command of the joint army was to be held by the two monarchs on alternate weeks. If one of them should be with the fleet, he would be in supreme authority there while the other enjoyed complete command on land. Because the two monarchs feared that France might make a diversion in favor of Sweden while the Dano-Russian army was in Skåne, both rulers were to obtain positive declarations from the kings of Prussia and England as to the strength of the forces they would put on the field if such an apprehension became an actuality. The latter two sovereigns were bound to act in such a contingency according to the treaties they had signed in 1715. Details of the invasion plan were to be kept a secret unless both monarchs agreed upon what was to be communicated to another power. For the guarantee desired by the king of Denmark concerning the permanent possessions of the occupied regions at a future peace, that given by the Czar in his treaty of alliance of 1709 was deemed sufficient.[1] Such was the convention which was the basis for Danish action both militarily and diplomatically throughout the remainder of 1716.

The Danes immediately took steps to procure the desired transport ships and naval protection necessary to insure the complete success of the great plan. A commission, which included in addition to Meyer, Privy Councilor Massow and War Commissar Sasson, was sent to Stettin to draw up terms by which transport ships belonging to Frederick William would assist in the campaign. On June 27 an agreement was reached between the two countries. A Danish commission under Sasson was to choose fifty Prussian transport ships, which were to be assembled at Rügen (in a seaworthy condition) not later than July 15. The crews and equipment for these ships was to be provided by the Prussian king. In order that the Danish troops might have the best transportation facilities possible, Frederick IV pledged himself to pay in advance a monthly payment of four *reichthalers* per last.[2] All payments after the first one were to be weekly and were to be paid from the time that the ships were ready for sea until they had returned home.[3] It was

---

[1] *Loc. cit.*

[2] A last equals 4,000 pounds.

[3] The contract of June 27, 1716; Holm, 'Studier,' V, iii, 159–160 prints this contract in full. The coinage of Stettin was to be the monetary basis of the transaction.

estimated that the initial payment would total around 12,000 *reichthalers*.[1]

It was one thing to receive a promise of ships from the Prussian king and another thing to obtain them. Throughout July and early August, Frederick William made all sorts of excuses for not sending the pledged transports and soon the Danes began to feel that he was purposely trying to retard the invasion.[2] For that reason the new Danish envoy to London, Söhlenthal, was instructed to ask Whitehall to accelerate the Prussian ruler.[3]

There may have been some justification for the Danish complaints because Frederick William never was whole-heartedly anti-Swedish, and all that he desired was peace for northern Germany and the possession of Stettin for the Hohenzollerns.[4] Motivated perhaps by the above reasons or perhaps by his well-known penuriousness, he continually jacked up the amount of the first payment due him. First he demanded 20,000 *reichthalers* for the initial requital and finally his pretensions reached the sum of 30,000 *reichthalers*.[5] On August 23, Colonel Paul Lövenörn, who in July had been sent to Frederick William to provide an impetus to the transaction, succeeded in having the fifty Prussian ships handed over to Denmark.[6] Thus Denmark obtained the ships needed to transport Russian and Danish soldiers from Pomerania to Zealand, but she received them a full month and a half after the specified time.

The Danes had commenced soliciting English naval coöperation long before the convention of Altona was signed. In March, 1716, Frederick IV had sent a new envoy to Great Britain, one Baron Henrik Frederik von Söhlenthal. His initial instructions, which were dated March 18, had told him to press

---

[1] Frederick IV to Meyer, August 21, 1716, Rigsarkiv, Söhlenthal Correspondence, T.K.U.A., England, C. Cf. Holm, 'Studier,' V, iii, 60.

[2] Frederick IV to Frederick William I, August 18, 1716, and to Söhlenthal, August 25, 1716, Rigsarkiv, Söhlenthal Correspondence, T.K.U.A., England, C.

[3] Frederick IV to Söhlenthal, *Ibid.*

[4] Holm, 'Studier,' V, iii, 59.

[5] Frederick IV to Meyer, August 26, 1716, Rigsarkiv, Söhlenthal Correspondence, T.K.U.A., England, C.

[6] Geheimeregistratur der Anno 1716. Entry for July 6, 1716. Rigsarkiv, T.K.U.A., Vol. 258. A. P. Tuxen, *Poul Vendelbo Lövenörn* (Copenhagen, 1924), pp. 80–81.

for English naval aid without any loss of time, pointing out that without such assistance it would be impossible for Frederick IV to save his lands and people from Swedish subjugation.[1] Aided by his predecessor, Justitsraad van Holtz,[2] Söhlenthal asked for seventeen ships which would carry eighteen pound guns. Such was the need of the Danes if they expected to be as strong in sea power as the Swedes,[3] who according to the Danish admiral, Ulrik Kristian Gyldenlöve, had assembled at Karlscrona twenty-four or twenty-five vessels, some of which carried eighteen to twenty-four guns.[4] Söhlenthal had been instructed to add weight to his arguments by pointing out that it was necessary for England to prevent Norway from falling into Swedish hands, lest Charles XII and the Pretender to the English throne, James Edward Stuart, use Norwegian harbors to embark upon an invasion of Scotland.[5]

Söhlenthal worked for aid other than the coöperation of the English fleet. He was instructed by Frederick to work for the money owed Denmark by England, which, according to a report made by the Danish Chamber of Finances, amounted to 311,095 *riksdalers*.[6] Although arrangements had been made in the treaty of 1715 for the payment of this sum, due to Denmark ever since the Peace of Utrecht, a year and a half had elapsed without any English action. This money was especially important to Denmark because of the heavy financial burdens that the Skåne invasion entailed.[7] George I blamed his English subjects for the delay, and claimed that he was doing all in his power to bring about a settlement of the question.[8] Söhlenthal also tried unsuccessfully to bring Denmark into the Treaty of Westminster, which England was in the process of making with the Empire.[9] By such a move,

---

[1] Söhlenthal Instructions, March 18, 1716, Rigsarkiv, Söhlenthal Correspondence, T.K.U.A., England, C.

[2] Frederick IV to Söhlenthal, March 31, 1716, *Ibid.*

[3] Gyldenløve to Söhlenthal, March 30, 1716, *Ibid.*

[4] *Loc. cit.*

[5] Gyllenborg to Sparre, April 21, 1716, *Handlingar*, X, 297. Frederick IV to Söhlenthal, March 18 and 28, 1716, Rigsarkiv, Söhlenthal Correspondence, T.K.U.A., England C.

[6] Frederick IV to Söhlenthal, April 18, 1716, *Ibid.*

[7] Idem to Idem, May 11, 1716, *Ibid.*

[8] George I to Frederick IV, June 5, 1716, *Ibid.*

[9] Frederick IV to Söhlenthal, July 11, 1716, *Ibid.*

Denmark hoped to win Imperial guarantees for the conquests in the Empire that she had made at Swedish expense.[1]

England and Denmark did agree on Wismar. Both countries were in favor of making the fortress an Imperial town, and neither of them wanted the Duke of Mecklenburg in possession of the disputed citadel.[2] George I, however, was against demolishing the fortifications, and had obtained an express order from the Emperor forbidding it. Their efforts went for nought because in the spring of 1716 the kings of Prussia and Denmark had agreed to the contrary,[3] and it was those two monarchs whose troops controlled the city.

Russia too prepared for the coming assault. Even before the waters of the Baltic had been freed of ice, Peter had assembled his transports and men-of-war at Reval awaiting spring and the approaching campaign.[4] This convoy required Danish naval protection. Peter in addition to outfitting his own ships, gave Denmark 3,000 pounds of hemp and a great many masts.[5]

Russia also rendered diplomatic assistance. On March 6, 1716, Prince Kurakin arrived in England hoping to bring about English participation in the Skåne operation.[6] The English conduct towards the Russian minister was very cool and was undoubtedly influenced by Bernstorff's displeasure over the quartering of Russian troops on his Mecklenburg estates.[7] Nikiforov, however, insists that it was not Bernstorff but Townshend who was dragging his feet, and that the threat of Sweden helping the Pretender and English trade and diplomatic interests in the Baltic called for a separate peace between George I and Charles XII.[8]

All that England was willing to offer was a commercial treaty in which 'Peter's obligations were set forth fully, but

---

[1] *Loc. cit.*

[2] Sehestedt to Söhlenthal, June 19/30, 1716, *Ibid.* Robethon to Polwarth, May 21/June 1, 1716, *Polwarth Papers*, I, 33.

[3] Chance, *George I and the Northern War*, pp. 108–110. Cf. Holm, 'Studier,' V, iii, *passim*.

[4] *Russian Navy under Peter I*, N.R.S., XV, 45.

[5] Sehestedt to Westphal, May 2, ¡1716, Rigsarkiv, Westphal Correspondence, T.K.U.A., Russland, C 122.

[6] Gyllenborg to Sparre, April 16, 1716, *Handlingar*, X, 298.

[7] Lamberty, *Mémoires*, IX, 556–557.

[8] Nikiforov, *Russische-Englische Beziehungen*, p. 175–181.

those of George were small and indefinite.'[1] On April 15, one day before Kurakin left London, Bernstorff and Bothmer handed the Russian envoy a guarantee treaty which was to serve as a basis for further discussion. Nothing came of it because Russia refused to enter into a commercial treaty unless a defensive and offensive alliance was signed at the same time.[2] Thus the presence of Russian troops in Mecklenburg broke down the Czar's negotiations to win English aid for the Skåne descent.[3]

Toward the end of March, the Danes, who had been working day and night in order to have fifteen ships seaworthy by the time that the English fleet approached the Baltic,[4] received information that Norris would weigh anchor for the Sound at the end of the month.[5] Frederick IV, who hoped that Norris had been commanded to blockade Karlscrona and take part in the Skåne invasion, requested on April 11 a copy of Norris' instructions in order that the Danish admiral Gabel might be sent a corresponding order.[6]

Norris had been scheduled to sail from England around the end of March, but in reality he did not clear the Nore until May 29. Ten days later he arrived at the Sound with nineteen ships of the line and two frigates.[7] In an interesting letter written on June 5, George excused the delay claiming it had been caused by circumstances over which the English had no control, namely contrary winds. Stung by charges that he was not fulfilling the treaty obligations of a true ally, George I asserted that it was not in his power to command Norris to veer off from convoying and to engage openly in hostilities against Sweden. The English king then implied that Norris

---

[1] Chance, *George I and the Northern War*, p. 103.

[2] Copy of treaty with Kurakin's remarks, Ny. Kgl. Saml. in Royal Library, Copenhagen, 696b.

[3] Reading, *The Anglo-Russian Commercial Treaty*, p. 86. Lamberty, *Mémoires*, 556–557. Nikiforov, *Russische-Englische Beziehungen*, p. 175–185 ignores the Mecklenburg factor so far as Kurakin's mission was concerned, but does give the Mecklenburg problem top priority for the worsening of relations between George I and Peter the Great.

[4] Frederick IV to Söhlenthal, March 18, 1716, Rigsarkiv, Söhlenthal Correspondence, T.K.U.A., England, C.

[5] Idem to Idem, April 11, 1716, *Ibid.*

[6] *Loc. cit.*

[7] Chance, *George I and the Northern War*, p. 118.

would shortly win the affection of Frederick IV and that soon all Swedish enterprises against Denmark would cease.[1] George I at this time also expressed regret that the matter of subsidies and arrears owed Denmark by the English had not been brought to a peaceful solution, and claimed that he had done all in his power to obtain the money.[2]

George I was engaging in his usual double-talk because the instructions given to Norris on May 10, 1716, definitely indicated that the British ruler intended to sell his Danish colleague short so far as British naval assistance was concerned. Undoubtedly conversations held between Townshend and Gyllenborg prior to the sailing of the squadron accounted for a softening toward Sweden on behalf of the English king. Gyllenborg had suggested that Bremen and Verden might be ceded to Hanover if George I as Elector and King would assist Sweden to recover some of its other possessions.[3] Actually Charles XII had asked for more specific guarantees than vague promises of good assistance,[4] and Gyllenborg had come to the conclusion that a peaceful cession of Bremen and Verden would be impossible. Nevertheless, he could dangle hopes before the Hanoverians, and he well knew that many people in England were seriously worried about the growing power of Russia in the Baltic. To some British ministers there was a definite fear that Russian dominance in the North would be opposed to British interests, and one British minister had informed the Spanish ambassador that if George I, because of his own private interests, went too far in his plans against Sweden, his English ministers would oppose him.[5]

Thus George I had his hands tied by his English ministers, and in early 1716 he did not want an open break with Sweden. If he could obtain Bremen and Verden without military actions, so much the better. Yet pressure might speed up

---

[1] George I to Frederick IV, June 5, 1716, Rigsarkiv, Söhlenthal Correspondence, T.K.U.A., England, C.

[2] Loc. cit.

[3] Various letters in Handlingar, X. Cf. Larsson, Gyllenborg, pp. 18–22 and Chance, George I and the Northern War, pp. 116–117.

[4] Intercepted Letters (Sweden), 1716–1717, P.R.O., State Papers Foreign, Confidential, 107/13. Cited hereafter as Intercepted Letters.

[5] Larsson, Gyllenborg, p. 22. Larsson bases his statement on a Gyllenborg dispatch dated May 14, 1716.

Charles XII, and some recognition of the desires of George I's allies had to be considered. The Norris instructions tried to realize these double objectives.

The British admiral upon arrival at the Sound was to send a message to the King of Sweden informing him of the presence of the British squadron in the Baltic. Jackson was to be instructed to do likewise at Stockholm. Both were to complain about Sweden's ignoring British trade grievances and to threaten reprisals. Those portions of the Norris instructions dealing with trade and commerce were secondary, however, to the other parts pertaining to power politics. By 1716, diplomacy outweighed commerce. George I suspected that that Charles XII had entered:

> into Measures with our Enemys highly Injurious to our Crown and Kingdoms; and in order to secure himself more Effectually the means of accomplishing these Designs, he [Charles XII] is now endeavouring to make himself Master of Norway, the Reduction of which Kingdom we look upon, besides the Loss of Trade of Great Britain thither, to be the most ready way both to enable him to cut off entirely the Commerce of our Subjects to the Baltick, and to afford him greater Opportunities of carrying on those Projects, which from good Grounds we cannot but apprehend he is forming against the Peace and Safety of our Kingdoms.

Norris was ordered to command Charles XII to call off the attack upon Norway and promise not to give direct or indirect aid to the Pretender.[1]

This portion of the Norris instructions was designed to prod Charles XII to make peace and to desist from negotiating with the Pretender. Also, it in part fulfilled George's commitments to aid Denmark, for the British admiral told Charles XII to withdraw from Norway, and if Charles XII attacked Norway or the Danish islands, Norris was 'to use all possible means to prevent the same.'[2] The belligerent tone in the Norris demands, especially regarding Norway, went far beyond the instructions of the Dutch contingent which was soon to join Norris. The

---

[1] Norris' Instructions, May 10, 1716, BM., Add. MSS., 28,145.
[2] Ibid.

States in 1716 as in 1715 wanted to limit naval activities solely to the protection of trade.[1]

Some of the less pugnacious parts of the instructions would in turn make the allies of the Northern Alliance unhappy. George I offered to mediate the Northern War and promised to procure for Sweden 'as good a Peace, as the present Situation of affairs will admit of,' and Norris was not to act offensively against the Swedes until he had received answer to the letter he had sent Charles XII. The only possible reason for offensive action was an attack upon Norway or the Danish islands by the forces of the Swedish king. While waiting for news from Sweden, if the King of Denmark and the Czar 'should offer to undertake a Descent upon Schonen,' Norris was to persuade them to delay the undertaking until he had heard from Charles XII. If Frederick IV and Peter persisted in the Skåne plans, Norris was to threaten 'to leave the Sound' with the British Squadron and 'to let the Fleet of Sweden act freely in their own Defence.'[2]

Norris upon arrival informed the Danes of his presence and sent off a memorial to Charles XII who at the moment was in Norway besieging the city of Frederickstadt. The Swedish fleet, which had been active off the coast of Zealand, withdrew higher up the Baltic.[3] With twenty-two ships of the line, it was impossible for Denmark to defend Norway without British assistance. In fact, it was extremely difficult for the members of the Northern Alliance to do anything without the coöperation of the twenty-one ships under the Norris command.[4]

Gyllenborg himself supplied Norris with his own secretary, a certain Stambke,[5] to carry the Norris note to Charles XII. The note itself conformed with the demands set forth in the

[1] Instructions to Hendrick Grave, June 10, 1716, Rijksarchief, Secrete Resolutiën, Staten Generaal, June 10, 1716. See also additional instructions, July 23, 1716, *Ibid.*

[2] Norris' Instructions, May 10, 1716, BM., Add. MSS., 28,145.

[3] Norris to Bernstorff, to Townshend, and to Burchett, May 29, 1716, *Ibid.*

[4] Chance, *George I and the Northern War*, p. 118. The list of ships in the squadron, BM., Add. MSS., 28,145 shows only twenty ships, but one might have been added before sailing. The British had intended to send just sixteen ships, but added to the strength of the squadron when they found out that the Dutch would contribute a mere six ships. *The Historical Register*, III, 352, says that the Norris squadron was made up of twenty-one ships.

[5] Rumpf to Fagel, June 20, 1716, Brieven van Willem Rumpf aan Staten Generaal, Rijksarchief, Liassen, Zweden, 1715–1718, Archief Staten Generaal, 6557. Cf. Chance, *George I and the Northern War*, p. 120n.

Norris instructions with the ousting of the Jacobites in Sweden and a withdrawal from Norway being emphasized. England's sovereign would employ 'all the means which God has put into his hands' to prevent the conquest of Norway and the Danish islands. On the other hand, if Charles XII were to give satisfaction on the diplomatic and economic points demanded by Norris, the English admiral promised that George I was ready and willing to use old friendships to iron out all existing differences between Charles XII and his enemies and to procure for Sweden 'as good a Peace as can be in the present Situation of affairs.' George I 'would esteem himself the most happy Man in the World' if he received a favorable answer as soon as possible; an answer he expected 'with an Impatience equal to the Importance of this great Affair.'[1]

On June 5, Jackson presented a memorial in a similar vein which contained a detailed list of the losses that the British merchants had suffered at the hands of the Swedish privateers.[2] He delivered his near ultimatum at the same time that information reached Sweden that Norris had arrived at the Sound coincident with the appearance of Muscovite warships. The English merchants at Stockholm were certain that an open rupture between England and Sweden would transpire and that the note would have a deleterious effect upon the property and the persons of the British merchants in Sweden.[3] Throughout the Swedish capital there was common talk of open hostilities between England and Sweden. Charles XII supposedly was highly incensed over the demand to withdraw from Norway, and gossip had it that the Swedish navy at the first opportunity would attack the British fleet and merchantmen.[4]

The public in Sweden was, however, unduly excited. Horn read the Jackson memorial to the Swedish Chancery which decided to send it on to Charles XII. Jackson was informed

---

[1] Norris to Charles XII, May 27, 1716, BM., Add. MSS., 28,145.

[2] Jackson to the Swedish Chancery, June 5, 1716, P.R.O., State Papers, Sweden, 95/22. A copy of the memorial can be found in Lamberty, *Mémoires*, IX, 650–652. *The Historical Register*, III, 325 erroneously claims that the memorial was delivered on June 15, 1716.

[3] Rumpf to Fagel, June 20, 1716, Rijksarchief, Archief Staten Generaal, Liassen, Zweden, 6557.

[4] Idem to Idem, July 1, 1716, *Ibid.*

that Müllern would personally go to the King's camp with the English note in order to ascertain the orders and wishes of the Swedish ruler.[1] Charles XII, for his part, threw the Norris memoir on a table and refused to read it on the ground that neither Norris nor his messenger were accredited agents to the Swedish court.[2] Furthermore, he placed an embargo upon all correspondence between his camp and Norris' fleet.[3] By June 12, 1716, Jackson could write Townshend: 'By what Count von der Nath said, as I am assured before I [had] spoken to him, there is not much probability the King will return any answer at all either to Sir John Norris' Memorial or mine.'[4]

Meanwhile in Denmark, Norris was having his troubles with the Danish Court and with Püchler, the Hanoverian minister to Denmark. The Danish Court had taken the letter of George I, promising help and assistance to Denmark at face value. As the days passed and there was still no news from Sweden, Norris' position became much more difficult. On June 19, Sehestedt asked Norris to merge the British fleet with the Danes in order that the joint fleet drive all Swedish ships from the Baltic. By so doing, Norris would be able to compensate for his lateness in coming to the Baltic.[5] Nine days earlier, Püchler had written Norris in a similar vein, stressing the danger that the Swedish fleet posed to Denmark and to the ships moving men and supplies from the mainland to Zealand destined to take part in the Skåne invasion.[6]

With such pressures the English admiral found himself in a quandary. He stalled by informing Sehestedt that he could not move without Dutch coöperation and that he had to wait for an answer from Charles XII. Consequently, he was forced to remain where he was, but if Charles XII attacked Denmark, Norris promised to do all in his power to ward off the Swedish

[1] Carl von Grooth (for the Swedish Chancery) to Jackson, June 6, 1716, P.R.O., State Papers, Sweden, 95/22. *The Historical Register*, III, 528, dates this answer June 16, 1716. For another copy, dated June 6, 1716, see Lamberty, *Mémoires*, IX, 650.
[2] Rumpf to Fagel, July 20, 1716, Rijksarchief, Archief Staten Generaal, Liassen, Zweden, 6557. Cf. Larsson, *Gyllenborg*, p. 24.
[3] Jackson to Townshend, June 12, 1716, P.R.O., State Papers, Sweden, 95/22.
[4] *Ibid.* Jackson sent letters in a similar vein on June 22 and July 3, 1716. *Ibid.*
[5] Sehestedt to Norris, June 8 and 19, 1716, BM., Add. MSS., 28,145. See also Rigsarchiv, Söhlenthal Correspondence, T.K.U.A., England, C.
[6] Püchler to Norris, June 11, 1716, n.s., BM., Add. MSS., 28,145.

onslaught and to defend the possessions of the Danish king.[1] Thus the English admiral was reduced to waiting upon the arrival of the Dutch squadron and upon some answer from Charles XII.

What to do with an unfavorable answer from Charles XII also harassed the British admiral for his instructions did not clearly cover such a contingency. He knew that Püchler's request to cover the convoys coming to Zealand would speed up the invasion plans.[2] On the other hand, if he joined the Danes, 'our Behaviour may break into War.'[3] His conferences with the Danish king had been plagued by such questions as to how long he would wait for an answer from Sweden, what he would do if the Swedes rejected his note, what was in the note to Sweden, etc. Norris himself pleaded with Townshend to clarify his instructions if Charles XII were 'so unreasonable, as not to permit any Answers to come to me.' If such happened 'I shall be in want to know from your Lordsp. how his Majty will please to have me behave myself.'[4]

He also went to the Hanoverians for some inkling as to how he should act. Turning to his father-in-law, Admiral Aylmer, upon whose influence he greatly relied, he asked him to find out from Bernstorff or Robethon just what was expected from him. 'I don't write to Mor. Berringsdorff till I hear he is o' this side the water, and pray you will make him my compliments. Robethon told me we were not to correspond this year, which is the reason I don't write to him, but you will please to make him my compliments that we may stand right with him.'[5] Aylmer was to acquaint Bernstorff that Norris was of the opinion that the Danes 'are very desirous to have us in some action that may draw us into War.' He had not written directly to Bernstorff, but Robethon could put his letter to Aylmer into French for Bernstorff. Norris' sole objective was to do his duty and to obey the King, and consequently, he desired to hear from Aylmer often. Fifteen days had elapsed and still no news from Sweden. Norris was coming to believe that like last year

---

[1] Norris to Sehestedt, June 9 and 20, 1716, *Ibid.* Also in Rigsarkiv, Söhlenthal Correspondence, T.K.U.A., England, C.
[2] Idem to Townshend, June 1, 1716, BM., Add. MSS., 28,145.
[3] Idem to Idem, June 9, 1716, *Ibid.*
[4] Idem to Idem, June 5, 1716, *Ibid.*
[5] Idem to Aylmer, June 12, 1716, *Ibid.*

Charles XII might 'send no Answer. I therefore in that Case beg to know how the King will have me behave, and that shall be done.'[1] 'So while I am obeying my orders, which I endeavour strictly to observe, I shall be complained against by the Danes and Muscovites, and perhaps the Swedes at last prove so stubborn, as not to admit the offers of coming to an accommodation. Thus between Sila and Caribbis, I am like to give neither content.'[2]

The attitude of the Hanoverians apparently was to win Bremen and Verden by diplomacy if possible and to prevent the dismemberment of Sweden by Russia and her allies. Yet if a complete upsetting of the balance of power in the North were necessary to obtain Bremen and Verden, George I was willing to gamble. It was an Hanoverian adventure all the way. Robethon on June 1 sent the following memorandum to Polwarth, the British minister to Denmark:

> Should the Danes complain because he, [Norris] does not assume the offensive immediately on his arrival your lordship will represent how that the Admiral has instructions to protect their lands, their fleet and their commerce against the Swede, and that his Britannic Majesty cannot justly commence war with Sweden without such good causes as Parliament cannot fail to approve, which will be given should the King of Sweden refuse a satisfactory answer.[3]

There can be little doubt that Robethon was sure of his man.

On June 30, Norris held a conference with the Danish court, hoping that he might persuade Frederick IV to call off the invasion of Skåne. Hannekien, the British Secretary at Copenhagen had briefed him ten days earlier that the invasion could not get under way until the 'middle of August or September' because preparations for the great undertaking were moving slowly.[4] Pressure from Sehestedt and Püchler, however, had caused him to call the conference and to ask Frederick IV if there might not be some way other than the invasion of Sweden to relieve Norway—a way in which Norris might be able to take part and not violate his instructions. The Danish king,

[1] Idem to Idem, June 9, 1716, *Ibid.*
[2] Idem to Idem, June 16, 1716, *Ibid.*
[3] Robethon Memorandum, May 21/June 1, 1716, *Polwarth Papers*, I, 33.
[4] Hannekien to Norris, June 20, 1716, n.s., BM., Add. MSS., 28,145.

however, remained adamant in his request for British ships to assist in the invasion plans.[1]

Norris' inept attempts to have the Danes abandon the Skåne project came as a bombshell to the assembled Danish diplomats. His arguments as to why his request should be adopted were specious and based upon deliberate prevarications. Norris claimed that he had received news from Jackson at Stockholm which had informed him that Sweden was about to sue for peace and that the consummation of the invasion plan would destroy all hopes for a speedy termination of the war.[2] All of Jackson's correspondence in that period actually gives a contrary opinion as do Norris' own dispatches to Townshend, Aylmer, and others.[3] By the end of June, Norris was so confused as to how he could get the Swedes out of Norway, sabotage the invasion of Sweden, and assist his master to get Bremen and Verden that he was reduced to lying. His proposal was strongly rejected by Sehestedt, who refused to even consider it. The Danish plans, said Sehestedt, were too far advanced to allow for a postponement of the attack at such a late date. The conference adjourned with the puzzled Sehestedt wondering about what to him appeared to be a sudden change in British policy.[4]

His confusion was justified. George I had promised one thing which seemed to be substantiated by his Hanoverian minister at the Hague, while his British admiral seemed to be following an entirely different policy. Meanwhile, Alexander, Lord Polwarth, his new English minister to Denmark, appeared to be going in two directions. He was ardently pro-Hanoverian but reduced to explaining why George I as English king could not carry out the commitments he had made as Elector of Hanover.

On one point, however, Norris was quite clear and that was that he did not intend to engage the Swedish fleet before his Dutch reinforcements arrived. He had received information

---

[1] Chance, *George I and the Northern War*, pp. 121–122, and Holm, 'Studier,' V, iii, 53–57 have good accounts of these discussions.

[2] Sehestedt to Söhlenthal, June 30, 1716, Rigsarkiv, Söhlenthal Correspondence, T.K.U.A., England, C.

[3] Jackson Dispatches in June, 1716, P.R.O., State Papers, Sweden, 95/22. Norris' Letter Book, BM., Add. MSS., 28,145.

[4] Sehestedt to Söhlenthal, June 30, 1716, Rigsarkiv, Söhlenthal Correspondence, T.K.U.A., England, C.

that the Swedes under Admirals Wachmeister and Sparre had 1,362 guns as opposed to his own 1,070, and he was of the opinion that the Swedes probably outmanned the British in approximately the same proportion. Believing that the Swedes had orders to attack—and his information was as bad as it had been the year before on this score—Norris did correctly analyze the attitude of George's allies:

> The Danes and Muscovites have nothing so much to wish for as that we may be engaged alone with the Swedes, in which Action let the Advantage be as it will, we shall be both so dis- abl'd as that after it they will be entire Masters of these Seas and have their own Advantage to pursue at pleasure.[1]

Reminding Townshend that he had asked for sufficient strength to meet the Swedes alone if they were in force, Norris awaited the arrival of the Dutch contingent.[2] With its arrival the tempo of Britain's Baltic diplomacy became accelerated.

[1] Norris to Townshend, June 30, 1716, BM., Add. MSS., 28,145.
[2] *Ibid.*

IX

THE ANGLO-DUTCH
SQUADRON OF 1716

NEGOTIATIONS by England to bring about Dutch coöperation in a Baltic squadron had been in progress since the
first of the year. In February both Townshend in England and
Horatio Walpole at the Hague were doing much to persuade
the Dutch to take part in next summer's Baltic operations.
Townshend insinuated to Duivenvoorde, the ambassador of the
States, that the French were receiving favored treatment under
the Swedish privateering edict. By the end of the month his
representations on this score helped win Duivenvoorde over to
the British way of thinking.[1] The chief reason, however, for the
Dutch envoy being in favor of the squadron was that he was
of the opinion that Dutch-Baltic trade had to be protected at
all costs, and the most reasonable way to protect that trade
was through a joint squadron.[2]

Horatio Walpole at the Hague, meanwhile, was appealing
to the pennypinching Amsterdam burghers. In addition to the
usual arguments he pointed out that if England and Holland
united and made 'a right use of our Squadrons design'd for the
Baltick' they could win the friendship and assistance of
the Northern Allies and thereby frustrate all activities of the
Pretender.[3] By a 'right use,' the Northern Alliance of course
wanted naval coverage for its proposed invasion of southern
Sweden.

[1] Duivenvoorde to Heinsius, February 11, 24, and 28, 1716, n.s., Rijksarchief,
A.A.H., 1972.
[2] Idem to Idem, February 28, 1716, n.s., *Ibid.*
[3] Horatio Walpole to Townshend, February 21, 1716, n.s., Walpole Letters,
Indiana and Murray, *Honest Diplomat*, pp. 153ff.

The Walpole and Townshend insinuations that the French would receive favored treatment from Swedish privateers, and that the Maritime Powers might be excluded from the Baltic trade, moved a group of Amsterdam merchants to request in February protection for their Baltic merchantmen. The States General agreed that naval cover was necessary, but they were hard put to raise the funds needed to equip ships for convoy duty. There was a strong rumor in the United Provinces that the merchants themselves would outfit the ships, but such private aid as might be expected was not interested in George's Baltic schemes. So shaky were Dutch finances, that the States could not have carried on an aggressive foreign policy in the Baltic even had they so desired.[1]

While the States of Holland tried to find the money for the squadron, their diplomats were in conference with the British regarding the aims and purposes of the naval units. 'Townshend felt keenly and perhaps guiltily the deceit over Norris' instructions in 1715, and was anxious to avoid definite commitments with George I's Hanoverian allies as to the plans of the British Navy for the 1716 campaign.'[2] This attitude can definitely be seen in the ambiguous character of Norris' instructions as they were finally drafted.[3] Duivenvoorde, for his part, was sure toward the end of March that Norris' 1716 instructions would be approximately the same as they had been in 1715.

Orford and Townshend conferred with Duivenvoorde on March 24, 1716, n.s., and insisted that the Dutch would have to contribute more ships than planned if the convoy were to be effective. Townshend warned that the French might try to send a squadron to protect French commerce but that this should not be permitted because France 'by contract' had already provided for her Baltic trade.[4] The danger that the French ships might unite with those of Sweden was in British eyes a real one and steps would have to be taken to forestall it. If the States refused to coöperate then Britain would equip

[1] Idem to Idem, February 21, 1716, n.s., P.R.O., State Papers, Holland, 84/253. *Cf.* Murray, *Honest Diplomat*, p. 153, note 2.
[2] Hatton, *Diplomatic Relations*, p. 121.
[3] See previous chapter.
[4] Duivenvoorde to Heinsius, March 24, 1716, n.s., Rijksarchief, A.A.H., 1972.

fifteen ships, prevent the Swedes from aiding Wismar and at the same time protect its own commerce.[1] Because of the differences of 1715 Duivenvoorde and Townshend found conversations over Norris' instructions highly embarrassing. The subtle separation of the King of England from the Elector of Hanover differed slightly from the situation that had existed the previous year. Justitsraad von Holtze had been hurriedly sent from Denmark to expedite the sending of the Baltic squadron, but as he had come as an envoy to George I as elector, Townshend had not spoken with him and would not converse with Duivenvoorde about Holtze or about his mission. The Dutch envoy was convinced that George I's engagements committed him to blockade the Swedes at Göteborg or Karlskrona. As to what diplomatic effect and explanations to be given this operation, Duivenvoorde had come to the conclusion that perhaps the British Court itself did not know its own mind.[2] Duivenvoorde by late April, however, had become convinced that Norris' instructions would contain secret clauses which would make it possible for George I to carry out his promises to Denmark and the other members of the Northern Alliance.[3] The Dutch envoy was positive that the squadron up to the fall of Wismar would cruise before that city as it had before Stralsund and Rügen the previous year. The termination of the Wismar siege and the city's capitulation left Duivenvoorde wondering as to the next move of the Hanoverian-British party.[4]

Walpole in the latter part of April had acquainted Heinsius with the British concern over the Swedish invasion of Norway and asked if there were any possibility that the Dutch ships might be given orders to act with those of the British to prevent Norway from falling into Swedish hands. The Pensionary had answered him with the supposition that Charles XII would fare poorly in his Norwegian adventure, and that it would be

[1] Idem to Idem, March 27, 1716, n.s., *Ibid.*: 'Ome de Zweden te beletten Wismar te secourene.'
[2] Idem to Idem, April 14, 1716, n.s., *Ibid.*: 'Evenwel weet ik dat het engagement van de koning leit om door het engelse esquader de Zweden te beletten of uit Gottenburg of uit carelscroon te loopen, dog men dit sal effectieren en wat couleur men den het werk sal geven, weten sij misschien hier selfs nog niet.'
[3] Idem to Idem, April 21, 1716, n.s., *Ibid.*
[4] Idem to Idem, May 1, 1716, n.s., *Ibid.*

difficult 'to dispose the States to engage themselves in ye Northern troubles, and they were equipping fast as they can six men of War for ye Security of their trade in those parts.'[1] Duivenvoorde at London endeavored to keep his conversations in the same vein.

On May 4, 1716, he asked Townshend a series of questions concerning Britain's Baltic policy now that Wismar had fallen. Would she help drive Charles XII from Norway? Would she assist the Danes and Russians in their plans to drive the Swedes from Skåne? Faced with straight-forward questions, Townshend as was his custom gave his answers in double-talk. He claimed to know nothing about the situation in Norway, but added that surely people did not want the Swedes to be masters of Norway. To allay Dutch concern over the changing balance of power in the Baltic, Townshend went on to assure Duivenvoorde that no one in England would give the least assistance to Sweden's enemies, and that above all George I's plans were good for both Sweden and Holland. All that the English ruler desired was peace in the North, and he was, so Townshend claimed, genuinely unhappy about the sufferings of the Swedish people.[2]

The Dutch diplomat was, as noted above, not impressed with Townshend's professions of British friendship toward Sweden. He went to Lord Orford, the First Lord of the Admiralty, who was among the small group in England opposing the Hanoverian attempts to embroil England in Baltic politics. It will be remembered that it was Orford who had tied Norris's hands in 1715.

The First Lord of the Admiralty stressed to Duivenvoorde the twin necessities of preserving the balance of power in the North and of protecting trade and commerce. Orford was of the opinion that the Maritime Powers should compel Charles XII to grant them freedom of commerce. On the other hand, he was opposed to any further meddling by them in Baltic affairs other than using their good offices to bring about peace.

---

[1] Horatio Walpole to Townshend, April 24, 1716, n.s., Walpole Letters, Indiana, and Murray, *Honest Diplomat*, p. 222.

[2] Duivenvoorde to Heinsius, May 5, 1716, n.s., Rijksarchief, A.A.H., 1972. Townshend told Duivenvoorde that he 'versekeert konde wesen dat Engeland geen de minste assistentie soude geven aen de vijanden van Zweden om iets ter werelt tege dat rijke te onderneme.'

He was concerned over Danish and Russian statements that until Charles XII allowed freedom of commerce in the Baltic, he would not be permitted to negotiate with anyone. Orford thought that to prevent such negotiations the Danes would start taking Dutch and British ships.[1]

The long dispatches of Duivenvoorde to Heinsius were carefully considered by the States before they drafted the instructions for Captain Hendrick Grave, the commander of the Dutch ships destined for Baltic duty. Grave was to sail to Elsinore and rendezvous with Norris. The main concern of the Dutch Commander was again to be the trade. He was to allow no warships to approach the merchant ships under his convoy, and if unfriendly vessels approached, 'he was to meet force with force.'[2] If necessary, Grave could stay in the Baltic throughout September.

If on arrival in the Baltic he could not find Norris, he was to ascertain the strength of Swedish sea power in those parts of the Baltic whither the merchantmen were bound. He was then to call a council of war, and if it was evident to the council that he could freely convoy the ships to their destination, he was to do so at once. If such a course were decided by the council as too dangerous, Grave was to await the arrival of Norris. If the British joined the Danes, Grave was to see if he could act alone. If the Dutch council felt its ships too weak for unilateral action, Grave was to unite with the Norris command.[3]

Grave, with six warships and over 200 merchantmen, arrived in Danish waters off Elsinore on July 2, 1716. A council of war was held the next day between British and Dutch naval officers. Norris wanted Grave to join him in bringing 'the King of Sweden to reason,' which of course Grave could not do. The British commander then proposed to send three British ships along with the Dutch six to convoy the merchant shipping to its respective destinations. With so many ports of call to make, Grave was of the opinion that nine ships would be insufficient for the task of covering the merchantmen. With so many Swedish ships ready for sea duty, and the Swedish refusal to

[1] Idem to Idem, May 8, 1716, n.s., *Ibid.*
[2] 'sal hij geweld met geweld keeren.'
[3] Instructions for Grave, June 10, 1716, and additional instructions, June 13, 1716, Rijksarchief, Secrete Resolutiën, Staten Generaal, June 10 and 13, 1716.

allow any dispatches to land at Elsinburgh, Grave feared a Swedish attack upon the convoy which might end up in disaster for the allied ships. Furthermore, inclement weather might prevent the joint fleet from keeping the station off Bornholm. It was thus decided that the two commanders would wait for additional orders from home.[1]

Söhlenthal from London meanwhile had sent word to the Danish Court that Norris had received new orders. He had obtained this information directly from Bernstorff. Consequently, Sehestedt asked Norris when he would begin blockading Karlscrona now that the Dutch fleet had arrived. If the British did not get to work soon, Sehestedt felt that Sweden would 'become more obstinate, and the Peace farther off than ever.' It was necessary that Norris declare himself as soon as possible 'in a manner agreeable to the Common Interest of the Allies.'[2]

Norris answered Sehestedt at once, and his letter well expresses the problems facing the British commander. He admitted that he had been instructed to go with the Dutch and take a station near Karlscrona and then to proceed up the Baltic with the trade. Afterwards he was to remain near Bornholm or Karlscrona to observe the Swedish fleet so that it could not molest the trade. These orders, however, had been overruled at the council of war for Grave's instructions commanded him to remain at Elsinore until further notice. Norris himself had no freedom to take the offensive against the Swedes, and unless the ships of Sweden made war by attacking the commerce, he could do nothing. If he could have moved, he would already have been off Bornholm. As George I had already left for Hanover, Norris suggested that Frederick IV write him there to learn what the next move of the British fleet was to be. After he found out, Norris hoped that the Danish king would fill him in as to details. Norris especially wanted to know what would be expected of the Anglo-Dutch squadron and how many Danish ships would assist it in any future under-

---

[1] Norris to Townshend, July 3, 1716, and to Stanhope, same date and Minutes of the Council of War, July 3, 1716, BM., Add. MSS., 28,145. See also Grave to Fagel, July 14, 1716, n.s., copy in Rijksarchief, Secrete Resolutiën, Staten Generaal, July 21, 1716, n.s.

[2] Sehestedt to Norris, July 3, 1716, BM., Add. MSS., 28,145.

takings against Sweden.[1] By the beginning of July then, Norris was looking towards the Danish king for instructions.

The vacation trip of George I to his beloved Hanover did not begin until July 7, and his leaving England gave a new twist to Baltic affairs. Townshend had opposed the trip and maintained that it would not only weaken Britain's Baltic policy, but also that it would give malcontents within the kingdom an opportunity to criticize the sovereign.[2] George I recognized the difficulty of conducting Britain's Baltic policy during his absence, and to remedy the situation took Stanhope with him. Henceforth he was to transmit directly through Stanhope all orders to Norris and to England's new envoy to the Baltic, Alexander, Lord Polwarth, who was to arrive at his post at the beginning of August. Norris still sent Townshend duplicates of his dispatches, but more and more the play revolved around Hanover and Stanhope so far as the Baltic squadron was concerned.

'For the rest, George conducted his negotiations with the czar and with the kings of Denmark and Prussia to a great extent through his German ministers.'[3] The Walpole-Townshend forces in England were already beginning to fear the influence of Bernstorff, Robethon, and the Duchess of Münster, and they were also uneasy about the political aspirations of Sunderland.[4] Little did they realize that Stanhope too was moving into the camp of the Hanoverians.

Meanwhile Norris waited. On the fifth he heard that the Swedes had been near Bornholm with twenty-eight ships. By the seventh he learned of a Danish victory over the Swedes before Fredrickshald, which alleviated the danger in Norway as Charles XII would be forced to withdraw to his supplies in Skåne. On that day he wrote Stanhope at Hanover for more explicit instructions. If it were George's pleasure he, Norris, was ready to 'act in Concert with the Danes' so that 'they will be the sooner able to make their Descent upon Schonen.' Norris admitted that there was little likelihood that Charles XII would negotiate with the English commander and already

---

[1] Norris to Sehestedt, July 3, 1716, *Ibid.*
[2] Townshend to Bernstorff, May 19, 1716, Coxe, *Walpole Memoirs*, II.
[3] Chance, *George I and the Northern War*, pp. 124–125.
[4] Robert Walpole to Stanhope, July 30, 1716, Coxe, *Walpole Memoirs*, II, 59.

'The Season of the Year is so far advanced that the Trade which goes to Petersburg will hardly be able to return before the Frost comes.' Norris thought that the Dutch ought to join the English and the Danes and assume the offensive, 'and if this Method were to be taken, the Swedish Fleet should be first attackt and forced into Port, the Descent make, and then the Trade to proceed their Voyages, and what could not return this Year might safely do it the next.'[1]

While Norris and Grave waited for news from home, some Russian troops began to arrive in Denmark. Peter himself anxious to reach Denmark travelled to Falster on a hoy and arrived there July 14. His galleys came the next day, and on the seventeenth he was able to appear at Copenhagen with his troops. Earlier ships destined for Russian service purchased in Holland and England had already reached the area in June. Other Russian ships had wintered in Norway and Denmark, and soon seven ships of the line with three frigates and three schooners were to join them from Reval. All in all by the end of the month the Russian admiral Scheltinga found himself in command of an excellent fleet which included fifteen ships of the line.[2]

On July 24 Norris received both a public and private dispatch from Townshend in answer to his letters of June. Sehestedt again knew of Norris' new instructions as soon as the admiral did because he had been advised of their contents by Söhlenthal on Bernstorff's authority.[3] It is doubtful, however, whether Söhlenthal could make any more out of his information than could the British admiral, for the new material contained a good deal of conflicting material. The public dispatch, for example, congratulated Norris on his 'steddy Conduct,' and expressed George's pleasure that his admiral had not been prevailed upon by any 'plausible Insinuations to deviate in the least from his instructions'.

Townshend admitted to Norris that there was considerable danger in trusting the merchant ships solely to Dutch protection and consequently he ordered Norris to join a detachment of

[1] Norris to Stanhope, July 7, 1716, BM., Add. MSS., 28,145.
[2] Chance, George I and the Northern War, p. 125; Holm, 'Studier,' V, iii, 45; Hartman, Tzar Peter's underhändlingar 1716 om landgång i Skåne, pp. 62–65.
[3] Holm, 'Studier,' V, iii, 56.

sufficient strength to the Dutch naval units so that the merchant fleet would be adequately covered. By so doing Norris would weaken his squadron and expose it to attack if it stayed in the Sound. He was, therefore, instructed to withdraw the rest of his ships to 'Kiog Bay' or some other station of less danger. Being so protected he was to await an answer from the Swedish king.

If Norris had 'any Apprehension of Danger to the Squadron remaining' with him from the superior naval strength of the Swedes, it was 'his Maj't's pleasure' that Norris 'should join the Fleet⁀of Denmark for his own better security.' 'And as the King of Sweden has hitherto protracted his returning an Answer, and probably will not give any, his Majty therefore directs that you should not give any Hinderance to the Danes in the Descent upon Schonen, either by Representation, or otherwise.'[1] Even as Townshend was writing about his apprehensions that Charles XII might ignore the British note, he received news from Jackson which shattered any hopes that he might have had on that score. Consequently he added a postscript to Norris informing him that he might have orders to act with less reserve towards Sweden.[2]

Townshend's private dispatch to Norris of the same date in part summed up the situation as Townshend saw it, and also illustrates the dilemma of the English ministers. News from France indicated that a Swedo-Jacobite treaty had been signed whereby the Swedes would take Jacobites into the Swedish army at the same rank and station that they had enjoyed under the Pretender. Charles XII by allowing Sparre to make such a treaty had added this new low blow to his refusals to answer English notes and to forgo his depredation upon English commerce. In British eyes if he became master of Norway he would be in an even better position to exploit his animosities against England.

Norris thereupon was to take still another tack regarding the Skåne invasion. 'To this purpose it is the King's pleasure that you should not only forbear to hinder the intended Descent in Schonen, but as that seems the only Expedient left for obliging the Kg. of Sweden to retire out of Norway & that

---

[1] Townshend to Norris, July 3/14, 1716 (Public dispatch), BM., Add. MSS., 28,145.
[2] *Ibid.*

you should make such Movements with that part of your Squadron which shall remain with you after you have made the necessary detachmt for the Security of the Trade as may facilitate and cover that Attempt.' If the Swedish fleet interfered with the invasion, Norris was to join the Danes and attack 'as the Success of this Descent appears now to be of more immediate concern to the safety of his Maj't's Dominions.'[1]

Yet even these instructions were qualified:

> His Maj't's Intentions being that you should observe no measures toward Sweden in any case where the assistance of his Fleet shall be necessary to deprive them of any Signal Advantage, or where your joining the Danes may procure them some Signal Advantages. But without one or the other of these two Cases, you are not to give the Danes such a degree of assistance as may be interpreted to amount to an open rupture with Sweden.[2]

Norris by now at least had orders to move, but he still was dependent upon the Dutch if the guise of neutrality were to be maintained. Consequently after he arrived at Copenhagen on Sunday, July 26 and conferred with Peter, Frederick IV, and their ministers, he refused to answer their specific statements regarding the transport of troops from Mecklenburg and the covering of the descent upon Skåne pleading that first he had to have answers to questions he had sent to the States and to George I at Hanover. Once having received these, Norris was of the opinion that if the entire naval forces of Russia and Denmark could join him off Bornholm or Karlskrona, and if it appeared that the Swedish fleet was harmlessly in port, then the traders could be sent on to their destination under a detachment and the remaining ships could participate in the Skåne adventure.[3] He summed up his feelings to Stanhope shortly after his conference with Peter and Frederick IV:

> The latter part of my Lord Townshend's directions seems to be very cautious of any offensive Action against the Swedes,

[1] Townshend to Norris, July 3/14, 1716 (Private dispatch), BM., Add. MSS., 28,145.

[2] Ibid.

[3] Questions given to Norris by Peter and Frederick IV, July 15/26, 1716, and Norris' answers on the same date, BM., Add. MSS., 28,145. Cf. Norris to Townshend and to Stanhope, July 17/28, 1716, Ibid.

and yet if our Trade proceed as I have mention'd and we in Company of the Danes and Muscovites should meet the Swedes, it would be impossible to protect the Trade and Cover the Descent without an attempt upon them to force them into Port, which if his Majty thinks must be done, I pray you to signify the same.[1]

Meanwhile back at the States all was not well between England and those controlling the affairs of the United Provinces. Stanhope had not informed the States General that Norris was to remain stationary while Grave, with his six ships and three hundred and eight guns, was to do convoy duty alone. Actually, it was Görtz, the first minister of Charles XII who alarmed the Dutch with the news that George I planned a descent upon Skåne in conjunction with his allies.[2] Consequently, the Dutch in no uncertain terms informed Stanhope that they would 'never agree to offensive orders for Captain Grave, nor let him convoy the combined merchant fleets without some co-operation from Norris.'[3] Thus the men in charge of the affairs of the States made it unequivocally clear to Stanhope that they would never agree to Grave's taking offensive action against Sweden nor would they allow him to convoy the Anglo-Dutch merchantmen to their Baltic destinations without some coöperation from the British admiral.

Grave, on July 23, 1716, was therefore sent additional orders. The safety of the merchantships had to be the chief aim of the squadron. To that end Grave was to persuade Norris to convoy the merchantmen far up into the Baltic past Sweden and to send detachments to the ports to frustrate the work of the Swedish privateers. All six Dutch ships were to accompany the detachments with as many British warships as Norris might be disposed to contribute. The remainder of the English squadron was to observe the Swedish fleet so that it could not detach large units which might be employed against the merchant shipping. Grave was to assist Norris in this task if the English acted alone. Should Danish warships join Norris in order that the Swedish fleet might be observed with greater security,

---

[1] Norris to Stanhope, July 17, 1716, *Ibid.*
[2] Hatton, *Diplomatic Relations*, p. 122; Jägerskiold, *Sverige och Europa*, pp. 20ff.
[3] Hatton, *Diplomatic Relations*, p. 122.

Grave was not to oppose the merger but he was to refrain from participating in a combined Anglo-Danish squadron.[1]

These new orders for Grave were evidently a compromise worked out between Stanhope and the State because on July 24, when he arrived at George's Court at Osnabrück, 'additional orders were sent to Norris roughly conforming to Grave's instructions as far as the convoying of trade was concerned.'[2] These new orders George I regarded 'as purely temporary, forced upon him by the stubbornness of the Dutch, and the regard he was forced to take to British public opinion.'[3] They also show that at this point the commands were coming from Stanhope with Townshend relegated to the position of asking that he might be notified so that he could inform the Prince Regent and so that he could give Norris 'such Directions, as may sometime happen to be proper to come from this side of the Water.'[4]

Norris received his new instructions on July 30, instructions which could only make George's allies think that he was hedging on his promises. Using the excuses that Charles XII had returned the Norris letter unopened and that Sweden's ruler had given orders for his privateers to seize all Anglo-Dutch ships, George I commanded Norris to join the Dutch ships and proceed eastward with the merchantmen until he was free from all danger of Swedish attacks. Then with the joint fleet he was to keep the Swedish fleet under observation and take reprisals. In order to be 'better able to perform the two services recommended to you of securing the trade . . . and of making reprisalls,' Norris was to press the Danes to join him in the eastward cruise.

> In consideration of which service being performed, you may give his Danish Majesty, his ministers or admirals, assurance of your being ready to act in concert with the Danish squadron

---

[1] Orders to Grave, July 23, 1716, Rijksarchief, Secrete Resolutiën, Staten Generaal. Copy in Walpole Letters, Indiana and in Murray, *Honest Diplomat*, pp. 330–332. 'Capiteijn Grave in gedagten sal houden, dat haer Hoog. intentie niet verder gaet, als om de Coopvaerdij Scheepen te protegeren, en de geweld met geweld af te weeren, sonder eenige feijtelijchsheden eerst te beginnen, en de dat hij vooris in alles soldaet en Zeemanschap sal gebruijken.'

[2] Hatton, *Diplomatic Relations*, p. 122.

[3] *Ibid.*, p. 123.

[4] Townshend to Norris July 17/28, 1716, BM., Add. MSS., 28,145.

to oblige the Swedish fleet to retire into their ports, and thereby, as by such other methods as shall be judged practicable to secure a free passage and navigation to all ships belonging to his Danish Majesty or to his allys; and you will accordingly use your best endeavours so to doe, and will continue and act with our squadron in such manner and place as shall most effectually answer these ends, until the season of the year shall require your attendance upon the trade homewards.[1]

Stanhope also informed Polwarth, Britain's new ambassador to the Danish Court, to do all in his power to move Frederick IV to coöperate with the Anglo-Dutch squadron in covering the merchantmen.[2] Polwarth was also instructed to persuade Peter the Great to join his ships with those of Norris and to sail under the command of the British admiral. Speed was of the essence as the season was already well advanced and the passage of each day posed a danger to the merchantships destined for the upper Baltic.[3]

Norris at once informed the Danish and Russian ministers about his new instructions although Sehestedt already knew about them through Söhlenthal who had acted upon Bernstorff's authority.[4] On July 31 the English seaman held a conference with Peter and Frederick IV and suggested that all the allies join forces, go to Bornholm to search out the Swedes, attack them and drive them into port, and then proceed up the Baltic with the trade leaving sufficient ships behind to contain the Swedes and cover the descent.[5]

The Czar was quite willing to participate in the course of action as outlined by Norris, but the Danes dragged their feet. First they wanted to assume command of the joint squadron,[6] and second they felt that they should not weigh anchor until ships under the command of Admiral Gabel had been added

[1] Copy of Norris' instructions enclosed in Stanhope to Polwarth, July 13/24, 1716, *Polwarth Papers*, I, 40–41. See also orders for Norris from Osnaburgh, *Report on the Manuscripts of Charles, Viscount Townshend*, Historical Manuscripts Commission, *Reports* (London), 1887, Report II, Appendix, Part 4, p. 100.

[2] Stanhope to Polwarth, July 13/24, 1716, *Polwarth Papers*, I, 40.

[3] *Ibid.*, p. 41.

[4] Holm, 'Studier,' V, iii, 56. *Cf.* Chance, *George I and the Northern War*, pp. 125–126.

[5] Norris to the Russian and Danish ministers, 20/31 July, 1716; and to Stanhope July 21/August 1, 1716, BM., Add. MSS., 28,145.

[6] Norris to Stanhope, July 21/August 1, 1716, *Ibid.*

to the joint squadron, 'but that is mere pretence, for so soon as the Fleet sails from this place, the Russian Troops will come hither from Mecklenburgh, which is what the Danes would avoid till they be ready for the Descent.'[1]

Norris then turned his attention to the Dutch while Peter took off in a sloop to view the mouth of the Sound.[2] Walpole had already briefed Norris on Grave's instructions, which were not to the admiral's liking, for he looked with a jaundiced eye upon Buys, Fagel and others at the Hague who were tying Grave's hands. Norris' dislike stemmed from diplomatic and strategic reasons, but he still hoped to circumvent Dutch caution and timidity:

> And yet it is impossible for their [the Dutch] Ships to go safely up the Baltique, before the Swedes be forced into Port, and therefore I shall use all the means, I am able, if it must come to an Action, to do it before the Dutch part from me, that their State may share in the Rupture, as well as in the Safety the Action, whenever it happens, will procure to their Commerce.[3]

Norris, however, reckoned without taking into account the sentiment of Robert Goes, the envoy of the States at Copenhagen. Grave, concerned only with protecting the commerce, had been won over to Norris' arguments that the safety of the merchantmen depended upon a sweep before Bornholm in conjunction with the Russian and Danish fleets. While Grave wrote home for permission to follow British leadership, Goes suggested that the Russians and the Danes contain the Swedish fleet while the Maritime Powers took the merchantmen to their destinations. Goes countered Norris' excuse that such an action was contrary to British orders with the suggestion that he thought that the safety of the trade was the reason for the joint convoy.[4]

On August 3 bitter words were exchanged between Norris and Goes which well indicates the differences in opinion between the two men. With the rumor rampant in Copenhagen

---

[1] Norris to Townshend, July 24/August 4, 1716, *Ibid.*
[2] Norris to Stanhope, July 24/August 4, 1716, *Ibid.*
[3] Idem to Idem, 21 July/August 1, 1716, *Ibid.*
[4] Goes to Fagel, August 1, 1716, Rijksarchief Secrete Brieven Denemarken, Archief Staten Generaal, 7278. Grave to Fagel, August 4, 1716, Rijksarchief, Secrete Resolutiën, Staten Generaal, August 11, 1716.

that Goes had offered 1,000 ducats to have the invasion called off,[1] and with Goes confirmed in his suspicions that Norris wanted to command an allied invasion fleet to assist Hanoverian aspirations, it is no wonder that tempers flared. Goes hotly suggested that the Russians and Danes, who were at war with Sweden, attack the Swedes, or that the English, who were committed to reprisals, do it, but all this was no concern of the States. Norris snapped back that the Northern Alliance did not exist to bring Charles XII to heel, so that the Dutch shipping could enjoy free passage in the Baltic.[2]

Goes might be correct in his opposition to Dutch coöperation in the invasion on the grounds that if it were successfully carried out it would ruin the balance of power in the Baltic, but he indulged in considerable wishful thinking when he claimed that many people in Denmark were pleased with Dutch neutrality.[3] Actually, public opinion ran sharply against the Dutch in all quarters. There were rumors, probably fostered by the Danish Government, that if it had not been for the States, the invasion would not be necessary and Charles XII would have been brought to terms. The Dutch purposely let the Swedes take their ships and thus Sweden could continue the conflict. If the States really meant what they professed about freedom of commerce, the Danes asserted that they should have sent a naval squadron of sufficient strength to cover their merchantmen. The Danish Court was also irked that at a time when the States were letting the Swedes take their ships and run a debt up into the millions, they consistently refused to pay just debts due to the Danish king.[4]

The Dutch were faced with a number of hard facts: They did not have enough ships to cover their merchantmen without help; there was considerable danger from Denmark and Russia in allowing a large number of merchant ships to lie at anchor in waters which were not too friendly and which would shortly be the scene of an invasion convoy; they had either to go along with Norris or take a chance and sail into the Baltic alone. This last decision Goes considered but did not dare make on

[1] Holm, 'Studier,' V, iii, 70.
[2] Goes to Fagel, August 4, 1716, Rijksarchief, Secrete Brieven, Denemarken, Archief Staten Generaal, 7278.
[3] Idem to Idem, August 8, 1716, *Ibid.*
[4] Idem to Idem, September 8, 1716, *Ibid.*

his own.[1] Norris for his part refused to protect Dutch shipping unless the States acted on their own behalf.[2] He could not understand Grave who refused to render any assistance in forcing the Swedes into their ports and yet who agreed that Dutch commerce would not be safe unless some other nation did it, 'which is so extraordinary a proceeding of the States.'[3] Norris' superior fleet, however, gave him the bargaining power and even before new orders came from the Hague, Goes and Grave decided to attach the Dutch contingent to the joint squadron.[4] Unless they dared gamble, they could not do otherwise. Back at the Hague the reaction to Baltic events was what one might expect. The States had thought that the compromise worked out among their representatives, Walpole, and Stanhope would solve everything, and were surprised to learn that the merchant ships were not enroute to their Baltic destinations. Grave they felt should sail because whatever the hazards looming ahead of him in the Baltic, they did not compare with the present danger of letting a large merchant convoy remain as a sitting duck. The season was already advanced and the ships for safety's sake had to move up the Baltic. Nevertheless, the Dutch warships were again cautioned not to begin any offensive action against Sweden and were to use force only when force was used against them. The sea deputies of the States intended somehow through diplomacy to force Norris to move the convoy. Grave was instructed not to remain in the Baltic beyond the end of September, and if he could not get all of the ships entrusted to him out of the Baltic, he was to leave them in some Baltic port, so long as it was not in the possession of Denmark.[5] On August 11 and 12 Fagel, Buys, and other deputies of the States had conferred separately with Walpole and had reasserted the Dutch stand on trade and on acting offensively against Sweden.[6] Buys' protests against Dutch participation in

[1] Idem to Idem, August 4, 1716, *Ibid*.

[2] Norris to Horatio Walpole, August 1, 1716, BM., Add. MSS., 28,145; Norris to Townshend, August 1, 1716, *Ibid*.

[3] Norris to Stanhope, July 24/August 4, 1716, *Ibid*.

[4] Minutes of Anglo-Dutch council of war, August 1 and August 12, 1716, *Ibid*.

[5] Additional orders to Grave, August 12, 1716, and report of same to Goes, Rijksarchief, Secrete Resolutiën, Staten Generaal, August 12, 1716. Walpole to Townshend, August 11, 1716, n.s., Walpole Letters (Indiana), and Murray, *Honest Diplomat*, pp. 340–343.

[6] *Ibid*. Walpole to Norris, August 12, 1716, BM., Add. MSS., 28,145.

active hostilities against Sweden were in British eyes considered
to have 'a particular and extraordinary turn in them,' but
'exactly agreeable to the old way of ratiocination used by that
Gentleman.'[1] Nevertheless, Fagel, usually pro-British, warned
Walpole that the sea deputies of Rotterdam and the traders of
Amsterdam were especially upset about the Baltic situation
and that he 'apprehended ye clamours of ye Merchants might
occasion a difference between ye two nations in disputing where
ye blame of their losses is to be layd.'[2] And losses there were
bound to be because of the delays resulting from British-
Hanoverian Baltic diplomacy.

In the meantime, the allies awaited the return of Danish
Vice-Admiral Gabel who was covering convoys from Pomerania. Actually the addition of his ships was not necessary, but
Frederick IV would not consider any operations until they
arrived on the scene.[3] Gabel, delayed by adverse weather
conditions,[4] did not reach Copenhagen until August 7, at
which time he united his squadron with that of Admiral
Gyldenløve.[5] On the tenth Norris and Polwarth conferred with
the Danish and Russian representatives in a council of war.
The Danes had eighteen ships, the Russians fourteen, and
Norris nineteen, some of which were later to be detached to
cover the Baltic trade. Eventually it was decided after protest
that Peter would personally command the Russian and Danish
ships and that Norris would act in conjunction with them but
not under the Czar's command. After the fleets were joined,
there were to be no detachments without a council of war.[6]

On the twelfth Norris acquainted Grave with the results of
his council with the Danes and the Russians. The joint squadron

[1] Walpole evidently discussed this conversation in a letter to Townshend dated
August 16, 1716, which is not in P.R.O., State Papers, Holland, 84/254. Cf. Townshend to Walpole, August 10/21, 1716, P.R.O., F.E.B., State Papers, 104/81.

[2] Walpole to Townshend, August 11, 1716, n.s., Walpole Letters (Indiana),
and Murray, *Honest Diplomat*, pp. 340–343.

[3] Holm, 'Studier,' V, iii, 70.

[4] Danish Manifesto, October 10, 1716, *The Historical Register*, III, 530–533.

[5] Holm, 'Studier,' V, iii, 70–71. Chance, *George I and the Northern War*, p. 128
says that Gabel arrived with seven warships on August 8, 1716.

[6] Minutes of Council of War, July 30/August 10, 1716, BM., Add. MSS.,
28,145. In addition to differences over the command, the Danes were of the
opinion that Norris should salute the Danish flag, an act which he avoided even
in the Road of Copenhagen. Norris to Polwarth, August 4/August 15, 1716, and
Gyldenløve (Guldenleu) to Norris, August 16, 1716, *Ibid.*

agreed to sail at the first good weather, and the British were to detach five ships and a frigate to help the Dutch ships with convoying.[1]

Four days later the convoy with the British and Dutch merchantships left Copenhagen. On the first night they ran into heavy winds and strong currents and were forced to anchor, but the next morning saw them under way toward the rendezvous with the Danes and the Russians. These two were not there when the Maritime ships arrived and they did not come into view until the next morning. By the next night the juncture of all ships was accomplished. On the evening of the twentieth they reached Bornholm. The Swedes had been at sea but retired when they sighted the joint squadron. The trade was sent up the Baltic with the covering warships, and on the twenty-fourth at a council, the Danes announced they would neither chase the Swedes, blockade Karlskrona, nor go beyond the island of Oeland. Peter, therefore, on the next day decided to return to Copenhagen leaving Norris to wait until the twelve ships convoying the merchantmen could rejoin the united squadron.[2]

The merchantships made the passage up the Baltic in safety. On the return, they were to rendezvous on September 15 at Danzig.[3] Norris stoutly maintained that 'if the ships had been sent in the manner the States mentioned, before the United Force had come with them, the States might have lost most of their Ships, and a'helped the K. of Sweden to have carry'd on his War with their Booty.'[4] He honestly held to the opinion that the Dutch and the British could not have protected the merchantships without Danish and Russian assistance and did not like the attitude of the men at the Hague at all. 'And if the States will please consider that the value of their Trade is at least ten times more than ours, and the small Number of Men of War they sent to their Protection, they will have no Reason to find fault, but be thankful to the King for his Assistance.'[5]

[1] Minutes of Council of War with the Dutch, August 1, 1716, *Ibid.*
[2] Norris to Townshend, to Bernstorff, and to Stanhope, August 17/28, 1716, and various minutes of Councils of War, *Ibid.* See also extract Grave to Goes, August 31, 1716, Rijksarchief, A.A.H., 1957.
[3] Extract, Grave to Goes, August 31, 1716, Rijksarchief, A.A.H., 1957.
[4] Norris to Polwarth, August 26/September 6, 1716, BM., Add. MSS., 28,145.
[5] Idem to Horatio Walpole, September 2/13, 1716, *Ibid.*

By September 19 the combined fleet was back in 'Kioger-bocht.'[1]

The correspondence of the various principals during the period is highly illuminating. Stanhope in the main along with the various members of the Hanoverian junta approved of Norris' actions. Townshend's approval was more cautious, however, and he showed a much greater concern for the trade than did Stanhope, a concern which was to deepen as winter approached. In August Townshend became aware of the uneasiness of British traders because of the various delays, but he rationalized: 'the Several Circumstances of Affairs in the Baltique have rendered those Delays unavoidable.'[2] Norris by early September was in a great hurry to get the invasion under way: 'and what is the hindrance of it, good Weather passes quick, and no time should be lost.'[3] The men at the States and their representatives in Denmark were also concerned about time, but not in the same way that Norris was. Heinsius hoped for a speedy return of the merchantships,[4] and the States, fully aware that Norris' projected time of return was not feasible, ordered Grave to stay in the Baltic only so long as the weather permitted. He was to make sure that he would be back home before the advent of winter. He was to bring with him those ships which were ready and leave the rest behind. To the governors of the States, the British vessels were remaining in the Baltic far longer than the protection of the merchantmen required.[5] So far as Goes was concerned, Norris wanted to lead the united squadron against Sweden,[6] and that Anglo-Dutch coöperation actually meant conforming to the view of the English Court, which in turn represented the interests of the court of Hanover more than it did either England or the United

[1] Goes to Heinsius, September 19, 1716, Rijksarchief, A.A.H., 1957. Chance, *George I and the Northern War*, p. 130, says that they were back in Copenhagen on the 20th.

[2] Townshend to Norris, July 31/August 11, 1716, and various letters between Stanhope and Townshend, BM., Add. MSS., 28,145.

[3] Norris to Polwarth, August 26/September 6, 1716, *Ibid*.

[4] Heinsius to Goes (Minutes), August 29, 1716, Rijksarchief, A.A.H., 1982.

[5] Orders to Grave, Rijksarchief, Secrete Resolutiën, Staten Generaal, August 26 1716.

[6] Goes to Heinsius, September 19, 1716, Rijksarchief, A.A.H., 1957. Idem to Fagel, Rijksarchief, Secrete Brieven Denemarken, Archief Staten Generaal, 7278.

Provinces.[1] His conversations with Norris and Polwarth about the possible return of the merchantships must have been quite discouraging. Both Britishers were more interested in the projected invasion of Skåne than in the shipping. According to Norris, the States had the most merchantmen and they should have sent sufficient protection for them. Goes did not even press the issue.[2] To him no one cared much about commerce unless to prey upon it. Dutch traders were suffering at the hands of Russians and Danes as well as Swedes. No longer were the States free agents in the Baltic. All that they could do was wait and watch the development of the invasion plans.

[1] *Ibid.* 'Want dat men zonder bewimpeling zou zeggen dat het zelve Hoff [England] meer reflecteerde op de particuliere belangen van het hoff van hanover, als op die van beijde Natien.'
[2] *Ibid.*

X

THE INVASION THAT DID
NOT TAKE PLACE

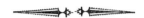

BACK at Copenhagen and elsewhere plans proceeded for the attack on Sweden, but mistrust and doubt grew between Dane and Muscovite. The Danes, whose fears of the Russians had increased throughout July,[1] became openly suspicious of the Russians during the next month. On August 15, Lord Polwarth wrote home, 'By what I can observe the Danish are not a little jealous of the Muscovites.'[2] Peter himself was not happy about the course of events, with Dane, Briton and Hollander showing varying degrees of hostility to his plans. It will be remembered that: first, Norris had tried in June to talk the Allies out of the invasion; second, that the Danes were postponing to the last moment the arrival of Russian troops in Denmark; and third, that the Dutch envoy at Copenhagen was rumored to have offered a substantial sum of money if the plans were cancelled.

Peter and Frederick IV were also at odds as to who would command the Danish troops. Peter was positively opposed to General Dewitz, who had stopped the entry of Russian troops into Wismar, and he did not like the Duke of Würtenberg or Admiral Gyldenløve. Frederick IV tried to ease the tension by having Dewitz remain upon his estate at Fyen, but refused to relieve him of his post. He was an excellent commander and Denmark needed him. Peter was also displeased because the Danes were not willing to send ships to the Gulf of Bothnia to

[1] Syveton, 'L'erreur de Görtz,' IX, 69–70.
[2] Polwarth to Robethon, August 4/15, 1716, *Polwarth Papers*, I, 53.

cover the Russian diversionary attack against Stockholm. Although there was nothing in the Altona Convention binding Denmark to such an action, Peter claimed that Denmark should participate in both operations. Frederick IV, for his part, wanted his ships to remain at home to cover the Skåne invasion. Peter evidently wanted to employ Danish ships in the attack on Stockholm to insure a trustworthy foreign policy from his ally, but it is possible as Frederick IV suspected, that the Czar wanted to make Danish naval units bear the brunt of the attack upon the Swedish defenses. Thus he would be able to alter the balance of naval power in the Baltic in his own favor. Whatever his reasoning Peter, because of the Danish reluctance to join him in the Bothnia diversion, threatened to call off the secondary attack.[1]

While the naval forces manoeuvered, the Russian troops had been on the march. The bulk of them had been assembled at Rostock and Warnemünde by the end of June when Peter returned from taking the waters at Pyrmont.[2] Here they had waited for the Danish transports and the covering transports. The impatient Peter, however, could not delay, and on July 15 sailed in a hoy to Falster,[3] and two days later as stated above he arrived at Copenhagen with fourteen battalions of land forces. On the next day twelve additional galleys had arrived, and Peter by that time had ready an estimated force of 10,000 men.[4] These men had camped near Copenhagen, a short distance from the city gates.[5] Peter had been received with considerable fanfare, although his wife had a much cooler reception, because her seamy past as a camp follower hardly made her acceptable to the ladies of the Danish Court.[6]

Danish and Russian troops were still expected from Pomerania, but they needed Gabel's naval units to cover them.[7] As the days slipped by with the bakeries feverishly making bread for the invasion forces,[8] it became apparent that it was necessary

[1] Holm, 'Studier,' V, iii, 84.
[2] Chance, *George I and the Northern War*, p. 125.
[3] Holm, 'Studier,' V, iii, 63. Chance, *George I and the Northern War*, p. 125 sets the date as July 14.
[4] *The Historical Register*, III, 529–530.
[5] *Loc. cit.*
[6] Holm, 'Studier,' V, iii, 67.
[7] See chapter 9.
[8] Hanneken to Norris, July 25, 1716, BM., Add. MSS., 28,145.

THE INVASION THAT DID NOT TAKE PLACE

for these troops to appear soon if the invasion were to start before winter.[1] On September 1, the day that Peter returned from a flying trip to Stralsund to inspect the transport ships,[2] the Ingenhaven regiment of Danes arrived from north Germany. It was the first of the regiments from Pomerania. Between the ninth and fifteenth of September, large contingents of Danish and Russian troops poured into the vicinity of Copenhagen, and all of the warships back from the Baltic were assembled at Copenhagen Roads to launch the invasion.[3] The land forces consisted of 30,000 Russians and 23,000 Danes.[4]

The great day approached; European diplomats speculated as to the outcome. On September 14 all of the Danish clergy were ordered to pray on the coming Sunday for the success of the campaign. By that time Frederick IV had selected September 21 as invasion day.[5] With everything ready, Peter changed his mind. He had come to the conclusion that the season was too late to attempt amphibious operations against Sweden with any real hope of success. The Russian decision announced on the seventeenth by the Russian minister and two days later by Peter himself,[6] was the result of reconnaissance sweeps made by the Russians upon Swedish coastal defenses. On September 10, the Czar's galleys landed sixty Cossacks with horses who overmastered two Swedish posts and returned with three prisoners. Peter himself sailed close to the Swedish defenses on a snow, and the land batteries scored a direct hit upon the Czar's ship. The shore guns were so cleverly hidden that the Russian gunners had not been able to spot them.[7] From the prisoners it was learned that any invasion force would not only encounter an army of 20,000 men, but also it would have to break through a coastal ring strongly fortified with redoubts and guns.[8] Furthermore, the Russian generals to a man were

[1] Polwarth to Robethon, August 7/18, 1716, *Polwarth Papers*, I, 59.
[2] Chance, *George I and the Northern War*, p. 129.
[3] *Russian Navy under Peter I*, N.R.S., XV, 48–49.
[4] Holm, 'Studier,' V, iii, 78. Chance, *George I and the Northern War*, p. 130 sets the number of Russians at 29,000 with between 3,000 to 4,000 of this number being noncombatants. The combined force according to Chance was 52,000 men.
[5] Holm, 'Studier,' V, iii, 79–80.
[6] *Ibid.*
[7] Goes to Heinsius, September 11, 1716, Rijksarchief, A.A.H., 1957.
[8] Chance, *George I and the Northern War*, p. 131. Holm, 'Studier,' V, iii, 83. Lamberty, *Mémoires*, IX, 624–625.

opposed to making a winter campaign in Sweden.[1] Although the Russians had brought with them considerable supplies, nearly enough for three months, the news that the grain in Skåne had already been cut and sent to various strongholds made it all too clear that the invasion armies would have trouble living off of the country.[2] This was a factor of considerable importance to men accustomed to winter fighting. In addition, Russian troops in Finland and Livonia were not strong enough to carry out the diversion.[3] For these reasons, Peter called off the invasion.

His decision was probably a wise one.[4] Although Charles XII would have been able to place only 22,000 men on the field,[5] in spite of rumors to double that number,[6] he would have had the advantage of fighting on his own terrain plus a superiority in military skill. He was a better general than any of his opponents, and Peter, who had been scarred by his claws at Narva and Pruth, had little desire to flush the Swedish lion out of his own den. Swedish garrisons for a change were well filled, having been furnished at a cost of 1,200,000 *riksdaler*, which had been wrung from the Swedish people. The fleet was provisioned until October and the troops had been paid up to the same date.[7] If the invading army had been able to storm the Swedish shore defenses, it would have had hard going through Sweden because Charles XII had ordered all grain to be moved from Sweden's southern provinces.[8] The Danes might claim that there was as much forage in Sweden as could be found in the spring,[9] but Peter well knew that early snows would make this difficult to come by. Little help could be expected from Denmark. The resources of Frederick IV were

[1] Holm, 'Studier,' V, iii, 83.
[2] Goes to Heinsius, September 15, 1716, Rijksarchief, A.A.H., 1957; Goes to Fagel, September 22, 1716, Rijksarchief, Secrete Brieven Denemarken, Archief Staten Generaal, 7278.
[3] *Ibid.*
[4] Chance, *George I and the Northern War*, p. 131.
[5] *Ibid.* Holm, 'Studier,' V, iii, 80–81, places the Swedish strength at about 20,000.
[6] Hartman, *Tzar Peter's underhädlingar 1716 om landgång i Skåne*, p. 106n.
[7] Report of General von der Nath, August 29, 1716, *Handlingar*, VIII, 267.
[8] Charles XII to Hesse, *Konung Karl XII's Egenhändiga Bref*, p. 209.
[9] Goes to Heinsius, September 22, 1716, Rijksarchief, A.A.H., 1957; Goes to Fagel, September 22, 1716, Rijksarchief, Secrete Brieven Denemarken, Archief Staten Generaal, 7278.

so taxed that he could hardly keep the joint army supplied as it lay before Copenhagen, let alone furnish it over a body of water during the winter months.[1]

Many reasons have been advanced for the abandonment of the invasion plans. Peter himself blamed it on the lateness of the season,[2] but as Holm has pointed out, the Danes in their conferences had inferred that troops could not embark for Sweden before the end of August at the earliest. Thus Sweden would have had ample opportunity to prepare for the assault even though the invasion date finally arrived upon was four weeks late.[3]

Distrust and suspicion were primarily the reasons that Peter altered his plans,[4] along with his healthy regard for the military abilities of Charles XII. A pamphlet entitled, *A Letter of a Gentleman of Mecklenburg to His Friend in Copenhagen* claims that Peter did what he did because his allies were getting ready to sell him to the Swedes. Allied policy was aimed more toward harming Russia than aiding it, and Denmark wanted to feather its own nest by gaining control of both sides of the Sound, an act not completely to Russia's interest in obtaining a Baltic outlet.[5]

Repnin's treatment at Wismar had left Peter with a scar which his own reception at Copenhagen had failed to remove.[6] The Danish handling of the Russian troops in Denmark had been such that the Czar had good cause to fear betrayal from his allies. On September 19, Polwarth wrote, 'I am told from good hands that after a part of the Muscovite Horse were at Korsör, the rest that were about to land were fired upon and obliged to go back again, and that the Czar had sent for *neuf vaisseaux de guerre d'advantage.*'[7]

Holm makes no mention of actually firing upon the Russian troops, but does say that on September 7, Frederick IV ordered Commander Schönfelt to double the watch on the east and

---

[1] Chance, *George I and the Northern War*, p. 132.

[2] Danish manifesto, October 10, 1716, *The Historical Register*, III, 530–533.

[3] Holm, 'Studier,' V, iii, 82.

[4] *Ibid.*

[5] Letter of a Gentleman of Mecklenburg to his son in Copenhagen, October 23, 1716, Lamberty, *Mémoires*, X, 628–637.

[6] Holm, 'Studier,' V, iii, 74–75.

[7] Polwarth to Robethon, September 8/19, 1716, *Polwarth Papers*, I, 78–79.

north gates of Copenhagen, and gave him orders to fire at the first sign of unrest among the billeted soldiers. Unfortunately for harmony, those two gates faced the Russian camp, and the order was issued on the day that Peter's troops were expected from Mecklenburg.[1] The burghers of Copenhagen were so afraid of the Czar's soldiers—and well they might have been after reports from Mecklenburg and elsewhere—that they armed themselves.[2] Furthermore, the Danes patrolled the island where the Russians were camped. Distrust on the one side could only lead to mistrust on the other.

It is possible that the Swedish minister, Görtz, through negotiations at the Hague had influenced the Czar through offers of a separate peace. On the other hand, he was also making suggestions to the Dutch that he favored a general conference to solve Baltic affairs. There seems little doubt that Görtz had made indirect contact with the Russians before Peter abandoned the descent, but to give Görtz credit for the decision is to overrate his abilities.[3] After all, Peter in September was still negotiating for a defensive alliance and a commercial treaty with England, although his high-handed actions toward the English merchantships at St. Petersburg could hardly expedite such negotiations.[4]

Denmark and Russia spent the rest of September in continual conferences. Peter, when he had thrown over the invasion plans, had offered fifteen battalions of foot and one regiment of dragoons if Frederick IV insisted on going ahead with the undertaking. To interested observers it was apparent that the Danes had to make a decision almost at once or it would be too late even to start the descent.[5] The Czar made many promises. In addition to the troops, he offered to attack eastern

---

[1] Holm, 'Studier,' V, iii, 90.

[2] Syveton, 'L'erreur de Görtz,' IX, 438.

[3] Holm, 'Studier,' V, iii, 130. Cf. Chance, *George I and the Northern War*, p. 133. Lt. General Rank, a native Swede in the army of the Prince of Hesse-Kassel, approached Kurakin on August 20 on the possibility of a Swedo-Russian peace, which Kurakin supposedly rejected. Yet earlier at Prymont, Peter had spurned Swedish feelers. Nevertheless early in September he told Kurakin not to close the door on Rank. Nikiforov, *Russische-Englische Beziehungen*, p. 193–194.

[4] Robethon to Polwarth, September 4/15, 1716, *Polwarth Papers*, I, 76–77.

[5] Polwarth to Robethon, September 11/12, *Ibid.*, I, 80. Polwarth felt that the Russians and the Danes would have to reach a decision within ten days or it would be useless to try the descent because of the lateness of the season.

Sweden if help were forthcoming from the Danish fleet, and he volunteered his galleys to transport the fifteen battalions.[1] Coincidental with these offers was the rumor that Peter had agreed to carry out the plan according to the original arrangements if Frederick IV would grant permission for the Russians to maintain a garrison in Copenhagen, and to control the east and north gates of the city.[2]

The Danish answer to the Russian compromise given on September 23 was about what Peter and others must have expected. Denmark could not see her way clear to carry out the invasion with the limited assistance that Peter was prepared to grant.[3] Denmark requested thirteen additional battalions, a boon which Peter refused.[4] Three days later Frederick IV asked Peter to withdraw his troops from Denmark, as it was impossible for Denmark to carry out military operations against Sweden with Russian troops encamped in Denmark proper. By the end of the month the Russian soldiers were waiting for a favorable wind in order to leave Denmark.[5]

Great was the consternation in Hanover when the news arrived that the invasion had been postponed. The Court there, especially Bernstorff, had been looking forward with great anticipation to the departure of the Russian troops from Mecklenburg.[6] Robethon well sums up this attitude in a letter to Polwarth:

It will be necessary to take vigorous measures in the affairs of poor Mekelbourg as soon as the Russians leave it, because of the umbrage that will be felt against the Czar. I think that we should do nothing to intensify this feeling in the Danes. It is better that things come about naturally, as they will do, than by our suggestion. We shall see what happens in Scania and let events decide.[7]

---

[1] Holm, 'Studier,' V, iii, 98–99.

[2] *Ibid.*

[3] *Ibid.*, p. 100.

[4] Polwarth to Robethon, September 11/22, 1716, *Polwarth Papers*, I, 80 claimed that the Danes were asking for between 28 and 30 battalions. Declaration of Frederick IV, October 10, *The Historical Register*, III, 530–533 and Lamberty, *Mémoires*, X, 626.

[5] Declaration of Frederick IV, October 12, 1716, Lamberty, *Mémoires*, X, 626.

[6] Chance, *George I and the Northern War*, pp. 133–134.

[7] Robethon to Polwarth, August 10/21 and 14/25, 1716, *Polwarth Papers*, I, 61.

As for Bernstorff, he 'quite approves what I wrote as to the propriety of not increasing the feelings of the Danes against the Muscovites.'[1] The Hanoverians evidently were hoping for a rift, but only after the invasion. Then George I would be strong enough to keep Russian troops out of Germany while Bernstorff and the Mecklenburg nobles could bring the Duke to heel once he lost the support of Russian troops.

A letter of Görtz to von Kochen dated August 8 is indeed curious and perhaps sheds some light on the growing rift between Peter and George I. Evidently Ostermann had told Görtz that England was pushing the invasion and had ordered Norris by a secret letter to sink all Russian vessels that refused to coöperate. Norris however refused to obey such orders saying he would not put his head on a scaffold to humor Bernstorff who wanted Norris to sink the Russian troops.[2]

The return of those troops into the Empire upset the plans of George I and the men around him. Furthermore, Bernstorff was out of pocket between 700 and 800 crowns a month,[3] and Russian assurances that the troops would not be quartered on his estates or those of his colleague Bülow were not sufficient to mollify him.[4] Bernstorff wanted Norris to join with the Danes and 'crush the Czar immediately' and even suggested the seizure not only of the Russian ships, but of the Czar himself, 'till his troops shall have evacuated Denmark and Germany.'[5]

An almost 'unbelievable hatred' toward Russia sprung up in Hanover.[6] George I and the Hanoverians, therefore, were highly receptive to Denmark's appeal for Hanoverian aid in persuading Peter to reverse his decision. Representations were made through the Russian envoy at Hanover, Baron Schleinitz,

---

[1] Idem to Idem, August 14/25, 1716, *Ibid.*, I, 64.

[2] Nordmann, *La Crise du Nord*, p. 175, N. 15, quotes from the *Handlingar*, IV, p. 301–302. 'C'est que lorsque le czar a été en Seelande et qu'il a refusé de faire la descente en Scania, le voix d'Angleterre à l'amiral Norris par une lettre de cachet de couler à fonds tous les bâtiments, qui refuseraient d'y aller Maris que l'amiral Norris n'avant pas voulu obéir à ces ordres, disant qu'il n'était pas d'humeur de porter sa tête sur un échafaud pour l'amour de M. Bernstorff. De sorte de M. Ostermann qu'il n'a tenu qu'à M. Norris de noyer par une trahison ennuyé toute l'armée du czar.'

[3] Chance, *George I and the Northern War*, p. 134n.

[4] Norris to Stanhope, October 9, 1716, BM., Add. MSS., 28,145.

[5] Stanhope to Townshend, September 25, 1716, n.s., Coxe, *Walpole Memoirs*, II, 84.

[6] Mediger, *Moskaus Weg*, p. 32.

and through George's representatives at Copenhagen, both Electoral and British.[1]

The attitudes of Stanhope and Townshend throw considerable light on the growing differences of opinion in England regarding Baltic affairs. The latter, relying upon Polwarth's dispatches which were giving him a jumbled account of the situation, looked upon a break with Russia apprehensively, for it could lead to the seizure of all the merchantships. If, in addition, Russia prohibited British trade to areas under its control, the fleet would suffer. Any miscarriage of the present Baltic merchant flotilla would make it impossible for England to fit out naval squadrons in the future—this at a time when there was a possibility of Sweden aiding the Jacobites. Townshend, who saw a Jacobite threat looming, now that Charles XII did not have to worry about an invasion of Skåne, wanted Norris to return as soon as possible with the trade, so that supplies to equip the warships would be available, and the country would not be without naval protection at a time when Charles XII might give full reign to his passion 'by pouring a body of forces into England.'[2]

He was worried about Norris being pushed into overt acts by the Hanoverians, and trusted Stanhope to cool down the tempers of the Electoral Court. His trust of Stanhope was perhaps somewhat naïve, for he wrote his colleague his real feelings about Baltic affairs, which when carried to the King against his wishes could only alienate both sovereign and minister:

> I cannot help writing this letter to you, which I beg may be seen by no one person living, but remain absolutely between you and me a secret for ever. My chief design is to beg of you not to consent to sir John Norris staying any longer than the first of November, nor to the king's engaging openly in the affair about the czar. This Northern War has been managed so stupidly, that it will be our ruin. Is it possible for the king to carry it on with Denmark only on his side, and the Muscovite troops against him, supposing even the intended project should succeed? Would it not therefore be right for the king to think

[1] Hartman, *Tzar Peter's underhändlingar 1716 om landgång i Skåne*, pp. 108–109; Chance, *George I and the Northern War*, p. 135.

[2] Townshend to Stanhope, October 6, 1716, Coxe, *Walpole Memoirs*, II, 87–89.

immediately how to make his peace with Sweden even tho' he shou'd be obliged to make some sacrifice in obtaining it?[1]

Stanhope, who abused Townshend's trust, was by this time in the camp of the Hanoverians, and had difficulty in checking his 'nature on this occasion, which was ever inclined to bold strokes.' He pointed out that pressure was being exerted upon him to send orders, but he did want Townshend's reactions.

> The truth is, I see no day-light through these affairs. We may easily master the czar, if we go briskly to work; and that this be thought a right measure. But how far Sweden may be thereby enabled to disturb us in Britain you must judge. If the czar be let alone, he will not only be master of Denmark, but with the body of troops which he hath still behind on the frontiers of Poland, may take quarters where he pleases in Germany.[2]

Stanhope worried about the attitude of Prussia and bemoaned the fact that a treaty with France had not been concluded. Although Stanhope admitted that at one time he had been adverse to making any treaty with France, he was now in favor of it and wanted full speed on the negotiations being carried on with the French Regent through Abbé Dubois.[3]

The representatives of George I at Copenhagen were indeed busy. To Norris and Polwarth had been added the Lieutenant-General Bothmer, brother of the Hanoverian minister to England who had been sent to Denmark as a military observer. He had been given special instructions to observe Peter's German policy and to beware of Prussian intrigues. He arrived just in time to hear that the descent had been postponed.[4] Polwarth had seen the growing suspicions between Dane and Muscovite mainly as a chance for the English fleet to play a more important role.[5] Norris, on the other hand, had been in close touch with Peter on logistic and other problems connected with the invasion, and saw matters a little differently.[6] All George's agents knew that there were troubles on the horizon,

---

[1] *Ibid.*, II, 86.
[2] Stanhope to Townshend, September 25, 1716, *Ibid.*, II, 85.
[3] *Ibid.*
[4] Chance, *George I and the Northern War*, p. 135.
[5] Polwarth to Stanhope, September 1/12, 1716, *Polwarth Papers*, I, 74.
[6] Norris to Townshend, September 8/19, 1716, BM., Add. MSS., 28,145. Norris to Stanhope and to Robethon, *Ibid.*

but only Norris had feared that the lateness of the weather would, 'Cause the laying aside the Descent.'[1]

When the news of Peter's refusal to go through with the descent broke, Lieutenant-General Bothmer began to plead the Danish case on his own and to object to the proposed return of the Russian troops to Germany.[2] It was Norris, however, who was to have the most voice because of his friendship with the Czar. Knowing this, Frederick IV called Norris, Bothmer, and Polwarth to a meeting of his ministers and generals, told them of Peter's offer of limited participation, and urged the three to persuade Peter to go along with the invasion as planned. Norris spoke with Peter who agreed that if the descent were taken, it had to be taken in full force, and asked for time in order to confer with his Vice-Chancellor, Shafirov, before he came to any fast decision.

Norris later met with Shafirov and the Russian council, which presented him with a number of written questions dealing with the feasibility of the invasion. Norris answered as best he could, and pointed out that Denmark would 'never be able to make the like effort if it were not done.' Sweden, if not crushed, might increase in power and once more become a formidable foe of Russia.

The Vice-Chancellor then returned to Peter, who met for a while with his council, and afterwards he came to Norris with a plan of the Sound in his hand and asked him at what point the landing should be made. The Czar then talked about the Swedish soldiers 'and the Opposition they might give to the Landing, and what a great Disgrace the Miscarryage of it would be.' Peter said that if the Danes had given him ships so that he could have made the diversion, they would not now be faced by such huge troop concentrations in Skåne. Peter again repeated his offer to leave fifteen battalions for a descent next year. Norris informed Polwarth and Bothmer of what had transpired and then took Peter's message to Sehested 'with an acknowledgement of my Concern, that I had not been further able to effect what he desired.'[3] Norris hoped that the Danes

---

[1] Ibid.

[2] Chance, George I and the Northern War, p. 135.

[3] Norris to Stanhope, September 15/26, 1716, BM., Add. MSS., 28,145. Polwarth to Robethon, September 15/26, 1716, Polwarth Papers, I, 84.

and the Russians would adjust their affairs sufficiently so that the joint squadron could get up into the Baltic and meet the returning trade.[1]

Meanwhile, the British and Electoral couriers had taken the news to Hanover and had returned with more instructions. On September 26, Stanhope wrote to Norris about his fears that the Muscovites intended to take winter quarters by force in Denmark, Mecklenburg and other territories in the Empire. George I considered this 'a very unjust and grevious Way' for Peter to treat his allies and felt called upon to use all his efforts to stop it. He had already delivered a strong protest to the Czar through his German ministers on this matter because he was a prince of the Empire. Norris was to inform Peter that should a rupture occur, George I would be bound to align himself on the side of the Danes.[2]

Upon receipt of Stanhope's instructions on what to do because of 'the unhappy Accidents which break up the Campaigns in these parts,' Norris conferred with Bothmer and Polwarth, both of whom had received similar advice. A real problem faced them: 'now the Czar's Troops are near all embark'd, to prevent them taking Quarters in Mecklinburgh and other parts of the Empire.'

The three decided that Norris should go to Peter to offer him British assistance in bringing about an understanding with Denmark and to find out what the plans were for next year. Norris was to suggest that the troops now leaving Denmark go to Åland and make a descent there while the Danes hit Skåne. On the previous day, Frederick IV had told Norris and Bothmer in his garden at Rosenberg that he might favor such a scheme if it came from Peter. This seemed to Norris and Bothmer the only practical way to keep Russian troops out of Mecklenburg and the Empire. Through Robert Erskine, Peter's physician, Norris on October 3 insisted upon the necessity for harmony among the allies and pointed out that the king of Denmark would not allow Russian troops to winter on his domains. Peter in answer sent Norris word that he would have Shafirov and his ministers meet with him so that some sort of a future project would be drafted.

[1] Norris to Stanhope, September 18/29, 1716, BM., Add. MSS., 28,145.
[2] Stanhope to Norris, September 15/26, 1716, *Ibid.*

Polwarth, Bothmer and Norris then went to see Frederick IV who said that in spite of his disappointments, he would work for the good of the whole. The Danish king did hold that as Peter had broken the last agreement, any proposals for the future should come from him. Then Frederick IV asked Norris to meet with his Admiral and Secretary of State 'to consult about the convoying the Russian Troops.'

Back to Peter's ministers went the three where much conversation but very little action took place. The Russians wanted to know how much authority Bothmer, Norris and Polwarth had from Frederick IV to negotiate. They ended up with presenting a project which the Russians promised to lay before Peter. 'Thus ended all the Efforts we were able to make, and the Jealousies and Chagrinz which have been between them will, I fear, prevent any hearty relyance on each other for the future.'[1]

At the request of the Russians, George's three envoys conferred with the Russians, Shafirov and Tolstoi, who said that Peter had told them the day before that he had given up the invasion for that year because of the season and because of the bad results which would be coincident with failure. Again he offered to leave fifteen battalions in Denmark and winter the rest in Mecklenburg so that the descent could take place next year. The English asked that the troops be removed beyond Danzig if the Danes could not supply the troops, and pointed out that the putting of troops in Mecklenburg would cause too great a disturbance in the Empire. Again they put forth the idea of the Åland descent while the Danes invaded Skåne and blockaded the Swedish fleet at Karlscrona.

The Russians returned for additional orders while the English went to the Danish Court. Here the Danes asked Norris when he could be able to convoy the Russians out of the area, and Norris said, 'at that moment,' but he wanted to know where they were going. When the Danes answered Rostock, Norris asked them to plead with Peter to keep his troops out of the Empire. Poland was suggested as an alternative place for the wintering of the Russian troops. In a personal interview with the Danish King, Norris brought up the Åland project. Frederick IV agreed to it if the Russians made a treaty to that effect, if they removed their troops from Denmark and the

[1] Norris to Stanhope, September 22/October 3, 1716, *Ibid.*

275

Empire, and if they made their attack first and had the Danish troops act only as a diversionary force aided by eight or ten thousand Russians. To Frederick IV this project was feasible and the only one that he and his ministers considered workable.[1] The Danes, who had the most to lose, did not want an open rupture with Russia or the break-up of the Northern Alliance. The most that they promised so far as Mecklenburg was concerned was to ask Peter not to interfere in Imperial matters.[2]

The fourth and fifth similar conferences resulted in Peter reiterating his desire to winter in Denmark and Mecklenburg and offering satisfaction for damages; in the Anglo-Hanoverian contingent trying to get the Russians to invade or to take themselves beyond Danzig; and in the Danes being anxious to get the Russians out of Denmark regardless of where they went. When Norris asked Sehestedt what measures the Danes were willing to take in order to keep the Russians out of Mecklenburg, the Danish minister answered, 'that there was no forcing of Princes and that it must be by request. There you see the Cautions they take.' The Danes had a real fear that the Russians would disembark and conquer Denmark, especially as their provisions were running precariously low. Norris failed in his efforts to persuade the joint squadron to go off Bornholm to observe the Swedish fleet.[3] To the Russian ministers, the envoys of George I might have had more weight in pressing for the descent if they had brought 20,000 men to assist in the operations.[4]

Norris was willing to use his ships to help escort the Russians out of Denmark, but would not cover them to Rostock, as George I did not want to be charged with having helped put Russian troops in the Empire. Norris was willing to watch the Swedes so that the two fleets might unite, go to Bornholm, and cover the trade. In this way he would be able to prevent the Swedes from moving around in the Baltic.[5]

[1] *Ibid.*

[2] Söhlenthal's Instructions, October 28, 1716, Rigsarkiv, Söhlenthal Correspondence, T.K.U.A., England, C.

[3] *Ibid.* Norris to Stanhope, September 25/October 6, 1716, BM., Add. MSS., 28,145; Polwarth to Robethon, September 22/October 3, 1716, *Polwarth Papers*, I, 86–87.

[4] Polwarth to Robethon, September 18/29, 1716, *Polwarth Papers*, I, 85.

[5] Norris to Sehestedt, September 28/October 9, 1716, BM., Add. MSS., 28,145.

Frederick IV wanted to know if Norris' orders were from George I as king of England, and Norris coupled his affirmation with a promise to prevent the Russians from wintering in Denmark. He then asked the Danish king to order the Danish admiral to take a similar stand regarding their, 'doing the like in Mecklenburgh.' Polwarth and Bothmer added their supplications to those of Norris, but the Danes only wanted the Russians out of Denmark and their king had given his word not to molest the Russian passage to the Empire.[1] In the Danish councils men like Wibe, Sehestedt, and Krabbe had carried the day against the Mecklenburg advisers. They insisted that an open rupture with the Czar could lead only to a separate peace.[2] They were not in line with the Electoral court whose wishes were expressed in a letter to Polwarth:

> His Majesty is perfectly satisfied with the way you have acted and bids me add that if the Russians come into the Empire it will be its ruin and we will inevitably be drawn into a war with them; so that to prevent such a misfortune the English and Danish fleets ought not only to threaten but use force if need be and escort these Gentlemen beyond the Vistula.[3]

Bothmer hinted that Norris had definite orders to post his ships so that the Russian transports would have to go beyond the Vistula, but Norris had no such orders to act without Danish coöperation, which was not to be forthcoming.[4] On October 9, Norris tried to induce Sehestedt to follow a plan, suggested on October 4 by Stanhope, for a joint attack upon Karlskrona, and then Norris took the proposition to the Czar who said that the conditions on board his troop ships made it mandatory that he go to Mecklenburg. He did promise not to winter his troops on the estates of Bernstorff and Bülow. This far would he go and no farther.[5] As it was the anniversary of a Russian victory over the Swedes, Norris dressed his ships and fired salutes. Peter was so pleased that he asked Norris

[1] Norris to Stanhope, September 29/October 10, 1716, *Ibid.*
[2] Holm, 'Studier,' V, iii, 116; Chance, *George I and the Northern War*, p. 138n.
[3] Robethon to Polwarth, October 1/12, *Polwarth Papers*, I, 97.
[4] Chance, *George I and the Northern War*, p. 138.
[5] Norris to Stanhope, September 29/October 10, 1716, BM., Add. MSS., 28,145.

to accept a decoration which the English Admiral would have accepted except that he was forbidden to do so by George I and the ministers around him. Meanwhile, George I began to mobilize his troops upon the frontier of Mecklenburg.[1]

For the next four days meetings were held, with little avail, regarding an attack against Karlscrona. For three weeks the negotiations had been kept secret, but most of Europe was wondering why the invasion had not taken place. The news of the rift was pretty well known, but all doubts were dispelled on October 10 at Hamburg where the Danish government published an account of the proceedings. Not only did this declaration set forth the Danish side so far as the invasion was concerned, but it also buttressed the Danish argument by pointing out that the ministers of Great Britain and Hanover had made every effort possible to persuade Peter to live up to his committments and to carry out the invasion.[2] This disclosure was perhaps more upsetting to Britain than it was to Russia, because Britain's diplomatic stand supposedly was limited to reprisals and to defense. The Hamburg publication, circulated throughout Europe, pretty well stripped the mask away from George's use of the fleet for electoral politics. The critics of his policy both at home and abroad had ample fuel for their propaganda guns. Furthermore, if the Swedes were toying with the idea of aiding the Jacobites, they would now have every justification to so do.

Throughout the next two weeks the English and the Hanoverians labored fruitlessly to alter the plans of the Russian Czar, while Peter reiterated his stand. The Danes strove to preserve the Northern Alliance and to get the Russian troops out of the country.

A break with Russia, however, was definitely not in the plans of the Danish government,[3] in spite of the Hamburg declaration. Actually, on the very day of its issuance, Westphal presented to the Russian ministers a statement of Denmark's willingness to enter into a plan of operations for the coming

---

[1] Chance, *George I and the Northern War*, p. 139.

[2] Hamburg Declaration, October 12, 1716, Lamberty, *Mémoires*, IX, 624ff. Chance, *George I and the Northern War*, p. 141n says that the declaration might have been published on the 10th. Cf. Droysen, *Geschichte*, IV, ii, 174 for a similar theory.

[3] Söhlenthal Instructions, October 28, 1716, Rigsarkiv, Söhlenthal Correspondence, T.K.U.A., England, C.

year,[1] and on the next day the Russians gave him a carefully drawn up project for future military adventures.

Russian troops numbering 20,000 men were to cross the Gulf of Bothnia and force an entry into Sweden. In order that troop movements might be made in comparative safety, a joint allied fleet was to blockade the Swedish fleet in Karlscrona and a detachment of allied ships was to oppose the Swedish squadron defending Stockholm. For an invasion against Skåne, Peter promised to give forty battalions of infantry and 10,000 cavalry which included two dragoon regiments. Fifteen of the Russian battalions were to winter in Denmark-Norway during 1716–1717 under the conditions stipulated at Stralsund on September 6, 1715, by Peter and Dolgorouky. By wintering the Russians in Danish possessions, the Danes would be spared the cost of transporting fifteen battalions from Denmark to the Continent and then back again. Denmark was to assume the responsibility of ferrying fifteen battalions of infantry and 1,000 horse from Rostock to Zealand in late May or early June and was to furnish forage for an additional 1,000 horse if they marched through Danish provinces in order to participate in the campaign. Peter himself was to pay for the rest of the transportation of troopers and dragoons. The Russians insisted that all this had to be accomplished by early June so that nothing except contrary winds could delay the attack on the Swedish mainland.

It was realized that such gigantic troop movements necessitated naval protection. Russia, therefore, suggested that both parties have their naval units assembled at Copenhagen Roads and ready to sail by the middle of April. Peter was to contribute seventeen ships of the line, five frigates, four snows and two bombardier galleys, while the Danes were to give twenty ships of the line. Pressure was to be exerted upon England to have Norris' squadron remain in Denmark throughout the winter so that it would be ready to cover the descent in early spring. If George I did not agree, Peter and Frederick IV were to persuade him to dispatch the English fleet to the Baltic as early in the year as it was possible. The Russian ships were to stay in Copenhagen, but a watch of only 400 sailors and marines was to remain with them. Part of the Russian naval force was to

---

[1] Frederick IV to Söhlenthal, October 11, 1716, *Ibid*. Cf. Holm, 'Studier,' V, iii, 103 for a detailed account of the Danish attitude at this time.

winter in Zealand where the Danish King was to give them shelter and the Czar their board. It was also planned that the combined Russo-Danish fleet would remain at sea as long as the weather permitted, in order to keep the Swedes blockaded at Karlscrona, and thus prevent them from coming out and threatening the war operations against Stockholm and Skåne.

The question of the command was to be as it had been agreed upon by the convention before Stralsund with Peter personally leading the attack against Stockholm and Frederick IV the one against Skåne. If for some reason the Russian troops had to be recalled from the Skåne campaign, they were to leave only after the consent of the Danes had been given. Denmark was to obtain Skåne, and both parties were to make no peace with Sweden without the consent of the other. Finally, Peter agreed to guarantee to Frederick IV the conquests that had been promised to the latter by the agreement of 1709.[1]

On the next day the Danes gave their counter-project. Peter should attack Sweden from the east with a force numbering between 30,000 and 40,000 men, while Frederick IV fell upon Skåne with twenty battalions of foot and horse numbering 10,000. The Danish force was to be strengthened by twenty Russian battalions which would winter in Denmark and Norway. Peter was to promise not to entertain any peace offers from Sweden without demanding as a preliminary to any negotiation that Sweden give up her exemption of the Sound dues, and that she cede to Denmark a part of Pomerania and the Island of Rügen. Sweden was also to give to Denmark the Skåne provinces of Helsingborg, Laholm, Engelholm, Halland, Båhus, Vigen and Jemteland, with their dependencies. In addition, Schleswig was to go to Denmark and the habor of Karlscrona was to be demolished.[2]

This project of the Danes and also the one of October 10 are interesting because they set forth the war aims of the Danes and show that the country was still interested in carrying out the Skåne plan, and consequently, had no desire to break with Russia. Peter, although seemingly willing to agree to the Danish

---

[1] Russian project for a 1717 campaign, October 11, 1716, Rigsarkiv, Söhlenthal Correspondence, T.K.U.A., England, C. Cf. Holm, 'Studier,' V, iii, 104–105.
[2] Holm, 'Studier,' V, iii, 106–107.

offers, made preparations to sail. On October 21, another Russian counter-project was drawn up,[1] but two days later the Russian troops departed for Mecklenburg.[2] On the twenty-seventh Peter and the Czarina embarked, with the British ambassador, Polwarth, remarking, 'The Czar and Czarina went from here this morning for Hamburgh under a brisk discharge of all the guns of the remparts. All his forces by sea and land are likewise gone; so there is an end of a project that made a good deal of noise without any agreement for the operations in time to come.'[3]

When Peter left Denmark, the Northern Alliance had begun to crumple, with the various members of the alliance seeking new alignments. After a short stay at Schwerin, Peter went about the end of November towards Havelberg to meet the King of Prussia, a man who valued his friendship and feared his enmity. The first was true because Russia would serve Frederick William well in case of trouble between him and other states in the Empire, especially Hanover and Austria. The Prussian king, however, had much to fear from a hostile Czar because the Hohenzollern province of Prussia, isolated from Brandenburg as it was, lay at the mercy of the Russian army stationed in those parts of Europe.[4]

The Prussian policy towards the invasion had been one of little aid, and consequently, Peter had been angered. When it appeared, however, that an open rupture might take place between Russia and Denmark, Prussia had attempted to mediate.[5]

In spite of Herculean efforts by Bernstorff, Prussia veered over to the Russian side and consequently, when the Czar and Frederick William I came to meet at Havelberg, the ground work for a rapprochement had already been laid.[6] The main difficulty between Hanover and Prussia had been the Mecklenburg question because Prussia had not only been in favor of the

[1] Russian project of October 21, 1716, Rigsarchiv, Söhlenthal Correspondence, T.K.U.A., England, C. Peter refused to pay board and fuel charges for troops to be wintered in Denmark.

[2] *The Historical Register*, III, 533.

[3] *Ibid*. Polwarth to Robethon, October 16/27, 1716, *Polwarth Papers*, I, 109. Polwarth to Tilson, same date, *Ibid*.

[4] Chance, *George I and the Northern War*, p. 147.

[5] Syveton, 'L'erreur de Görtz,' X, 239–240.

[6] *Loc. cit.* Chance, *George I and the Northern War*, p. 149.

Duke, but also had feared that King George not only hoped to possess Mecklenburg but hoped to use Prussian arms for that purpose.[1] Hanover, on the other hand, believed that the Skåne invasion had been called off because of Prussian instigation[2] and that Peter because he hated George I personally intended to invade Hanover.[3]

The Prussian attitude in November can be seen in a number of instances. Early in the month Baron Friedrich Ernst von Kniphausen, the Prussian envoy at Copenhagen, stated as he was leaving to join his master at the proposed meeting with the Czar, that Denmark was responsible for the rift between Peter and Frederick IV. According to the Prussian ambassador, Frederick IV should have allowed the Russian troops to winter in Denmark so that Sweden could be brought to terms in the next year. Denmark would not have suffered from such an act because England and Prussia were on hand to see that the Russian troops behaved themselves in a proper fashion.[4] Charles Whitworth, the English envoy to Prussia, summed up the Prussian attitude on November 4:

> This Court has at last formally declared that they will not make the least step which may disoblige the Czar, and that they think it adviseable his troops or at least a good part of them should stay this winter in Mecklenburg. The reason they give us is to be at hand to succour Denmark in case of necessity, but their real view is to clip the privileges of the nobility in favor of the Duke, in hopes, the succession of the duchy may one day fall to their share.[5]

On November 22, at nine in the morning, the King of Prussia set out to meet the Czar at Havelburg where it was expected that some plans for a future peace would be offered by the Czar.[6] On the twenty-fourth and the days following, the two monarchs conferred.[7] Although little material exists as to the

[1] Mediger, *Moskaus Weg*, p. 33.

[2] Chance, *Ibid.*, pp. 147, 149. Droysen, *Geschichte*, IV, ii, 187–188 claims that Bernstorff was manoeuvering with the Imperial Court to arrange a settlement of the northern question at the expense of Prussia. This negotiation in fact was a plan to dismember Prussia. Cf. Syveton, 'L'erreur de Görtz,' X, 240.

[3] Mediger, *Moskaus Weg*, p. 34.

[4] Polwarth to Robethon, October 23/November 3, 1716, *Polwarth Papers*, I, 115.

[5] Whitworth to Polwarth, October 24/November 4, 1716, *Ibid.*, I, 116.

[6] Whitworth to Polwarth, November, 11/22, 1716, *Ibid.*, I, 130.

[7] Chance, *George I and the Northern War*, pp. 149–150.

definite terms decided upon by the two, it is known that
Prussia and Russia agreed to defend each other from other
members of the Northern Alliance, who might try to make a
separate peace with Sweden at their expense. Such assistance
would be either by troops or by a diversion against the aggressor.[1] In addition, it was agreed that Wismar should be demolished as soon as possible,[2] and that Russia should do as Prussia
had done; namely enter into better relations with France.[3]
Whitworth summed up the results of the conference in the
following manner:

> As far as I can learn, the old alliances between the Czar and
> King of Prussia have been renew'd. They have again promised
> one another not to make a separate peace, not to abandon one
> another; and the King of Prussia had oblidged himself particu-
> larly not to meddle in the affairs of Mecklenburg, nor to enter
> into any concert on that occasion contrary to the interests of
> the Czar, who had, I believe, thereby gained the principal end
> of this meeting.[4]

While the conference was in progress, a great attempt was
made by Ilgen to win Denmark over to the side of Russia and
Prussia. Not only was the matter of a new invasion considered,[5]
but many innuendoes as to English infidelity were advanced by
the Prussian minister. It was claimed that Hanover would sell
out Denmark to Sweden if the latter would cede Bremen and
Verden to George I, and English inaction and failure to

---

[1] Droysen, *Geschichte*, IV, ii, 185. Syveton, 'L'erreur de Görtz,' X, 240 dates
the exchange of agreements on December 8, 1716. Polwarth to Stair November
27/December 8, 1716, *Polwarth Papers*, I, 140. Westphal relation, November 27,
1716, Rigsarchiv, Söhlenthal Correspondence, T.K.U.A., England, C.

[2] Polwarth to Stair, November 27/December 8, 1716, *Polwarth Papers*, I,
140.

[3] Chance, *George I and the Northern War*, p. 150 has a good explanation of
Prusso-Franco relations. Cf. *Recueil, Prusse*, XVI, xiii, and Droysen, *Geschichte*,
IV, ii, 184–185.

[4] Whitworth to Polwarth, November 28/December 9, 1716, *Polwarth Papers*,
I, 141. C. Wich, the English resident at Hamburg, has a somewhat different
outlook: 'The Czar, you will see, continues to disturb us more and more. He
believes he has found a confederate in the Empire in the person of the King of
Prussia, but I believe he will find it a different story if perchance someday he has
to depend on the King of Prussia.' Wick to Polwarth, December 14/25, 1716,
Ibid., I, 152.

[5] Polwarth to Stair, November 27/December 8, 1716, *Ibid.*, I, 140.

coöperate were used as examples to strengthen the insinuations.[1]

Neither Peter nor Frederick William I had completely abandoned the English alliance at this time because both of them made attempts to win the coöperation of the English fleet in a planned attack against the Swedish mainland. George I answered the Prussian request by saying that he had made no engagement to aid the Northern allies by the use of the English fleet, and had heretofore done so only because of his good will. If Prussia wanted action against Sweden, she could more properly obtain it by contributing soldiers. Whitworth comments on the English answer to Frederick William's request thus: 'After the conduct of the Czar and this court have affected in respect of his Majesty, they could not dare expect any other return.'[2] Russian attempts were similarly rejected.[3]

England's firm stand against the two was influenced by her rapprochement with France, which was to be culminated on January 4, 1717, by the signing of the Triple Alliance.[4] Thus the end of 1716 and the beginning of 1717 saw the break-up of the confederacy against Sweden. George I, strongly supported by Austria and France, was openly at odds with the Czar and the King of Prussia. Denmark, who had the most to fear from the train of events, went from one camp to the other and tried to preserve the alliance which was rapidly falling apart.[5] As Chance says, 'The way was opened for separate negotiation with Sweden for peace, and the coming year saw George and Peter actively engaged therein.'[6]

---

[1] Westphal relation, November 27, 1716; Meyer to Westphal, December 5, 1716; Sehestedt to Söhlenthal, December 5, 1716, Rigsarkiv, Söhlenthal Correspondence, T.K.U.A., England, C.

[2] Whitworth to Polwarth, December 9/20, 1716, *Polwarth Papers*, I, 148.

[3] Chance, *George I and the Northern War*, pp. 150–154.

[4] Emile Bourgeois, *Le Sécret du Régent* (Paris, 1909); and *Le Sécret de Dubois, Cardinal et Premier Ministre* (Paris 1910), *passim*.

[5] Söhlenthal's Instructions, October 28, 1716, Rigsarkiv, Söhlenthal Correspondence, T.K.U.A., England, C, and Sehestedt to Westphal, January 5, 1717, Rigsarkiv, Westphal Correspondence, T.K.U.A., Russland C 122.

[6] Chance, *George I and the Northern War*, p. 156.

XI

THE SWEDO-JACOBITE PLOT

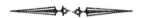

THE events of 1716 pushed George I and the men around
him into an awkward position. The approaching rupture
of the Northern Alliance and the growing predominance of
Russia in the Baltic caused many in England to feel that it
might be better to make concessions to Sweden at the expense
of Hanover than to raise a Frankenstein. A Russian trade
monopoly offered no more protection to English traders than
did a Swedish one, and it was apparent to many that Norris
had been more concerned with politics than with trade. There
was a real danger that the English Parliament would not allow
George I a fleet in 1717. Without the British Navy, George I
would have been clawless in the jungle of Baltic power politics.

While the Northern Alliance began to show wear and tear,
Gyllenborg back in London had taken his country's cause
directly to the English people. His sojourn in England had
convinced him of the importance of political pamphleteers in
eighteenth century English politics. In an anonymous pamphlet
entitled, *Remarks of an English Merchant*, he set forth Sweden's
position in a way that appealed greatly to the English populace
and caused no little embarrassment to those in power.

The 'merchant' pointed out that England was violating her
treaty obligations by withholding aid from Sweden. To be sure,
Sweden had promised freedom of commerce to the Baltic
provinces, but England in accepting this guarantee had agreed
to protect those provinces. Had England been in a similar
situation, she would have prohibited commerce as Sweden was
doing now, and as England had done in the wars against
Louis XIV. Sweden had £100,000 sterling due her for Swedish
ships seized by English naval vessels in previous wars, whereas

England's losses in 1715 were only £69,024 sterling, and it was unlikely that the 1716 losses would be higher. The cost of the squadron was £400,000 sterling while the trade was worth one-fourth of that.

The pamphleteer went on to show that it was absurd for England to use the treaty of 1700 to demand the arrest of the Jacobites when by the same treaty she had guaranteed Sweden's German provinces. Norway had been invaded only to cause a diversion of Danish troops, and if Sweden fell, the Protestant religion would take a severe blow. Because the Hanoverian policy could not be defended on religious, commercial, or 'free' principles, it could only be assumed by the 'merchant' that George's actions had one source of motivation, and that was the acquisition of Bremen and Verden to his electoral holdings.[1]

This work caused considerable furor in England as did various Tory criticisms of the Baltic policy. Furthermore, a growing section of the Whigs began to have doubts about the Baltic adventure. To have Parliament grant him supply for a squadron, George I required something sensational to use against Charles XII. He had to keep anti-Swedish sentiment alive in England. He was to find what he needed in the negotiations of Swedish ministers with Jacobite agents. Furthermore, it was necessary for him to strengthen his hand diplomatically. This he was to accomplish through the Triple Alliance of 1717 which brought Britain, France, and the United Provinces into a defensive alliance against Sweden and other enemies that Britain and Hanover might have indirectly.

The negotiations of the Swedes with the Jacobites and the British rapprochement with France are closely linked together as are events in the Baltic. The main figure bobbing in and out of all three strands was Görtz. His main area of operation was on the Continent, especially in the Low Countries.

Up to the sending of the fleet to the North, Swedo-Jacobite negotiations had not had any tangible results, although rumors of a Swedish-Stuart entente were circulated in order to dis-

[1] 'Remarks of an English Merchant upon a scandalous Jacobite piece published in the "Post Boy" July 19 under the title of memoir presented to the Swedish Chancellor by the Resident of Great Britain,' Lamberty, *Mémoires*, IX, 667–677. A copy is also in Abel Boyer (ed.), *The Political State of Great Britain*, XII (London, 1717), 306–318.

credit Charles XII in the eyes of the English people and in order to make it possible for George I to fulfill his promises to his allies. After April, 1716, the Jacobites increased their efforts to enlist Swedish aid, and Swedish ministers apparently became more open to Stuart overtures.

By late May, however, no answer had been received from Charles XII instructing his ministers as to their conduct regarding the Jacobites.[1] Robert Leslie and General Arthur Dillon, high-ranking officials of the Chevalier's court, wanted to send a man of good character to the Swedish king. Sparre, although he paid lip service to this plan, would not sanction it until he had heard from home.[2] John Erskine, Earl of Mar and chief of the Jacobites after the dismissal of Bolingbroke, felt that it would be more advantageous to the cause if Sparre received full powers to negotiate at Paris. According to Mar, any person sent to Charles XII would have to be of highest rank or the haughty king would feel slighted, and the sending of such an emissary would advertise the negotiation to all the world.[3]

Fortune intervened and presented the Jacobites with Sir John Erskine of Alva, a man of note, who could be sent to the Baltic safely without the rest of Europe knowing the true reason for his journey. Erskine was a brother to Sir Robert Erskine, Peter's private physician, and was a cousin to the Earl of Mar. He had left England during 'the Fifteen' to purchase war supplies in France,[4] and subsequently had been outlawed. He was reputed to have a silver mine of great value on his property about which the British government learned through a former employee of the owner.[5] The government, however, lacked information as to the exact location of the ore, and wanted the mine discovered and worked because a law passed in 1592 reserved one-tenth of all ore found in Scotland to the crown.[6]

[1] Dillon to Mar, May 15, 1716, *Stuart Papers*, II, 155.
[2] *Loc. cit.*
[3] Dillon to Mar, June 9, 1716, *Stuart Papers*, II, 213.
[4] Chance, *George I and the Northern War*, p. 167. Cf. James F. Chance, 'The Swedish Plot of 1716–1717,' *English Historical Review*, XVIII, 90.
[5] An anonymous letter, July 23, 1716, *Miscellany of the Scottish History Society* in *Publications of the Scottish History Society*, 3rd series, 30 vols. (Edinburgh, 1933), XXI, 414. Hereafter cited as *MSHS.*, XXI.
[6] *Miscellany of the Scottish History Society*, in *Publications of the Scottish History Society*, 1st series, 61 vols. (Edinburgh, 1904), XLIV, 384. Hereafter cited as *MSHS.*, XLIV.

Some of Erskine's friends had persuaded Townshend that it would be to England's advantage to pardon the exile so that the government's share of the supposed wealth could be realized.[1] Townshend had granted the request and had sent Sir Henry Stirling, nephew of Sir John, to find his uncle and to deliver the warrant permitting his return to England.[2] If Erskine travelled to Northern Germany to meet Stirling, it would not be considered a Jacobite move although such a trip would give him an excellent opportunity to open preliminaries with the Swedish Court. Young Stirling, another Jacobite, could aid in the negotiations and could use the pretext of carrying the pardon to Sir John as a cloak for his own Jacobite activities.[3]

Thus, when Sir John started north, he carried with him full powers to treat for James with the Swedish ministers.[4] The instructions to Erskine dated July 17, 1716, were as follows: as soon as he arrived at Hamburg, he was to find some way to write General Hamilton, a trusted Jacobite serving under Charles XII. Hamilton in turn was to inform the Swedish king that Sir John had come a considerable distance to treat and only awaited Charles' permission to proceed to Sweden.[5] After gaining an audience at the Swedish Court, Erskine was to point out that the House of Brunswick was trying to divest Sweden of her rightful possessions as it had already defrauded James of his heritage. Erskine was to obtain a refuge for James in Sweden, and was to ask if ships of the Royal Navy which might defect could use Swedish ports as bases. In exchange for aid in a Stuart restoration, Erskine was to promise Jacobite assistance to win back Charles' possessions which were now in the hands of Hanover.[6]

Erskine reached Brussels on July 26,[7] and continued on to Lübeck where he arrived on August 23. Here things were not

---

[1] Anonymous letter, July 23, 1716, *MSHS.*, XXI, 414.
[2] Patrick Campbell to Dr. Charles Erskine, *MSHS.*, XXI, 415.
[3] *MSHS.*, XLIV, ii, 385.
[4] James to Charles XII, July 16, 1716, *Stuart Papers*, II, 283.
[5] Mar to Erskine, August 4, 1716, *Ibid.*, II, 328. It appears that Sparre was of the opinion that the trip of Sir John Erskine could do no harm, and he approved of Erskine's writing to Hamilton before he tried to enter Sweden.
[6] James to Erskine, July 17, 1716, *Ibid.*, II, 288.
[7] Erskine to Mar, July 26, 1716, *Ibid.*, II, 311.

as he had hoped. The city was in Russian hands, and General Hamilton was stationed so far from the army of Charles XII that a letter from Hamilton to Charles XII would have taken a great deal of time. On the positive side, Erskine learned that Charles XII had refused to even open Norris' letter and that there was a growing dissension in the Northern Alliance. Consequently, he decided to proceed to Sweden without waiting for permission.[1]

At Lübeck, Erskine fell in with a colonel who was carrying Sparre's dispatches to Sweden. A subject of the Prince of Hesse-Cassel, the colonel would have made it possible for Erskine to get into Sweden. The plan had to be altered because the Czar, upon occupying Travemünde, refused to let anyone connected with the Prince of Hesse pass. With this news along with information that the Czar was half way between Wismar and Lübeck, Sir John considered visiting his brother, Dr. Erskine, to see if peace negotiations might not be opened between Russia and Sweden. He changed his mind, however, because he feared that the Russians would view such a mission with hostility. In addition, such activity would make him less acceptable to Charles XII when he finally arrived in Sweden.[2] Erskine then went to Travemünde to ascertain if some way might not be found to cross over to Sweden, but Russian military and naval power made such an attempt impossible.[3]

In the meantime, Mar had written commanding him not to go to Sweden unless so ordered by General Hamilton. He was to write General Dillon for additional instructions.[4] On the seventh of September he met Sir Henry Stirling, who had pushed on to see Dr. Erskine. Erskine decided that he could do no good to the cause at Lübeck, so he returned to Holland. From there he took passage late in the year to Scotland.[5] The first major Jacobite effort was unsuccessful.

Just before Erskine began his useless trip, Baron Görtz, the agent at large for Charles XII, who despaired of raising any more money in Sweden for his master, set out with General

---

[1] Erskine to Mar, August 23, 1716, *Ibid.*, II, 367.
[2] Erskine to Mar, August 26 and September 2, 1716, *Ibid.*, II, 371, 402.
[3] Mar to Erskine, August 27, 1716, *Ibid.*, II, 381.
[4] *Ibid.*, II, xxvii.
[5] *MSHS.*, XXI, 417n.

Stanislaus Poniatowski[1] for Holland and arrived at Amsterdam on July 13.[2] The trip from Sweden had been an eventful one, and the Baron had reached Amsterdam in a state of *omnia mea mecum porto* because his baggage and servants, as well as those of Poniatowski, were captured by a Danish frigate. Only by a stroke of luck had the two been able to escape with their papers.[3]

Görtz carried with him full powers to negotiate for financial assistance for Sweden.[4] He was supposed to raise 1,000,000 *riksdalers* in silver for Charles' badly depleted treasury.[5] Although he considered that his mission had little chance for success,[6] Görtz set himself to his task on such a grand scale that at one time he negotiated even with some Madagascar pirates for ships and money.[7]

All of his financial endeavors were not so far-fetched. While at the Hague, he asked the Dutch government for a subsidy offering the Swedish iron and copper mines as security. He also wanted the States to guarantee on the same basis any loans that might be made to Charles XII.[8] Both of these requests were denied, and he was referred to the moneyed men of Amsterdam. He tried to have naval stores sent to Sweden and to engage sailors for duty in the Swedish marine, offering them wages of five crowns per month plus maintenance.[9] He also issued passes to Dutch and Danzig merchantmen to protect them from the ravages of Swedish privateers, but such passes seemed to have made little difference to Swedish sea captains.[10]

---

[1] General Stanislaus Poniatowski (1677–1762) had been a Polish companion of Charles XII at Bender and had espoused Stanislaus Leszczynski's cause.

[2] Görtz to Sparre, July 16, 1716, *Handlinger*, VIII, 248.

[3] *Ibid.*

[4] Moser, *Rettung der Ehre und Unschuld des . . . Gortz*, Appendix ii: 'Plena, potestatem damus in usum. Nostrum conquirende comparandique pecunias in exteris Regionibus, deque conditionibus rite conveniendi, et accepta pecunia necessaria insuper instrumenta inque optima forma instructa autographa extradendi illis qui eam gratumque hatituros ac plenae executioi mandaturos quicquid praedictus . . . ea de re transegerit atque concluserit, rerum etiam debitam curam gesturos, de summae pecuniariae commadate acceptae justa solutione.' Cf. Görtz to Gyllenborg, February 24, 1716, *Handlingar*, VIII, 251.

[5] Westrin, 'Friherre . . . Görtz Bref,' XVIII, 98.

[6] Görtz to Sparre, July 16, 1716, *Handlingar*, VIII, 249.

[7] Voltaire, *Charles XII*, p. 433; Lamberty, *Mémoires*, X, 69n.

[8] Chance, 'The Swedish Plot,' XVIII, 87.

[9] *Handlingar*, VIII, 255. The sailors were to serve during 1717.

[10] Lamberty, *Mémoires*, X, 69. Letter of the States to Charles XII, September 23, 1716, *Ibid.*, X, 654–655. Some passports, however, were recognized, especially

Görtz not only had to contend with Dutch mistrust of his motives, but also he was hampered in his attempts to raise money by the ever-watchful English and Hanoverian ministers at the Hague, who dogged his footsteps and constantly aroused the authorities against him.[1] Their diligence can be seen in the Pieterman affair. In September an Amsterdam banker, Amiot, formed a company and registered it under the name of his valet, Francis Pieterman.[2] The company was to ship silver ingots to Sweden and to coin them there at a profit of two million *riksdalers*. In exchange, Amsterdam bankers were to purchase and to export iron, copper, wire, pitch, and tar. The undertakers, who might establish foundries of their own in Sweden, would be compelled to buy from Swedish subjects and to coin for them at six per cent profit all bullion offered. The contract was to be for three years and all contrary agreements previously made were to be annulled.[3] Görtz was to advance 150,000 florins to purchase the first consignment of ingots. The company would then coin them in Sweden, purchase goods for the Amsterdam market, and with the proceeds export further ingots. The object was to replace Swedish paper money with hard currency so that Charles XII could pay his debts. In addition, home industries would be fostered, something highly prejudicial to English commercial interests.[4]

The negotiation was exposed to Bernstorff by Dirck Wolters, a Rotterdam merchant in British pay. To thwart the scheme, Wolters put into practice means suggested by Robethon. First

[1] Chance, *George I and the Northern War*, p. 160.
[2] *Ibid.*, p. 161. Cf. Moser, *Rettung der Ehre, passim*, and Westrin, 'Friherre . . . Görtz Bref,' XVIII, 100.
[3] The contract, dated September 30, 1716, *Handlingar*, XXI, 358. *Handlingar* X, 388; Moser, *Rettung der Ehre*, appendices; Lamberty, *Mémoires*, IX, 656. The copies differ somewhat but they are all essentially the same.
[4] Chance, *George I and the Northern War*, p. 161.

those issued at Amsterdam. Attestation of some Amsterdam merchants, June 12, 1717, *Ibid.*, X, 72: 'Certifions pour la vérité à tous ceux qu'il appartiendra, que nous n'avons jamais entendu, ne trouvé, que les vaisseaux Hollandois, étans pourvûs de Passeport du Sieur Baron de Görtz, pour aller d'ice en Suède, aient été pris par les armateurs de Suède, n'y qu'ils aient été arrêtez ni confisquez: Mais qu'au contraire, il nous est très bien connu & que nous avons souvent entendu, & savons d'esperience, que lesdits Passeports ont été respectez en toute maniere, & que lesdits Vaisseaux, qui en ont été pourvûs, ont toujours été libres, sans etre molestez par lesdits armateurs Suedois, & par ainsi ont poursuivis franc & libre leur voiage aux portes de Suède.'

he tried intimidation by suggesting that the ships upon which the company's agents had to travel would be captured by the Danes. Expectation of profits, however, was stronger than fear, and the two agents sailed in spite of a temporary arrest of their ship.[1] Then Wolters tried something else. He distributed a pamphlet exposing the scheme in hopes of arousing the jealousies of Amsterdam merchants not in the company.[2] Not content with these efforts on behalf of the Hanoverians, Wolters wormed his way into the confidence of Görtz and Amiot and obtained charge of the first consignment of silver. Henceforth no matter what happened, George I and his ministers could be advised in time to take necessary action.[3]

Finances were only a portion of Görtz's commission. He was also empowered to treat for peace. The main reason that Görtz was so keen on building up the Swedish army and treasury was to have a good talking point at the conference table. He wanted to negotiate from strength.[4] It was obvious to him, Vellingk, Gyllenborg, Sparre, and Stiernhok—if not to the king—that it was absolutely necessary for Sweden to pacify some of her enemies if she were to survive.[5] It will be remembered that Gyllenborg had been of this opinion in the spring of 1716. Overtures had been made at that time to Russia viâ the mediation of the Landgrave of Hesse-Cassel, but then Peter was more interested in Wismar and the Skåne invasion than in peace talks. Consequently, the attempt came to naught.[6]

Peace talks and finances went together, and they both became entangled with the Jacobites. Soon after Görtz arrived at the Hague, he received overtures from the Jacobites. These seem to have been his first direct negotiations with the Stuarts, but he had undoubtedly discussed the possibility of a Scottish invasion, by Swedish troops, with Croissy while the two men had been at Stralsund.

The approach of the Jacobites was rather curious. An English officer approached the Baron and suggested that Sweden cede

[1] *Ibid.*, pp. 161–162. The text is a summary of Chance.

[2] 'Lettre d'Ami de Petersbourg à un Ami d'Amsterdam,' Lamberty, *Mémoires*, IX, 656.

[3] Chance, *George I and the Northern War*, p. 162.

[4] *Ibid.*, 163n.

[5] Vellingk to Müllern, April and May, 1717, *Handlinger*, VI, *passim*.

[6] Carlson, *Om Fredsunderhandlingarne*, pp. 92–93.

Bremen to Hanover. Görtz cut the conversation short because
he had an appointment with the French Ambassador Chateauneuf.[1] Fifteen days later the officer requested another interview
to which Görtz agreed. At that time, to the surprise of the
Baron, the supposedly loyal Englishman suggested that Görtz
accept a sum of money which was also being offered to Gyllenborg. Görtz pointed out that such a step would entail making
an alliance with the Pretender, a step that he was not empowered to take. He did agree to accept the money as a loan.
The English officer asked for time in which to think the matter
over, and Görtz (so he claims) warned Gyllenborg and Sparre
against negotiating with Stuart supporters at this time.[2]

Meanwhile, Sparre had become embittered at the French
who were, in his eyes, paying less and less attention to Sweden's
light. Although France was bound by treaty to give a subsidy
to Sweden,[3] money had not been forthcoming. The French
were offering only a small part of what was owed and pleaded
an exhausted exchequer, but Sparre considered the delay a
lack of good faith.[4] Because of his difficulties in France, Sparre
decided to confer with Görtz about finance and the feasibility
of raising ships and sailors in France for Swedish service.[5]

Görtz was anxious to please Sparre, and on August 2 left
Holland to meet him at Douai.[6] There he proposed that Sparre
seek to force France to hand over on account as much of the
subsidy as possible because Sweden was desperately in need of
money at that time.[7] Sparre, who was pro-Jacobite,[8] used the
first possible occasion at Douai to intercede for them and to
try to find out the sentiments of the Swedish Court toward the

[1] Westrin, 'En redogörelse af . . . Görtz,' XVIII, 276–286.
[2] *Loc. cit.*
[3] *Supra.*
[4] Sparre to Vellingk, *Handlingar*, VIII, 220: 'Quand j'insiste sur les subsides on
allegue l'epuisement des finances, mais les amis disent que c'est celuy de la volonté.'
[5] Westrin, 'Friherre . . . Görtz Bref,' XVIII, 101.
[6] Syveton, 'L'erreur de Görtz,' X, 47. Görtz to Sparre, July 17, 1716, *Handlingar*, VIII, 252.
[7] Westrin, 'Friherre . . . Görtz Bref,' XVIII, 101 quotes Görtz to Vellingk,
September 17, 1716.
[8] Westrin, 'En redogörelse af . . . Görtz,' XVIII, 280–283. Cronström to Müllern, March 7, 1716, quoted in Westrin, 'Friherre . . . Görtz Bref,' XVIII, 104:
'Le Régent scait que c'est Sparre que est l'auteur et l'instrument de l'affaire
d'Angleterre.'

Pretender.[1] The two ministers decided not to tell the King anything about their plans regarding either French money or the Jacobites because they feared that their dispatches would fall into the hands of Lord Stair, British ambassador at Paris.[2] By July 29, Görtz was back in Holland.[3]

Before he set out for Douai, Sparre had agreed that, upon his return, he would meet General Dillon ten leagues from Paris. Here in a spot supposedly free from Stair's spies, Sparre assured Dillon of the friendly disposition of Charles XII toward the Jacobites. He fortified his statement by pointing out that when Charles XII had gone to Norway he had left one of his chief ministers in Sweden to answer Sparre's questions on Jacobite matters. Sparre told Dillon that he personally was willing for the Stuarts to send an envoy to Sweden, and promised to inform the Jacobites as to the best time for dispatching such an emissary.[4]

During this conversation, Sparre requested that no information about the meeting be sent to the Courts of St. Germain and Avignon because he feared that news of the negotiation would fall into British hands. He also suggested that the Jacobites forward a sum of money to Sweden, although Sparre doubted that Charles XII would accept it.[5]

Upon returning to the Hague, Görtz endeavored to procure French financial and diplomatic assistance. On August 16, he saw Chateauneuf and asked him to approach Peter through Kurakin, the Russian minister who was at the Hague. Görtz wanted Chateauneuf to point out to Kurakin that it was to the interest of both Sweden and Russia to prevent the demolition of Wismar. The French ambassador refused Görtz's request because he lacked the necessary orders from home.[6]

To further the success of any negotiations that he might have

---

[1] Inese to Mar, August 18, 1716, *Stuart Papers*, II, 351–352.

[2] Chance, 'The Swedish Plot,' XVIII, 94; Lindeberg, *Görtz*, p. 58. This author claims that Charles XII was kept uninformed by Görtz so that the truth-loving king would not be implicated.

[3] Horatio Walpole to Polwarth, July 20/31, 1716, Polwarth Papers, I, 50: 'Baron Görtz returned hither again the night before last, having been at Avignon a league beyond Lisle, to speak with Baron Sparre or some other person that came from Paris to meet him there.'

[4] Dillon to Mar, August 20, 1716, *Stuart Papers*, II, 359.

[5] *Ibid*., Mar to Dillon, August 27, 1716, *Ibid*. II, 380.

[6] Görtz to Sparre, August 17, 1716, *Handlingar*, VIII, 253. Görtz to Sparre, September 24, 1716, *Ibid*., VIII, 276.

with the individual enemies of Charles XII, Görtz spread reports that Sweden desired peace,[1] and that negotiations to that end were already in progress with Russia. The Amsterdam *Gazette* announced that Prince Kurakin had already received the Swedish agent. If this did happen, nothing immediate resulted. It is more than likely that Görtz himself supplied the paper with the paragraph inserted.[2] In November Kurakin denied that he had had any diplomatic intercourse with the Swedish minister.[3]

This statement, however, applied only to Görtz. There were Russo-Swedish negotiations through other channels. Toward the end of the month, the Landgrave of Hesse-Cassel made another attempt at mediation, this time through General Rank, a Swede by birth. Peter received news of this overture on September 15, just when he was contemplating abandoning the Skåne invasion. Consequently, he authorized Kurakin to discover what Sweden's *sine qua non* was.[4] Kurakin was to do this in secrecy and on his own responsibility.[5] A month later, Peter, to Görtz's surprise,[6] haughtily rejected the Swedish feeler.[7] The probable reason for the Russian change in attitude was the developing joint effort of Russia and Prussia to form a block against Hanover and England. By November, when the alliance with Prussia had become an actuality, Peter firmly rejected Swedish advances proposed by Kettler, another statesman serving Hesse-Cassel.[8] After futile efforts to approach Russia

[1] Horatio Walpole to Polwarth, August 14/25, 1716, *Polwarth Papers*, I, 64.
[2] Chance, *George I and the Northern War*, p. 164.
[3] Hartman, *Tzar Peter's underhändlingar 1716 om landgång i Skåne*, p. 148. A letter of Görtz's dated November 20, 1716, in Moser, *Rettung der Ehre*, appendix xix gives the opposite viewpoint but both Holm and Hartman feel that Görtz was lying. See also a letter of Görtz dated November 25 in *Ibid.*
[4] Westrin, 'Friherre . . . .Görtz Bref,' XVIII, 110–111; Carlson, *Om Fredsunderhandlingarne*, p. 90; Lamberty, *Mémoires*, IX, 681. Hesse-Cassel was also trying to mediate between England and Sweden at this time.
[5] Chance, *George I and the Northern War*, p. 164.
[6] Westrin, 'Friherre . . . Görtz Bref,' XVIII, 110–111. Görtz to Vellingk, November 20 and 28, 1716, Moser, *Rettung der Ehre*, pp. 490–491: 'J'ai la satisfaction d'apprendre à votre Excell., que notre negociation avec la Pr. Kurak, est actuellement en train, et que du côté du Czaar l'on montre autant d'empressement pour un accomodement que nous scaurions en avoir du nôtre.'
[7] Westrin, 'Friherre . . . Görtz Bref,' XVIII, 110–111; Carlson, *Om Fredsunderhandlingarne*, pp. 93–94; Lamberty, *Mémoires*, IX, 637 ff.
[8] Chance, *George I and the Northern War*, p. 164. Cf. Carlson, *Om Fredsunderhandlingarne*, p. 93.

through Hesse-Cassel and later through Mecklenburg-Schwerin,[1] there still remained one avenue open to approach Peter. That was through his Jacobite physician, Dr. Charles Erskine.

During these negotiations, Görtz made a flying trip to Paris, arriving there early in September.[2] There is considerable mystery shrouding this trip, and there are some who doubt if it were even made.[3] The motives for the trip also remain in the dark. It is known that Görtz had planned to go to Vienna, and upon hearing that he would not be well received at the Imperial Court, decided to go to Paris.[4] It would appear that the main purpose of the journey was to solicit the French subsidies due Sweden,[5] although Horatio Walpole at the Hague thought that the Baron was going to settle differences which had arisen between Sparre and Görtz. The Englishman also thought that Görtz was going to reassert his commission which gave him sole charge of money matters.[6] Lamberty is of the opinion that Görtz, while at Paris, conducted a full negotiation with the Regent,[7] but Syveton discards this on the basis that the Chateauneuf–d'Huxelles correspondence contains no information of this nature. Furthermore, there are no traces left in France of Görtz's having had any relations with the cabinet of Paris. Syveton claims that the trip was a repetition of the trip to Douai, and its chief result was another cabal in which Sparre and Görtz arranged the project for an entente with the Jacobites.[8]

The *Calendar of Stuart Papers* substantiates the fact that Görtz's visit gave a decided impetus to Swedish-Jacobite negotiations, but it does not throw any light on other movements of the

---

[1] Görtz and Vellingk correspondence, October and November, 1716, Moser, *Rettung der Ehre*, appendices XIII ff.; Carlson, *Om Fredsunderhandlingarne*, p. 94; Chance, *George I and the Northern War*, p. 165.

[2] Dillon to James, September 12, 1716, *Stuart Papers*, II, 427. *Memoirs of St. Simon*, XXV, 67–68. Görtz left the Hague on August 28, 1716, Görtz to Sparre, August 28, 1716, *Handlingar*, VIII, 265. Poniatowski went with him, Lamberty, *Mémoires*, IX, 655. Sparre to Vellingk, September 17, 1716, *Handlingar*, VIII, 210. Görtz arrived on September 1, 1716.

[3] Syveton, 'L'erreur de Görtz,' X, 226. Cf. Westrin, 'Friherre . . . Görtz Bref,' XVIII, 101.

[4] Görtz to Sparre, August 28, 1716, *Handlingar*, VIII, 264.

[5] Syveton, 'L'erreur de Görtz,' X, 227.

[6] Horatio Walpole to Polwarth, September 5, 1716, n.s., *Polwarth Papers*, I, 71.

[7] Lamberty, *Mémoires*, IX, 637–638.

[8] Syveton, 'L'erreur de Görtz,' X, 227.

Baron.[1] The day after his arrival, Dillon and Sparre conversed for two hours. Sparre wanted Dillon to draw up a memoir for James which would be sent to Charles XII, and this had to be ready by the ninth, as Görtz planned to return to Holland on the tenth. Sparre informed Dillon that he was acting without Charles' consent, but that he was willing that the memoir be forwarded to Sweden. When, in the conversation, Sparre discovered that the Queen Mother, Mary of Modena, knew about their conversation, he flew into a rage, claiming that soon Lord Stair would be well informed. Although Mary was in charge of Jacobite activity in Paris, Sparre did not think that the people around her could be trusted.[2]

By the next morning Sparre had calmed down, and once more he sent for Dillon who brought the requested memoir with him.[3] Sparre, upon studying it, claimed that there was little in it to Sweden's advantage, while Dillon insisted that the memoir was only for the purpose of having the two monarchs unite and was not a binding treaty. Consequently, neither party was compelled to state specifically what it would concede to the other.[4]

Sparre evidently had hoped to receive a formal treaty draft which he could have sent to his master for approval.[5] The Jacobites on their part seem to have been of the opinion that Sparre had been given full powers to negotiate, although he would not admit it.[6] According to Jacobite reasoning:

> The king of Sweden is in absolute need of money for his troops . . . if your Majesty [James], by means of your friends in England would satisfy him on that point, it is the essential stroke and one that will engage the prince to make the utmost efforts to restore you to the throne of your ancestors.[7]

Mar was displeased with the memoir that Dillon had drawn up for Sparre, and thought that 8,000 men should have been asked for instead of 6,000. With his customary optimism, he

[1] Sparre to Vellingk, September 18, 1716, *Handlingar*, VIII, 210.
[2] Dillon to James, September 12, 1716, *Stuart Papers*, II, 427; Lindeberg, *Görtz*, p. 58, credits Görtz with making a toast at a banquet where the Queen Mother was present. Görtz drank to a happy conclusion of the projected enterprise.
[3] The Memoir, *Stuart Papers*, II, 429–430.
[4] Dillon to James, September 12, 1716, *Ibid.*, II, 427.
[5] Dillon to James, September 26, 1716, *Ibid.*, II, 477.
[6] Dillon to James, September 12, 1716, *Ibid.*, II, 429.
[7] Mar to Dillon, September 18, 1716, *Ibid.*, II, 447.

stated that the Jacobites could have obtained 10,000 to 12,000 troops from Charles XII just as easily as 6,000.[1] Perhaps he would have been nearer the truth if he had said that there was as little chance of getting 12,000 men as 6,000. Mar was also overly hopeful as to the amount of money that could be raised in England. His Scottish agent, Lockhart, wrote that most of the persons, 'who formerly would have contributed to the king being exiles or forfeited, and such as were not so, nevertheless in great straits by the losses sustained and depredation of their estates during the war and by the charges they were at in supporting their distressed friends abroad and at home.'[2]

By the middle of September, Sparre became concerned over the silence from home on the various memoirs and letters that he had forwarded to Charles XII on the matter of the Jacobites. He came to wonder if any of his countrymen had received permission to enter into negotiations with the Stuarts. On September 25, he wrote Gyllenborg asking him whether there was any foundation to the rumor that he had been authorized to enter into Jacobite plots and cabals.[3]

Two days later, Gyllenborg answered, informing Sparre that the report that the King of Sweden had committed himself to the Pretender's cause was false. Gyllenborg himself when approached on the subject always said that he did not know his master's wishes in the matter, but added that Sweden had many reasons to espouse the Stuarts. Gyllenborg pointed out that conditions were such that Charles XII could not help James even had he so desired, and went on to warn his colleague to be cautious in dealing with the Jacobites because they were prone to exaggerate. As to his own feeling concerning James, Gyllenborg asserted that an English king with interests in the Empire would never be in favor of Sweden and, 'we should try to replace him.' He also pointed out that it would be to the advantage of the Emperor to back James, a prince without power to dispute the Emperor on the Continent.[4]

---

[1] *Ibid.*

[2] George Lockhart of Carnworth's account of affairs, *Lockhart Papers*, II, 7-8.

[3] Sparre to Gyllenborg, September 25, 1716, *Handlingar*, X, 363. Letters are also to be found in Cobbett, *Parliamentary History*, VII, 397 and in C. S. Terry (ed.), *The Chevalier de Saint George and the Jacobite movements in his favor*, 1701-1720 (London, 1901).

[4] Gyllenborg to Sparre, September 27, 1716, *Handlingar*, X, 317-318.

While his colleagues discussed the Jacobites, Görtz who had returned to the Hague on September 18, was sending Sparre urgent appeals for money and pointing out that Sweden had to appear powerful so that her friends could procure her a favorable peace.[1] His correspondence continued in a similar vein throughout September and October.[2] The tenor of the letters shows that Sweden's financial and military resources were temporarily in excellent shape, but that Görtz was reaching the end of his rope. It was absolutely necessary that Sparre raise money somewhere, money so vital if Sweden were to profit from the rupture beginning to show in the Northern Alliance.

The wily Görtz had been closely watching the pending rupture in the Alliance, and hoped that Sweden could forestall any hostile move that the Czar might make against Sweden. The Swedish minister predicted that the dissenting allies would soon endeavor to reach separate agreements with their common enemy, and that Sweden stood to profit from the situation. To exploit events to the fullest, it was necessary for the Swedes to iron out all differences that existed between them and the Emperor, and to strengthen the French alliance. Furthermore, Sweden would have to appear in a dignified and a strong position when negotiations opened.[3] Görtz labored for a rapprochement with the Emperor and the Regent of France because he was of the opinion that neither would allow the other the sole prestige of being arbiter of the Northern War.[4]

Although Görtz had considered the Northern Question accurately, he underestimated the rapprochement that was taking place between England and France, a change in French policy

---

[1] Görtz to Sparre, September 18, 1716, *Ibid.*, VIII, 266.

[2] *Loc. cit.*, and Görtz to Sparre, October 1, 1716, *Ibid.*, VIII, 289–291.

[3] Görtz to Count van der Nath, October 3 and October 27, 1716, Moser, *Rettung der Ehre*, p. 132: 'Il est absolutement nécessaire, que pendant l'hiver nous fassions tous les efforts imaginables par rapport aus préparatifs pour l'année prochaine, si nous voulons, qu'entre ce tems la négotiation aille bien ci-dehors, pour sortir, une bonne fois d'affaire et pour parvenir à une fin heureuse. . . . J'aporteroy avec moi un plan pour la paix, qui sera au goût du Roi à ce que j'espère. Pour le faciliter d'avantage il est absolument necessair que Sa Majesté se mettre en état de se faire respecter et craindre.'

[4] Görtz to Sparre, October 9, 1716, *Handlingar*, X, 364.

definitely not to Sweden's advantage.[1] Much credit for the bringing together of the traditional enemies must be given to Stanhope and Abbé Dubois, trouble shooter for the Regent.[2] Their task had not been easy. French sentiment was in favor of the Stuarts rather than the Hanoverians. Marshal d'Huxelles and the Marquis de Torcy, two leading French ministers, opposed the English alliance and were of the opinion that a Franco-Spanish treaty should be the basis of French foreign policy. Public opinion in both countries had been against the alignment of old enemies, and Dutch sensibilities were suspicious of joining with France and England if it meant involvement in the North and a weakening of Dutch defenses in the Barrier towns.

The Peace of Utrecht could not be utilized as the basis for a new treaty, because George I as king was an ally of the emperor who had not recognized that settlement. French aid to the Jacobites in the 'fifteen,' and their construction of a canal at Mardyke to make a naval base were other bones of contention. Stanhope, in a letter to Stair dated May 31, 1716, summed up three points upon which England was insistent.

> That the Pretender shall be obliged to go beyond the Alps, that the Regent shall declare that none of His Majesty's Rebel Subjects shall be suffered to continue in, or to return to France on any Pretence whatsoever, and that Mardyke shall not be suffered to continue or be made capable of receiving any Vessels of War[3]

Stanhope had been aided in negotiating the Triple Alliance by the ardent desire of George I to obtain allies who would either aid him or promise not to succor Hanover's enemies in the Great Northern War. George also wanted to insure his dynasty upon the English throne. From the French side, Stanhope was aided by the dynastic situations in France and in

[1] Görtz to Gyllenborg, October 13, 1716, Cobbett, *Parliamentary History*, VII, 398. In this letter Görtz makes the statement that the Swedes 'need not be much disturbed about the treaty between France and Great Britain.' Carlson, *Om Fredsunderhandlingarne*, p. 86.
[2] Williams, *Stanhope, passim*; Bourgeois, *Le Sécret de Dubois* and his *Le Sécret du Régent* deal with the negotiations of the Triple Alliance.
[3] Stanhope to Stair, May 31, 1716, *British Diplomatic Instructions, France*, XXXV, 105. Cf. Townshend to Stanhope, July 27, 1716, Wiesener, *Le Régent et les Anglais*, I, 475.

Spain. Philip V, grandson of Louis XIV, had ascended the Spanish throne according to the Treaty of Utrecht. He had married for the second time, taking for his bride, Elizabeth Farnese, niece of the Duke of Parma.[1] The uxorious Philip had come very much under the influence of his dynastically minded wife and her adviser in foreign affairs, Cardinal Alberoni, one of the shrewder actors on the diplomatic scene. Furthermore, Philip had never entirely renounced his claim to the French throne.

The young king, Louis XV, was a sickly boy, and both the Regent and Philip realized that he might die. If he did, Philip was the next hereditary claimant, but he had technically forfeited his right by accepting the throne of the Spanish Hapsburgs, because of the clause in the Utrecht settlement which stated that the thrones of France and Spain could never be united. Thus, in European eyes, the Regent was next in the line of succession. The Regent, however, had seen wills involving successions violated before, and there was the possibility that Philip might prefer the throne of France to that of Spain. Consequently, Orleans was amenable to overtures made by the English ministers around the Hanoverian elector.[2]

After the Skåne affair, that group feared that France might join a Russo-Swedish bloc, which it believed that Görtz was trying to effect. Consequently, England was willing to lessen its demands on the matter of Mardyke in order to expedite the conclusion of the treaty. Speed was of the essence to the pro-Hanoverian group surrounding the King, even though English interests might suffer, and even though England might have to ditch the States because they moved so cumbersomely when it came to making a diplomatic decision.[3]

On October 10, the Convention of Hanover was signed between England and France, and the results were noteworthy

[1] Edward Armstrong, *Elizabeth Farnese*, 'the *Termagant of Spain*' (London, 1892), gives an excellent account of Spain during this period.

[2] Charles Peneau Duclos, 'Mémoires sécrets sur les régnes de Louis XIV et de Louis XV,' in *Collection complète des mémoires relatifs à l'histoire de France*, Ser. 2, Vol. 78, Alexander Petitot (ed.) (Paris, 1819–1929), pp. 232–235.

[3] Stanhope to Methuen, September 25, 1716, Wiesener, *Le Régent et les Anglais*, I, 491–492: 'Et en considerant le danger immediat ou il semble que nous mettent les troubles du Nord, je dirai franchement que dans mon opinion, nous devons nous assurer, s'il se peut, l'amitié du Régent.'

so far as northern affairs were concerned. Robethon, in a letter to Polwarth, pointed out the immediate effect that the treaty had upon Sweden:

> The Regent rejoices greatly at the conclusion of the treaty with us, believing he is now assured of the succession, and seeing himself much strengthened in the regency. He has laid an embargo upon those in the French ports who took privateering commissions for the King of Sweden, some of which Mr. Sparre, the Swedish minister at Paris, wished to distribute. In a word, the Regent is at present so strongly attached to the King and it is so much his interest to be so, that if the Czar and his Shaffiroff wish to go to Holland and France to endeavour to draw the latter into the affairs of the North they may save themselves the trouble.[1]

Sweden's position was also weakened by a Franco-Prussian treaty, which had been signed on September 14, 1716. The new French diplomatic line, which Görtz did not wholly appreciate, did not deter him in his efforts to negotiate an honorable peace and to strengthen Sweden's military and diplomatic hand. Soon he was sounding out Russia in order to ascertain what that country would concede to Sweden in order to bring an end to the long war. Baron Ostermann, the Muscovite minister of state, was not impressed by some of Görtz's grandiose schemes. He was as cautious as Görtz was bold and daring, and feared that some of the Swedish plans might be adopted by Peter and thus cause him to grant Sweden a more favorable peace than the situation warranted.[2]

It was to be a Jacobite who helped Görtz drive an opening wedge in the Russian negotiations, and it was to be the Jacobites who might supply some of the money necessary for Sweden to keep going. Some time in October, Görtz wrote Sparre a letter, the contents of which were to be forwarded to James at Avignon. Görtz said that the more he considered the Scottish plan, the better it 'tasted to him.' Vessels to transport the soldiers were fundamental to the success of the undertaking. As Gyllenborg had written from London that the plan would

---

[1] Robethon to Polwarth, October 6/17, 1716, *Polwarth Papers*, I,102–103.
[2] Voltaire, *Histoire de Charles XII*, p. 453. La Vie on Osterman, *Sbornik*, XXXIV, 326. Osterman was a very wise man, knew all the languages, and was in charge of Russian foreign affairs.

have to be put into action next spring, it was necessary to have the ships at once. Görtz did not think that the time was ripe to inform Charles XII of the negotiations, but promised to inform the King of the entire project as soon as it was possible to win his approval.[1]

Görtz, who at that time was in Amsterdam, said that nothing could be accomplished in 1716, but if they were to be successful in 1717, money was needed immediately.[2] Such money could also pave the way to winning a separate peace with one of Sweden's many enemies.[3] For the latter reason, he urged Sparre to raise money in France by bending every effort to obtain the French subsidy. To stir Sparre to action, Görtz dwelt at length upon the privations of the Swedish king, and suggested ways and means by which France could fulfill her treaty obligations.[4] Görtz in addition worked to destroy French doubts that Charles XII opposed a reasonable peace.[5]

There seems to be no doubt that by the end of October Görtz was seriously negotiating with the Jacobites, and that he was more interested in Jacobite money than in the Jacobite cause *per se*. Pressed as he was for money, Görtz found a Jacobite offer of £160,000 sterling too tempting to ignore.[6] For that kind of cash, he would at least pay lip service to Jacobite hopes and dreams.

While Görtz vainly tried to raise money, plans for a Jacobite rebellion took shape. Colin Campbell of Glenderule wrote to Mar and advised him that the best place to land invading troops was somewhere near Glasgow. If this were not possible, some place near Inverloch was to be an alternative.[7] One of Charles' minor transport fleets, under a famous privateer captain named Gatenhielm, was to supply between 4,000 and 10,000 troops, to be commanded either by Charles himself or Major-General Hamilton. Volunteers from France and Irish

[1] Görtz to Sparre, October 29, 1716, *Handlingar*, X, 370.
[2] Görtz to Sparre, October 9, 1716, *Ibid.*, X, 366.
[3] Görtz to Sparre, October 9, 1716, *Ibid.*, X, 367.
[4] Görtz to Sparre, November 12, 1716, *Ibid.*, X, 374–375.
[5] *Ibid.*
[6] Westrin, 'Friherre . . . Görtz Bref,' XVIII, 105ff. Cf. Gyllenborg to Görtz, October 27, 1716, Cobbett, *Parliamentary History*, VII, 400.
[7] Mar to the Bishop of Rochester, October 2, 1716, *Stuart Papers*, III, 13. Mar to Dillon, October 4, 1716, *Ibid.*, III, 17.

troops in the service of the King of Spain were to participate in the venture. Scotland was to furnish the necessary horses and the Jacobites the money. An easy victory was expected in Scotland, but Ireland would be more difficult. James' presence in the Highlands before the arrival of the Swedes was mandatory if the invading soldiers were to be received by the natives. If James could not do this, Campbell felt that it was a requisite that he at least be with the Swedes.[1] Gyllenborg was enthusiastic over the plan and commented: 'In short, it will be a glorious enterprise, which will put an end to all our misfortunes by ruining those who are the authors of them. As to what I have to say of the time, the sooner the better.'[2]

The Jacobites dubiously hoped for French assistance.[3] Oxford was hoping that Orleans would help in 'his beloved sneaking underhanded way,' while Mar did not dare approach the Regent, because of his inability to keep a secret.[4] A man named Olgrive did, however, try to approach the Regent through De Torcy, but had little success because De Torcy was afraid of Lord Stair and his spies, and would not venture any move which the English ambassador might label a Jacobite intrigue. Olgrive wanted Oxford to have some English nobles with Jacobite leanings approach the French ambassador in London in order to see if something might not be done from that quarter. All was in vain. By early October, Dubois and Iberville had won the ear of the Regent, and France was drifting towards Hanover and the Triple Alliance.[5] Not only were the Jacobites to lose all hopes for French aid, but also they were soon to be requested to leave Avignon.

As Orleans moved toward Brunswick, Sparre and the Jacobites approached each other more closely. Dillon wrote:

[1] Lindeberg, *Görtz*, pp. 57–59. Cf. Gyllenborg to Görtz, October 23, 1716, Cobbett, *Parliamentary History*, VII, 399 claims that fifteen to twenty thousand men were needed. Lindeberg, *Görtz*, p. 57 says that the Spanish fleet was to help.

[2] Gyllenborg to Görtz, October 23, 1716, Cobbett, *Parliamentary History*, VII, 399.

[3] Gyllenborg to Gustaf Gyllenborg, October 27, 1716, Cobbett, *Parliamentary History*, VII, 400: 'One of them [the Jacobites], who is the chief promoter of this affair, assured me, that we had nothing to apprehend from the Regent on this occasion.' Evidently the informant of Gyllenborg was unduly optimistic and was not in step with the changes taking place in Franco-Swedish relations.

[4] Mar to Oxford, September 21, 1716, *Stuart Papers*, II, 415.

[5] Inese to Mar, October 27, 1716, *Ibid.*, III, 142; Olgrive to Mar, October 8, 1716, *Ibid.*, III, 43; Dillon to Mar, October 6, 1716, *Ibid.*, III, 26.

I find Jeoffrey [Sparre] more willing than I am able to express, to unite Arthur [James] and Humphrey [Charles] in a solid manner ... the latter's being abandoned in the treaty 'twixt Edgar [the Regent] and Kendrick [King George]. The descent in Schonen [Skåne] is laid aside as I already informed you, which will make matters more feasible, and perhaps determine Humphrey to take the only party that can retrieve his losses, and at the same time augment his glory, which he often preferred to his interest.[1]

Dillon also thought that if the Jacobites furnished money in time for Charles XII to act against his enemies, an agreement might be reached. Görtz had placed the amount necessary before Charles XII could assist James in the recovery of the British throne at £50,000.[2]

The more that the French Court attempted to persuade James to leave Avignon, the more Sparre urged him not to depart until he was forced to do so.[3] In the meantime, the Jacobites had sent a man named Downes to England to see if the sums requested by the Swedish ministers could be collected. Before Downes departed, Sparre conversed with him, but there were no ensuing communications between the two because of the fear of exposure.[4] In late October, Sparre was down five days with a fever, and so the month ended with negotiations in Paris at a standstill.[5]

November saw both parties straining every sinew to realize an agreement, and it was during the early days of this month that the two came to understand how each might be advantageous to the other. Görtz, meanwhile, learned that Peter had signified his hatred of George I to Sir Henry Stirling, who was visiting his uncle, the Czar's physician. Stirling wrote that Peter had said that nothing would please him more than to have the Chevalier made king of England.[6] Görtz held Dr. Erskine responsible for cultivating the Czar's friendly disposition toward the Jacobites, and was of the opinion that the Stuart

---

[1] Dillon to Mar, October 17, 1716, *Ibid.*, III, 90.
[2] Dillon to Mar, October 17, 1716, *Ibid.*, III, 91.
[3] *Ibid.*
[4] Mar to Dillon, October 23, 1716, *Ibid.*, III, 129.
[5] Dillon to Mar, October 27, 1716, *Ibid.*, III, 141.
[6] Gustavus Gyllenborg to Carl Gyllenborg, November 17, 1716, *MSHS.*, II, 420.

adherents should return this good will and assure Peter that he would not find them wanting should he put them to the test.[1]

The Swedish minister did not implicitly trust his information, but it is possible that, at this time, he constructed a plan for uniting Peter and Charles XII in a joint effort to expel George I from the British throne and to substitute James.[2] In November he wrote:

> I believe, however, that by means of the confidential physician, the good will of the Czar could be cultivated, if it be such as has been represented. If the Czar comes here, and there were any means of having a conversation with the confidant, we should certainly advance affairs considerable, supposing, as I have said, that what the confidant wrote was well founded. Meanwhile, I am trying to find some other way.[3]

Hearing that Peter was to visit the Hague while en route to Paris, Görtz asked Gyllenborg to arrange a meeting for him with Dr. Erskine.[4] Gyllenborg obtained the requested letter of introduction, but did not dare send it to Görtz, because he feared that it would be seized by the English postal authorities.[5] Peter arrived at the Hague about December 6,[6] and in two interviews with Russian ministers, Görtz made more progress toward bringing Sweden and Russia together than he had in all of his negotiations with Ostermann.[7] Unfortunately for the Jacobites, however, the Baron missed Dr. Erskine by two days, so there were no conferences held between the two during this critical stage of Swedo-Jacobite diplomacy.[8]

While he waited for Peter, Görtz, and the Jacobites through Sparre, carried on a voluminous correspondence. James, sick with a fistula and about to be forced to leave France, had his agents try to gain him sanctuary at Deux Ponts. Görtz said that

[1] Görtz to Sparre, November 12, 1716, *Handlingar*, XVII, 380.
[2] *MSHS.*, XLIV, 386.
[3] Görtz to Sparre, November 12, 1716, *MSHS.*, XLIV, 419.
[4] Görtz to Gyllenborg, December 1, 1716, *Ibid.*, XLIV, 421.
[5] Gyllenborg to Görtz, December 29, 1716, *Ibid.*
[6] Görtz to Sparre, December 6, 1716, *Handlingar*, XVII, 401.
[7] Voltaire, *Histoire de Charles XII*, p. 436.
[8] Sir Hugh Paterson to Mar, January 11, 1717, *Stuart Papers*, III, 381: 'This is a misfortune, but it cannot be helped and it was not my fault that the visit was not made sooner, but others thought it not fit till Davies [the Czar] consented to it, and I cannot say they were much wrong in that since this accident was not to be supposed.'

such a measure would defeat the hopes of both parties by betraying all to England. The sole result would be the raising of a fleet by England to frustrate the contemplated invasion.[1] Consequently, he instructed Sparre to stick to his instructions. If not, Görtz threatened to wash his hands of the entire affair. He denied that Charles XII had been informed about the plot,[2] and refused to sign any sort of formal treaty with the Stuarts. Such a move would be harmful to both sides, as it would disclose the secret to all of Europe.

Sparre was ordered to inform Dillon and his friends that they would have to trust the Swedish ministers and furnish them with a loan large enough so that Charles XII could be in a position to help the Pretender, should a suitable opportunity arise. At least 300,000 *écus* were needed at once to reinforce the Swedish fleet at Göteborg. To allay Jacobite suspicions, Sparre was instructed to tell them that Charles XII as yet knew nothing of the plot, and if he could not be persuaded to throw his

---

[1] Görtz to Sparre, December 6, 1716, *Handlingar*, XVII, 401.

[2] Westrin, 'Friherre . . . Görtz Bref,' XVIII, 105–106 quotes a letter showing that Gyllenborg had informed Charles XII about the Jacobite negotiation, November 7, 1716: 'Einige der fürnehmsten Toris aus England haben mich durch die dritte hande antragen lassen, sie zu Ew:r Konigl. Maj:tt dienst wohl eine summe von 300,000 Rohler hergeben wollten, wenn ihnen gezeigt werden könte, das sie von Ew:r Konigl. Maj:tt sich einer assistentz könte zu erfahren haben, dafern sie dazu einen soliden plan fournirten. Da nun Ew:r Konigl. Maj:tt hohe gedanke hierüben mir gantz unbekant sind, so habe ich mich auch keines weges ermächtigen wollen mit diesen seuthin auf einen solchen fuss in irgent ettwas einzutreten. Doch habe ich ihnen zu erkennen geben lassen, E. K. Maj:tt hätten mich allergnädigst bevollmächtiget, auf leidliche conditiones einige gelder zu dero dienst aufzuhandeln. Wann demnach sie darauf ein darleih zu thun geneigt wären, könte ich die sache wohl mit ihnen richtig machen. Wollten sie übrigens mir über ihr ander werck einen plan zufertigen, so wollte ich nicht ermangln E. K. Maj:tt denselben gebührend einzusenden. Ich vermeine hierunter nichts gethan zu haben, welches E. K. Maj:tt missfallen könte, angesehen deroselben wohl indifferent seyn wird, von was für particulieren man einige gelder für dieselbe aufzuhandeln gelegenheit finden möchte, wie dann der könig vor Frankreich wohl ehe bei privatleuthen hier in Holland gelder hat negotiiren lassen. Ich solte auch sonsten dafür halten E. K. Maj:tt besagter partheiij vorschläge ohne consequentz anhören könten. Der Englische hof verdienet wenigstens nicht, das E. K. Maj:tt einig menagement für ihn haben solten, denn derselve es wohl nicht ungern sehen würde wen E. K. Maj:tt um crohn und scepter könten, gebracht werden.' Cf. Görtz to Sparre, November 12, 1716, Cobbett, *Parliamentary History*, VII, 403: 'But I will not venture to convey anything of this to his majesty otherwise than by word of mouth. It is satisfaction enough to me to know originally that I am in no danger of giving offence to Sweden by the part I take upon me to act in this affair.'

lot in with that of James, the money would be returned to the Jacobites by May, 1717.[1] The tenor of Görtz's letter gives the impression that he wanted to procure a loan from the Jacobites sufficient to outfit the fleet and thereby put the country in a position to negotiate successfully for peace in the following spring. Having gained that long desired objective, Sweden would reimburse the Jacobites and thus could not be accused of having obtained the money under false pretenses.

As stated above, the bulk of Görtz's correspondence to Sparre during November contained urgent demands for money. On the twentieth, he sent to Sparre a memoir which was to be presented to the King of France, reminding him that four subsidies of 300,000 *écus* each were due Sweden by treaty. Görtz realized that a lack of specie had been advanced by France as an excuse for her failure to pay, but he felt that perhaps the real reason for nonpayment was diplomatic pressure from London. To circumvent French excuses, Görtz proposed that France give Sweden 500,000 *écus* in bills of exchange payable on sight within four and six months. This plan, according to Görtz, would put to bed French refusals to meet treaty obligations.[2] The Baron had little hope that France would assist in the Jacobite plot because of the Regent's desire for the English treaty. On November 17, 1716, Görtz wrote: 'I am persuaded that France will not take any step that may disgust England before they have finished the treaty of alliance that is now depending.'[3]

Görtz wanted at least 100,000 *écus* in order to purchase three ships from Antoine Hogguer, a French banker, who on several occasions had come to Sweden's aid. Not only had he sent large sums of money to assist Stenbock at Tönning, but he had also contributed to the garrisons of Wismar, Stralsund, and Stettin. For these services he had been made a Swedish baron.[4]

---

[1] Görtz to Sparre, November 12, 1716, *Handlingar*, X, 377. Idem to Idem, November 12, 1716, Cobbett, *Parliamentary History*, VII, 403 expresses the need of the Swedish fleet: '300,000 crowns may satisfy us at present to augment our naval forces at Gothenburg.'

[2] Görtz to Sparre, November 20, 1716, *Handlingar*, X, 386.

[3] Görtz to Sparre, November 12, 1716, Cobbett, *Parliamentary History*, VII, 402.

[4] Görtz to Sparre, December 12, 1716, *Handlingar*, X, 375. Chance, 'Swedish Plot,' XVIII, 89, claims there were four ships. Cf. Westrin, 'Friherre . . . Görtz Bref,' XVIII, 102.

As purveyor of masts for the French navy, Hogguer had succeeded in obtaining three warships of sixty to seventy cannon, for use in protecting his commerce and his cargoes of masts.[1] Hogguer promised those ships to Sweden along with a crew of 600 men.[2] Sparre was urged to obtain the ships not only because the King wanted them, but also because the 'safety of the King of Sweden depends upon this acquisition.'[3]

Sparre's inability to raise money caused relations between him and Görtz to become somewhat strained.[4] Sparre also objected to the purchase of the Hogguer ships, fearing that such an act would cause trouble between Sweden and the French Court. He also thought that if the Regent reached an agreement with England, the ships would not be allowed to leave France. Consequently, Swedish money invested in them would be lost. Görtz, on the other hand, felt that the probable rewards justified an embroilment with France, and pointed out that France had neither pact nor treaty which prevented Swedish armament construction in France.[5]

In addition, Görtz accused Sparre of receiving money from the French Court and not sending it on to him at the Hague.[6] Another cause for friction may have been that Sparre, who was more amicable to the Jacobites than was Görtz, disliked being implicated in a negotiation which might dupe them.[7] Furthermore, Sparre's brother Axel, like many prominent Swedes, hoped that Görtz would fail in his efforts to raise money, and thus Charles XII would be coerced into suing for peace. Görtz suspected that Sparre had joined the camp of his brother and

---

[1] *Ibid*. Cf. Chance, 'Swedish Plot,' XVIII, 89.

[2] Westrin, 'Friherre . . . Görtz Bref,' XVIII, 102. Görtz to Sparre, August 11, 1716, *Handlingar*, VIII, 255 contains information on paying and feeding French sailors serving in the Swedish fleet.

[3] Görtz to Sparre, November 12, 1716, *Handlingar*, X, 375: 'Il semble que toute la resource de la Suède depend maintenant des subsidies de la France malpayes.' Görtz's ardent desire for a strong Sweden can be seen in Görtz to Petkum, October 6, 1716, *Ibid*., VIII, 294: 'Mais il me semble, qui si l'on souhaitte notre conservation, l'on n'y scauroit contribuer plus a propos, que presentiment, ou il s'agit de mettre le Roi en etat pendent l'hiver qu'on gagne, de figurer encore mieux l'année prochaine et de se rendre encore plus respectable. Je me preserve l'honneur de m'etendre d'avantage la dessus.'

[4] Westrin, 'Friherre . . . Görtz Bref,' XVIII, 103.

[5] Görtz to Sparre, November 12, 1716, *Handlingar*, X, 378.

[6] *Ibid*., X, 384.

[7] Mar to Dillon, November 27, 1716, *Stuart Papers*, III, 263.

this added to the existing tension. Sparre was recalled from his post sometime in January on the grounds of ill health, but the main reason was that Charles XII was displeased with his failure to raise funds in France.[1] A by-product of that failure was a more concerted effort made by Görtz to obtain money from the Jacobites.[2] Unable to realize his hopes so far as the French subsidy was concerned, Görtz had practically no other alternative.

The Jacobites, meanwhile, had been watching the trend of European diplomacy, and had come to the conclusion that their best hope for success lay in a reconciliation between Charles XII and Peter the Great. To bring Charles XII over to the Stuart cause, John Menzies, the chief Jacobite agent in England, suggested that the Shetland Islands be ceded to Sweden.[3] Although there was considerable grumbling in England as to the way that the Earl of Mar was conducting the negotiations with Sweden,[4] nevertheless, Herculean efforts were begun in November to raise the necessary funds.

The British group which furnished the bulk of the money wanted tangible assurances from Görtz before any financial transaction was made. Menzies tried to win from the Baron a flat promise that 12,000 men and 4,000 horse would be sent to England in the following spring. Menzies and his English friends were also concerned as to how the money could be sent to Sweden with the English fleet controlling the sea lanes.[5]

A conversation held December 4, between Gyllenborg and one of the leading Jacobites, well illustrates Jacobite fears and aspirations. It appears that the Jacobite was of the opinion that a treaty had already been concluded at Avignon between Charles XII and James. Learning that things were to the contrary, he became highly indignant and suggested that if Görtz was negotiating solely for a loan, Gyllenborg had better keep the matter quiet so as not to endanger Swedo-Jacobite friendship. He pointed out that if the Jacobites were interested in

[1] Chance, 'Swedish Plot,' XVIII, 79.
[2] Westrin, 'Friherre . . . Görtz Bref,' XVIII, 103. Westrin calls this negotiation 'Ett spel, som han börjada i hopp om at fanga dessa [Jacobites], men slutade med att han själf vardt fanga.'
[3] Menzies to Mar, November 8, 1716, *Stuart Papers*, III, 237.
[4] Menzies to Mar, November 22, 1716, *Ibid.*, III, 285.
[5] Menzies to Mar, October 29, 1716, *Ibid.*, III, 196.

loaning money for profit, England would be a better investment because of her higher interest rate. To Jacobite thinking a project dependent upon the whims of Charles XII was a shaky one, to say the least. Görtz was accused of using the Jacobites to obtain better peace terms, and the Jacobites in England refused to give any money to Sweden without positive guarantees of military assistance to the Chevalier.[1]

A week later, Görtz answered the Jacobite complaints and implied that 10 to 12,000 Swedes, including 4,000 cavalry might be sent to England. He promised to go to Sweden himself to make the necessary arrangements as he did 'not like to rely upon the care of others in such a particular.' As for the transaction of the money, the English Tories could give it under the name of a Dutch merchant and consequently risk nothing. Insisting that the word of Charles XII was as good as any written guarantee, Görtz said that ships were necessary for any invasion of England, and if the invasion were to be successful, the ships had to be procured immediately. The Swedish agent threatened 'that they [the Jacobites] must come to a resolution speedily, or think no more of the affair for all the next year.'[2]

The Jacobites still wanted more than threats and promises. The growing strained relations between Sparre and Görtz increased their suspicions of the latter. Dillon, sensing disharmony, grilled Sparre about his relations with Görtz and learned that his fears were justified, and that a rift did exist between the two Swedish ministers. Dillon did not think that James played any role in the split, but he could not help but see that the Jacobite cause would suffer by it. Even though Sparre assured Dillon that Görtz was as much for the Pretender as he was, and that Görtz in Holland was trying to hog the negotiation, the Jacobites were not mollified. Heretofore they had considered Sparre, rather than Görtz, as their friend.[3]

With the situation deteriorating at Paris, Görtz decided to

[1] Gyllenborg to Görtz, December 4, 1716, Cobbett, *Parliamentary History*, VII, 405–408.
[2] Görtz to Gyllenborg, December 11, 1716, *Ibid.*, VII, 410.
[3] Dillon to Mar, January 2, 1716, Stuart Papers, III, 385: 'Görtz seems so cautious in the affair concerning Arthur [James] as indeed Jeoffry [Sparre] does too, but I believe by the influence of the other, that it makes me think I have found for this suspicion, and it ought to be watched.'

go there and to take matters into his own hands. The main object of his visit was to ascertain the true attitude of France toward Sweden in order to plot the future course of Swedish action.[1] The Regent's new alignment with England had to be studied and investigated carefully. While at Paris, however, Görtz continued to negotiate with the Jacobites as a part of his overall financial plan.

Sparre had assured Görtz that 100,000 crowns awaited him at Paris, but Görtz was destined to be disappointed.[2] It does appear, however, that by the middle of January a sum of money was about to change hands. On the first, Gyllenborg at London had been told that £20,000 were ready for Sweden. All that the Swedish minister had to pledge was that the funds would be used for the benefit of Charles XII. An additional £8,000 had been sent to Sparre from Avignon. Görtz, however, had asked for £70,000, but by January 12, 1717, only £30,000 had been raised. Mar, moreover, was stalling and trying unsuccessfully to get some sort of a written agreement from Görtz.[3]

Noticing that the Paris Jacobites were cooling, Görtz demanded instant action. Gyllenborg was instructed to have the London element order the Paris group to pay Görtz so that money for the Hogguer ships would be available. To drive home the need for speed, Görtz warned: 'If they will not, this business ought to be broken off entirely, without thinking further of it. To lose four weeks more would be losing all, for this year at least; and afterwards the circumstances of affairs will so change, that there can be no thinking of it any longer.'[4] At the same time, he sent Sparre a definite plan for an invasion of Scotland.[5] On the other hand, he cautioned Gyllenborg about divulging any information about the invasion plans to the Swedish Court.[6]

[1] Görtz to Sparre, December 25, 1716, *Handlingar*, X, 399.

[2] Görtz to Gyllenborg, January 8, 1717, *Ibid.*, VIII, 406 and in Cobbett, *Parliamentary History*, VII, 414. Chance, *George I and the Northern War*, p. 175.

[3] Gyllenborg to Görtz, January 1, 1717, Cobbett, *Parliamentary History*, VII, 413. James to the Bishop of Rochester, January 26, 1717, *Stuart Papers*, III, 475; and Mar to Jerningham, January 12, 1717, *Ibid.*, III, 436.

[4] Görtz to Gyllenborg, January 8, 1717, Cobbett, *Parliamentary History*, VII, 414.

[5] Görtz to Sparre, January 8, 1717, *Ibid.*, VII, 414-415.

[6] Görtz to Gyllenborg, January 8, 1717, *Ibid.*, 415.

At that point, George Jerningham was put in charge of the Jacobite side of the negotiations.[1] On January 11, Görtz signed a note which made it possible for the Swedes to borrow money from the Jacobites. Loans were to be repaid in two years with one-sixth of the principal to be paid every four months. Interest was set at six percent.[2]

About January 27, Görtz made a verbal agreement with Jerningham. James was to give Görtz £70,000 as soon as possible, and Charles XII by April 20, 1717, was to transport to England 8,000 foot soldiers and 3,500 horse completely equipped with everything except mounts.[3] The Jacobites in England were to do all in their power to work for the cashiering of half of the English army and to prevent the fleet from sailing to the Baltic the next year.[4] Up to this point Görtz had received only 50,000 crowns from the Stuarts. He hoped that Gyllenborg would confer with him at the Hague at an early date and bring the money expected from the English side. At such a meeting the two Swedish diplomats could work out details for the great enterprise.[5]

While they joined in revolutionary plots, Görtz and Gyllenborg had by no means neglected the safer and saner methods of diplomatic procedure. One of the chief reasons for Görtz's Paris trip had been to sound out the Regent's policy toward Sweden.[6] Basic disagreements between France and Sweden were readily apparent. France wanted to play the role of mediator at a general peace conference,[7] whereas the Swedes

[1] Mar to Jerningham, January 27, 1717, *Stuart Papers*, III, 480. Cf. Westrin, 'Friherre . . . Görtz Bref,' XVIII, 112.

[2] Copy of acquittance given by Görtz to the French Jacobites, January 11, 1717, Cobbett, *Parliamentary History*, VII, 418.

[3] Jerningham to Mar, January 27, 1717, *Stuart Papers*, III, 480.

[4] Görtz to Gyllenborg, January 16, 1717, Cobbett, *Parliamentary History*, VII, 418. Cf. Chance, 'Swedish Plot,' XVIII, 97.

[5] Mar to Jerningham, January 27, 1717, *Stuart Papers*, III, 480. Westrin, 'Friherre . . . Görtz Bref,' XVIII, 113 claims that from January to February Görtz while he was in Paris was able to raise only £75,000. This was done under conditions put forth by the Jacobites. See Görtz to Gyllenborg, January 8, 1717, Cobbett, *Parliamentary History*, VII, 415.

[6] *Supra.*

[7] De la Marck Instructions, Recueil, II, 281: 'Il est aisé de juger, lorsque l'on fait attention à l'état présent des affaires générales de l'Europe, de quelle importance il est pour les interêts de Sa Majesté que la paix du Nord se fasse par ses offices; l'on sait qu'Elle désire le maintien de la paix, et qu'au contraire la cour de Vienne, croyant la conjoncture favorable pour ses desseins ambitieux, n'oublie

were of the opinion that they had more to gain from a separate peace, especially one with Russia.[1] On January 17, Görtz conferred with Marshal d'Huxelles and asked for French mediation in a separate peace with the Czar. The marshal pointed out that such a move would expose France to the reproaches of the Northern Alliance and consequently render her ineffectual to assist Charles XII. Furthermore, France absolutely refused to take any steps contrary to the Triple Alliance, which she had just concluded with England and the United Provinces.[2]

Syveton is of the opinion that when Görtz saw that French policy was veering toward England, he should have taken cognizance of the fact and arranged an entente with Peter, who was without any allies except Prussia. Instead, Görtz spent valuable time listening to Jacobite intrigues, for which Syveton condemns him. This to Syveton was the 'erreur de Görtz.'[3] It must be remembered, however, that Görtz, in order to negotiate a favorable Russo-Swedish peace, first needed ships and money. He undoubtedly had such an agreement with Russia in mind while he negotiated with the followers of the Chevalier.

Görtz and Gyllenborg also worked for accord with Hanover-England at the expense of Russia and Denmark.[4] Hanover's insistence on Bremen and Verden made any real hope of success improbable. Görtz feared that once George I obtained his aims, neither he nor his subjects in Hanover or Britain would concern themselves with gaining compensations for Sweden at Russian expense.[5] Without real assistance from the Hanoverian army and the British navy, Sweden had little to gain by accepting the terms of the British king. The Görtz-Gyllenborg correspondence shows that both men gradually became more anti-

[1] King to Chateauneuf, January 5, 1717, *Ibid.*, VIII, 139–140.
[2] De la Marck Instructions, May 7, 1717, *Ibid.*, II, 278–280.
[3] Syveton, 'L'erreur de Görtz,' X, 223.
[4] De la Marck Instructions, *Recueil*, Hollande, II, 281.
[5] Chance, *George I and the Northern War*, pp. 179–180.

rien pour se préparer les moyens de les exécuter, aussitôt qu'elle sera délivrée de la guerre contre les Turcs; et il n'est pas douteux que, si elle parvenoit à régler par ses offices seuls ou par son autorité les interêts des princes engagés dans la guerre du Nord, elle sauroit bien profiter de cette ouverture pour se ménager des alliés, en sacrifiant a ceux qu'elle croiroit desposés à s'unir avec elle ce qui pourroit flatter leu ambition.'

Hanoverian and more pro-Stuart. They came eventually to the conclusion that unless the Hanoverian party was ruined in England, Swedish possessions in Germany, and even Sweden itself, would be lost.[1]

Both Görtz and the Stuarts had stressed the importance of secrecy throughout their negotiations. Both knew that if the Whigs heard about what was being planned, all would be lost.[2] In spite of all precautions, however, the news leaked out. The British government had known for some time that the Swedes and the Jacobites were having conferences with each other, but it had not been sure just what the exact relationship was. As indicated in previous chapters, Swedo-Jacobite coöperation of one sort or another had continually played a role in British diplomacy.

Back in July, 1716, Townshend had written Norris that: 'His Majesty is well assured that the Swedish Minister at Paris has concluded a Treaty with the Rebels in France, by which they are to be admitted into the service of the King of Sweden in the same rank and stations they enjoyed respectively under the Pretender. . . .'[3]

In August, Lord Polwarth had been informed that the King of Sweden was planning to invade Scotland and put the Pretender on the throne. Then Sweden, France, and England would unite against the Northern Alliance. France was to furnish money, and Spain, Bavaria, and Hesse were to be invited to join the new alliance. Polwarth felt that the details were invented, but that there was something to the rumor.[4] In addition, as pointed out above, Lord Stair and his spies in Paris were well informed and consistently caused Sparre to deny that he was in communication with Stuart supporters.

In October, some letters between Gyllenborg and Görtz had been stopped by London officials and deciphered. Action on the matter was delayed until January 29, 1717, when Stanhope laid the matter before the Council of State and proposed that Gyllenborg be arrested and his papers seized. When General

[1] Gyllenborg to Görtz, November 4, 1716, Cobbett, *Parliamentary History*, VII, 400–401.
[2] James to the Bishop of Rochester, January 26, 1717, *Stuart Papers*, III, 475.
[3] Townshend to Norris, July 3, 1716, *Townshend Papers*, p. 100.
[4] Extract of a letter by Sehestedt, *Polwarth Papers*, I, 32.

Wade arrived at the home of the Swedish minister, he demanded not only those papers that were on the table, but also those in a cabinet. Countess Gyllenborg claimed that the questioned *escritoire* contained only her plate and linens, but when it was broken into, it was found to be filled with papers. Wade sealed them up and carried them away with him. On the same day a Mr. Caesar, M.P. for Hereford, and Sir Jacob Banks, formerly a member from Minehead, were arrested because of their Jacobite activities.[1]

The next day Stanhope sent instructions to William Leathes, now the British Resident at the Hague, to press the States for the arrest of Görtz and his secretaries.[2] Stanhope and other Englishmen in his camp considered that such an action would not be contrary to international law, because Görtz had shown no credentials which could give him diplomatic immunity.[3] Before Leathes could obtain the order, Görtz had come to the Hague after an errand to Paris regarding Hogguer's ships. No news of Gyllenborg's arrest had preceded him, and he evidently did not anticipate any danger. On February 18, he interviewed Baron Heems, the Imperial minister, and departed on the next day for Amsterdam with General Poniatowski. The reason for his going was a business transaction with a merchant named Hooker.[4]

Görtz left for Amsterdam about noon, and at two his house was beset with soldiers and his papers confiscated. Stambke, his most trusted secretary, had accompanied him to Amsterdam, but his second secretary, Gustavus Gyllenborg, had remained behind, and as a result he was taken into custody. A third secretary named Preis, who was also the Swedish Resident at the Hague, set out to warn the Baron, but his trip was useless

---

[1] Wiesener, *Le Régent et les Anglais*, II, 1; *Historical Register*, IV, 66; Cobbett, *Parliamentary History*, VII, 393–394.

[2] Chance, 'Swedish Plot,' XVIII, 104; Lamberty, *Mémoires*, X, 23–24.

[3] Whitworth to Polwarth, May 18/29, 1717, *Polwarth Papers*, I, 249. Whitworth points out Görtz's lack of credentials. All that Görtz carried was a letter of attorney from Charles XII. This point will be developed more fully in the next chapter. Wiesener, *Le Régent et les Anglais*, II, 5 was of the opinion that the Dutch had no legal right to seize Görtz as he was not plotting against the United Provinces.

[4] Jerningham to Mar, February 22, 1717, *Stuart Papers*, III, 532. Cf. Chance, 'Swedish Plot,' XVIII, 104 claims that Görtz went to the Hague in order to send dispatches to Sweden.

because neither he nor Leathes, who was in pursuit of Görtz, were allowed to enter Amsterdam until the following morning.[1]

Görtz, meanwhile, through Hooker had learned of the design to seize his person and papers. He therefore decided to spend the night at the tradesman's home rather than in a public lodging house. Although he felt it necessary that he go into hiding at once, he delayed long enough to see Dr. Erskine, who by chance happened to be in Amsterdam. The following morning the inn at which Görtz had planned to stay was surrounded by a troop of soldiers led by Leathes.[2] The English Resident then went to Hooker's house where he found twelve packets of papers which were placed in close custody, but were not opened. By this time the wily Swede was en route to the border with Stambke. He did not quite make it, for at Arnheim he was betrayed by a man named Willem Vleertman and captured on February 22.[3]

[1] Lamberty, *Mémoires*, X, 23–24.
[2] Jerningham to Mar, February 22, 1717, *Stuart Papers*, III, 532.
[3] Lamberty, *Mémoires*, X, 23–24.

XII

THE ARRESTS AND THE
FINAL COMMITMENT

T HE apprehending of Gyllenborg caused a good deal of
speculation and discussion throughout London. With the
news the stock market fell six percent. There were no immediate particulars given to the public, but rumors abounded.
Some gossips had James in Göteborg waiting to lead 12,000
Swedish soldiers into England while others had no less than
twenty-two messengers being sent abroad to arrest various 'Persons of Distinction in sundry places.'[1] Nathaniel Mist summed
it up in his *Journal* of February 2, 1717: 'The Seizing of Count
Gyllemberg Envoy of Sweden and others, has made the greatest
Noise about the Town that has been known, and afforded
matter enough for the greatest Speculation.'[2] London was not
the only place stunned by the news. 'The whole world talkes
about this matter, and everyone judges and speakes according
to his inclination and the Party he imbraces.'[3]

This partisan attitude was well reflected by the diplomatic
colony in London. All of the diplomats seemed to have been
concerned about the treatment meted out to Gyllenborg, but
Sweden's friends were naturally the most indignant. One group
of them, under the leadership of the Spanish ambassador, Isidor
Cassado, Marquis de Monteleone, went immediately to the
Court of St. James' to demand an explanation. Monteleone also

---

[1] *Mist's Journal*, February 9, 1717, II, 52; Sir Gustavus Hume to Polwarth,
January 27/February 7, 1717, *Polwarth Papers*, I, 176; Robethon to Polwarth,
February 8/19, 1717, *Ibid.*, I, 177.
[2] *Mist's Journal*, February 2, 1717, II, 17.
[3] Wich to Stanhope, March 5, 1717, P.R.O., State Papers, 82/34.

delivered a protest on his own initiative wherein he opposed the British arrest of Gyllenborg and the impounding of his papers on the ground that the British had violated the principle of diplomatic immunity.[1] The majority of the diplomats, however, preferred to watch events closely and to do nothing until after the British had explained their apparently precipitous actions.[2]

They did not have long to wait. On February 17, 1717, Stanhope informed all of the foreign ministers in London that Gyllenborg had violated public faith by negotiating with the Jacobites and had thus rendered himself, 'unworthy of the Protection and the Privileges due to his Character.' Consequently, the English government had found it necessary to apprehend him in order to preserve peace and tranquility in England and to bring to an end practices which were in direct conflict with international law.[3]

Monteleone was not satisfied with the British explanation and clung to the opinion that the peace and tranquility of England (and of Europe, as Stanhope had suggested) were not contingent upon a direct violation of the law of nations and the denial to an ambassador of the immunity inherent in his office.[4] At Vienna the Imperial Court took a different attitude. It admitted that, 'the Proceeding was indeed extraordinary against the Person of a Foreign Minister, but own'd that the case was so too.'[5] Meanwhile, all of the Courts in Europe were expectantly waiting for England to substantiate the charges levelled against the Swedish ministers.

Proof was forthcoming shortly. The papers commandeered

---

[1] *Historical Register*, IV, 66–67. *Mecurius Politicus*, February, 1717, p. 67 asserted that all of the foreign legations had asked for the release of Görtz, but as Wiesener, *Le Régent et les Anglais*, II, 4 points out, only Monteleone made a formal protest. His protest and observations on the arrest did receive a rather wide circulation in both British and European news outlets.

[2] Borsselle to the States, February 12, 1717, Rijksarchief, Archief Staten Generaal, Liassen, 6955.

[3] Stanhope to the Foreign Ministers, February 12, 1717, *Ibid*. A French copy can be found in Lamberty, *Mémoires*, X, 19 and an English one in *The Historical Register*, IV, 67.

[4] Borsselle to the States, February 16, 1717, Rijksarchief, Archief Staten Generaal, Liassen, 6955.

[5] Stanyan to Stanhope, March 3, 1717, P.R.O., State Papers Foreign, Empire, 80/34.

from Gyllenborg at the time of his arrest and the subsequent publicity given them strengthened the government's hand considerably, for they revealed that Görtz, Sparre, and Gyllenborg had all been in communication with Jacobite agents.[1] Gyllenborg's implication could be magnified by the press because he had a Jacobite wife,[2] had close Jacobite friends,[3] and had carried on pamphleteering activities of a libellous nature against the Hanoverians[4]—libellous that is, in so far as George I and his friends were concerned.

Stanhope initially read certain of the letters to Parliament,[5] and then in late February issued a 'Whitebook' entitled, *Letters which passed between Count Gyllenborg, the Barons Gortz Sparre and others relating to the design of raising a rebellion in His Majesty's Dominions to be supported by a force from Sweden.* Copies of this book were sent by Stanhope to all foreign diplomats in London,[6] and translations were distributed throughout Europe.[7] Compiled and edited mostly under Robethon's direction,[8] the letters showed that money between the Swedes and the Jacobites had been about to change hands and that Görtz had promised the Jacobites to set plans for an invasion of Britain before Charles XII. Coupled with the publication of this 'Whitebook' was a letter which claimed that Britain's policy toward Sweden was completely justified and that all of the Courts in Europe owed

[1] Intercepted Letters (Sweden), 1716–1717, P.R.O., State Papers Foreign, Confidential, 107/13.

[2] Lindeberg, *Görtz*, p. 58.

[3] Mahon, *History of England*, I, 206n pointed out that Gyllenborg had spent the summer at the home of Charles Caesar, who was arrested at the time of the disclosure of the Jacobite plot. Caesar and Gyllenborg were related by marriage.

[4] Various letters of Gyllenborg to his publisher in Intercepted Letters, P.R.O. State Papers Foreign, Confidential, 107/13. The Gyllenborg pamphlet which caused the most furor was *Remarks of an English Merchant upon a scandalous Jacobite piece published in the 'Post Boy,' July 19 under the title of memoir presented to the Swedish Chancellor by the Resident of Great Britain*. An English copy is in Boyer, *The Political State of Great Britain*, III, 306–318 and a French version is in Lamberty, *Mémoires*, IX, 667–677.

[5] Cobbett, *Parliamentary History*, VII, 397; *The Historical Register*, II, 66; *Mist's Journal*, February 23, 1717, II, 64.

[6] Borsselle to the States, March 5, 1717, and copy Stanhope to Borsselle, February 21, 1717, Rijksarchief, Archief Staten Generaal, Liassen, 6955; and Stanhope to the Spanish ambassador, Lamberty, *Mémoires*, X, 19.

[7] Wich to Stanhope, March 16, 1717, P.R.O., State Papers, 82/34 and Stanhope to Polwarth, January 19/30, 1717, *Polwarth Papers*, I, 173.

[8] Murray, 'Eighteenth Century Whitebook,' XIII, 376.

Stanhope and the Hanoverians a vote of thanks for having preserved peace on the Continent by their vigilance.

One important item was missing from the British brief and that was concrete evidence linking Charles XII with the activities of his ministers. The British hoped that the Görtz dispatches seized by the States might supply this vital propaganda material.[1] Their attempts to obtain these documents involved Britain in a considerable amount of diplomacy with the Dutch government, which will be elaborated upon below. It was one thing to arrest a diplomat, but it was something else again to seize his papers and to publish them. It would have been common practice to have asked that Gyllenborg be recalled and to have sent him home with his papers intact. Many diplomats in London who supported George I had some doubts about his actions. This in part may explain the Dutch reluctance to turn Swedish dispatches over to their British allies.

If some of the diplomats at London and at the Hague were upset over events, their governments back home were even more concerned. A letter of Gustavus Gyllenborg which incriminated Dr. Erskine in the plot forced Peter to disclaim any understanding with either Charles XII or the Jacobites. Duivenvoorde, 'who combined intimate relations' with Russian agents and a 'proved devotion' to the House of Hanover, protested that Peter wanted nothing more than a closer union with George I, while Baron Johann Christoph von Schleinitz, the Russian envoy to Hanover, offered his congratulations to Robethon that the plot had been discovered. Meanwhile, Theodor Pavlovich Veselovsky, the Russian resident at London, delivered a formal memorial testifying to Erskine's good conduct and asserted, furthermore, that it was impossible for the doctor to implicate Peter in such a conspiracy, as Erskine was not admitted to any of the Czar's state councils. Erskine himself pledged on his life that he had written Mar no letters of an incriminating nature. Although the Russians and the Czar's physician might protest, the fact remains that Erskine at times had been admitted to council meetings, as Norris' negotiations with Peter in 1716 so well illustrated.

England coolly received the various protestations, both formal

---

[1] Bothmer to Polwarth, April 23/May 4, 1717, *Polwarth Papers*, I, 222; and Whitworth to Polwarth, April 24/May 5, 1717, *Ibid.*, I, 222.

and private, delivered on behalf of Erskine and the Russian Czar. The presence of Russian troops in Mecklenburg and George's fears of a separate Russian peace were hardly conducive to good relations between the two. Indeed, these factors were in part responsible for the arrests. There can be little doubt that German affairs were Hanover's chief motivating force, and this was reflected by George I and the men around him.[1]

In addition to distrusting Peter's moves in Germany, George I was also suspicious of Frederick William I of Prussia. The latter, George's nearest relation, 'was the first who publickly express'd his Resentment of that wicked Attempt,' and harmony did appear on the surface. On February 24, Bonet, the Prussian minister, had an audience with George I and offered him Prussian assistance against the Jacobites.[2] Meanwhile back in Berlin everyone was talking about the 'traitrous' Swedish design.[3] Here Whitworth entered into conversations with the Russians wherein England on the one hand promised to guarantee Russian conquests, but on the other demanded that Russian troops withdraw from Mecklenburg. 'So rough an overture was justly rejected,' but afterwards there was some agreement on two main points: the Russians were to evacuate Mecklenburg in return for the assistance of another Baltic squadron. 'But as the Muscovites thought the first condition was too positive and the other too loose and uncertain, the whole Treaty and Interview came to nothing.'[4]

France, always suspect where Jacobites were concerned, took special pains to disavow any connection with the triumvirate of Sparre, Görtz, and Gyllenborg. Dubois even went so far as to assert that had the Regent known of Görtz's plans he would have been much more careful in giving him letters of exchange for part of the subsidy due Sweden. Dubois, however, was of

[1] For Peter's denial of plotting with the Jacobites, see Chance, *George I and the Northern War*, pp. 187–189. For Wesselowsky's memorial of March 12, 1717, and Stanhope's answer on the same date, see Boyer, *The Political State of Great Britain*, XIII, 248–362. Defore, *Mercurius Politicus*, March, 1717, p. 179 summarizes the Wesselowsky-Stanhope negotiations.

[2] Boyer, *The Political State of Great Britain*, XIII, 247.

[3] Whitworth to Stanhope, February 16/27, 1717, P.R.O., State Papers Foreign, Prussia, 90/7.

[4] Whitworth to Tilson, February 16/27, 1717, *Ibid.*

the opinion that France had the best opportunity to find out the true intentions of Charles XII, and to use that information in a way most conducive for George I to bring about an advantageous peace in the North.[1]

Actually Dubois' approval of the British measures taken against Gyllenborg did not represent French public opinion. A great furor against the arrest arose in France touched off by the pro-Jacobite French majority. The Abbé was criticized for having compromised the Regent with his own opinions, and D'Huxelles claimed that the Gyllenborg affair was an invention of George I to keep a standing army in being. As a result of the opposition, Dubois, who did not weather moments of stress well, was more dejected than he had been for ten years.[2] France did hope to gain from the affair by acting as mediator between England and Sweden. To do so she would have to steer a tight course between an alliance of short duration, the one with England, and an alliance with Sweden which had been a guiding beacon of French foreign policy over a long period of time.

The most important reaction to the arrests so far as England was concerned was of course that of Sweden. Stanhope almost immediately sent Jackson news as to what had transpired in England with the pious hope that the information would be received by the British minister before it reached the Swedish chancery so 'that you may consult your own Security, which you are left at liberty to do in the way you shall think best.' Charles XII was to be informed by 'the Surest Channel,' and Gyllenborg was to be kept in custody 'till we know that you are in Safety, perhaps then his Majty may think fit to order him to be released.'[3]

In reality, the diplomatic grapevine proved to be more effective than 'the Surest Channel.' While Jackson was engaged in the never ending process of trying to obtain damages and to secure the release of British shipping, mail from Karlscrona reached Stockholm. It included newspapers from Lübeck and Königsberg

---

[1] Dubois to Bernstorff, March 10, 1717, BM., Hanover Papers, Stowe Manuscripts, 230.

[2] Wiesener, *Le Régent et les Anglais*, II, 10.

[3] Stanhope to Jackson, January 30, 1717, P.R.O., F.E.B., State Papers, Foreign, 104/155.

which carried the story of the Gyllenborg arrest.[1] Jackson had no doubts as to the authenticity of the news release. Consequently he removed his more important papers to the house of Rumpf, the Dutch resident, 'so I am in no pain happen what may.'[2]

The Swedes at first wanted to set a guard over Jackson's house, but cooler counsels prevailed on the ground that the story appeared in what was ordinarily an enemy publication.[3] When proper verification did arrive, it was decided that Jackson should suffer the same fate as Gyllenborg—close arrest with a denial of mailing privileges, plus a tight scrutiny of all his servants.[4] In Rumpf's case, the Swedes decided to wait for additional clarification from Holland. The Dutch resident was forbidden the right to negotiate, but he was allowed his mail, although it had to be opened in the presence of a Swedish secretary in order to see that no correspondence for Jackson was included. Reprisals, however, were indicated if proper satisfaction was not forthcoming.[5]

The arrest of Görtz and the seizure of his papers caused considerable surprise in Sweden, but the majority of the Swedes felt that the affair was a personal matter between Görtz and the States because the person and papers of Preis, the Swedish minister to the States, had not been violated. Furthermore there was real optimism in Sweden that Preis would be able to iron out Swedish differences with the Low Countries. Rumpf personally felt that the Görtz arrest was unfortunate as it came just at a time when Holland was in a position to reap concrete economic advantages from Sweden.[6]

By April 14, n.s., Rumpf was able to have printed in Sweden the published intercepted letters of Gyllenborg. After reading them, the Dutch minister could come to no other conclusion but that the plot was at most a means to raise money from the Jacobites without any actual involvement or commitment on

[1] Extract of Königsberg *Gazette* giving the details of the arrest enclosed in Jackson to Townshend, March 6, 1717, P.R.O., State Papers, Sweden, 95/22.

[2] Jackson to Townshend, March 6, 1717, *Ibid.*

[3] *Ibid.*

[4] Rumpf to Fagel, March 31, 1717, Rijksarchief, Archief Staten Generaal, Liassen, Zweden, 6557; and Swedish Chancery to Rumpf, March 19, 1717, enclosed in *Ibid.*

[5] Rumpf to Fagel, March 31 and April 14, 1717, *Ibid.*

[6] Rumpf to Heinsius, May 22, 1717, Rijksarchief, A.A.H., 2002.

the part of Sweden. Görtz was too penetrating in his thinking not to comprehend that such an undertaking as an invasion of Britain was in view of English naval preponderance completely impracticable.[1] Up to the time of the arrests, neither Jackson nor Rumpf had ever heard anyone in Sweden even mention such a proposition, nor did they and the Swedes think that such a project was anywhere near feasible.[2]

If Rumpf and Jackson had heard no inkling of the negotiations, and if the plot were incapable of consummation, just what was behind the arrests and the hyper-drastic steps taken by the Anglo-Hanoverians early in 1717? The answers perhaps lie in events that took place between the cancellation of the Skåne invasion and the arrests.

In October there had been considerable excitement in England over Northern affairs. Herman Petkum, the Holstein minister in London, had answered Townshend's complaints about the taking of an English ship bound for Archangel with the terse statement that Britain was lucky that Sweden had not seized all British effects in Stockholm. Petkum was close to Görtz, and at that time personally held the opinion that Sweden would soon come to some agreement with the Czar.[3] Petkum some days later had a conversation with Bothmer who advanced the theory that a rapprochement between Russia and Sweden would be effected during the winter months. Bothmer had a real fear that Peter would receive concessions in Germany. Because of Bothmer's jitters and those of other Hanoverians, and because of the situation in general, Petkum felt that only money was wanted to mount a propaganda offensive capable not only of sowing disunity among the members of the Northern Alliance, but sufficient to tear the Alliance asunder.[4]

There can be little doubt that Sweden in the fall of 1716 was

[1] Rumpf to Heinsius, April 14 and May 22, 1717, *Ibid.*

[2] Rumpf to Heinsius, April 14, 1717, *Ibid.*: 'Vous pouvant assurer qu'avant la nouvelle de l'arrêt de Monsr. Gyldenbourgh ni Monr. Jackson ni moi n'avons jamais etendu parler d'un pareil projet, ni crû qu'il seroit possible de la mettre en oeuvre.'

[3] Petkum to Görtz, October 2/13, 1717, P.R.O., Foreign ministers in England book, State Papers, 100/1.

[4] Petkum to Görtz, October 12/23, 1716, *Ibid.* Petkum said to Görtz that with money he could serve the Swedes almost according to his own inclination as 'il me seroit tréz facile a mettre de la jalousie parmy le alliez du Nord, et de les desunir.'

in a position to bargain with her opponents. Görtz himself was in favor of playing England off against Russia. He feared Russia more than he did England, and he doubted the effectiveness of British aid in any war against Russia, although there were many men around Charles XII, including the King himself, who placed a great emphasis upon the strategic power of the British fleet.[1] Görtz in addition was not afraid to antagonize George I, because he considered British military blustering to be only diplomatic chess moves. As Görtz analyzed the situation, George I was too much hampered by parliamentary restrictions to do little more than protect the commerce and the economic interests of his subjects.[2] Görtz throughout this crucial period and later held to the opinion that Russia constituted the greatest threat to Sweden's security, and thus peace with her was mandatory. He intended to play one set of enemies off against the others. In the back of his mind, he perhaps toyed with the possibility that once peace was established, Charles XII could rebuild his arms and his country, and then find an opportune occasion to rewin what he now had to concede to his Russian foe.

Jägerskiold considers Peter's instructions to Kurakin in the fall of 1716, in which the Russian diplomat was told to prepare for peace negotiations, to be much more than mere caprice on the part of the Czar. From the beginning of September, the rumor circulated throughout Europe that Görtz had made contact with Kurakin at the Hague.[3] Although Görtz as late as October was still searching for a way to open negotiations with Peter,[4] Danes, Saxons, Prussians, Russians, Hanoverians and Jacobites all discussed with certainty that a meeting between Görtz and Kurakin had actually taken place. Görtz never did meet Kurakin personally, but he did carry on some diplomatic correspondence with him through mediators. Naturally he encouraged the rumors, and he probably helped to blow

[1] Jägerskiold, *Sverige och Europa*, pp. 90–91.

[2] Görtz to Vellingk, November 24, 1716, *Ibid.*, p. 95n.: 'Le dessein du Roy d'Angleterre de susciter les Anglois contre Nous ne seroit ce pas plustot une menace de sa part qu'un sujet d'allarme pour Nous? Quoy qu'il tienne a sa devotion le Ministere et le Parlement, la guerre a proposer est bien chatouilleuse, puisqu'elle choque directement les interests du commerce de ses sujets.'

[3] Jägerskiold, *Sverige och Europa*, pp. 36–37, 54.

[4] Görtz to Vellingk, October 17, 1716, Moser, *Rettung der Ehre*, 470–471.

them up to where they were badly out of proportion with the facts.[1] At the same time that the rumors of a Russo-Swedish peace abounded, Görtz, Vellingk, and Gyllenborg were constantly stressing the danger inherent to England resulting from the growth of Russian strength in the Baltic. Not only would Russian sea power be a threat to British commerce, but Russia would be in a position to establish trade monopolies which would not only damage British trade but would threaten the fleet's supply of naval stores as well. In addition, the Swedes depicted Bremen and Verden as menaces to British liberties because from those places Hanoverian troops could embark against England to Germanize the nation.[2]

Thus a good part of Europe believed that negotiations between Sweden and Russia had taken place, the facts to the contrary. After Peter refused to go along with the Skåne invasion, it was assumed by many that peace had already been secretly concluded. Danish spies in Sweden branded such rumors as authentic, as did the English public.[3] So artfully did Görtz exploit the bizarre situation that Defoe[4] and subsequently other historians gave him full credit for forestalling the invasion itself.[5]

Görtz, however, actually did want to negotiate with Russia, and considered Erskine, Peter's physician, as a real possibility to pave the way to Moscow for him.[6] To the Swedish minister, Erskine and the Jacobites were a means to an end. They could supply him with money so that he could operate from strength, and they could give him his entrée to the Russians. Sparre on the other hand also hoped that Erskine would be the 'kanal' to Peter, but he considered the Russian negotiation only as a

---

[1] Jägerskiold, *Sverige och Europa*, pp 36–37, 42.

[2] Görtz to Gyllenborg, October 27, 1716, P.R.O., State Papers, Confidential, 1a.

[3] Gyllenborg to Müllern, November 6, 1716: 'Man wysar här ey mindre längtan att förnimna rätta orsaken hwarföre Czaren ey welat i åhr i wärcket ställa langstigningen i Skåne, i synnerhet synes man sig mycket bekymbrat öfwer det rycket som går, att Een hemlig fredshandling emellan Hans Kongl. Maytt. och Honom skulle hafwa warit därtill orsaken.' Quoted in Jägerskiold, *Sverige och Europa*, p. 74. *Cf.* Holm, 'Studier,' V, iii, 123 and the *Stuart Papers*, III, 55.

[4] Defoe, *Görtz*, p. 8.

[5] See the chapter on the Skåne invasion.

[6] Görtz to Vellingk, 14 November, 1716, Moser, *Rettung der Ehre*, p. 479.

preliminary to the 'engelska affärena.' He was hopeful of a quick Swedo-Russian peace, as were many people in France, but to him the Stuart restoration was the chief objective.[1]

Sparre, moreover, was prone to give credit for frustrating the Skåne invasion to the friends of Crown Prince Frederick of Hesse-Cassel rather than to Görtz and the Holsteiners.[2] Although he was incorrect in this assumption, it is well to remember that it was through Vellingk and Baron Johann Reinhard Dalwigks, minister of Landgrave Karl Leopold of Hesse-Cassel, that Swedish contacts with Kurakin were first made. Jacobite agents assisted in these initial stages, and Karl Leopold did claim later the palm for forestalling the attack upon the Swedish mainland.[3]

The rivalry between Hessians and Holsteiners in Swedish politics is well illustrated by the fact that Crown Prince Frederick of Hesse-Cassel asked Dalwigks not to tell Görtz about his negotiations with Russia.[4] Differences between these two groups were also apparent in the Mecklenburg situation. Karl Leopold wanted Russia out of the Empire,[5] while the Holsteiners were not so anti-Russian.[6] Early in 1717, the rumor persisted that Peter wanted to marry his daughter to the Duke of Holstein, and that he was willing to use Muscovite troops to restore to the Duke those territories taken from him by Denmark.[7] The passage of the Czar's troops from Denmark to Mecklenburg was to increase Hessian and Holstein differences as it did those that existed among the members of the Northern Alliance.

The presence of Russian troops in Mecklenburg gave Peter 'a strong trump in his hand' because from that territory he could pose a threat to Denmark, Hanover, and Prussia. After the Treaty of Havelberg in November, 1716, his position became

---

[1] Jägerskiold, *Sverige och Europa*, p. 43. Sparre wrote to Müllern on November 16, 1716: 'on continue a assurer icy que le Czaar arrivera le 17. en Hollande . . . on pourra le sonder de prez sur ses intentions pour la paix, a la quelle on assure de touttes parts qu'il penche sincerement.'

[2] *Ibid.*, p. 48.

[3] *Ibid.*, pp. 48, 50.

[4] *Ibid.*, p. 48.

[5] *Ibid.*, p. 49.

[6] Görtz to Vellingk, November 3, 1716, Moser, *Rettung der Ehre*, p. 475.

[7] Robethon to Polwarth, February 26/March 9, 1717, *Polwarth Papers*, I, 186.

even stronger especially in his relationship to George I.[1] Sweden also profited from the Mecklenburg situation. Vellingk was pleased with the Czar's stand on Wismar, and had spoken to the Duke of Mecklenburg in order to stress to him that his safety was contingent upon the continuation of Russian troops in his domains. In addition Vellingk sounded out the Duke on the possibility of his aid to bring about a reconciliation between Sweden and Russia.[2] Görtz too hoped for great things from Mecklenburg, and it is possible that even Charles XII was pleased with the shape that events were taking.[3] Had the Swedish king not been elated over the troubles resulting from the Russian thrust into the Empire, he should have taken comfort that a rupture was developing between his British and his Russian foes.

Only with Prussia would Peter discuss driving Sweden from the Empire. Jealous of her gains in Pomerania, Prussia not only refused to work for the expulsion of the Russian forces from Mecklenburg, but on the contrary asked Peter to keep them there as a possible solution to the eastern question. High diplomatic circles in Saxony and Prussia urged the Czar to make a separate peace with Sweden and to forge an alliance with France. Thus a power bloc would be forged strong enough to control central Europe and to protect the allied countries from all contingencies.[4]

Thus George I in late 1716 found himself in a squeeze. He wanted the Russian troops out of Mecklenburg; he wanted to curb the rising power of Russia in the Baltic; and he wanted to add Bremen and Verden to his electoral dominions and to disengage England from the Swedish conflict. To accomplish these aims, he needed allies and a position of strength from which to bargain. That bargaining position among other things necessitated either a fleet or a separate peace with Sweden. The latter was becoming more elusive, for Görtz, perceiving that England might now apply further pressure upon Sweden even to the risk of open war, had decided that it was better to stand

---

[1] Jägerskiold, *Sverige och Europa*, p. 52: 'en stark trump på hand.'
[2] Vellingk to Görtz, October 28, 1716, Moser, *Rettung der Ehre*, pp. 472–474.
[3] Idem to Idem, November 3, 1716, *Ibid*.
[4] Jägerskiold, *Sverige och Europa*, pp. 53–54.

up to George I than to appease him.[1] Thus the attaining of a fleet became a prime consideration no matter in what diplomatic direction George I went.

To make matters considerably worse for the English king, a substantial number of his subjects holding high places were becoming disgusted with Baltic affairs, and they wanted to withdraw from what they considered to be an impossible position. On October 4, 1716, Townshend wrote the following to Stanhope in confidence and was promptly betrayed to the King:

> My chief design is to beg of you not to consent to Sir John Norris staying any longer than the first of November, nor to the king's engaging openly in the affair about the Czar. This Northern war has been managed so stupidly, that it will be our ruin—would it not therefore be right for the king to think immediately how to make his peace with Sweden even tho' he shou'd be obliged to make some sacrifice in obtaining it.[2]

In the same month Townshend's brother-in-law, Horatio Walpole, wrote to Stephen Poyntz from the Hague:

> I dont doubt but ye letters wch ye messenger carrys on this occasion from Hanover to England will bring you an account of ye great confusion ye affairs of ye North are at present in; and how extremely frightened our Ministers at Hannover are; and indeed wth very good reason; but I could wish they would not propose things wch seem to be impracticable; or if put in execution would rather increase, than remedy ye mischiefs we apprehend; if we are to change our measures here with soe much precipitation on every alarm we shall expose our weakness.[3]

Townshend was of course dreaming if he expected that George I and his associates would make sacrifices at Hanover's expense, and his brother-in-law had every reason to be perturbed at the impracticable flounderings of the ministers around

---

[1] Görtz to Charles XII, December 5, 1716, quoted in Jägerskiold, *Sverige och Europa*, p. 96: 'Was Ich hierunter gethan ist in der persuasion geschehen, das man bey den Engländern durch ein standhafftes bezeigen und durch vorstellung ihres eigenen Nutzens mehr gewinnen dufte, alss wenn man ihnen die wache Seithe geben wolte.'

[2] Coxe, *Walpole Memoirs*, II, 86.

[3] Horatio Walpole to Poyntz, October 10, 1716, n.s., in Murray, *Honest Diplomat*, p. 348.

the King, whose schemes included everything from a hair-brained plan to seize Peter and hold him as a hostage until his troops left Mecklenburg to an order that Norris should reject all customary and other gifts from the Czar, for George I promised to take care of his admiral in such a way that he would 'never want the favor of any other Potentate whatsoever.'[1] One result of the 'percipation on every alarm' was the speeding up of negotiations intended to bring Great Britain, France, and the States into a triple alliance.[2] The center of the negotiations to achieve this aim changed from the Hague to Hanover. Meanwhile Walpole in Holland constantly showed a deep concern over the steps that Stanhope and Abbé Dubois were taking to exclude the Dutch from playing an active role in the diplomacy. Consequently he did all in his power to keep Heinsius informed as to what was transpiring at Hanover.[3] As he wrote Townshend: 'Were it not done by his Majt's Directions, I would venture to say to your Lrsp alone, I think it must be extreamly prejudicial to the King's Interest, and I am afraid must end with a great deal of Confusion & uneasiness between us and the States.'[4]

George I, however, could not wait for England's old ally 'on account of the slow forms in Holland,'[5] while Abbé Dubois feared that if the signing of a separate Anglo-French treaty were deferred to the opening of Parliament, the entire treaty might well founder in the Commons.[6] Walpole, having promised the States that England would not act without them, was chagrined at developments, and he fought to save face not only for himself but also for his own and Britain's Dutch friends.[7]

[1] Stanhope to Methuen, October 16 and to Townshend, September 29, 1716; copies in Stanhope to Norris, September 26 and October 16, 1716, and in Stanhope to Polwarth, September 26, 1716, P.R.O., State Papers Domestic, Regencies, 43/1.
[2] See Hatton, *Diplomatic Relations, passim.*
[3] H. Walpole to Heinsius, October 14, 1716, Rijksarchief, A.A.H., 1971; Townshend to H. Walpole and Cadogan, October 5, 1716, P.R.O., F.E.B., State Papers Foreign, 104/81; and various letters of H. Walpole to Stanhope, P.R.O., State Papers, Holland, 84/254.
[4] H. Walpole to Townshend, October 14, 1716, in Murray, *Honest Diplomat,* p. 352.
[5] Townshend to H. Walpole and Cadogan, October 9, 1716, P.R.O., F.E.B., State Papers Foreign, 104/81.
[6] Hatton, *Diplomatic Relations,* p. 55.
[7] Various letters of H. Walpole to Townshend in Murray, *Honest Diplomat,* pp. 352–361. See also Hatton, *Diplomatic Relations,* pp. 132–143.

The efforts of Townshend and Walpole to have the States included in Anglo-French negotiations did not set well at Hanover. Walpole shortly became suspect in Hanoverian circles, and Cadogan superseded him in the negotiations at the Hague.[1] Furthermore the Dutch knew full well that they were being duped by their English ally in order to aid Hanover in its Baltic adventures. They would have agreed with Walpole:

> this morning . . . a Messenger arrived from Hannover wth repeated orders to us to sign with ye Abbe; and the only reason that I find for it, is least ye Czar would become master of ye Nobility of Mecklenbourgh; I can't for my life see ye connection between our immediate signing & that affair; or why ye whole System of affairs in Europe must be entirely subverted on account of Mecklenbourg; God knows what will be ye consequence of such Politicks; but I lay that aside; being sensible that it is not for me to judge of his Maj'tys reasons for these proceedings. . . .[2]

Having bludgeoned the English ministers into line, Hanover began to encounter delays from France. Dubois refused to sign on October 30 because of difficulties involved with the removal of the Pretender.[3] On November 5, Cadogan had to request new full powers from Townshend to conclude a separate Anglo-French treaty because Dubois insisted that the general terms used in the British instructions were not acceptable to France.[4] New powers arrived at the Hague ten days later, and again Dubois dragged his feet. This time he insisted that the powers were not valid because they had not been countersigned by a secretary of state. Cadogan might argue well and long that the British plenipotentiaries who had handled the treaties of Ryswick and Utrecht had not had countersigned powers, but Dubois refused to budge.[5] Once more the packet boats went back and forth while time dragged interminably for George I and his ministers at Hanover, who were all on edge because of Baltic affairs. To the Hanoverians speed was of the

[1] Hatton, *Ibid.*, p. 132.
[2] Walpole to Townshend, October 21, 1716, in Murray, *Honest Diplomat*, p. 359.
[3] Hatton, *Diplomatic Relations*, p. 139.
[4] Copy of Dubois' objections, enc. in Cadogan to Townshend, November 5, 1716, P.R.O., State Papers, Holland, 84/255.
[5] Cadogan to Townshend, November 17, 1716, *Ibid.*

essence in order to prevent France from becoming involved in the Baltic crisis either on the side of George I's open enemies or those who hid within the compass of the Northern Alliance.

It is possible that Dubois was stalling in order to give the States opportunity to come into the treaty. In November, France had agreed to two items upon which the Dutch had insisted, and with these concessions, the Amsterdam burgo-masters, who were fearful of being embroiled in the Baltic, began to show an inclination not only towards the French treaty, but also toward one with the Empire. Meanwhile new full powers arrived from London with all the proper signatures, and on November 28, an Anglo-French treaty was signed. One noteworthy provision was a clause agreeing to keep the treaty secret for a month in order to give the States time to join the alliance.[1]

Throughout December, Cadogan labored to obtain full Dutch participation in the treaty. Finally, on January 4, 1717, the Triple Alliance between Britain, France, and the States was signed; and Cadogen, Dubois, and Chateauneuf formally burned the Anglo-French treaty of November 28.[2] George I at long last felt free from the threat of trouble from France as he pursued Hanoverian policies in the North.

He had obtained this objective at the price of disunity among his British ministers. Both Stanhope and Sunderland had used George I's impatience with the seeming procrastination of Townshend and Horatio Walpole to increase their own posi-tions with the King. Even before the Triple Alliance had been signed, Walpole had been relieved of his post at the Hague, and Townshend had been dismissed from the office of Secretary of State and had been kicked upstairs to the empty and dubious honor of the Lord Lieutenancy of Ireland. George I was not known for his forgiving nature as his wife and son could well testify. He blamed Townshend for delaying the culmination of an alliance that was dear to his German heart.

As J. H. Plumb has pointed out in his masterly study of Walpole there were many factors behind the Whig split. First Townshend had 'fobbed' Fraulein von Schulenberg off with an Irish title rather than an English one. She, the German

---

[1] Idem to Idem, November 27 and December 1, 1716, *Ibid.*
[2] Idem to Idem, December 8 and 18, 1716, and January 12 and 15, 1717, *Ibid.*

advisers, along with Sunderland and his mother-in-law Sarah, Duchess of Marlborough, all lined up against the Townshend–Walpole group. Stanhope, fearing the Walpoles might join other Whig groups, betrayed them. But it is evident that the chief motivating factor was Hanoverian diplomacy which placed an inordinate importance on the Anglo-French treaty.[1]

Townshend on the other hand always insisted that he had done everything within his power to expedite the diplomacy, and charged that the Dubois-Stanhope negotiation in Hanover had made a separate signing at the Hague unnecessary. He admitted that he had considered the King's policy to be wrong, but he claimed, and rightly so, that he never intended to circumvent George I's wishes 'by such a mean pitiful artifice' as deliberately sabotaging the negotiation by drafting inadequate full powers. When Dubois had protested the general terms which Townshend had used so that it would have been easier to have come to terms with the States, Townshend on receiving news of the French protest had had new full powers passed through several offices and sent off to Holland in a single day. To Townshend, it was the ambitions of Sunderland which had caused his loss of favor with the King. With his eclipse, Townshend threatened to withdraw from public life. With this threat was the probable withdrawal of many of his relatives and friends.[2] Consequently it was only with a great deal of difficulty that the Government was able to persuade Townshend to accept the Irish post as a show of Whig harmony.

The split, however, was widening. The two Walpoles and Townshend were against declaring war on Sweden, and Orford in the Admiralty was notoriously set against the use of British ships and seamen to foster Hanoverian aspirations. Moreover Norris' squadron of 1716 had taken a good deal of punishment from the weather on its trip home, and the loss of British ships, seamen, and naval stores was something that was not taken lightly by the British populace. It well knew that it was Baltic politics which had delayed the squadron and which had exposed the squadron to late-season storms.

On the other hand, Gyllenborg had hoped that the split

---

[1] Plumb, *Sir Robert Walpole*, p. 225–242.
[2] Townshend to Slingelandt, January 1, 1717, Rijksarchief, Archief **Slinge-**landt, 119.

developing among the Whigs might prevent an open declaration of war by Britain against Sweden. In the last letter that he
was able to write home as a free agent, he recounted his efforts
to forestall the attack upon Sweden which he expected in the
next parliament, an attack which he feared could lead to open
hostilities.[1] Only the anti-Hanoverian Whigs could prevent this
from happening. Gyllenborg then feared open hostilities even
before his arrest. Furthermore he was not relying upon a weak
reed so far as the anti-Hanoverians were concerned. By the end
of April, 1717, the division among the Whigs would widen to
the point that the Tory, Erasmus Lewis, could inform Swift:
'Morally speaking, nothing but another rebellion can ever unite
them.'[2]

George I did not have a rebellion to unite his Whig ministry,
but he did have rumors of a Jacobite rising which was to be
assisted by aid from Sweden. By a skillful use of the rumors, he
might have his way with the Parliament. As soon as the Triple
Alliance was signed, and as soon as Townshend had agreed to
the Irish post, Stanhope dramatically revealed the existence of
a Swedish-Jacobite plot in order to rally sympathy for George's
diplomacy. The timing of the disclosure was geared to the
King's wants and desires in the Baltic.

George I needed naval support to frustrate Peter's ambitions
in the Baltic and in Mecklenburg. He needed naval support to
hang on to Bremen and Verden. He needed naval support
to wield a strong hand in subsequent Baltic negotiations and to
force Sweden either to make a separate peace with Hanover or
at least to prevent her from making one with Russia. Furthermore, as usual, it was to George's interest to embroil the States
in Baltic affairs, and this was becoming increasingly difficult to
do. The Amsterdam burghers, who held the greater part of
the purse strings belonging to the States, had been most unhappy about British policy in 1716.

In spite of the differences resulting from the postponement
of the Skåne invasion, the Hanoverians were still anxious to
engage Britain openly in their war against Sweden. Both
George I and Bernstorff were willing to promise Peter naval
coverage for a 1717 invasion, but they wanted him to withdraw

[1] Jägerskiold, *Sverige och Europa*, pp. 98–99.
[2] Williams, *Stanhope*, p. 251.

his troops from Mecklenburg before any hard and fast commitment was made. Bernstorff, Mecklenburger that he was, did not want an open rupture between Hanover and Russia. Furthermore the Russians by the end of July, 1717, would withdraw most of their forces from Mecklenburg. This would be accomplished by Bernstorff's diplomacy which in turn relied on British naval units.[1] Thus in early 1717 the Hanoverian advisers of George I had to come up with a British naval display in the Baltic to strengthen their position with all members of the Northern Alliance.

To Hanoverian thinking, a public disclosure of the long-known conversations between Swedish diplomats and the Jacobites would provide propaganda material of sufficient appeal to persuade Parliament to send additional and perhaps stronger squadrons to the Baltic. The arrest of Görtz under a treaty agreement which was in force between Britain and the States might provoke Charles XII into actions sufficiently rash to embroil the States in a war against Sweden. Furthermore by seizing and reading the papers of the arrested diplomats, the Hanoverian Court would be able to find out just how far negotiations had progressed for a separate peace between Sweden and Russia. Consequently the diplomatic exchanges of Sparre, Gyllenborg, and Görtz with the Jacobite leaders played directly into the hands of George I and his ministers. Stanhope, a former general, was a man who well knew how to exploit a tactical advantage.

Notwithstanding these factors, the Anglo-Hanoverians still had their work cut out for them. The British public ever since the War of the Spanish Succession had been adverse to military adventures on behalf of another country, albeit the King's own homeland. British suspicions towards the Hanoverians had been further heightened by George I's attempts to find peerages for his German friends, actions in direct contradiction to the terms of the Act of Succession. Such fears and misgivings needed to be allayed. Abel Boyer as early as September, 1716, had been white-washing Hanoverian policy by insisting that George I had no designs on the territories of Charles XII, 'whom, by the strictest and most solemn Treaty, he is obliged to defend.' Boyer even went so far as to slough off George I's hopes for

[1] Mediger, *Moskaus Weg*, p. 34.

Bremen and Verden by insisting that the King would never violate the Acts of Succession.[1]

The real propaganda offensive, however, came after the arrest of Gyllenborg and the confiscation of his letters. These were translated and prepared for the press apparently by a team of writers and officials headed by Jean Robethon, George I's private secretary. They were printed in February, 1717, by Samuel Buckley, publisher of the London *Gazette* and friend of Joseph Addison, under the title: *Letters which passed between Count Gyllenborg, the Barons Görtz and Sparre and others relating to the Design of Raising a Rebellion in His Majesty's Dominions to be Supported by a Force from Sweden.*[2] There was also a Dublin edition farmed out to Thomas Hume and sold by a Patrick Campbell 'at the *Bible*, the lower end of Cork-Hill.'[3] Both editions of the deciphered and translated letters included in general more material treating Baltic diplomacy than the plot itself. Special attention for example was given to Gyllenborg's pamphlet which was circulating widely throughout Europe and which vigorously defended Swedish policy and violently attacked that of George I. It was not until the seizure of the letters that the identity of the author was authenticated.

The Anglo-Hanoverians not only appealed to the public and to the Courts of Europe, but they also based their conduct on international law. The leading contemporary writer on the subject of ambassadors and diplomatic immunity was Abraham de Wicquifort, whose work *The Embassador and his Functions* had been translated into English by John Digby in 1716. Although De Wicquifort labelled ambassadors who threatened the state to which they were accredited as 'traitors from whom there is no Fence,' and who 'violate the Law of Nations,' he did not favor punishing them.[4]

Consequently it was to Dr. Richard Zouche, 'sometime Professor of the Civil Law in the University of Oxford,' that the defenders of British-Hanoverian policy turned for the

---

[1] Boyer, *The Political State of Great Britain*, XII, 305–320.

[2] *Letters which passed between Count Gyllenborg, the Barons Görtz, Sparre and others Relating to the Design of Raising a Rebellion in his Majesty's Dominions to be Supported by a Force from Sweden* (London, 1717). Cited hereafter as *Whitebook*.

[3] Title page, Dublin edition of the *Whitebook*.

[4] Abraham de Wicquifort, *The Embassador and his Functions*, trans. into English by John Digby (London, 1716).

majority of their arguments. Although Zouche had based much of his work on Grotius, he disagreed with his Dutch predecessor on the treatment of ambassadors, and he insisted that those guilty of conspiring against the state to which they were accredited should be brought before the bar of judgment. Zouche's arguments and his citations of cases in English history in which guilty ambassadors had been brought to trial under common law supplied the legal protective coat for the actions of George I and his ministers. So much emphasis was placed upon Zouche that one of his works written in the middle of the seventeenth century came out in a new edition and in an English translation just when the controversy over the arrest of Gyllenborg was at its highest. Entitled *A Dissertation concerning the Punishment of Ambassadors*, the new translation from the Latin was intended to reach a larger number of persons than other works treating diplomatic immunity, and it was dedicated to none other than Stanhope, the chief British minister behind the arrests.[1]

The propaganda offensive went far beyond legal and diplomatic word-splitting, as the press devoted most of its space to Baltic matters. Boyer, for example, had paid very little attention to Northern affairs throughout 1716, but in February, 1717, he devoted two thirds of *The Political State of Great Britain* to Baltic diplomacy.[2] Defoe in April, 1717, could write in the *Mercurius Politicus*: 'Things growing ripe now for a Breach with Sweden, everything was done both publick and private, that might provoke the People against the King of Sweden; as first a Book was published, Entitled, *The Narrative of the Life and Death of John Rhindolt, Count Patkul*, etc.' Included among the materials published were an account of the losses sustained by merchants trading to the Baltic and a petition of the Muscovy company demanding satisfaction.[3]

The treatment of Patkul by Molesworth in his account of the life and death of Patkul, and the handling of the Livonian by

[1] Richard Zouche, *A Dissertation concerning the Punishment of Ambassadors*, done into English by D. J. Gent (London, 1717). For the legal arguments pro and con connected with the arrests, see John J. Murray, 'The Görtz-Gyllenborg arrests— a problem in Diplomatic immunity,' *The Journal of Modern History*, December, 1956, XXVIII, 325–337.

[2] Boyer, *The Political State of Great Britain*, XIII, 100–246.

[3] *Mercurius Politicus*, April, 1717, p. 255.

other writers makes for interesting reading indeed. Molesworth
pointed out that even Defoe, the pro-Charles XII author of
The History of the Wars of Charles the XII, had been forced to
admit that the death of Patkul had not been just. From this
starting point, Molesworth takes off on a bitter tirade against
the Swedish king.[1] Patkul, it will be remembered had been the
Livonian noble who had helped forge the ring of enemies
against Sweden, a country to which he at least in name was a
subject. Upon his capture he had been broken at the wheel, a
common punishment in the Swedish army for treason. Few
historians have much respect for Patkul, but during this period,
he suddenly becomes 'brave General Patkul,' who defended
the brave Livonians from an oppression which was so brutal
that even the Queen Mother of Sweden was moved to tears.[2]
Charles XII in turn becomes 'a ravenous Beast of Prey' and
a bigot—this the man that the English Jacobites desired as the
'Preserver of our Religion, Properties and Liberties.'[3]

Patkul emerges at the hands of his Anglo-Hanoverian biographers as a Livonian Whig, and the descriptions of his
leadership of the Livonian nobles in their selfish drive to be
exempt from taxes and in their opposition to the Swedish
resumption of Crown lands become something at which to
marvel. Swedish taxation one learns was so heavy that persons
of the best quality in town and in country were known to
perish for want of bread. The English could expect a similar
fate should the Swedes come.[4] The account of Patkul was
written in haste as its author admitted, but done at the request
of the bookseller, Thomas Goodwin, 'knowing how great the
Expectations were of some ill-minded Men among us, and
how great the Apprehensions of many good ones, from this
King of Sweden, and his designing Expedition, I would not
delay it.' Molesworth hoped that all groups in England 'may
from hence learn, what they are to fear, or hope for, from a
Magnanimity so wronged turn'd; and an utter ignorance of all

[1] Robert Viscount Molesworth, *A Short Narrative of the Life and Death of John
Rhindolt Count Patkul* (London, 1717), pp. 26–30. Cited hereafter as *Patkul Narrative*.
[2] *An Account of Sweden and the Jacobite Plot* (London, 1717).
[3] Molesworth, *Patkul Narrative*, pp. 57–58.
[4] *Ibid.*, pp. 1, 3. Benson as early as 1711 in a *Letter to Sir J . . . B . . .*, p 21
had referred to 'Brave Patkul (that noble foreign Whig).' This interpretation found
a good deal more credence in 1717 when the *Letter* was reprinted.

Laws and Liberties; with an impatience of Contradiction, beyond what has appeared in this World these Five Hundred Years past.'[1]

Epithets other than those of 'tyrant' and 'oppressor' were levelled at the Swedish king. To the argument that the plot was too unsound to be accepted by a man of Charles XII's military skill, George I's hacks answered with the question 'what Action can be so hardy, so daring, or so desperate, but what may be expected from a King that sleeps in his Boots and lies in the Straw.'[2] Even Charles XII's well-known reputation for austerity and chastity were used against him. He was a 'stockfish lunatic' who never changed his linen, who let his hair grow long, and who used his dirty thumb to butter his bread.[3] He was taunted on the one hand:

> Can we our GEORGE and his lov'd Race disown
> To find thy barren Chastity a throne

On the other hand, he was told that the beautiful ladies of England would never 'Fall to thy Gothic Rage a Sacrifice,' for he was much too wild and much too rude for the gentile tastes of British womanhood.[4]

The Swedish troops were 'Slavish and Barbarous,'[5] and these 'Codsheads'[6] were northern 'Mohocks' who would be more savage than Saxon or Dane, and who would be as bad as the foreign troops of John 'who ravaged ENGLAND from one end to the other in such a cruel and brutish manner. . . .'[7] There would be 'Virgins ravished,'[8] and the Swedish soldiers accustomed to barren northern climate and terrain would not go home once their mission was completed. Even the English Tories would have to 'Be content to make way for them, and to remove their Habitations to Cornwall and Wales . . . and

---

[1] *Ibid.*, introduction, no pagination. Cf. Daniel Defoe, *A Short View of the Conduct of the King of Sweden* (1717), pp. 1–40. Goodwin also printed in 1717 a third edition of Robinson's *Account of Sueden.*

[2] *Mercurius Politicus*, February, 1717, p. 64.

[3] Daniel Defoe, *The Plot Discovered* (1717), p. 12.

[4] *An Epistle to the King of Sweden from a Lady of Great Britain* (London, 1717), pp. 6–8.

[5] *An Account of Sweden and the Jacobite Plot*, p. 8.

[6] Defoe, *The Plot Discovered*, p. 6.

[7] *Ibid.*, p. 32.

[8] *What if the Swedes should come* (1717), p. 8.

bless their Stars if they come off so easily.'¹ At best Charles XII
was considered to be an atheist, and at worst a papist.²

One of the chief problems of the British who defended the
arrests was how to implicate Charles XII personally in the
Jacobite negotiations. Furthermore, as the Government found
it difficult to arrest additional conspirators in England because
there was insufficient evidence, rumors abounded that the
exposure of the plot was party politics and nothing more.³
Opposition newspapers such as the *Weekly Journal* of Nathaniel
Mist made much of this,⁴ but the silence of Charles XII played
into Hanoverian hands. When the British insisted that he
formally deny any connection with the plot, Charles XII with
his customary stubbornness refused to make any statement
whatsoever. Thus the propagandists of George I could say that
the Swedish king was guilty or he would have repudiated
Görtz, Gyllenborg, and Sparre and asserted his own innocence.⁵
To many Whigs the situation appeared urgent, and they like
John Toland even though they were opposed to standing arma-
ments considered the country's danger as such that they felt
that they should grant the King's wishes 'sufficient to maintain
our reputation abroad, and tranquility at home, without any
diminution of our Liberty.'⁶

The extreme wing of the Jacobites did little to help Charles
XII, for it went to great lengths to show that the plot had
validity and that James' bid for the throne of his father stood
to profit from Baltic affairs. Whether the Jacobite leadership
took this stand for propaganda purposes is problematical. With
the usual hopes and dreams of exiles, the Jacobites were probably converting wishes into realities. Two toasts going around
Jacobite tables could be used by the Hanoverians against both
Charles XII and Peter the Great. One was to the 'valiant
Swede' with the fervent wish that 'no oppressors him invade,'
while the other was to the 'mysterious Czar' with the hope that
he would 'send us help from far.'⁷

¹ *An Account of Sweden and the Jacobite Plot*, p. 23.
² *Steadfastness to the Protestant Religion*, pp. 1–28.
³ *Mercurius Politicus*, March, 1717, p. 127.
⁴ *Mist's Weekly Journal*, II, *passim*.
⁵ *Mercurius Politicus*, February, 1717, pp. 98, 119–120.
⁶ John Toland, *The State-Anatomy of Great Britain* (1717), p. 58.
⁷ Hogg, *Jacobite Relics*, II, 44–45.

The friends of Sweden along with the anti-Hanoverians also made an appeal to public sympathy. Nathaniel Mist was extremely active, and he not only attacked the arrests in his *Weekly Journal*, but he also advertised such anti-Hanoverian pamphlets as *The Northern Crisis* and *The Gottemburg Frolick*, both printed and sold by J. Morphew 'near Stationer's-Hall.'[1] The latter, a real burlesque on the plot begins:

> Muse, if thou can'st awhile assist
> And laugh with me till thou'rt bepiss'd
> To see the diff'rent Schemes are hit on
> To ward off Blows design'd at Britain:
> And hear the several Conjectures,
> Of Cowards, Sinners, Saints and Hectors:
> Of all Degrees, and each Persuasion,
> About this Comical Invasion.[2]

To the writer, the idea of Rome working with Sweden and conversely was as far-fetched as having the English Puritans make an alliance with Philip II during the period of the Armada. As for James's preparing to make a landing or going to Sweden, he actually was 'on the Strole' in another direction from the 'Northern Pole.' The purpose of the proposed naval squadron to be sent to the Baltic under Admiral Sir George Byng was to prevent Sweden from retaking Bremen from 'well-arm'd *Hanoverian* Bands,' and to prevent Charles XII from making reprisals against Denmark.[3]

> May *Bing* his Canvas Wings display,
> The Fears for *Zealand* to allay,
> And through the *Sound's* rough Surges ride,
> Born swiftly by the Wind and Tide,
> To scatter Troops that may engage in,
> The Siege of threatened *Copenhagen*,
> And give fresh Courage to a Prince,
> That merits *England's* sure Defence.[4]

Mist in his own writings cast doubts upon the plot, and agreed with the author of the *Frolick* that Charles XII had designs not upon England but upon Denmark or the Baltic

---

[1] *Mist's Weekly Journal*, II, 95, 108.
[2] *The Gottemburg Frolick* (London, 1717), p. 2.
[3] *Ibid.*, pp. 11, 28, 33.
[4] *Ibid.*, p. 33.

coast.[1] An anonymous letter dated February 12, 1717, expressed surprise that at a time when Britain was faced with the prospects of peace because of former victories and 'from the additional strength of our alliance abroad' a guard was necessary to arrest Gyllenborg and to impound his papers. It also pointed out that the law of nations was being breached by a nation that prided itself on liberty and justice.[2]

Another anonymous letter supposedly addressed to Petkum and dated a week earlier, which was privately circulated in both English and French, had a bigger play in the press.[3] It showed surprise at Stanhope's personal activities at the time of the arrest, and commented that his defense of the arrest on the grounds that Gyllenborg's papers would reveal something was 'precisely the same as to hang a Man first, and try him afterwards.' It asked when Gyllenborg began to listen to the Jacobites: whether if it were after the Hanoverian declaration of war on Sweden, or after the seizure of Bremen and Verden by Hanover; after the Hopson squadron and the blockade of Stralsund:

> Or if it was since last Summer, when the Czar, Sweden's most formidable Enemy, had the Command of the English Fleet and Admiral Norris, together with the English Minister pushed on by all possible Ways and Means, the Invasion which the Northern Allies design'd to compleat its utter Destruction, the same Admiral being at hand to countenance that Expedition, had it been put in Execution.

Under the circumstances, Gyllenborg had every right, even a duty, to work against George I. Even if the Swedish minister had been guilty without the real provocation which had been his, all that George I should have done was to have asked for his recall. The papers of the Swedish minister should never have been confiscated. After all Gyllenborg had every right to speak his mind as to what he thought was the true interest of Sweden. Other ministers more suspect than Gyllenborg had never suffered the indignity of having their papers taken. A

---

[1] *Mist's Weekly Journal*, II, 68, 89.

[2] Anon., *A Letter from a Gentleman in the Country to his Friend in Town relating to the Seizing of the Swedish minister and his Papers* (London, 1717), pp. 3-5.

[3] Anon. to Petkum, February 5, 1717, printed in Boyer, *The Political State of Great Britain*, XIII, 238ff. and in *The Historical Register*, IV, 69ff.

dangerous precedent had been established which would make it possible to seize a minister's papers 'upon any frivolous pretext whatsoever.'[1]

A third letter, which circulated mostly on the Continent, said that the exposure of the plot to the Parliament consisted of 'belles paroles' and 'grande promesses,' but on the whole the Hanoverian case was vague and of little significance. It questioned whether George I as he claimed had saved a Protestant kingdom from destruction or had prevented a general war in Europe. It chortled sarcastically over George I's claim to have saved Sweden also, and wondered how much assistance from Britain would be forthcoming once Hanover possessed Bremen and Verden. It accused the British government and the Parliament of being directed by Hanover, and held up the sceptre of absolutism to the British people. It pointed out that George I was an absolutist by nature, and it brooded ill for British law and liberties so long as George I held the throne and had arms and money to carry out his purposes.[2]

The English antipathy toward standing armies was a real stumbling block in the path of the Hanoverians, and the opposition used it for all that it was worth. As one pamphleteer pointed out, Russia, Sweden, and Denmark were countries whose people lived in slavery because of standing armies, while the people of Poland were free because there no standing armies existed:

> The Story of Denmark is so well known, and so well related by an excellent Author [Molesworth, who wrote the atrocity account of Patkul to help the Hanoverian cause] that it would be Impertinence in me to repeat it; only this I will observe, that if the King had not had an Army at his Command, the Nobles had never delivered up their Government.

In the eyes of the author, for George I to ask for a standing army under the existing circumstances was utterly absurd.[3]

Thus the pamphlet and propaganda war swirled as Parliament prepared to debate the supply bill, and as the Whig party split into factions. Obviously the biggest weapon in the Hanoverian arsenal was the publication of the Gyllenborg letters,

[1] *Ibid.*
[2] *Lettre d'un Gentil-home . . . Stockholm, Londres,* pp. 1–4.
[3] *Reasons against a Standing Army,* n.p.

and George I and his advisers hoped to deliver the *coup de grâce* to the opposition by a second publication, that of the Görtz letters. They reckoned, however, without the Dutch. Heinsius had been willing to go along with the arrest of Görtz and his secretary, and he justified his action on the grounds that the States had treaty commitments to England, and that Görtz was not an accredited diplomat to the States because he had never formally presented his full powers.[1]

The Dutch, however, were fearful that the arrests might lead to an open war with Sweden, something that they intended to avoid at all costs.[2] Consequently they used one pretext after another to delay turning the Görtz letters over to the English.[3] In April, 1717, just when the battle in the Parliament was at its height, Stanhope strongly expressed his master's surprise over the Dutch attitude on the matter of the seized dispatches 'for which there seems no manner of Colour, since without the Examination of those Papers, all the Advantage that could be expected to his Majty & the Publick Service from the Seizing of Goertz & his Secretarys must be entirely lost & I am afraid is already too much so by the Delay.'[4] By June, the States had come to the conclusion that the real danger to England, if any, had ended with the arrests, and that further steps could only make matters worse. By that time the States were anxious to get their unwelcome prisoners off their hands.[5] Also by that time, Parliament had met and had adopted measures against Sweden.

Charles XII in his own way upset the plans of the British propagandists. They had expected him to go into a rage and commit some rash act that might be grist for their mills. Instead he placed Jackson under the same close arrest as was Gyllenborg. Rumpf on the other hand, unlike Görtz, had

---

[1] Declaration of the States on the Görtz arrest, June 3, 1717, Rijksarchief, Secrete Resolutiën, Staten Generaal, and Reasons put forth by Heinsius for the seizing of Görtz, Rijksarchief, A.A.H., 2288.

[2] Leathes to Stanhope, February 26, 1717, n.s., P.R.O., State Papers, Holland, 84/255.

[3] Various letters of Leathes to Stanhope, March, 1717, *Ibid.*

[4] Stanhope to Leathes, April 12, 1717, P.R.O., F.E.B., State Papers, 104/82 and Whitworth to Polwarth, April 12/23, 1717, *Polwarth Papers*, I, 214.

[5] Report of the Deputies for Foreign Affairs of a conference held with Chateauneuf, Whitworth, and Preis, Rijksarchief, Secrete Resolutiën, Staten Generaal, June 8, 1717.

considerable freedom of action. To be sure he had to open his mail in the presence of a Swedish secretary to see that no news was being smuggled into Jackson, and until Charles XII had satisfaction for the treatment of Görtz, whom Charles XII insisted was his plenipotentiary, Rumpf was forbidden to transact business in the Swedish Court.[1] By April, 1717, Rumpf was given enough freedom to have the Gyllenborg papers printed and distributed in Sweden,[2] and by May he was calling the arrest of Görtz unfortunate because it took place just at a time when the Dutch were moving into a position to reap certain economic advantages from Sweden.[3] Charles XII's policy of ignoring events in this case had stood him in good stead. It prevented him from assisting his enemies in the British Parliament as they debated what action to take against him and his country under the pretext of reaction to the Jacobite plot.

The battle in the Parliament was an arduous one, as party politics and foreign policy intermingled. The government in power was difficult to beat in the eighteenth century. Furthermore it held a tight rein on the opposition press. John Morphew of the *Post Boy* and publisher of *The Northern Crisis* and *The Gottemburg Frolick* was imprisoned for inserting a paragraph in his journal as to the probable fate of Jackson. Morphew rashly pointed out that Gyllenborg had been harshly treated by the English for no valid reason whereas Jackson had 'advised the Danes and Muscovites how and where to undertake Descents in *Sweden*; and *that his Original Letters* upon this Subject were intercepted, and are forthcoming.'[4]

Notwithstanding the fact that the Hanoverian party held all of the trumps, some of their anti-Swedish measures passed Parliament by only the narrowest of margins. On March 4, 1717, after thanking the King for preserving England from the Swedes, Parliament voted the estimated amount for the land force. In this case all went well for George I for his cohorts carried the vote 222 to 57. An additional supply bill to send the fleet to the Baltic once more ran into trouble. This time

---

[1] Swedish Chancery to Rumpf, March 19 and April 14, 1717, enc. in Rumpf to Fagel, March 31 and April 14, 1717, Rijksarchief, Archief Staten Generaal, Liassen, 6557.

[2] Copy of a letter, Rumpf to Heinsius, May 5, 1717, Rijksarchief, A.A.H., 2002.

[3] Rumpf to Heinsius, May 22, 1717, *Ibid.*

[4] Printed in Boyer, *The Political State of Great Britain*, XIII, 241.

the opposition was more dogged and more determined, and the bill passed by only eight votes.[1] George I in addition hoped to starve the Swedish people into submission. Knowing that Sweden was facing acute food shortages with the loss of the Baltic Provinces and the long war, he had Parliament pass a bill prohibiting all trade and commerce with Sweden until March 31, 1718. On March 13, n.s., a Royal proclamation to that effect was issued,[2] but it was never enforced effectively.

Thus George I and the Hanoverians had in the main won the day. England was committed to the Baltic, and the Stanhope–Sunderland Whigs were in the saddle. Yet the tactics had been too much for old friends to stomach. On April 20, 1717, Robert and Horatio Walpole, Methuen, Orford, Devonshire, and Pulteney withdrew from public service in protest of the treatment of Townshend. The trade prohibitions needed Dutch support which was not forthcoming. The Dutch merchants did not want an open rupture with Sweden, for by a war they had everything to lose and little to gain.[3] 'The Swedish partisans' in Holland antagonized Stanhope who began to lose what little patience he had with the Dutch.[4] The latter in turn, who had been more than tried by Hanover's adventures began to look for some sort of an agreement with Sweden.[5] It was only with difficulty that Leathes and Whitworth were able to keep Görtz imprisoned.

Görtz was finally released on August 1, 1717, by an independent action on the part of the States of Gelderland,[6] much to the disgust of the British.[7] The States General themselves were probably highly relieved to see the end of the affair. The Dutch

[1] Cobbett, *Parliamentary History*, VII, 422–433.

[2] The Royal Proclamation, February 24, 1718, *The Historical Register*, V, 138–139.

[3] Various letters of Leathes and Whitworth to Stanhope, P.R.O., State Papers, Holland, 84/255 and 84/256.

[4] Stanhope to Leathes, April 12, 1717, and April 12, 1717, P.R.O., F.E.B., State Papers, Holland, 104/82.

[5] Various letters of Leathes and Whitworth, P.R.O., State Papers, Holland, 84/255 and 84/256. For the best account of Anglo-Dutch relations during this period see Hatton, *Diplomatic Relations*, pp. 147ff.

[6] Landdags Recessen van Gelderland, 1717–1719, Rijksarchief, Provintie Resolutiën, G. 26.

[7] Sunderland to Whitworth, August 10, 1717, copy in Rijksarchief, A.A.H., 2288.

part of the arrest left a bad taste in the mouths of both the British and the Dutch.

George I, however, by the arrest of Görtz had gained time. He had kept Sweden's most able diplomatist from negotiating at a critical point in the Great Northern War, but with the stubbornness of Charles XII, there is considerable doubt as to whether Görtz could have won his sovereign over to any sort of an equitable solution. Thus the net results for the Anglo-Hanoverians were hardly worth the loss of trust in the eyes of an old and trusted ally. By the end of the century, England and the States were at war.

England on the whole suffered from the Hanoverian domination of British foreign policy. Admittedly Stanhope later took issue with Bernstorff and other Hanoverian advisers of the King, but in early 1717, either because he was greedy for power or because he was duped by Sunderland, Stanhope played into Hanoverian hands.

Until late summer 1718 Bernstorff was to dominate Hanoverian and British Baltic policy. After that time Stanhope attempted to unify anti-Russian sentiment among the European nations and to bring about a separate peace. Part of this policy called for a rapprochement between George I and Frederick William of Prussia whom Bernstorff loathed. But at the time of the Whig split, Bernstorff used British political animosities and ambitions to achieve his aims.[1] A division among the Whigs resulted which later aided Robert Walpole in his rise to supreme political power.[2]

George I committed England to a policy in the Baltic from which it was difficult to withdraw. No formal declaration of war was declared against Sweden, but the Baltic squadron made an annual appearance in Northern waters until peace was finally achieved. That settlement gave Hanover the principalities of Bremen and Verden. Prussia's share, a part of Pomerania, greatly enhanced the power of the Hohenzollerns, who now superseded the House of Brunswick as a dominant power in the Empire, and who eventually came to rival even the Hapsburgs. Even more important the settlement led to the rise of a new Baltic power, Russia, who was ready and anxious

[1] Mediger, *Moskaus Weg*, pp. 41-43.
[2] Plumb, *Sir Robert Walpole*, pp. 243ff.

to challenge British and Dutch naval and commercial supremacy in those waters. Without Hanover, England might in part have alleviated the humiliating surrender of her ally Sweden, and thus helped maintain Sweden as a counter weight to Russia. Thus the overall advantage accruing to England through Hanoverian diplomacy can be argued. There can be no argument, however, regarding George I's skillful use of his subjects, their press, their money, and their fleet for the benefit of Hanover.

INDEX

INDEX

Baltic Sea, 4, 6, 16, 20, 22–23, 25, 28, 33, 35, 40–45, 53, 57–58, 65, 72, 87, 89, 92, 106, 108, 110, 117, 154, 163, 167, 169, 171, 173, 176, 179, 181–83, 186, 188–89, 192, 208, 211, 219, 224–25, 232, 247–49, 253, 255–59, 261–62, 264, 265, 267–68, 271, 274, 279, 285–86, 313, 322, 329–30, 332, 334–36, 338, 342, 348; balance of power in 69, 71; commerce of, 30, 36, 102, 105, 243; crisis in, 333; diplomacy, 1715, 16; English on, 81, 86; Nobles, 6; policy, Maritime Powers, 79; seaports, 29; tar ports, 43, 46; provinces, 5–6, 30, 33, 43–44, 47, 137, 347; Russia in, 234, 327; shipping, 80, 238; squadrons, 36, 68, 104–5, 115, 140, 161, 163, 169, 171–72, 178, 181, 203, 212–13, 228, 233, 235, 243, 245, 248, 250, 254–55, 258–59, 260, 274, 348; squadrons, Swedes on, 167 (*see also* Fleet, Swedish); Swedish naval forces in, 228, 236
Bang, Nina, author, 28n., 29n.
Banks, Sir Jacob, 12, 316
Barrier towns, 300
Barrier treaty, 3, 89, 127
Batavia Illustrat, 29
Bavaria, 315
Bender, 46, 47, 72, 290n.; debacle at, 8
Benson, William, 12–13, 339n.
Berlin, 137–38, 141, 153, 322
Bernstorff, Andreas Gottlieb, baron von, 75, 92–94, 96, 99, 102, 113–15, 166, 184, 221, 222, 225, 232, 236n., 239, 248, 249–50, 255, 260n., 269–70, 277, 282n., 291, 323n., 335–36; split with Stanhope, 348
Besenval, Jean Victor de, 66
Berwick, duke of, *see* Fitzjames
Bible, bookstore, 337
Blathwayt, William, secretary of war, 55n.
Bleking, 6
Board of Trade, British, 34, 40
Boëthius, Bertil, historian, 32n., 33n.
Borssele van der Hooge, Philip van, 105, 115n., 116n., 175, 319n., 320n.
Bolingbroke, Viscount, *see* St. John, Henry
Bonet de St. Germain, Louis-Frederic, Prussian resident in London, 84, 114, 322
Bourgeois, Émile, historian, 2n., 284n., 300n.
Bornholm, island of, 114, 166, 172, 173, 174, 180, 184, 248, 249, 252, 255–56, 260, 276
Bothmer, Baron Hans Caspar von, 233, 272–75, 277, 321n., 325

Bothnia, Gulf of, 29, 227, 263–64, 279
Bourbon, house of, 3, 125
'Boy Patriots,' 23
Boyer, Abel, writer, 1n., 286n., 320n., 322n., 337n., 343n.; defense of George I, 336
Boyle, Henry, secretary of state, 67n.
Brandenburg, electorate of, 135, 137
Brandenburg-Prussia, 6–7, 93, 143, 152, 281
Brandt, Otto, historian, 56n.
Brasch, C. H., author, 14n.
Bremen, 4–5, 7–8, 23, 28n., 57, 86, 94, 96–98, 103–4, 126–27, 143, 151, 154–56, 177, 182–85, 187, 202, 208, 209, 215, 234, 240–41, 283, 286, 293, 314, 327, 329, 337, 343–44, 348; George I on, 82; Hanoverian purchase of, 93; importance to England, 97, 204
Breslau, town of, 128
Breton, William, English minister to Berlin, 77n., 83–84
Brihuega, 90
Bromley, William, British secretary of state, 48–53, 77n., 78n., 80n., 81n., 82–83, 84n., 121n.
Brunswick-Luneburg, 1, 3, 57, 69, 81, 88, 97, 99, 126–29, 148, 191, 212, 288, 304, 348, Congress at, 80, 126, 136, 154, 156
Brussels, 288
Buckley, Samuel, publisher, 337
Bülow, Joachim Henry, Mecklenburger, 270, 277
Burchett, Sir Josiah, secretary of the admiralty, 20, 28, 59n. 67n., 115n., 172n., 187n., 236n.
Burrish, Onslow, writer, 29n., 35–36
Bussemaker, Theodore, historian, 3n., 89n., 102n., 104n.
Butler, James, duke of Ormond, 51, 203, 211–12, 256, 258
Byng, Sir George, British admiral, 23, 203, 342

Caeser, Mr., M. P. for Hereford, 316
Cadogan, Lord William; 102, 104–5, 331n., 332–33
Calendar of Stuart Papers, 296
Calvinists, Silesian, 64, 125
Campbell, Archibald, duke of Argyle, 207
Campbell, Colin, 303–4
Campbell, Patrick, 288n., 337
Campredon, Jacques de, French minister to Sweden, 119n., 120n., 121
Capers, Swedish, 171; *see also* Privateers, Swedish
Carelia, 138, 157
Carlson, Ernst, 57n.

INDEX

Melville, Lewis, historian, 95n.
Memel, 28n.
Memoire of a Person interested in Baltic Commerce, 28
Menshikov, Prince Alexander, 135
Menzies, John, 310
Merchants, Anglo-Dutch, 253; British, 19, 26, 30, 34–35, 42, 44, 167, 191, 237; Swedish, 35, 40
Methuen, Paul, 301n., 331n., 347
Meyer, General Bendix, 153, 219n., 229–30n., 284n.
Meyerfield, Count Johan August, governor-general of Pomerania, 121, 134–35
Michael, Wolfgang, historian, 4n., 10n., 82n., 88n., 89n., 93, 96n., 97n., 101n., 102, 103n., 104n., 113n., 114n., 138n., 161n., 173, 179n., 182, 186-87
Milne, June, historian, 62n., 63n., 66n.
Minehead, 316
Ministers, British, 184
Ministry for Foreign Affairs, French, 137
Mist, Nathaniel, journalist, 318, 320n., 341–42, 343n.
Molesworth, Robert, first viscount, 10–11, 14–18, 20, 31, 56, 338–39, 344
Monteleone, 318, 324
Montgomery, Isabel, historian, 89n.
Morphew, J., printer, 342
Moscow, 5, 327
Moser, Baron F. C. von, historian, 290n., 291n., 295n., 296n., 299n., 327n., 328, 328n.
Müllern, Wolfgang, 45n., 47, 70n., 72, 73n.,74,86n.,119n.,122,124n.,201n., 206, 208–9, 238, 292n., 293n., 327n.
Münster, duchess of, 126, 249
Murray, Sir George, 65n.
Murray, John J., 10n., 37n., 77n., 89n., 94n., 127n., 243n., 244n., 246n., 254n., 258n., 259n., 320n., 330n., 331n., 332n., 338n.
Muscovites, 22, 30, 129, 240, 242, 253, 263, 270–72, 274, 322, 328; *see also* Russia
Muscovy, 18
Muscovy Company, 338

Narrative of the Life and Death of John Rhindolt, Count Patkul, 338
Narva, port of, 138, 266
Nath, Count von der, 238; 266n., 299n.,
Naval: demonstrations, British, 188; security, British, 43; stores, bounties on, 42
Navy, British, 8, 39, 129, 191, 285, 288, 349

Netherlands, 74; Spanish, 127
Neukloster, Amt of, 156
Newcastle, 32, 208
New England, 40
Newfoundland, fisheries of, 25
New World, 42
Nikiforov, L. A., 86n., 92n., 114n., 223, 225, 232, 233n., 268n.
Nimwegen, Treaty of, 54, 147, 150
Nordberg, Jöran, 56n.
Nordmann, Claude J., author, 6n., 119n., 124n., 150n., 223n., 270n.
Nore, 161, 233
Norris, Admiral Sir John, 67–68, 86, 96, 105, 114–16, 160–74, 176–77, 179–88, 191–92, 203, 208, 233, 235–39, 242, 246-63, 264n., 270–72, 277–78, 285, 289, 315, 321, 330–31, 334, 343; councils on invasion, 241, 273–76; instructions to, 106, 112–13, 214, 234, 244–45, 250–51
Norrlandska Tjäruhandelskompaniet, 36; *see also* Tar Company of Stockholm
North America, 40, 42
North Sea, 67, 182, 225
Northditmarsen, fortress of, 57
Northern Alliance, 41, 84, 86, 115, 130, 132, 143, 146–47, 151, 159–60, 163, 173, 177, 180, 189, 192, 201, 216–17, 222–26, 236, 243, 245, 257, 263, 267, 276–77, 281, 283, 285, 289, 299, 314–15, 325, 328, 333, 336
Northern allies, 228, 343
Northern Crisis, The, 342
Northern Germany, 230
Norway, 31, 36, 38, 214, 219, 223, 227, 235–37, 241, 245–46, 249–51, 280, 286, 294; coast of, 161; defense of, 231; relief of, 240, Swedish attack on, 202, 216, 218, 220
Nystad, peace of, 69

Oberg, Count Bodo d', 63
Odense, Treaty of, 60
Oder River, 135
Oeland (island), 260
Oldenborg, 154
Olgrive, Jacobite agent, 304
Oliver, Frederick S., author, 209n.
Oliva, Treaty of, 150
Oncken, Wilhelm, author, 7n.
Orford, Earl of, *see* Russell, Edward
Orléans, duke of, *see* Philip
Ormond, duke of, *see* Butler, James
Osgood, Herbert L., historian, 37n., 40n., 41n.
Osnabrück, 254
Ostermann, Baron Heinrich Johan Friedrich, Russian minister, 270, 302, 306

360

INDEX

INDEX

Puchler, Gottlieb Justus, Hanoverian resident, Copenhagen, 113, 162–63, 166, 172n., 173n., 175, 179n., 180–81, 184–86, 238–40

Pulteney, David, English minister to Copenhagen, 51–52, 8on., 82, 83n., 347

Puritans, English, 342

Pyrmont, 218, 226, 264

Queensbury, duke of, 72n., 73n.

Raben, 175n., 186n.

Raby, 43n., 66n., 67n., 69n.

Rank, Baron Konrad, general in service of Prince of Hesse-Cassel, 207, 295

Reading, Douglas K., author, 22n., 23n., 27n., 30n., 32n., 33n., 75n., 157, 233n.

Remarks of an English Merchant, 285

Repnin, General Prince Nikita Ivanovich, 220, 222, 267

Reval, 138, 157, 172–76, 232, 250

Review, 65

Rex Legis, 15

Richelieu, Loyis François Armand Du Plessis, 147

Richmond, ship, 112n.

Riga, 28, 33, 47–48; "Riga Wainscot," 33

Robethon, Jean de, 9, 63, 91–2, 94–5, 113, 158n., 161n., 162n., 166, 172n., 176n., 177n., 232n., 239–40, 249, 263n., 265n., 267n., 268n., 272n., 273n., 276n., 281n., 282n., 291, 302, 318n., 320–21, 328n.; influence on British diplomacy, 94; letters of, 96, 269; on Triple Alliance, 302; papers of, 94; propaganda of, 337

Robinson, Dr. John, 10–14, 34, 35n., 38–40, 55n., 61–66, 67n., 69n., estimate on trade, 43; Hamburg activities, 67; on Sweden, 10–14, 31; return to England, 68; Utrecht Settlement, 76

Rochester, bishop of, *see* Atterbury, Francis

Romanoff, House of, 117, 136

Rooke, Admiral Sir George, 58–59, 6on.; squadron of, 85

Rosén, Jerker, 76n., 81n.

Rosenberg, 274

Rosenkrantz, M. de, minister of Denmark, 84, 189n.

Rostadt, city of, 3

Rostock, 28, 223, 264, 275–76, 279; Danish exclusion from, 222; Russian battalions at, 228

Rottembourg, Count Conrad Alexander de, 137–39, 141, 144; mediation attempts of, 138

Rotterdam, 259, 291

Rousseau, Jean-Jacques, 9n.

Rowe, Nicholas, 46n., 190n., 342

Rügen (island), 151, 154, 156, 180, 186, 189, 229, 245, 280; campaign for, 187; capture of, 188

Rumpf, Willem, Dutch minister at Stockholm, 45–47, 88, 167–68, 209n., 236n., 238n., 324–25; protests to Swedish authorities, 48; restrictions on, 345–46

Russell, Edward, earl of Orford, first lord of admiralty, 115, 161n., 162n., 176, 182, 244, 246–47, 334

Russia, 2, 6–7, 19–20, 23, 29, 32, 38, 41, 43–44, 48, 59, 62, 66, 68, 73, 82, 84, 112, 117, 129–31, 133, 135–40, 143–44, 146–48, 150, 152, 154, 156–60, 174, 214, 219, 232–33, 240, 246–47, 255–57, 259, 262, 264–71, 273, 278–81, 283, 285, 289, 292, 295, 302, 306, 314, 322, 325–26, 329, 335–36, 344, 348, brutality of, 20; Frederick IV on, 216; growing power of, 215, 234; institutions of, 19; naval forces of, 252; Swedish diplomacy, 130; Swedish peace rumors, 326–27; Polish treaty, 81; proposed treaty with Hanover, 184; Prussian treaty, 138; restrictions on foreigners, 18; trade of, 19, 30; Turkish war, 71; warships from England, 51; Wismar affair, 221

Russia Company, 43

Ruyk, Bay of, 165n.

Rydberg, S., author, 12n.

Ryswick, peace of, 55, 148, 150, 332

Sacheverell, Henry, 12n.; trial of, 71

Saint-Germain, Court of, 294

Saint James, Court of, 318

Saint James's, Palace, 1

St. John, Henry, Viscount Bolingbroke, 1, 8n., 11, 46n., 47n., 49, 69n., 70n., 71n., 74, 75–77, 79–80, 82–86, 126, 203, 287; Baltic policy of, 85; Polish affairs, 81; Sweden, 118

Saint Petersburg, 20, 43, 130, 137–38, 158, 250, 268

Saragossa, 90

Saxony, 7–8, 59, 61–65, 70, 132–33, 135, 138, 143, 146, 152, 326, 329; Augustus II, elector of, 131; Charles XII's invasion of, 125; return to belligerency, 69; Swedish diplomacy with, 132

Scandinavia, 10

Schack, Baron von, minister of Russia, 84, 154

Schartau, Sigurd, historian, 200n.

INDEX